A Guide

to Forecasting

for Planners

and Managers

Raymond E. Willis
University of Minnesota

Prentice-Hall, Inc., Englewood Cliffs, New Jersey 07632

Library of Congress Cataloging-in-Publication Data

Willis, Raymond E. (Raymond Edson), (date)
    A guide to forecasting for planners and managers.

    Includes bibliographies and index.
    1. Forecasting. 2. Management. 3. Planning.
I. Title.
HD30.27.W55 1987   658.4'0355   86-25532
ISBN 0-13-369539-5

Editorial/production supervision: Bernie Scheier and Mary Miller
Cover design: George Cornell
Manufacturing buyer: Ed O'Dougherty

To Libby and the boys

© 1987 by Prentice-Hall, Inc.
A Division of Simon & Schuster
Englewood Cliffs, New Jersey 07632

Printed in the United States of America

10 9 8 7 6 5 4 3 2 1

ISBN 0-13-369539-5 01

PRENTICE-HALL INTERNATIONAL (UK) LIMITED, *London*
PRENTICE-HALL OF AUSTRALIA PTY. LIMITED, *Sydney*
PRENTICE-HALL CANADA INC., *Toronto*
PRENTICE-HALL HISPANOAMERICANA, S.A., *Mexico*
PRENTICE-HALL OF INDIA PRIVATE LIMITED, *New Delhi*
PRENTICE-HALL OF JAPAN, INC., *Tokyo*
PRENTICE-HALL OF SOUTHEAST ASIA PTE. LTD., *Singapore*
EDITORA PRENTICE-HALL DO BRASIL, LTDA., *Rio de Janeiro*

Contents

Preface

"We have made these remarks because we believe a little reflection upon the subject will be useful at this season to men of business as well as politicians. They are both obliged to act more or less as if the usual must happen, and they are right in doing so, but they should never forget that the usual is not the inevitable, and is less so just now than heretofore. . . . Of this we are quite sure, that a double conviction of the necessity for forecast and of its futility begins to daunt the strongest."

"The Futility of Forecasts,"
The Economist, *January 2, 1897*

Planners are concerned with the future, forecasters are concerned with the past. The job of the forecaster is to examine the past for patterns which are likely to persist or for analogous situations which are likely to recur. Armed with this information, the planner is then in a position to deal with the uncertainties of the future.

The interface between the planner and forecaster is critical and not always completely understood, even when the forecaster and the planner are the same person. It is the intent of this book to examine that interface. In the process we will do less than complete justice to either. The planning situations examined are relatively simple and were chosen to be illustrative of the types of problems that planners face. On the other hand, this is not a book on the methodology of forecasting. While we touch on most of the methods in common use, the technical detail necessary to the professional forecaster is absent.

This book has a threefold purpose:

1. To show how the different approaches to forecasting must be matched to the specific needs of the planner and to aid the planner and manager in evaluating the forecasts with which they are presented. 2. To present in simple form a few forecasting techniques that the planner-manager can use initially or as a "quick-and-dirty" check on the more sophisticated forecasts of the technical analysts. With rare exceptions I have limited this to "back of the old envelope" methods; that is, they require no more than paper and pencil and a hand calculator. At the same time it should be noted that all of them can be readily adapted to use with a personal computer spreadsheet program such as Lotus ®1-2-3®. Most of the calculations and graphics in the book have been developed in this way. 3. To emphasize the importance of graphic presentation of data in developing and interpreting forecasts. The increasing availability of graphics programs gives forecasters and planners access to a very powerful tool that is too often underutilized.

The book is divided into five parts. Part I introduces forecasting as one of the many ways managers have of dealing with uncertainty, with the planning process seen from the viewpoint of the planner, and with some of the principles of rational decisional analysis. Part II develops the statistical background necessary for understanding the rest of the book. The reader who has had some introduction to time series analysis may want to skim this material rapidly and then move on to Parts III or IV.

The emphasis in Part III is on relatively short-range, quantitative types of planning and the forecasting techniques needed for their support. Part IV focuses on the special problems that arise in forecasting for strategic planning and management. The problems here are more qualitative and less formally structured and lead to different attitudes and approaches to forecasting. Depending on the reader's interest, Parts III and IV can be read in any order, with a rare cross-reference between the two.

Part V summarizes the book through an informal set of "check lists." These should prove helpful to the manager who would like to experiment with some of the ideas contained herein.

As with any book, this can only be read with the *active* participation of the reader. Whether you are a student with assigned readings or a manager working through the material on your own, you should read with pencil and paper, hand calculator, and graph paper at hand and reproduce *on your own* the calculations and graphical analyses presented. The first few times you try them, the procedures will seem tediously detailed. In time, they will come to be second nature and will greatly strengthen your ability to interpret historical data in your capacity as manager and planner.

The seeds for this book were sown more years ago than I like to remember. The people who have contributed to it have been so many that it is impossible to list them all. A few that I would like to single out must include Professors Edna White, Marius Janson, and Dean Schroeder, all of whom at various stages alternately acted as critic and cheerleader; John McCanna of Prentice-Hall, who kept me from forgetting that I was supposed to be working on this project; and my wife, who put up with the way that it sometimes interfered with vacations and family activities. I can only hope that the final product will live up to their expectations.

Raymond E. Willis

CHAPTER 1

The Nature of Forecasting

The term *forecasting* means different things to different people. For some it refers to something very close to prophesy or to a psychic ability to foresee future events. For others it is more closely allied to concepts of creativity or imagination and to an ability to imagine the different ways in which the world may evolve and how those different worlds might be achieved (or avoided). For still others it may only mean a way of anticipating the effects of present decisions or actions. Perhaps the only common element in these varying views is that, in every case, the term somehow relates to the future.

This book is concerned primarily with the problems faced by the manager/planner in applying forecasting to planning and decision making, rather than with the needs of the technical analyst. The effects of any decision must, of necessity, occur in the future, whether it be years or only seconds away. It follows that every decision implicitly or explicitly is based on assumptions about the form that the future will take. It makes no sense to argue, in this context, whether it is or is not possible to forecast; a forecast is inescapably embedded in the action or decision itself. The only real question is whether the embedded assumptions will be made explicit and explicitly evaluated or left implicit and thus unquestioned. The planner/manager may wish to deal with these assumptions personally, and we will consider some simple forecasting techniques which, in many cases will require little more than paper and pencil. In other cases the manager will need to call on the assistance of the professional forecaster. This book describes and gives simple examples of methods available to the forecaster and explores how they relate to the needs of the planner/manager.

Forecasting approaches can range from simple graphics and hand calculations to mathematically sophisticated techniques which require large data bases and complicated computer programs. With rare exceptions, the methods presented here involve no more than a hand calculator and a few sheets of graph paper. They can also be easily adapted to use with PC or desktop computer software packages. With one minor exception (the three-dimensional graph in Chapter 9), all the calculations and graphs in this book were developed using the popular and widely available spreadsheet program Lotus 1-2-3® Release 2. Many other spreadsheet, statistical, and graphics programs are available and more are released almost daily. Many have features that make them even easier to use than Lotus 1-2-3. No attempt is made to cover the range of possibilities. At various points in the book hints are given that should help the interested reader in replicating the results shown and in applying the methods to new problems.

FORECASTING

A forecast is a description of a possible future. A related idea, common in fantasy fiction, is that of the sudden acquisition of the ability to learn the future through a device such as time travel or the unexpected obtaining of an advance copy of a future newspaper. (A rather delightful example of this is John Buchan, *The Gap in the Curtain,* noted in the readings at the end of the chapter.) For a manager, such an opportunity would not be unwelcome. A plan must be developed or a decision made. There are factors involved in the decision that will only be known at some future date. If the manager could somehow obtain an advance copy of the *New York Times* or the *Wall Street Journal,* it would probably contain information that would be of great use in making that decision. In the absence of such an event, however, the manager must do the best that he or she can and rely on forecasts.

Imagine that you live in a small town that, each August, has a day-long celebration of the town's founding, ending with a chicken barbecue and fireworks. Each year people who have moved away return for the day and others come from neighboring towns to join in the festivities. Planning for the big day starts in April. Suppose that this year you are in charge of the chicken barbecue; it is now April and you are beginning the planning process. By some magical device you suddenly have access for a few minutes to copies of the town newspaper for next July and August. What are some of the things that you would look for? The first would probably be any reports of the number of people who actually attended the celebration as a way of estimating the likely demand for dinners. Next you might look for the weather report for the day of the celebration; if it will be cold you'll need lots of coffee and hot chocolate; if it will be warm you'll want cold drinks instead. If it's going to rain, you may plan to have it indoors or to rent a tent or canopy. Finally, you will probably look at the grocery store ads for the prices of chicken and the other things you will need to help you in setting the price of the dinner.

Unfortunately, there is no current procedure for obtaining future newspapers. The fact remains that, as the planner and manager, you must make assumptions in April about all these factors: weather, demand, and prices. These assumptions will be based on forecasts. To be useful the forecasts must address all the aspects of the external environment relevant to the plan in an integrated and internally consistent way.

DEALING WITH UNCERTAINTY

Uncertainty enters the planning process in many ways. We may be unsure of specific events, such as the passage of a new law or the introduction of a new technology. We can be uncertain of whether the events will occur, of when, or of the exact forms that the events will take. We may be uncertain of the magnitude of future changes in quantitative variables such as price levels or population movements. We may be unsure of the exact nature of relationships among variables: the effect of a price change on the demand for a product or the effect of a specific new government regulation on costs. We may be unsure of some specific external event or variable, of its internal impact within the organization, or of the importance that that impact will have to the organization.

Such uncertainty about the future is inevitable in any decision making or planning. Attempting to foresee or forecast the future is only one possible response. In most situations a manager has alternative ways of dealing with uncertainty. Galbraith (1973), for example, suggests that organizations can

1. increase their ability to preplan (decrease the uncertainty)
2. increase their flexibility to adapt to their inability to preplan
3. decrease the level of performance required for continued viability

Forecasting is one aspect of preplanning and thus of decreasing uncertainty; it is not the only possibility. In many cases a manager or organization can choose the business it wishes to be in or the approach that it wishes to use in a particular situation. Some businesses are inherently more uncertain than others. Operating a hardware store would seem to involve less environmental uncertainty and be more predictable than would operating a store selling computer software or women's fashions. In the same way, a plant manager setting up a new production line may have a choice between using a well-tested and established process and using a newer technology, which may be more efficient but may also be more subject to breakdowns.

Uncertainty can also be reduced by having better and more timely information on the current situation. Particularly in the short run, environmental conditions may change very little. From the manager's point of view, the problem may be less one of forecasting and more one of receiving timely feedback on changes as they occur. Even when some form of forecasting is crucial, a first step in developing a forecast must be knowledge of current conditions and circumstances.

To the extent that the level of uncertainty cannot be reduced, actions must be taken to counteract the effects of the uncertainty. The effects of environmental uncertainty can be reduced in different ways. Three of the more common devices are

1. *Redundant Resources.* This can take two forms, use of safety stocks (or other types of safety margins) and use of multiple or parallel approaches. When future demand is uncertain, extra inventories can be carried to reduce the chance of a stockout; when future production requirements are uncertain, excess capacity can be designed into a production process. In research programs or in designing a new technology where the success of any particular approach may be uncertain, several different approaches can be simultaneously pursued to increase the probability that at least one of them will be successful.

2. *System Flexibility.* The effects of environmental uncertainty can also be eased by designing elements into the system to reduce its sensitivity to the uncertainty. In inventory control, an alternative to maintaining large safety stocks may be to reduce order lead times, perhaps using shipments by air freight rather than by truck. Leasing equipment or space, rather than buying or building, can increase the man-

ager's ability to deal with uncertainty. Similarly, flexibility can be increased by using multipurpose rather than specialized equipment.

3. *Organization Design*. Galbraith (1973) has suggested a number of ways that organizations can deal with uncertainty. These include creation of slack resources, structural self-containment, vertical information systems, and the development of lateral relationships. In general, these have the effect of increasing the flexibility of response or of decreasing response lead times.

As a final alternative, management may simply accept the fact that less than ideal performance may result because of unexpected or random changes in the environment. As a practical matter, no response to environmental uncertainty is costless. Developing forecasts requires time and resources. Maintaining safety stocks or other redundant resources costs money. Leasing is normally more expensive than buying. Multipurpose equipment is less efficient than special-purpose equipment. It is up to the manager to balance these costs. In some cases it may be less expensive to accept a reduced level of system performance than to spend resources on forecasting or on other alternative ways of coping with the existing uncertainty.

THE METHODS OF FORECASTING

While a forecast must deal with the future, we can never observe the future; the raw material for forecasting must lie in the past. At its most basic level, the process of forecasting is really that of historical analysis and the forecaster is a sort of historian. Historical data (that is, records describing the past) as well as data describing the present are used by the forecaster in two ways: analogy and extrapolation.

Forecasting by analogy involves the search for similar situations in the past (or present), whether incidents, markets, events, or organizations. The forecaster must try to decide to what extent it is valid to draw these analogies and thus to what extent it can be expected that the events of the future will resemble the past. For the individual (including the manager) analogy is the most common basis for informal forecasting. The current situation reminds us of something similar in the past and we therefore tend to believe that the future will unfold in a similar way. As we shall see later, many of the newer approaches to forecasting are basically attempts to formalize this process of reasoning by analogy.

Extrapolation as a forecasting approach normally occurs in conjunction with the analysis of historic (usually quantitative) time series. We formally or informally examine the time series to look for patterns which have tended to persist in the past; then, in the absence of reasons to believe that the underlying conditions have changed, we project those patterns into the future. Indeed, in many fields the terms forecasting and extrapolation are essentially equivalent.

The process of studying the past and applying the results to the future in itself can be a major source of our uncertainty. We can be unsure of the future because we lack knowledge of the past, because we do not completely understand the events of the past, or because the past, in itself, is not sufficient to an understanding of the future.

Depending on the specific decision situation, we may need to develop forecasts because

We lack adequate knowledge or understanding of the natural or physical world. A good example would be the uncertainty involved in forecasting weather. Even if we assume that, in some ideal sense, weather should be completely predictable, we simply do not have sufficient data or adequate understanding of weather phenomena to calculate exactly future weather conditions. In some cases the event or variable to be forecasted may already exist, as, for example, in projecting future oil reserves. A similar problem exists in forecasting new technological inventions and developments. In fact, when we understand (or think we understand) a phenomenon, we rarely use the term "forecasting," even for events many years in the future. We normally do not say that we are "forecasting" the time that the sun will rise tomorrow.

Human behavior, even with complete information about the past, may never be completely predictable.[1] It is useful, however, to distinguish the problems of forecasting the individual behavior of people, governments, and companies from that of forecasting the aggregate behavior of groups such as customers, voters, or employees where the averaging tendencies of groups may make aggregate behavior more predictable than that of any individual.

To the problems of forecasting individual events or variables, we must add that of forecasting the implications of these events and variables. A company may feel that their sales should be affected by consumer disposable income or by interest rates. It is not enough, however, to simply

[1]We will have to admit that this is a matter of personal opinion. Some would argue that, with sufficient data and understanding, forecasting human behavior should, in theory, be no different than forecasting the weather.

develop forecasts for these external variables. In addition, it is necessary to forecast the exact relationship of these to company sales.

Because different academic disciplines tend to be interested in different aspects of the future, they have tended to develop different approaches to forecasting. To a meteorologist, forecasting means something quite different than it does to a psychologist and something different still to a political scientist. Because of this we often tend to categorize forecasting methods according to the type of phenomenon studied, sometimes referred to as different environments. Five are frequently cited:

1. *Economic Environment*. This includes regional, national, and international economic institutions both in the context of individual markets and in broad summary measures, such as price-level indicators, employment, and industrial production.

2. *Social Environment*. This environment is first characterized by the broad demographic measures of population, including breakdowns by age, education, geographic location, and other similar social descriptors. In addition, the social environment encompasses existing and changing social institutions and the cultural characteristics of populations.

3. *Political Environment*. As with the economic environment, this includes elements of local, regional, national, and international politics and the actions of legislative, executive, and judicial branches of governments.

4. *Technological Environment*. This environment encompasses the physical elements of human invention and innovation, including new products and processes. More and more as we move into a world dominated by service industries and activities, the concept of the technological environment has been expanded to include new services and organizational forms as well.

5. *Natural Environment*. Natural resources, raw materials, geography and land use, and weather and climate are all elements of the natural environment. In recent years, with increased interest in environmental quality and the problems of pollution, the term "ecological environment" is now frequently used.

In practice, there is a great deal of overlap among these five different environments, and it is difficult to find factors which are only economic or political or social. On the other hand, particular forecasting techniques do tend to be identified with different environments, and there are enough differences in approach to warrant making the distinctions.

OUTLINE OF THE BOOK

In this book, the term forecasting is used in the widest possible sense. We will be interested in the problems of developing descriptions of possible futures for use in planning and decision making and will not be overly concerned with whether a particular method or application is or is not "forecasting" in some narrower sense of the word. Thus the use of the term differs slightly from the way it is sometimes applied by other writers. Many authors, for example, prefer to limit the term forecasting to descriptions of the "most likely" future state of the environment and to use another term, such as "alternative futures," for other applications. In a similar way, some writers limit the use of the word forecasting to quantitative descriptions of the future. For more general qualitative descriptions, another term, such as "scenarios," would be used. In practice, there is a great deal of overlap among these different concepts, and it is convenient to have some general umbrella term to describe the entire area. We have chosen to use "forecasting" for this purpose, modifying it as necessary in discussing narrower concepts.

Since the emphasis in the book is on managerial decision making and planning rather than on techniques of forecasting, the division of the material focuses on different aspects of the planning process, rather than on differences in the forecasting methods used. Those topics that are common to several sections will be treated separately in Parts I and II.

Part I: Introduction (Chapters 1–2).   In addition to this brief introductory chapter, the first section examines some of the fundamental concepts of planning and decision making. Much of this material is covered in detail in books on planning and management science. The reader familiar with this literature may wish to skip the remainder of this section, referring back to it only if the need arises.

Part II: The Analysis of Time Series Data (Chapters 3–4).   In forecasting, the single most important source of data is the quantitative time series. As a prelude to our consideration of the applications of forecasting to planning, it will be useful to spend some time on the issues involved in analyzing this type of data. The intent of this section is twofold: (1) to introduce some of the basic concepts that will be used in the following sections of the book and (2) to develop some simple techniques of data analysis (requiring no more than paper, pencil, and hand calculator) that a planner/manager can use either to develop simple preliminary forecasts or as a check on the conclusions obtained from more complex (and presumably better) methods of analysis.

Part III: Operational Forecasting and Planning (Chapters 5–9). A large part of a manager's time tends to be spent on the planning and control of ongoing operations. An important aspect of this type of activity is the existence of a strong sense of continuity between past, present, and future. This sense of continuity means that this type of planning tends to be relatively structured and systematic. From the point of view of the forecaster, continuity lends itself to the use of extrapolation and time-series approaches to forecasting. In this section we explore a number of different types of operational planning and consider the applicability of different forecasting models and methods.

Part IV: Forecasting for Strategic and Project Planning (Chapters 10–12). The class of problems that, in this book, are referred to as "strategic" are those that emphasize change and a lack of clear continuity with the past. These situations include the starting of new businesses or the changing of the basic mission of old ones, the introduction of new technologies or new products, and the opening of new markets. It will be seen that an important characteristic of such problems is that the project or program falls outside the usual course of current operations and, since something new is being tried, the sense of historical continuity explored in Chapters 3 through 9 either does not exist or is considerably weakened. Techniques of forecasting here must rely more heavily on the use of analogy and judgmental analysis.

Part V: Epilogue (Chapter 13). A common theme underlying this book is that planning and decision making require the making of assumptions about the future. Since the planner/manager bears the ultimate responsibility for the success or failure of those plans and decisions, it follows that he or she would be wise to play an active role in the development of the underlying assumptions and forecasts. As a sort of summary of the entire book, Chapter 13 gives a few hints on being your own forecaster.

READINGS

The last 20 years have been a period of high and general interest in the future. The 1960s saw, among other activities, the "Futuribles" project in France under Bertrand de Jouvenel and the "Commission on the Year 2000" chaired by Daniel Bell. This period also produced a number of books and articles on the nature of forecasting. The emphasis was not on the direct needs of the planner/manager as stressed in this book. Instead it was directly primarily toward understanding the potential problems, threats, and opportunities that appeared to be facing society in the future. Despite this difference in emphasis, many of the issues raised by these authors have relevance to the problems of the planner/manager. As examples you might look at

> BERTRAND DE JOUVENEL, *The Art of Conjecture*, New York, Basic Books, 1967.
>
> DANIEL BELL (ed.), *Toward the Year 2000: Work in Progress*, Boston, Beacon Press, 1969.
>
> FRED CHARLES IKLÉ, "Can Social Predictions be Evaluated?" pp. 101–126 in Bell (1969).
>
> HERMAN KAHN and ANTHONY J. WIENER, *The Year 2000*, New York, Macmillan, 1967.

For some contrasting views, see

> SEHDEV KUMAR GUPTA, "Does Future Exist?" *Canadian Forum*, January 1975, pp. 13–16.
>
> ROBERT A. NISBET, "The Year 2000 and All That," *Commentary*, June 1968, pp. 60–66.

Three relevant journals are *Futures* (British), *The Futurist* (USA), and *Technological Forecasting and Social Change* (USA).

Utopian and Disutopian Literature

Utopian fiction can be traced back at least to 1516 with the publication of Sir Thomas More's *Utopia*. Although written in the form of forecasts, the true intent is to focus people's attention on the shortcomings and problems of the present. At the moment, one of the best-known examples of this type of writing is

> George Orwell, *1984; a Novel*, London, Secker & Warburg, 1949.

Other well-known examples include

> SIR THOMAS MORE, *Utopia*, Louvain, 1516.
>
> FRANCIS BACON, *New Atlantis*, 1629.
>
> EDWARD BELLAMY, *Looking Backward: 2000–1887*, Boston, Houghton, Mifflin, and Co., 1887.
>
> ALDOUS HUXLEY, *Brave New World*, London, Chetto & Wendus, 1932.

H. G. WELLS, *The Shape of Things to Come*, New York, Macmillan, 1933.

B. F. SKINNER, *Walden Two*, New York, Macmillan, 1948.

Economic Forecasting and Econometrics

The literature in this area is extensive. While the issues of forecasting the economic environment are of central interest to the planner/manager, space limitations have dictated that it be a topic which is not really addressed in this book. Two relatively brief and interesting readings are:

DEBORAH DeWITT MALLEY, "Lawrence Klein and his Forecasting Machine," *Fortune*, vol. 91, no. 3 (March 1975), pp. 152–157.

DALE G. BAILS and LARRY C. PEPPERS, *Business Fluctuations*, Englewood Cliffs, N.J., Prentice-Hall, 1982 (Part I).

Two relatively simple introductions to econometrics with relevance to the needs of the planner/manager are

JAMES P. CLEARY and HANS LEVENBACH, *The Professional Forecaster*, Belmont, Calif., Lifetime Learning Publications, 1982 (Part 3).

H. RUSSELL FOGLER and SUNDARAM GANAPATHY, *Financial Econometrics*, Englewood Cliffs, N.J. Prentice-Hall, 1982.

Journals that will be of interest include *Business Economics, Journal of Business Forecasting, Journal of Business and Economic Statistics, Journal of Forecasting*, and *International Journal of Forecasting*. The first two are intended for the practitioner; the others are more technically oriented.

What Is a Forecast?

JOHN BUCAN, *The Gap in the Curtain*, Boston, Houghton Mifflin, 1932

is written in an entertaining way but relates directly to the problems of the manager who must make decisions based on incomplete and often garbled information.

Magazines that in various ways explore alternative futures include *Analog: Science Fiction/Science Fact, OMNI*, and *The Futurist*.

Dealing with Uncertainty

Some basic references would include

PAUL R. LAWRENCE and JAY W. LORSCH, *Organization and Environment*, Homewood, Ill., Irwin, 1969.

JAY GALBRAITH, *Designing Complex Organizations*, Reading, Mass., Addison-Wesley, 1973.

PROBLEMS

1. One of the standard themes used in science fiction involves the obtaining of exact (but frequently incomplete) knowledge of future events through time travel, "time warps," the accidental obtaining of an as yet unprinted copy of a newspaper, or some similar literary device.

   For this exercise, suppose that you have a friend who can travel into the future and can bring back any information from written records that you request. (No original data collection or visual observations allowed.) For example, you could request GNP by quarters for the next 15 years, sales records from the future files of a company, election results for 1988, or weather reports from the daily papers.

   For each of the following situations, indicate the information that you would ask your friend to obtain and how you would use it in the indicated planning. Remember that the information requested must be available in written form, and your instructions must be complete enough so that your friend can locate it rapidly. (You cannot, for example, ask that the person page through two years of newspapers and bring back "anything interesting.")

   a. You are in charge of production planning for a manufacturer of a variety of personal-care products (hair sprays, deodorants, shampoos, etc.). The company buys bulk chemicals and then mixes and packages them. Each month you must develop production plans and schedules by the 25th for the coming month for each of the products and for both the mixing and the packaging departments. The company is currently in a rather tight cash position and management has therefore been somewhat critical of the high inventories that are carried and the amount of overtime that has been scheduled. On the other hand, the sales manager is a suspicious type who tends to be quite nasty when there is any delay in filling orders (as a rule of thumb, they should have gone out yesterday). At the same time, it is practically impossible to get the plant manager to agree to any changes in the production schedules once they have been agreed on. At this point, you are looking for anything that will help you develop more accurate production schedules.

b. A company supplying business forms and other specialized printing has three plants serving their three major market areas. All three plants currently have some excess capacity, but sales are increasing in all three areas and the company expects capacity problems to begin arising in all three plants within the next two to four years. Available capital is very tight and this situation is not expected to improve in the foreseeable future. Because of shipping costs and the need to maintain a high level of customer service, it is impractical to try to balance work loads among the three plants. You have been given the assignment of developing capital budgets for the next three years.

c. A. M. Loisir, Inc., started in 1951 as a carpentry shop. They began by manufacturing garden furniture, expanded to indoor informal furniture, and in 1965 added game tables of various types. In 1972, they acquired a small manufacturer of outdoor game equipment and have since expanded rapidly in the area of outdoor sport and camping goods, including archery, fishing, boating, and camping equipment. A. M. Loisir, the president, feels that continuing to put resources into both furniture and camping goods means that neither of the businesses will receive the management attention and capital needed for real growth and proposes in the future to concentrate resources in one of the businesses and to phase out the other. You are to prepare recommendations on which of the two business areas has the most potential for future growth and profitability.

2. You own a small factory that subcontracts the manufacture of a variety of stamped metal parts. In your spare time you have developed a new product to conserve and reduce fuel consumption in the home. This would be used primarily by owners of existing homes rather than in new construction and would be sold through hardware and discount stores. The manufacturing process is similar to the existing one but would require new and additional equipment, space, and capital. It would also require a distribution system which the company, at present, does not have. Exactly what would be needed depends on the long-run demand for the product. Since the product is new, there are no past sales records to use to forecast future demand. Discuss the ways that you as owner could deal with the uncertainty presented by this problem.

CHAPTER 2

Decision

Making

and Planning

Before we begin a study of the methods of forecasting, it will be helpful to introduce some of the basic concepts of planning and decision making that are used in later chapters. Many readers will already be familiar with the ideas summarized here and will want to skim rapidly through or even skip much of the chapter. Those for whom the material is new should spend a bit more time because these concepts and terms are referred to frequently in the chapters that follow. This is particularly true in Chapters 5 and 10 where the forecasting needs of specific planning models are developed.

The view of decision making employed here is often referred to as the *rational-choice* model. We will argue shortly that, from a managerial point of view, this model is incomplete because it tends to emphasize only the formal, analytic aspects of the overall decision process. At the same time, because the intent here is to examine some of the formal tools that are available to the forecaster, the approach is useful.

Major Points To Be Noted

1. *The framework and stages in the formal planning process and the specific forecast needs that arise at each stage.*

2. *The structure and elements of the rational-choice model of decision making and the particular role played by environmental uncertainty in that model.*

3. *The structure and elements of outcome and payoff tables as a formalization of the rational-choice model.*

4. *The concept of opportunity cost or regret and its interpretation in comparing choice alternatives.*

5. *The implications of the different choice criteria, including min-max opportunity cost and expected opportunity cost.*

6. *The use of the concept of expected opportunity cost in estimating the potential benefits of searching for better forecasts.*

7. *The extension of the basic concepts of payoff models and opportunity costs to the case of the continuous variable.*

THE PLANNING PROCESS

Decisions are choices among alternative actions. *Planning* is sometimes referred to as "anticipatory decision making." That is, a *plan* is a tentative framework for a sequence of possible future decisions, a framework based on the goals to be achieved, on assumptions about other related future events, and on the anticipated effects of other preceding decisions and actions. To explore the different stages of the planning process, we introduce here a hypothetical example of a young couple, husband and wife, who decide to buy and operate a small-town hardware store. In later chapters, we will return to this example to illustrate various aspects of the planning and forecasting process.

The Hardware Store

Our hypothetical couple live and work in a large city but have had a longstanding dream of owning and operating a small-town business such as a hardware store. They have read all sorts of books on the subject and subscribe to a number of trade journals and small-business-oriented magazines.

One day they see an ad; a hardware store is for sale in a small town in southern Wisconsin that sounds like just what they have been looking for. They contact the seller; after some correspondence, they decide to go and look at it. They like the store and the town. The price seems negotiable.

Let us now follow them through an imaginary series of decisions that must be made and plans that must be developed. At each stage we will see that they face questions which are technically unanswerable because they concern events that have not yet happened and may never happen. At the same time, we will see that "answers" to these questions are needed if the necessary decisions are to be made. This is the essence of forecasting, to describe events that have not yet and may never occur. Although this example is that of a very small business, the issues are, in fact, much the same in organizations of all sizes and degrees of complexity.

Direction.   What is the long-range potential of the business? Is it a type of business in which they would wish to be involved? Will it provide the life-style that they want and the necessary income?

Such questions involve the basic direction of a business. Sometimes this choice of direction is referred to as the development of a *mission statement*. In this case, let's assume that the town is in the middle of a dairy farming area and that currently much of the business is with the local farmers. The town and the business have been quite stable for many years but, depending on what happens in the dairy industry, this could change.

There is a small co-op creamery in this town, but there is a good chance that it will go out of business in the next few years. If this were to happen, there is some question of what, if any, industry or business would replace it.

Although the current owner of the hardware store has never tried to tap this market, there are a number of local lakes with vacation cottages on them, many owned by people from Chicago and Milwaukee. On one lake there is a state park that attracts campers and fishermen. A nearby river has been suggested as the site of a flood-control dam. If it were to be built, this would create another large lake, which could develop into another tourist and vacation area.

Any of these possible events or changes could affect the long-run potential and direction of the hardware store. While none of them is certain, some changes are bound to occur. Even if one of these events were certain to occur, its impact on the community and the hardware store could not be completely foreseen. For example, suppose the creamery were to close and be replaced by a hi-tech electronics firm. What would be the implications of this for the town and for the store? Would it bring more people or fewer? Would the character of the town and the need for different types of hardware change? In what ways?

Strategy.   Suppose our hypothetical couple decide to buy the store. What next? How much should they be willing to pay? How will they finance the purchase? What will be their other capital needs? What initial actions will they need to take?

The mission or desired direction for an organization can rarely be achieved by simply continuing the current business with existing resources and by the present methods. Even if the mission is to maintain the current business, the external environment is changing and the owners will have to respond to those changes. It is necessary to have a strategy—objectives, policies, and programs—which will move the organization in the desired direction. Here, the current owner is planning to retire. His health has not been good and the business has been allowed to deteriorate. There is good reason to believe that, under new ownership, profits should improve. But this will not happen without some form of strategic program.

The store will need remodeling. In addition, our prospective buyers would like to build an addition to attract the vacation traffic. This cannot all be done at once; time, money, and study of the market will be needed. A long-range development and building program will be necessary.

To determine a price that they can afford and a loan repayment schedule that they can handle, the buyers will need estimates of probable earnings and profits over the life of the loan. This cannot be simply a projection of the store's past earnings; the buyers are planning to make changes. In any case, profits and cash flow will depend not only on the actions that the new owners take, but on local and national economic conditions, on local demographic conditions, on changes in the market for dairy products, and on what happens in the vacation and travel business. Future profits can even be affected by technological changes which will introduce new products and cause present products to become obsolete. Because of the possible effects of these factors, the past profitability of the store is, at best, only a partial and incomplete indicator of future profits.

Operations.   In addition to financing the purchase and expansion of the store, our buyers will need to arrange for working capital. For this it will be necessary to develop budgets and cash-flow estimates for the coming year for the existing business. This, in turn, will require sales estimates for the various lines of farm and nonfarm equipment and supplies that are currently stocked, together with sales estimates for any lines that will be added. These estimates will have to be adjusted for the effects of any changes in operations that are planned, such as increases in advertising or changes in the hours the store will be open.

Sales for the existing business will be directly affected by economic conditions and prices as these affect both their customers and their suppliers. Estimates of long-run profitability will depend on which new businesses the owners decide to enter and on environmental factors that cannot be foreseen. By contrast, short-range profitability, which will be particularly important to them, will depend on a different set of factors. The types of shorter-range changes which may occur will in most cases be relatively clear, although the directions and magnitudes of those changes will not.

Development.   Let's assume that the new owners decide to expand the business to include an increased emphasis on the tourist business. When the time comes to start construction for the building remodeling and addition needed for this, it will be necessary to develop time schedules to coordinate building activities, equipment purchases, and the ordering of new inventories. They will need to time these in order to be ready for the start of the spring fishing season and to develop advance publicity.

As compared to the broad issues involved in the development of strategic programs, here we are dealing with planning for specific developmental projects. The uncertain elements that must be estimated or forecasted will be, for the most part, the times that will be necessary for the completion of the various stages of the project and the costs of the component activities. These, in turn, will be affected by economic conditions and conditions in the construction industry.

Activities.   As the business develops, many routine decisions will have to be made. Stock will have to be ordered on an item-by-item basis. Because of the seasonal nature of the demand for many items, decisions will be necessary on both the size and the timing of orders. The owners will also have to estimate their short-term cash and staffing needs so that necessary lead times on obtaining these can be maintained.

In this brief example we have outlined a number of the different types of managerial decisions which would have to be made as part of the overall planning process for a small hardware store. The types of decisions are very much the same as those faced by managers in all kinds of organizations, large and small. Some deal with the management of ongoing operations, as in the development of operating budgets and the maintaining of inventories. Others deal with change and new activities, as with the original decision to enter a specific business, the decision to increase emphasis on serving vacation and leisure markets, and the development and implementation of a program of construction and expansion. The effectiveness of all these decisions will be affected by events that will occur in the future and that are now, at the time the decision must be made, inherently unknown and uncertain. It follows that all these decisions and plans involve some form of forecasting.

A Framework for Planning

The different plans and decisions just described are not independent. They can be thought of as elements of six distinct stages in an integrated planning process:

1. The formulation of a mission statement and its development into strategic objectives and policies.
2. The translation of the strategic objectives and policies into specific strategic programs and operating business units.
3. The development of tactical objectives and budgets for the programs and business units.
4. For the existing businesses, the development of operating plans and budgets and of specific operating policies and procedures.
5. For new programs, the establishment of developmental plans and budgets and the design of specific projects.
6. Within and between both operating businesses and new programs, the coordination and control of specific activities and component program elements and the monitoring of the external environment.

In later chapters we explore each of these stages in greater detail and examine the forecasting approaches that have been developed for each.

THE NATURE OF A DECISION

If we think of planning as "anticipatory decision making," then we must recognize that decisions are almost never made as isolated events; almost every decision is the start of a process that creates the need for further decisions, which in turn engender still other decisions. Viewed in this way, the consideration and evaluation of any decision must, to the extent possible or practical, anticipate some future decision stream that will follow the initiating action. Only when the future decision stream is effectively predetermined by the initiating action can we realistically speak of "the" decision in isolation.

In those cases where it is possible to analyze a decision as a single isolated event, it is often helpful to think of it as a formal act of rational choice from a set of alternative possible actions. If we must choose between going to the mountains or to the seashore for vacation and if there are no other second-order implications to this choice, then the question may only be: Which will we probably enjoy more? Here, however, we are more concerned with the process of decision making within organizations where decisions rarely take this simple form. The problem becomes complicated by the second- and third-order decisions that follow from the initial choice and that in most cases will be made by other people, under different and perhaps unanticipated environmental conditions and with no guarantees that the others will have exactly the same interpretation of the goals or objectives. Under such circumstances, the concept of rational choice based on explicit goals will not always form an adequate framework for analyzing the problems of planning.

In considering problems of complex decision making, Allison (1971) has suggested the use of three different frameworks or models for decision analysis:

1. *The Rational Actor.* Decisions are considered as reasoned, analytical choices among alternatives based on the explicit objectives or goals of the organization.
2. *Organizational Process.* Decisions can only be understood in the context of the organization. Decisions are not "made" in some unique identifiable sense. Rather they are an outgrowth of a process and can only be understood in that context. To say that the vice-president of sales "decides" to introduce a new product to the market can only be understood as the last stage in a process consisting of many other preliminary decisions and in the context of existing procedures and programs.
3. *Political Process.*[1] A decision is not made by an individual or organization with one clear identifiable set of goals or objectives. Rather it grows out of a process of negotiation in which no one person "makes" the decision, but where many people influence the decision. The decision can be thought of as the outcome of a game between specified players and within a particular framework of game rules.

Each of these views of decision making suggests a different dimension to the planning process and presents different ways of looking at the planner/manager's needs for forecasts within that process. No one of these different views can be said to be inherently the best or most useful. On the other hand, as we study different types of planning we may find that, in a particular context, each of these ways of thinking about a "decision" may be more or less useful.

Activity planning, to be discussed in Chapter 5, for the most part deals with a large number of small decisions which are made more or less independently within a broader organizational framework. No one decision

[1]Allison actually uses the term "governmental politics model." The term "political process" has been used here instead because the concepts involved can easily be applied in a much broader context.

is large enough to have major implications for the organization as a whole. It follows that little will be lost by thinking of these decisions as individual rational choices within a specified framework of organizational objectives.

By contrast, the annual or biennial budget process (also a topic for Chapter 5), although it can certainly be hoped to be at its base a rational process, is probably better understood as a complex organizational process designed for the communication of goals and the coordination of future activities, rather than as a static rational choice among a set of specified alternative budgets.

Finally, strategic and project planning that involves change—new products, processes, new ways of doing things, or new organizational forms—can best be viewed as a process of political negotiation among individuals and groups within the organization with different degrees of power or influence. We will turn to this topic in Chapter 10.

These distinctions are relevant to the subject of forecasting. Since we are concerned with forecasting as an element in the planning process, our view of what makes a good forecast will in each situation depend on how we view the planning process of which it is a part. At the same time, our primary focus in every case will be on the analytical tools available to the forecaster. For this reason, we will find it helpful to concentrate primarily on the rational-actor or rational-choice model of decision making.

THE RATIONAL-CHOICE MODEL OF DECISION MAKING

The rational-choice or rational-actor model of decision making and planning assumes that we are dealing with an analytical process where options and alternatives can be identified, objectives or goals are known, and the connections between the two can be formally modeled and analyzed. While only rarely is this completely true, as an abstraction it can be very useful in understanding many of the underlying issues.

The Basic Model

Figure 2–1 is a flow chart of the rational decision process designed to highlight the elements of the process that are most directly related to the development and use of forecasts. The starting point in this process is the decision maker (1), which may be a person but can also be some form of computer or automated choice generator. Based on some specified choice criterion, the decision maker generates a decision (2), that is, a specific choice of an action, which is then implemented. The action taken interacts (3) with forces in the external environment (4) to create an outcome (5). It

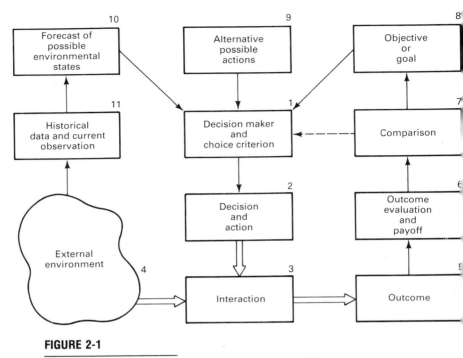

FIGURE 2-1

The rational decision model

is assumed that there is some basis for evaluating the outcome in terms of its payoff (6) so that it is possible to compare (7) the outcome with the decision-maker's goal or objective (8).

Supporting this choice process, it is assumed that the decision maker has a base of information that can be used for the analysis and the decision. This would include

the goal or objective (8),

an understanding of the underlying process (9), including both a list of the alternative available actions and knowledge of the ways in which these choices would interact with alternative possible states of the external environment to produce different possible outcomes,

forecasts of possible alternative environmental states (10) based on an analysis of historical data and on current observations (11).

The part of this model of most direct interest to the forecaster is in boxes 4, 10, and 11. The core of the model for the planner/manager, however, lies in boxes 2 through 5, the process by which the chosen action and the environment interact to produce the outcome. It is the modeling of this interaction that is considered here.

Outcome and Payoff Tables

The relationship between the action taken, the environment, and the outcome can be summarized in a two-dimensional form called an *outcome table* (Table 2–1). To construct this table, for each action (a_i) and each state of the external environment (s_j), it is necessary to describe the outcome (O_{ij}) that will occur. Clearly, this assumes that the structure of the underlying process is known, an assumption that is not always realistic but that, for the moment, we will accept. It is usually also assumed that it is possible to attach numbers to the different outcomes expressing their relative value or desirability. These numbers are termed *payoffs* and the table is then called a *payoff table*.

The easiest way of developing the idea of outcome and payoff tables is through an example. For this, we will temporarily leave our example of the hardware store and consider instead a larger and more established company that is installing a new computerized order-processing system. Since they are not yet completely familiar with the system, they are trying to decide on the best way of handling any maintenance problems that may arise. Three alternatives are being considered:

a_1 To obtain repairs locally as they may be needed.

a_2 To sign a service contract with the manufacturer, which would provide repair parts and repair personnel from the manufacturer's factory as necessary.

a_3 To set up a special repair shop within the plant, and buy repair equipment, hire repair personnel, and stock the necessary repair parts.

TABLE 2–1

Structure of an Outcome Table

Action	State of the Environment			
	s_1	s_2	s_3	s_4
a_1	O_{11}	O_{12}	O_{13}	O_{14}
a_2	O_{21}	O_{22}	O_{23}	O_{24}
a_3	O_{31}	O_{32}	O_{33}	O_{34}

In such a situation, descriptions of the outcomes would involve a number of different dimensions, including the costs of actual repairs and overhead, the amount and cost of downtime, and, in the case of the in-plant repair shop, the value of any additional benefits that might arise because the shop could be used for other repairs when it was not performing its major function. If we limit the description of the environment to the two issues of the number and cost of breakdowns and the total amount of downtime per year, it might be possible to simply characterize the three possibilities as high, medium, and low breakdown levels.[2] These, combined with the three alternative actions, would lead to the outcomes in Table 2–2.

If the manager were to completely describe each of these nine possible outcomes, it would take a substantial amount of space (and in some of the cases some rather colorful language.) To keep the example simple, only the essence of each description is given in the table.

In a case such as this, it is reasonable to assume that the goal of management is to minimize overall costs, including the costs of repairs, the repair parts, and the time lost to the company because of system downtime. If this is true, it will be possible for the manager to "cost out" each of the outcomes, giving the numbers or payoffs of Table 2–3.

If it were possible for the manager to determine in advance (forecast) the number of breakdowns (low, medium, or high) over the relevant planning horizon, the choice would be easy; it would only be necessary to choose the action with the lowest cost. Indeed, the forecaster may attempt to supply just such a forecast. If (as is usually the case) the forecaster cannot be completely certain of the answer or if the manager has less than complete confidence in the forecaster's abilities, some way of dealing with this forecast uncertainty must be found.

Decisions Under Uncertainty and Risk

Books on management science and statistics often distinguish between two situations: the case where the decision maker is able to generate a complete list of all possible states of the environment and attach probabilities to each indicating their relative likelihoods of occurring (referred to as decision making under *risk*) and the situation where this listing or probability assignment is not possible (called decision making under *uncertainty*). As we shall see in Chapter 5, most operational planning tends to

---

[2]To assume that the complex of issues involved in the breakdown pattern of this system can be captured in only three words, "high," "medium," and "low," is clearly unrealistic and in fact is unnecessary. We will treat this issue in a more realistic way in Chapter 5; for now, limiting the table to these three alternative states of the environment keeps the problem from becoming overly complicated.

TABLE 2-2

Outcome Table for an Equipment Maintenance Decision

	State of the Environment: Level of Maintenance and Repair Needed		
Alternative Action	Low	Medium	High
Obtain repair services as needed	Overall costs are low; little downtime	Repair costs about average; downtime is a significant factor	Repair costs are high; downtime adds a significant cost element as well as problems in production planning, requiring major management attention
Purchase a service contract from the manufacturer	Overall costs are increased by the cost of the service contract which is relatively unused; little downtime	Cost of the service contract is approximately covered by the reduction in repair costs covered by the contract; downtime is significant because repair personnel must come from the factory.	Because of the high repair needs substantial interaction with the equipment manufacturer is required; despite special efforts by the manufacturer, downtime is still high
Set up a repair shop in the plant	Costs are increased by the capital costs of setting up the repair shop; this is partially offset by using the shop for other work; little downtime.	The repair shop is used but there is still slack time for other work; downtime is shortened because the repair personnel are near the equipment	Repair shop is heavily used; Repair personnel begin to learn the idiosyncracies of the equipment and are able to reduce downtime per breakdown, although the number of breakdowns is still high

TABLE 2–3

Payoff Table for an Equipment Maintenance Decision (all costs are in $1000)

	State of the Environment		
Number of breakdowns/year:	Low 2	Medium 12	High 42
Alternative action			
Repair as needed	10	60	210
Service contract	61	91	181
Repair shop	90	110	155

fall into the category of "risk." Planning and forecasting in the case of "uncertainty" are explored in Chapter 10.

Minimum/Maximum Criteria.   In cases where it is not possible to assign probabilities to the alternative states of the environment, managers often tend to concentrate on the best and worst outcomes. Criteria of this type are referred to collectively as *min-max criteria*. Although they have a certain intuitive appeal, they should be used with caution. On the one hand, they enable us to put an upper or lower bound on the potential payoff, which can be helpful in planning. At the same time, they tend to focus our attention on only one state of the environment (a single forecast) and to ignore the full range of possible future conditions. In Chapter 10, however, we explore a modified use of the min-max criteria with particular applicability to problems of strategic planning.

To illustrate the use of this approach, suppose in this example that the forecaster is completely unable (or unwilling) to pick any of the three environmental states as more or less likely than any other. The manager might choose to look at the worst (maximum cost) outcome for each alternative action as identified in Table 2–4. It can be seen that the "worst of the worst" happens when repairs are ordered as needed and repair needs are high. The "best of the worst" (also called the min-max cost) occurs when the repair needs are high but the manager has decided to set up an in-plant repair shop. The argument underlying the min-max cost approach is that the manager, in the absence of any forecast to the contrary, would decide to set up the in-house repair shop in order to be protected against the worst that could happen.

Alternatively, the manager might concentrate on the best outcomes (also listed in Table 2–4). Here the "best of the best" occurs if the manager decides to obtain repairs as needed and needs turn out to be low

TABLE 2-4

Payoff Table for an Equipment Maintenance Decision: Min-Max Criteria (all costs are in $1000)

	State of the Environment			Worst Case: Maximum Cost	Best Case: Minimum Cost
Number of breakdowns/year:	Low 2	Medium 12	High 42		
Alternative action					
Repair as needed	10	60	210	210	10[b]
Service contract	61	91	181	181	61
Repair shop	90	110	155	155[a]	90
			Minimum	155	10

[a] The min-max cost
[b] The min-min cost

(the min-min cost).[3] Notice in both cases that the effect is that the planner considers only one forecast and ignores other possible environmental outcomes.

Opportunity Costs or Regrets.   One problem with using criteria based on actual costs (or profits) is that they mix two different issues. In forecasting and planning, the evaluation of any actual outcome should be separated into two distinct parts: (1) the payoff which results from the manager's decision and is therefore under her or his control and (2) the payoff which is environmentally determined and not under the manager's control. In this example, the cost of $210,000 associated with the outcome "make repairs as needed and high repair needs" is large for two different reasons. In retrospect, we would agree that the manager would have made a better decision in choosing to set up an in-house repair shop. At the same time, if repair needs turn out to be high, costs are going to be high as well, no matter what the decision. Conversely, if repair needs had turned out to be low, costs would have been low no matter what the manager decided. To separate these two factors, it is helpful to think in terms of opportunity costs or regrets.

For any state of the environment, the *opportunity cost* or *regret* associated with an outcome is defined as the difference between the actual payoff for that outcome and the payoff that would have occurred had the best action been chosen. For the outcome "purchase a service contract and repair needs turn out to be high," the cost is $181,000. Even with the best choice (the repair shop), the costs would have been $155,000. The most that the manager could have saved is the difference: $181,000 − $155,000 = $26,000. From the manager's point of view, this can be thought of as the "cost of the lost opportunity" or opportunity cost. Similar calculations can be applied to each of the other outcomes, giving the values shown in Table 2–5. Notice that every column has at least one zero opportunity cost since for each environmental state there will always be at least one "best" action. This is not true of the rows, as can be seen for the action a_2, the service contract.

If we now apply the min-max cost criterion to the opportunity costs, the action chosen is to purchase the service contract, even though that action would never be the best if the actual repair needs could be known in advance. Such a decision choice is sometimes referred to as *hedging*, for although the service contract is never the best choice, at the same time it is never the worst.

---

[3]When a payoff measure (such as profits) is used where large values correspond to favorable outcomes, the equivalent concepts are max-min profit and max-max profit.

TABLE 2–5

Payoff Table for an Equipment Maintenance Decision: Opportunity Costs (all costs are in $1000)

	State of the Environment			Worst Case: Maximum Opportunity Cost
Number of breakdowns/year:	Low 2	Medium 12	High 42	
Alternative Action				
Repair as needed	0	0	55	55
Service contract	51	31	26	51[a]
Repair shop	80	50	0	80
			Minimum	51

[a]The min-max opportunity cost

Expected Values.   When it is possible to assign probabilities to the states of the environment, the appropriate criterion is the *expected value,* which is sometimes defined as the long-run average value of the decision choice.[4] An expected value for each action alternative (row) is obtained by multiplying the payoffs by their probabilities of occurrence and then summing.

In Table 2–6, a forecast is given that the probability of low repair needs is 0.2, of medium, 0.3 and of high 0.5. The expected value of the action "purchase a service contract" is

$$0.2 \times 61 + 0.3 \times 91 + 0.5 \times 181 = \$130 \quad \text{(thousands)}$$

The expected opportunity cost is

$$0.2 \times 51 + 0.3 \times 31 + 0.5 \times 26 = \$32.5 \quad \text{(thousands)}$$

Similar calculations for the other decision alternatives are shown in the right column of Table 2–6. The best action according to the expected-value criterion is to obtain repairs as needed with an expected cost of $125,000. Unlike the case with min-max criteria, the use of either payoffs or of opportunity costs will lead to the same conclusion. Notice that the "most likely" outcome is that repair needs will be high, which would suggest setting up an in-plant shop. Since there is a substantial probability that the needs could be low or medium, the first option, getting repairs as needed, is the one with the lowest expected cost.

The Value of a Forecast.   From the point of view of the expected-value criterion, the job of the forecaster is to supply the planner or manager with the probabilities necessary for these calculations. From that perspective, the ideal forecast would be one with a probability of 1 assigned to the correct environmental state and 0 assigned to the other two. As a practical matter, such an ideal is never completely attainable. Forecasts can, however, frequently be improved so that the probability assigned to the correct state is increased and the others reduced. A question which often arises in this regard is how much time and effort should be put into developing a better forecast.

The concept of the expected opportunity cost can give a partial answer to this. First imagine that such an ideal forecast could be obtained. Since the correct action would then always be taken, the expected opportunity cost would be zero. On the other hand, suppose the manager were to decide to simply obtain repairs as needed. Based on the given probabili-

---

[4]It can be appropriate to use expected values even when a decision will never be repeated and when there may even be no meaning to the idea of a long-run average. For a discussion of this, see Levin and Kirkpatrick, pp. 194–198.

TABLE 2-6

Payoff Table for an Equipment Maintenance Decision (all costs are in $1000)

Expected Values

	State of the Environment			
	Low 2	Medium 12	High 42	
Number of breakdowns/year				*Expected Cost*
Alternative Action				
Repair as needed	10	60	210	125.00[a]
Service contract	61	91	181	130.00
Repair shop	90	110	155	128.50
Probability of occurrence	0.2	0.3	0.5	Minimum 125.00

[a]Minimum expected costs

Opportunity costs

	State of the Environment			
	Low 2	Medium 12	High 42	
Number of breakdowns/year				*Expected Opportunity Cost*
Alternative Action				
Repair as needed	0	0	55	27.50[b]
Service contract	51	31	26	32.50
Repair shop	80	50	0	31.00
Probability of occurrence	0.2	0.3	0.5	Minimum 27.50

[b]Minimum expected opportunity cost

ties, the expected opportunity cost is $27,500. It follows that $27,500 per year is the most that could be saved (on the average) and no forecast could be worth more than that amount. As a practical matter, ideal forecasts are unattainable; a more realistic goal might be a 10% improvement in the forecast accuracy. This presumably would save 10% of $27,500 or $2750 per year. Such a saving might be worth 3 to 4 weeks of a forecaster's time but probably not more.

The State of the Environment as a Continuous Variable

As developed so far, the payoff table has one major artificiality: the idea that the complexities of the possible states of the future environment can be captured by listing a relatively small number of alternatives, in this case three, low, medium, or high. Even if we were to assume that a single variable such as "number of breakdowns per year" would be adequate for describing the relevant environment, such a variable would have many more than three possible values. Although it will increase the complexity of the calculations, the concepts of expected cost and expected opportunity cost can easily be extended to cases where the environment is described by a (more or less) continuous variable. In Chapters 5 and 10, we will extend this to considering cases where many different variables may be needed to describe the relevant environment.

As an example, suppose that a manager is faced with choosing a production process for a new product and has two available alternatives. The first (I) involves hand assembly. The costs are $1000 per day plus $3 per unit. If the average production level required is above 4800 units per day, however, an additional $2.50 per unit is required to cover the cost of overtime. Alternative II is a more mechanized process. The costs are $5000 per day plus $2 per unit. Capacity is such that overtime would not be necessary. It can be seen in Figure 2–2a that the break-even point is at a daily production of 4000 units.

Opportunity costs can be calculated for each output level exactly as in the payoff table. Below 4000 units, the better choice is process I, so the opportunity cost of using it is zero. For process II, the opportunity cost is the additional cost that would arise from its use. Thus, at 2500 units, process I would cost

$$\$1000 + 3 \times 2500 = \$8500$$

whereas process II would cost

$$\$5000 + 2 \times 2500 = \$10,000$$

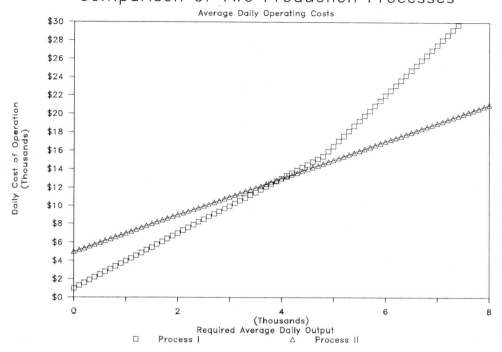

FIGURE 2-2a

Comparison of two production processes: Average daily operating costs

The difference of $1500 is the opportunity cost of using process II. Other points on the two lines are similarly calculated and shown in Figure 2–2b (p. 34).

As we will see in Chapter 5, the forecaster needs to supply a probability distribution of demand so that expected values can be calculated. The planner, in turn, will use this distribution to calculate the necessary expected opportunity costs. Although the full calculation is beyond the scope of what can be covered here, a few general illustrations can be given. Figure 2–3 shows the opportunity cost graphs from Figure 2–2b overlaid with several alternative probability distributions. Try to imagine in each case that you are adding up the opportunity cost for all the values of daily output under the probability curve, giving heaviest weight in the center of the distribution, where the probability curve is highest, and least weight to the opportunity costs toward the tails. In Figure 2–3a (p. 35), almost the entire distribution lies between 2000 and 5000 units. Even though the forecast, as represented by that distribution, is not particularly accurate,

Comparison of Two Production Processes

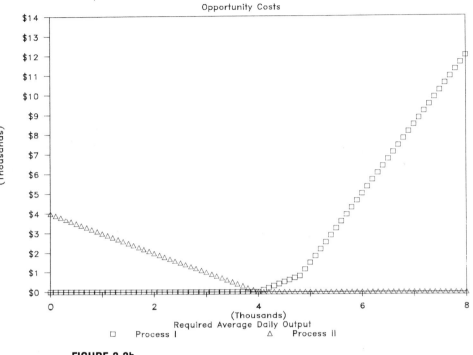

Opportunity Costs

FIGURE 2-2b

Comparison of two production processes: Opportunity costs

the potential costs of using process II, given the probability that the output will be below 4000 units, can be seen to be greater than that of using process I, given the probability that production will be over 4000 units. The manager would feel comfortable using process I; improving the accuracy of the forecast is unlikely to change that decision.

Now compare Figures 2–3b and c. In both cases the "most likely" required output is about 3800 units. In Figure 2–3b (p. 36), this can be seen to be a very accurate forecast, leading again to the conclusion that process I is preferable. By contrast, in Figure 2–3c (p. 37) the "point forecast" of 3800 units would be the same. At the same time, the forecast accuracy is much lower. Here the manager might prefer process II because the risk of incurring the high overtime costs if output turns out to be over 4800 units is substantially greater that the risk of incurring the high daily fixed costs of process II if output is less than 4000 units.

This highlights a central problem faced by the forecaster. In many cases the choice of an action by a manager can depend as much on the expected accuracy of the forecast as on the forecast itself. Point forecasts

Comparison of Two Production Processes

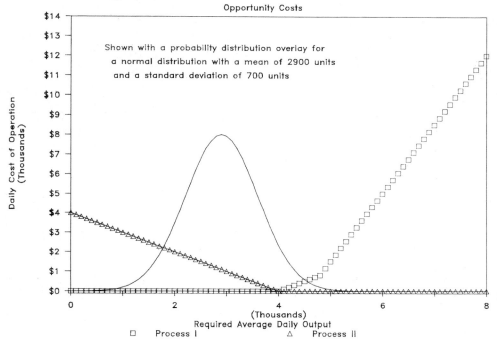

FIGURE 2-3a

Comparison of two production processes: Opportunity costs

will not be adequate. In the same way, presenting the forecast in a way that makes it appear to be more accurate than it really is can hinder rather than help the decision-making process.

SUMMARY

Chapter 2 introduced a model of the planning process that illustrates the range of different decisions that must be made within any organization and the different ways that environmental uncertainty can influence that decision making. The concepts of outcome and payoff tables were used to introduce the way that the manager's decisions interact with the external environment.

In supporting the planner or manager, the job of the forecaster is to generate alternative states of the future environment and, in those cases where it is possible, to estimate the probabilities that each of the alterna-

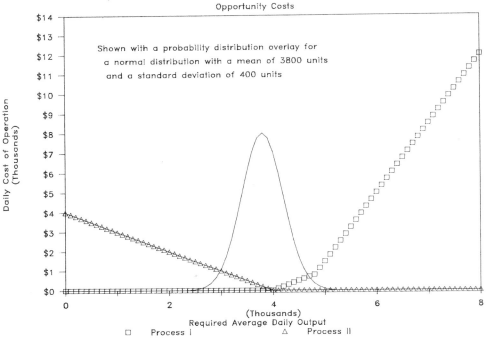

Comparison of Two Production Processes
Opportunity Costs

FIGURE 2-3b

Comparison of two production processes: Opportunity costs

tive futures generated may be the correct one. In Chapters 5 to 9 we consider in more detail planning situations where the environmental descriptions are relatively simple and the emphasis is on the estimation of probabilities. Chapters 10 to 12 are concerned with cases where the environmental descriptions are much more complex and the challenge to the forecaster is in conceptualizing the range of possible future states. In preparation for this, in Chapters 3 and 4 we begin to examine some of the basic tools of the forecaster.

READINGS

The Planning Process

Many books have been written on the planning process as illustrated in the hardware store example of this chapter. The topic is also a central element in most books on the fundamentals of management. For example, see

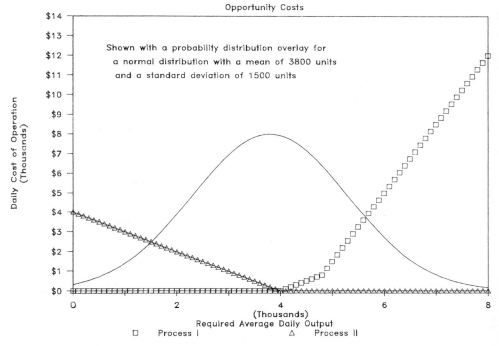

FIGURE 2-3c

Comparison of two production processes: Opportunity costs

JAMES A. F. STONER and CHARLES WANKEL, *Management,* 3rd ed., Englewood Cliffs, N.J., Prentice-Hall, 1986.

The Nature of a Decision

For a description of the different views of decision making introduced in this chapter, see

GRAHAM T. ALLISON, *Essence of Decision,* Boston, Little, Brown & Co., 1971.

Rational-Choice Model of Decision Making

Material on rational decision models and decision criteria are now standard in all books on management science. A good presentation can be found in

RICHARD I. LEVIN and CHARLES A. KIRKPATRICK, *Quantitative Approaches to Management,* 5th ed., New York, McGraw-Hill, 1982.

One classic in this area is

ROBERT SCHLAIFER, *Probability and Statistics for Business Decisions,* New York, McGraw-Hill, 1959.

PROBLEMS

1. Select some activity that you have always dreamed of doing and that would make a major change in your life-style. Examples might include opening a small business, sailing around the world in a small boat, becoming a homesteader in Alaska or a painter in Paris. In preparing for and carrying out your dream, what plans would you have to develop? What assumptions would you have to make about the future? As a general guide, use the hardware store example from the text.

2. The Miller Company has some available capital and is considering alternative uses for it. Management has agreed that the appropriate measure for evaluation is the net present value of the return over a 5-year planning horizon. They can acquire a small manufacturing company which is for sale, expand their existing operations, or keep the capital in more liquid investments.

To evaluate these alternatives, management has constructed three scenarios for the future economic and political climate, which they have termed (A) stagnant, (B) expansionary, and (C) variable and uncertain. For each of these scenarios, the planning staff has estimated returns as follows:

Strategy	*Estimated Returns*
Acquisition	$80 million for A
	$200 million for B
	$15 million for C
Expansion	$85 million for A
	$150 million for B
	$30 million for C
Liquid investments	$90 million for A
	$95 million for B
	$85 million for C

a. Set up a payoff table for this problem.

b. Using the criteria of max-min profit and max-max profit, which alternatives would you choose?

c. Set up an opportunity cost table.

d. Using the criterion of min-max opportunity cost, which alternative would you choose?

e. What issues might be involved in deciding on an appropriate decision criterion?

3. Planners for the Smith Division of the Jones Company are preparing budgets for the upcoming quarter. The Smith Division makes a food product that is packaged in bulk and needs to determine the aggregate amount of production to be planned for the quarter in order to set budgets for materials, personnel, and other production and shipping costs. You are given the following information:

Selling price:	$20 per unit volume
Fixed costs:	$3.5 million per quarter
Variable costs:	$6 per unit to 350,000 units
	$9 per unit for units over 350,000
	$12 per unit for units over 450,000

Average quarterly demand is 330,000 units

Because of policy and physical restrictions, *planned* production cannot be less than 300,000 or more than 500,000 units. Once the plan is set, the production quantity cannot be increased because ordering commitments will have been set. If planned production exceeds demand, production can be cut back, but at a cost of $6 per unit for the difference between planned production and actual demand.

a. If planned production is 300,000 and demand is 400,000 units, calculate the profit.

b. Repeat part a for production of 500,000 and demand of 300,000 units.

c. For convenience, assume that only three levels of production are to be considered, 300,000, 400,000 and 500,000 units, and that demand can only take on four values: 200,000, 300,000, 400,000 and 500,000 units. Set up the payoff table for this problem.

d. Demand probabilities are

Demand	Probability
200,000	0.2
300,000	0.4
400,000	0.3
500,000	0.1

What level of production should be planned using the expected-profit criterion?

e. Develop an opportunity cost table.

f. Calculate the expected opportunity cost. How might this calculation influence the amount that you would be willing to spend on obtaining a better forecast of demand?

4. A company is becoming concerned because their production facilities are old and, while almost fully depreciated, are relatively inefficient. A recommendation has been made that the current facilities be closed and a new plant built, but management feels that this is a bit extreme and has asked whether it might not be possible to just modernize the present facilities.

The following information has been obtained:

With the present plant, fixed costs are $5000 per week and variable costs average $4 per unit.

A new plant would reduce variable costs to $2 per unit, but fixed costs are estimated at $25,000 per week.

Modernization would raise fixed costs to $10,000 per week and would reduce variable costs to $3.40 per unit.

Weekly demand for the product is expected to remain relatively stable and average somewhere between 7000 and 15,000 units per week.

a. Graph total weekly (fixed + variable) cost as a function of average weekly demand over the applicable range.

b. It has been decided to simplify the problem by assuming that demand can only take on one of four values: 8000, 10,000, 12,000, or 14,000 units. Set up a payoff table based on this assumption. How realistic do you think this modification is?

c. From the payoff table in part b, develop a table of opportunity costs. Current forecasts available to the company indicate that there is a probability of 0.2 that average weekly demand will be 8000 units, 0.4 that it will be 10,000, 0.3 that it will be 12,000, and 0.1 that it will be 14,000. Determine the expected costs for each of the three alternatives and discuss how this would influence the decision.

d. It has been suggested that, before any decisions are made, better forecasts of future demand should be obtained. What are the issues involved here? Based on your analysis in part c, how much do you think should be paid for an improved forecast? (*Note:* You will not be able to come up with a specific numerical answer but should consider the elements involved in the decision.)

5. The Gotham City Business Association is planning a public seminar on "Planning Your Personal Finances" and is trying to decide on a location in which to hold it. Two halls are available. One holds 500 people and rents for $200; the other holds 1500 people with a rental of $400. Other costs are $2000 for the speaker and $1000 for miscellaneous costs such as advertising and printing. Tickets will sell for $10. Assume no tickets can be sold beyond the capacity of the hall.

   a. Graph as a function of ticket demand the profits associated with each of the three actions: rent the small hall, rent the large hall, or do not hold the seminar. On this graph show the ranges of possible ticket demands for which each of the three actions is optimal.

   b. Graph as a function of ticket demand the opportunity costs for each of the three actions.

   c. For each of the following forecasts, indicate from your answer to part b which action you think would have the highest expected profit. Give reasons for your answers.

Forecast	*Expected Demand*	*Range*
A	450 tickets	350–550
B	450 tickets	250–800
C	350 tickets	50–650

CHAPTER 3

Data Analysis

for Forecasters

This book looks at the place of forecasting in the broader context of managerial planning and decision making and does not attempt a detailed examination of the many forecasting techniques that are available to the professional forecaster. At the same time, it is important to examine some of the technical aspects of forecasting as a way of understanding the issues involved in choosing and applying specific approaches or methods. Although forecasts are directed toward the future, the major source of data for forecasting is the past.[1] A forecaster can be thought of as a sort of historian, exploring the past for clues to what may occur in the future. In this, the single most important source is the quantitative time series: data

[1] In one sense, all data are historical. In forecasting, however, it can be useful to distinguish data that describe the present state of the environment from data that form the more extended historical record.

that are routinely collected at specific points in time and in a com
and format. Companies maintain records of weekly or monthly sal
ernments regularly report information on a wide range of social and eco
nomic factors, such as GNP and the Consumer Price Index. Indeed the
amount of data available to the forecaster can be somewhat overwhelming.
At the same time, the amount of *relevant* data may be very limited. To
decide what time-series information to use and how to interpret it is one of
the forecaster's major challenges.

This is a problem familar to anyone who has had a course in elementary
statistics: how do you summarize and interpret large masses of quantitative
data? In Chapters 3 and 4 we explore some simple techniques. In having to
choose among the many approaches available, we have been guided here, as
in the entire book, by two criteria: (1) the techniques presented should
illustrate the basic concepts involved and set the stage for the discussion of
specific forecasting methods and applications, and (2) the techniques should
be simple enough so that a planner/manager can use them without needing
large computers, specialized software, or the support of a technical staff. For
the reader with no previous introduction to statistics, the material presented
here should be enough to get started. One with a more extended background in statistics will be familiar with many of the ideas presented and will
probably be mystified by the omission of some of his or her favorite techniques. Despite this, we hope that they will find the techniques and the
different applications which are discussed of interest.

The material of Chapters 3 and 4 is so basic to the remainder of the
book that it has been deliberately collected here in one spot. The person
with little or no previous exposure to forecasting or statistics may wish to
spend some time in mastering these concepts before proceeding. Others
may prefer to jump immediately to Part III or Part IV and return to these
chapters only as specific questions arise.

Chapter 3 deals with a number of issues relevant to all statistical
analysis, not just time series. These include some hints on developing and
using graphs, on understanding and editing data, and on developing summary descriptions of large masses of statistical data—all basic concepts and
techniques that will be used throughout the book.

Chapter 4 addresses issues of time-series analysis more directly. In
modeling or describing movements over time in a time series, three specific types of patterns have been identified:

Trends. Long-term tendencies for a time series to increase or
decrease

Seasonal Movements. Short-term fluctuations around the trend that
are tied to specific calendar periods

Cycles. Fluctuations over varying periods not tied specifically to the
calendar

Because they are so fundamental, these patterns directly or indirectly underlie most of the approaches to forecasting in common use. They are introduced along with the related concept of time-series decomposition. Later chapters return to these concepts in particular applications.

DATA ANALYSIS

Forecasting is concerned with the future, yet the analytical interests of the forecaster lie not in the future but in the past, the only source of actual data. Forecasting has sometimes been compared to a person who is blindfolded driving down a winding mountain road at 65 miles per hour, while someone else gives driving instructions by looking out the rear window. It follows that the forecaster as an analyst has much in common with the historian. The historian's interest, however, normally centers on the study of specific major historical events and is not particularly concerned with whether these events are likely ever to recur. The forecaster, by contrast, is looking for historical patterns that are likely to recur in the future and tends for this reason to take a more quantitative and statistical interest in the past.

The data of interest to the forecaster take two basic forms: (1) *cross-sectional studies*, such as surveys or market studies carried out at a specific time, and (2) *time series*, which are data on a single variable collected in a consistent way over time and usually at equally spaced intervals.

Cross-sectional studies can be used as a basis for forecasting by analogy. For example, a market study conducted in territory A last year may be used to predict sales in territory B this year if the two territories seem relatively similar and if no study is currently available for territory B. The use of analogy in forecasting is, of course, enhanced when there are several different and comparable cross-sectional studies available.

In many cases, analogy is the only possible approach to forecasting. In anticipating the potential impact of a *new* technology, no directly relevant historical information can be available. We look instead for some similar past technology which may supply clues to the probable development of the new. New products, new markets, and new production processes can present similar challenges.

In operational planning and in circumstances where there is a sense of continuity between past, present, and future, time series are of major importance. Particularly when forecasting time horizons are relatively short, many (although not all) of the major patterns that can be observed in a time series will tend to persist. The problem for the forecaster is to decide which historical patterns will continue into the future and which are transitory.

In this chapter and the next, we will temporarily put aside the topic of forecasting in order to consider some approaches that can be used in searching for patterns in time series. This is not intended to be an exhaustive coverage of the topic. The techniques described have been chosen with two purposes in mind: that they be illustrative of types of procedures that are commonly used by forecasters and that they be simple enough so that the manager or planner who would like to be his or her own forecaster can apply them using nothing more than paper, pencil, a simple calculator, and a few sheets of graph paper. As discussed in the introduction, this does not mean that application of these techniques will not be facilitated by use of the many spreadsheet, graphics, and statistical software packages now available for microcomputers. There will always be occasions, however, in the middle of a meeting or at one's desk, when the ability to rapidly generate a graph or to summarize some statistical data will prove invaluable.

Major Points To Be Noted

1. *The components of a time series: trend, cycles, seasonal and residual.*
2. *Graphing as a tool in data analysis and data presentation.*
3. *The things you should know about any data that you are working with.*
4. *Techniques for summarizing and analyzing residuals.*

PATTERNS IN TIME SERIES

Time-series analysis is a search for patterns. Many of the techniques used in this search involve some form of data decomposition. That is, patterns in the data are identified and studied in sequence. As each component pattern is determined, it is removed from the data. The *residual*, that is, the data with that pattern removed, is then examined for other possible patterns. As a prelude to our discussion of data analysis, it will be helpful to examine a typical time-series decomposition.

The search for component patterns is not a completely haphazard process; certain types of patterns are routinely observed in many different time series, and it is thus possible to develop a general search strategy. To illustrate one possibility, consider the time series shown in Figure 3–1. A visual examination of the graph should suggest the existence of several different types of movement.

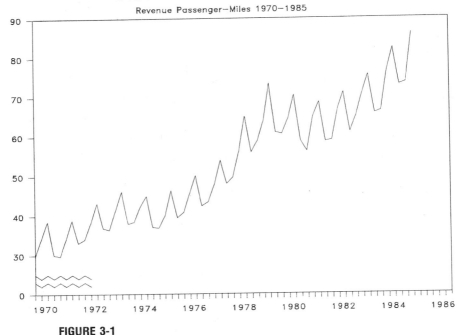

FIGURE 3-1

U.S. scheduled airlines: Revenue passenger-miles, 1970–1985 (*Source:* U.S. Department of Commerce, Bureau of Economic Analysis, *Survey of Current Business,* various issues, 1971–1985)

The Trend.   Trends are systematic tendencies for a time series to increase or decrease over time. Series which show a trend are sometimes referred to as *nonstationary* or *nonstationary in the mean* because a trend can be interpreted as a systematic shifting of the mean or average value of the time series. In the date shown in Figure 3–1, the trend appears as an underlying upward movement, with the data fluctuating between 30 and 45 billion passenger-miles per year in the early 1970s and fluctuating between 70 and 90 billion passenger-miles per year 15 years later.

Fluctuations around the Trend.   In addition to this general upward movement, other systematic movements or fluctuations around the trend can be seen. Some of these appear to be tied to the calendar, to specific dates, holidays, times of day, or season of the year. Others, while showing some regularity, do not seem to be so tied to the calendar. The first of these are called *seasonal* patterns and the second are called *cyclical*. Here the seasonal appears as a systematic tendency for third quarters to be relatively high or above the underlying trend, while first and fourth quarters are correspondingly low. The cyclical can be seen by comparing the periods 1973 to 1974 and 1979 to 1983 (where the underlying movement was either horizontal or sloping downward) with the rapid increases that took place between 1975 and 1978 and again since 1983.

When the term seasonal is used by itself it normally refers to patterns that recur annually. Particularly in very short range forecasting, there can be important seasonal patterns that recur over other periods of time. For example, highway traffic or the use of public transportation will show patterns which reoccur on daily and weekly bases. In such cases, reference is made to a daily seasonal or a weekly seasonal pattern.

Although it is usually relatively easy to determine the social or climatic reasons for seasonal fluctuations, the analysis of cyclical patterns presents more of a challenge. Indeed, for many managerial decisions the analysis and forecasting of the business cycle can be the single most important concern of the forecaster.

The Residual. The term residual is used in two different ways. At each stage in the process of decomposition, the unanalyzed remainder of the time series is referred to (temporarily) as the residual as it waits for further analysis. At some point, however, no apparent systematic patterns will remain; the time series will appear to be (at least on the surface) simply random or unpatterned "noise." This (final) residual is the part of the data that would seem to be inherently unpredictable. We need to stress "seem to be," because frequently potentially analyzable patterns will still remain; it will just not be economically or technically practical to spend any more time or resources on the analysis.

Decomposition

Patterns in Single-variable Time Series. The process of decomposition starts with the removal of the most obvious components, the seasonal and the trend. With these removed, the search for other patterns proceeds. Figure 3–2 illustrates graphically a decomposition of the time series of Figure 3–1. In your previous visual examination of that time series, the two most obvious patterns were probably the general tendency for the series to move upward to the right (the trend) and the systematic annual pattern, with the first and fourth quarters being relatively low and the third quarter high (the seasonal).

Techniques for analyzing (and removing) the seasonal component are developed in Chapter 4. One possible approach is to think of the different quarters of each year in relation to the pattern that would exist if there

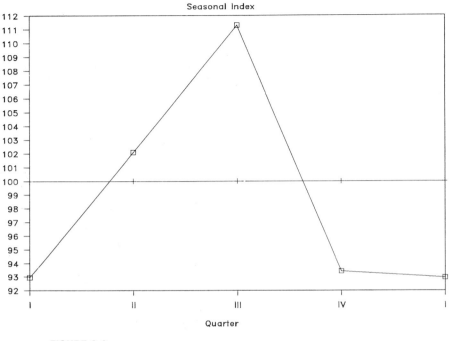

Airline Revenue Passenger—Miles

FIGURE 3-2a

Airline revenue passenger-miles: Seasonal index

were no seasonal component. As we will see, the difficulty is in separating, for each year, the seasonal from the random noise. We need to look for a sort of "average" seasonal, as shown in Figure 3–2a. Thus, if we think of 100 as a base with no seasonal pattern, then, over the 15-year period, third quarters have tended on the average to be approximately 11% above that base, whereas first and fourth quarters have been roughly 7% below it.

Removing this average seasonal pattern gives the graph of Figure 3–2b. This time series is referred to as *deseasonalized* or *seasonally adjusted*. With the seasonal component removed, it can be seen that the trend still appears much as it did in Figure 3–1, while the cyclical movement has become much clearer.

The trend component can be analyzed and removed in several different ways. For simplicity, it is shown in Figure 3–2b as a straight upward-sloping line. Figure 3–2c shows the data when the trend has been removed by taking the differences between the deseasonalized data and the trend

Airline Revenue Passenger−Miles
Seasonally Adjusted with Linear Trend

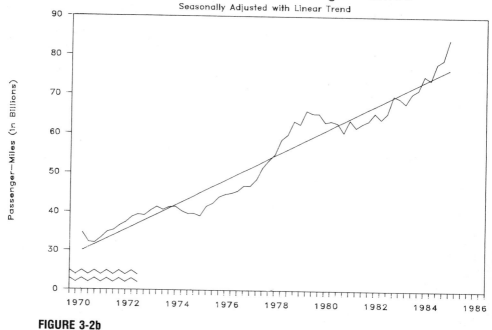

FIGURE 3-2b

Airline Revenue Passenger−Miles
Deviations from Linear Trend

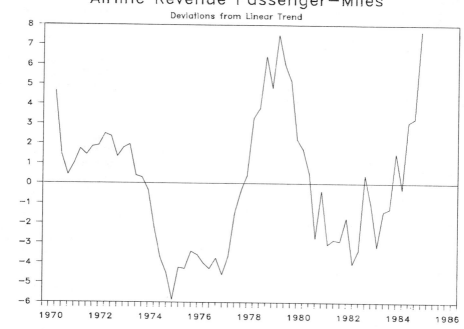

FIGURE 3-2c

line. The scale in Figure 3–2c has been expanded to emphasize the cyclical movement which now is shown as a fluctuation around a horizontal base line. In addition to this cyclical component, the graph continues to show some apparently random movements. If these are removed, the cyclical pattern appears as in Figure 3–2d. Notice that for the years shown the cyclical fluctuations seem to have a period that is around 5 to 6 years, but, in any case, is much less exact than the fixed 1-year period of the seasonal.

The (final) residual can be plotted as in Figure 3–2e (notice again the scale change). To emphasize the more or less random nature of the residual, the individual points have been left unconnected and replaced by vertical bars. Although the residual does not show any clear pattern of movement around this horizontal line, one additional pattern does appear: on the average the magnitudes of the residuals appear to be increasing over time. This is a topic that we will return to in Chapter 4.

Multivariate Patterns.   Up to this point we have considered only patterns in single-variable time series. It is also useful in forecasting to consider ways in which different time series can be interrelated. Two of these are of particular interest to the forecaster: (1) situations where different time series show similar cyclical fluctuations, and (2) those where there are relationships beween residuals from different time series.

Sometimes different time series exhibit cyclical patterns which are similar except that the timing of the cyclical peaks and troughs is different. That is, one series tends to reach its peaks and troughs before the other. If such a lagged pattern is observed consistently, it can be of value in forecasting the lagging series. When the first series passes a turning point, the forecaster can then expect that the other, after an appropriate time lag, will also show a peak or trough. In economic forecasting, frequent reference is made to *leading indicators*, that is, to series that tend to move ahead of movements in the overall economy and for that reason can be used in forecasting. We will see an example of this in Chapter 8.

Multivariate patterns can also be found between residuals. Residuals that can appear random and unpredictable when viewed as a single series may, in fact, be closely related to the residuals of a second series. If the residual movements of the second series are, for some reason, more predictable or if they lead the residual movements of the first series, such information can be useful to the forecaster. As an example, a wholesaler may find that demand at the retail level tends to lead demand at the wholesale level since retailers fill the immediate demand out of their stocks and then reorder to rebuild inventory. Consumer-level demand can thus act as a leading indicator for the wholesaler for both cyclical and residual movements in demand.

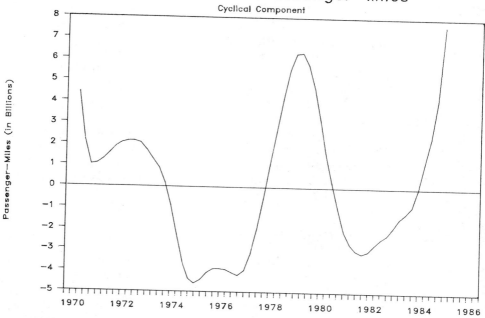

FIGURE 3-2d

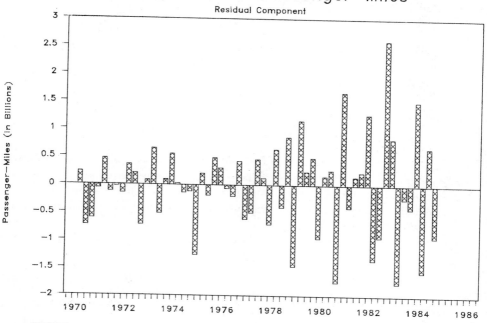

FIGURE 3-2e

GRAPHING TIME SERIES

In searching for patterns in time series, graphs can be particularly helpful. It is to the planner/manager's benefit to be able to interpret graphs rapidly and even to be able to draw or quickly sketch them to make a point in a discussion or as an aid to analysis. Even in working with computer graphics as in Lotus 1-2-3, not everything can be preprogrammed; an understanding of the structure and interpretation of graphs can be a useful skill and can aid in communication with technical analysts. This section gives a brief introduction to this important topic; more complete discussions are found in some of the references at the end of the chapter.

Choosing Graph Paper and Materials

A variety of different types of graph paper are commercially available. You will get best results using those types that are marked in small squares with heavier lines at every fifth and tenth square. Do not confuse this type of graph paper with quadrule paper, which has light blue horizontal and vertical lines spaced four or five to the inch. Although this is sometimes also referred to as "graph paper," the wider spacing of the lines makes accurate graphing difficult. Quadrule paper can be useful for making very rapid rough sketches and for tabular work where the vertical lines help in aligning columns of numbers. Also, don't use graph paper that has the heavier lines marked on every sixth or twelfth line in both the horizontal and vertical directions; this is intended for architectural drafting. If you are going to be doing a large amount of work with monthly data, however, special paper is available with the horizontal scale divided in groups of twelve and sometimes with months premarked.

Laying Out the Graph

Over time a number of conventions have developed to help in drawing and interpreting graphs. Although they are not sacrosanct, they can be useful in helping others in interpreting your data analysis and in understanding your forecast. You will probably also find them useful when you accidentally unearth a graph you drew six months before and try to remember what it was for. Figure 3–3a illustrates some of the basics of drawing time-series graphs.[2]

---

[2] In general, these same conventions should be followed in developing computer graphics. Unfortunately, the limitations of most graphics software make this difficult. The user must either modify the suggestions given here or resort to "cut and paste" methods for putting the graph together.

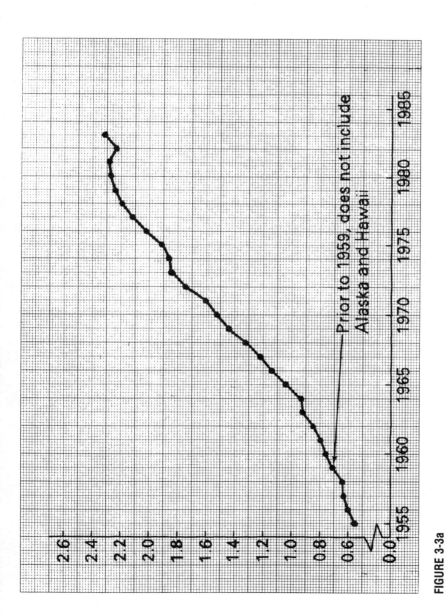

FIGURE 3-3a

Production of Electric Power by Electric Utilities: United States, 1955–1983. Excludes industrial facilities and railroads having own generating capacity. (*Source:* U.S. Department of Commerce, Bureau of the Census, *Historical Statistics Colonial Times to 1970* (Sept., 1975) and various issues of *The Statistical Abstract of the United States*.)

1. Every graph should have a heading. Even rough sketches should be labeled for future reference. This heading should include at a minimum:

A sequence number: Figure 3–3a

A title giving:

What data are plotted on the graph: Production of Electric Power

What geographic area or organizational group is represented or covered: Electric Utilities in the United States

What period of time is included: 1955–1983

Any additional information necessary should be put in a headnote directly below the title ("Excludes industrial facilities and railroads having own generating capacity") or in a footnote ("Prior to 1959, does not include Alaska or Hawaii") below the graph. If you want to make sure that the reader sees the information, put it in a headnote; if it is only "interesting" or only refers to a part of the graph, it should be in a footnote.

2. Show your source. When the data plotted have been obtained from some outside source (called secondary data), a source note should be placed below the graph (and after any footnotes). The information in the source note should be detailed enough so that the reader can locate the source if desired or necessary. It should cite the source where the data were obtained and not the original source. The source note should follow the same format as a bibliographic reference in a paper. Finally, the person preparing the graph should always put her or his name or initials and the date at the bottom of each graph.

3. Make your scales easy to read and understand. Vertical and horizontal scale lines should be marked on all graphs. Scales should follow the markings on the paper, with lines corresponding to multiples of 2, 5, or 10 units. Use of other multiples such as 3 or 4 generally leads to graphs in which it is difficult to interpolate between the scale lines. Numbers showing the scale units are placed only on the heavier lines and, as on the horizontal scale line in Figure 3-3a, need not be on every line. Some applications require the use of varying scale spacing, as in the log graph shown in the appendix to Chapter 4. In these cases, it is desirable to use specialized graph papers that have the scales premarked.

Each scale should be labeled in a prominent place with the name of the variable and the units of the scale. Occasionally it is necessary to plot two (or more) pairs of variables on the same graph but with different units. In such a case there should be a separate scale for each variable. Also, when a graph is unusually wide, it is common to include a duplicate scale on the right side of the graph. In plotting time series, the horizontal scale refers to historical or chronological time. In this case the scale units are shown, but the scale is not otherwise labeled.

4. Show the base line for the vertical scale.   Points on a graph are plotted relative to a base line that is normally at zero or (for ratios or index numbers) at 100. With rare exceptions, the horizontal base line should always be shown on the graph. Frequently, when all the values of the variable lie above the base line, it will be the same as the horizontal scale line.[3]

The scale units should be chosen so that the graph shows adequate detail. In many cases this would require an excessive amount of blank paper between the base line and the lowest plotted values of the variable. In such a case, part of the vertical scale should be omitted and replaced by some form of clearly marked scale break as shown at the lower left in Figures 3–3a and 3–3b. When plotting index numbers, notice that the base line is at 100 rather than 0 so that no scale break is needed, even though 0 is not shown. When plotting percents of a total, there should be two base lines, at 0 and at 100, so two different scale breaks may be needed. It is sometimes possible to add a scale break to a computer-drawn graph as in Figure 3–1. In these cases, a base line must still be created by adding a zero point to the vertical scale.

5. Make the intent of the graphs clear.   Normally, in plotting the data points they should be connected by straight lines. Although in engineering drawing smoothed curves are sometimes drawn through the points, this is neither necessary nor desirable in time-series analysis. In plotting residuals where the randomness of the points is to be emphasized, the points may be left unconnected. If it is desirable to emphasize the sequence in which the residuals occurred, the points can be connected by light lines to the base line, or a bar chart can be used as in Figure 3–2e.

It is usually best to plot a separate graph for each time series. Several different variables can be plotted on the same graph when it is necessary to compare patterns. Even here it is usually better, when possible, to use separate graphs placed one above the other. When two or more time series are plotted together, different types of lines such as dots, dashes, or combinations of dots and dashes should be used to distinguish among the variables. Computer graphics programs often use different symbols to mark the data points for the different series. Be cautious about using different colors. This can look attractive on the original but will not be distinguishable in black and white reproductions.

---

[3] A shortcoming of most computer graphics programs is that they show the horizontal scale line but not the base line.

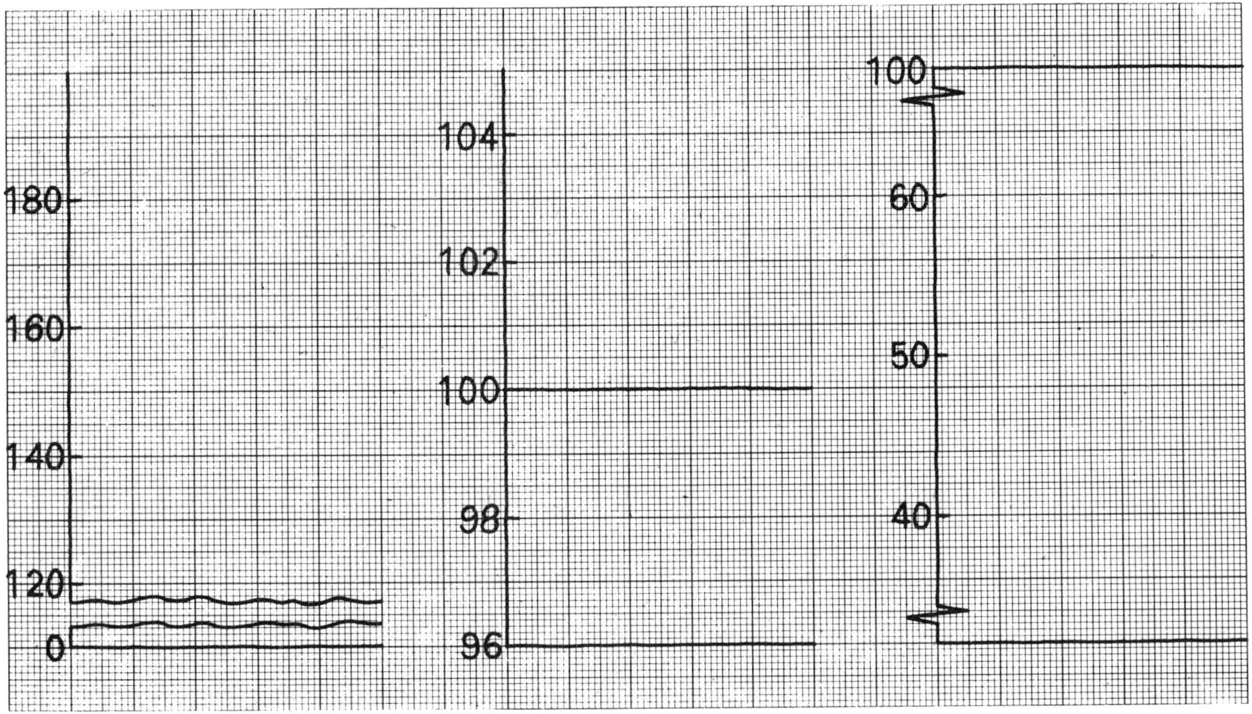

FIGURE 3-3b

Base lines, scale lines, and scale breaks

56

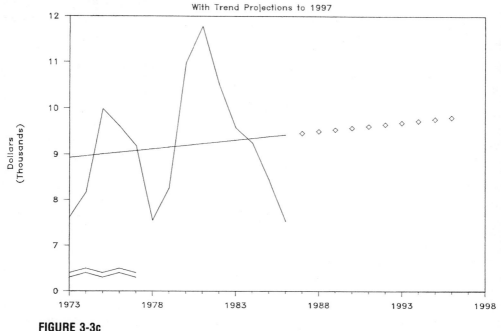

FIGURE 3-3c

A hypothetical time series, 1973–1986, with trend projections to 1997

When plotting both historical data and forecasted projections, a clear distinction should be made between the two. This can be done, as in Figure 3–3c, by using a different type of line marking or by using a dashed or dotted line.

FIRST STEPS: GETTING TO KNOW YOUR DATA

There is a failing that seems to afflict almost all forecasters, novice and experienced alike. You may be interested in forecasting, for example, the production of beer in the United States or the sales of automobiles. You locate a time series labeled "beer production" or "automobile sales" and, without further thought, begin the data analysis. Sometimes, if the data are available on tape or disk, you may simply "plug it in" as a variable in some computer program or model. One of the most important lessons that forecasters can learn from the historian is never to take any written record at face value. Each fact or piece of data should be examined in terms of its source, of how, why, and under what circumstances it was recorded, and of its relevance to the specific questions being researched. In the United States we have been spoiled by the generally excellent quality of collected historical statistics. Nevertheless, we would be wise to develop some skepticism in our use of data, especially when we have not been involved in its collection (and frequently even if we have). Rarely will we have to duplicate the detailed investigation required of a historian. At the same time, there are a few basic questions to ask and adjustments to consider as a prelude to any actual analysis of a time series.

What Does the Time Series Really Measure?

Many familiar time series have "common" names that may or may not completely reflect the actual nature of the series. A good example is the Consumer Price Index, CPI(W). This index takes a "market basket" of goods and services typical of the purchases of one segment of the population (urban wage-earner and clerical-worker families of two or more people) and measures changes in the amount that would have to be spent to buy this collection of goods and services. It may or may not reflect changes in the prices of goods typically purchased by unmarried college students, the elderly, or rural or farm families.[4] Also, as prices change they never all change at the same rate, and people tend to alter their spending patterns to reflect this. Thus, at best, this index reflects some past pattern of spending, not current expenditures. Having said this, the index has proved to be a very useful measure of consumer prices for many forecasting applications. Yet in each new application it is wise to explicitly consider whether it is really measuring the specific concept of interest to the planner/manager.

A related problem arises in many time series where some of the component elements must be estimated or measured indirectly. An example would be the Index of Industrial Production, which is released on a monthly basis by the Federal Reserve System. For some of the industries included, actual data on physical output are not available on a monthly basis. Instead they must be estimated indirectly by using data on hours worked in the industry or from total dollar sales or changes in inventories. These estimates are then adjusted as price or productivity information becomes available. For most applications this is still a very useful time series. It would not, however, be of much use in forecasting short-term changes in the productivity of labor in industry.

---

[4] This "market basket" is based on a periodic survey of the buying habits of a sample of households covered by the definition. This index only covers approximately 40% of the population. In January 1978, the index was revised and a second index CPI(U) was added to partially deal with this problem. This is intended to cover all urban consumers or about 80% of the population. The heterogeneity of this group is such, however, that the index still may not be representative of the prices paid by any one individual.

Who Collects the Time Series and Why?

Government statistics are, for the most part, intended for general application. In some cases, however, they are collected in connection with very specific legislation and for a very specific purpose. In a similar way, statistics published by individual companies, labor unions, trade associations, or community groups may reflect some very specific interests (or biases) of those groups. This certainly does not mean that the time series need be false or unusable. It does suggest that, no matter what the source, the potential user should be aware of the intent of the original source in collecting the data and be sure that the series, in fact, reflects his or her particular needs. If you have questions, do not hesitate to contact the organization indicated as the original or primary source. In most cases they will be more than happy to answer questions. In some cases they may have background or more detailed data that have not been published but that they may allow you to use.

What Is the Overall Character of the Data In the Time Series?

Seldom will the forecaster or analyst find all the data needed in one source and already edited. In compiling the 15 years of data on airline passenger-miles shown in Figure 3–1, it was necessary to refer to a number of different issues of the *Survey of Current Business*, as well as the biennial summary, *Business Statistics*. In this case the data have been routinely collected and published for many years, so there was little difficulty in doing this. In other cases, combining data from several different sources can cause some difficult problems of "splicing." In editing data, three types of problems can be anticipated:

1. *Clerical Errors.* Misprints can and do occur. Sometimes these are repeated; other times they are corrected immediately. When two reported values differ, deciding which is the misprint and which is the correct value is not always easy.

2. *Preliminary Estimates and Revisions.* Most time series must be published on a regular time schedule. If data are not available, they must be estimated. Published data are frequently identified initially as "preliminary" and later revised, sometimes several times. As with clerical errors, it is not always easy to decide which is the final version.

3. *Series Revisions.* Index numbers can shift to a new base period, and the weights used in the calculations can change; the definitions of time series can change; data may be aggregated in a different format

or the coverage may change.[5] Any of these can create what is a new time series, published, however, under the old title. Even if you are only shifting between succeeding issues of the same publication, it is necessary to check for changes in the definition of the series or to look for clues (such as a change in the format) that may signal some other important underlying change.

REMOVING NUISANCE PATTERNS

Time series are frequently collected in a form that is not directly related to the immediate needs of the forecaster. For example, many time series of production, inventories, or sales are given in dollar values. These series reflect changes in both physical levels of activity and in prices. If the forecaster is interested in studying only changes in levels of physical activity, the use of dollar values, particularly in inflationary periods, will distort the time series. Even when both types of change are important, their patterns of change may be very different and need to be analyzed separately.

A similar problem can arise when using highly aggregated series. For example, suppose a company sells to both consumer and industrial markets. It is probable that these two markets react in different ways to such things as inflation or changing levels of consumer disposable income. If over time the company's mix of sales in these two markets is changing, changes in patterns in the overall time series may be primarily a result of this changing mix. Forecasting total sales may be simplified by separating the two markets and analyzing each separately.

Preliminary Adjustments

Two adjustments arise frequently enough to deserve special mention: corrections for the varying numbers of days in a month and for price changes.

The Trading-day Adjustment.   The numbers of days in successive months can vary by as much as 10% (January to February or February to March are the most striking). For businesses which are active only five days a week it can be as much as 15%. This can cause substantial month-to-month changes in reported activity (production, hours worked, or sales), even though the actual levels of activity have not changed. The correction

---

[5] When the status of Alaska and Hawaii was changed from that of territory to state, many time series, such as that shown in Figure 3–3a, that had previously been limited to the 48 states were changed *under the same title* to include the new additions. The January 1978 revision of CPI(W) mentioned previously is another example.

for this is called a *trading-day adjustment*. In its simplest form this is done by dividing the reported monthly activity by the number of active days in the month. In cases where there are substantial changes in activity within the week (for example, most of the activity occurs on Monday), more detailed adjustments are possible and may be necessary.

  Price Adjustment.   One of the most frequent adjustments made is to convert time series expressed in monetary units such as dollars to series reflecting changes in physical volume or activity levels. This is sometimes described as giving the time series in *constant dollars*. The adjustment is carried out by dividing each data value in the series by the corresponding value of an appropriate price index.

  Figure 3-4a shows the effect of this adjustment on one particular series, "new construction in place." With the exception of 1975 and 1982,

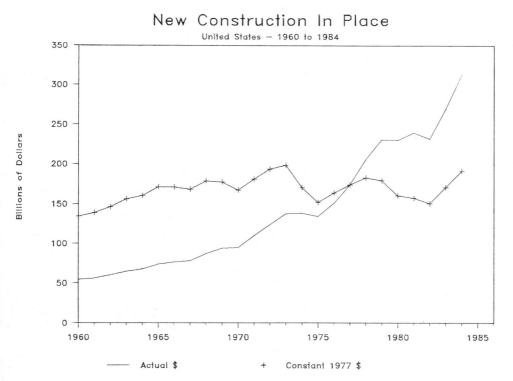

FIGURE 3-4a

New construction in place: United States, 1960–1984 (*Source:* U.S. Department of Commerce, Bureau of Economic Research, *Survey of Current Business,* various issues, 1962–1985)

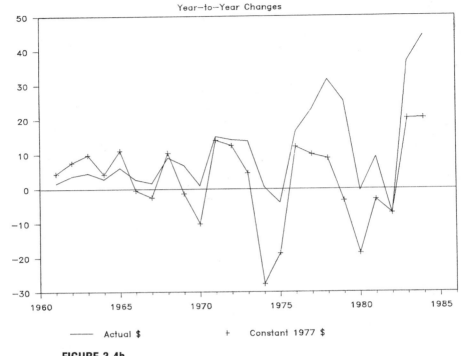

FIGURE 3-4b

New construction in place: Year-to-year changes

this series has shown a consistent upward trend since 1960. When this series is adjusted for changes in construction costs (by dividing by the U.S. Department of Commerce Composite Index of Construction Costs), the picture is quite different. Expressed in constant 1977 dollars, the actual physical volume of activity reached a peak in 1973, and only in 1984 is it approaching that level again. The difference is even more striking when considering the year-to-year percentage changes in the variable as in Figure 3–4b. The unadjusted data appear to have an upward trend. After price adjustment, the trend (at least through 1982) is downward.

Other Adjustments

A number of other adjustments can be helpful in special circumstances. A common one is a correction for the changing size of a population. For example, in a region where the population is increasing rapidly, total expenditures on medical care might be divided by the size of the population to obtain expenditures per capita. A similar correction might be made in analyzing output in an industry where the number of active firms is changing.

Where technology or product quality is rapidly changing, it can be useful to correct for these factors. As an example, in studying sales of computers for business or scientific applications, it is useful to adjust for the changing computing power of individual computer models.

As already noted, when dealing with time series of highly heterogeneous phenomena, such as the sales of a company making many very different types of products or operating in a number of different markets, it can be helpful to develop forecasts for each product and/or each market separately, even when the final forecast is intended to be one of total sales.

In many cases, knowing exactly how the variable is to be used for planning or decision making will suggest helpful adjustments. Figure 3–5 illustrates one such situation. The forecast required was of the present value of an individual's future earnings in a particular job. The individual requesting the analysis and the forecaster agreed to assume that future raises would only be related to cost-of-living adjustments as measured by the Consumer Price Index [CPI(W)] and that treasury bond yields would be used as the discount rate. These two time series are shown as Figures 3–5a (p. 64) and 3–5b (p. 65). Both series show substantial upward nonlinear trends, and CPI(W) shows large irregular movements as well. It can be shown, however, that in calculating the present value of future earnings these two variables never enter the calculations individually but only in the form of a ratio between the two. As can be seen in Figure 3–5c (p. 65) and 3–5d (p. 66), using this ratio changes the trend to what appears to be much closer to a simple linear form and substantially reduces the magnitude of the irregular movements. This is particularly noticeable in the first differences in Figure 3–5d. The apparently precipitous drop in the ratio following 1980 has a somewhat different appearance in the first differences, suggesting that care should be taken to not overreact to that drop in making long-term projections of the ratio.

The few adjustments described here barely touch on the range of adjustments that can arise in practice. If there is an overall theme, however, it is that time spent on these early adjustments will more than be returned in simplifying later analysis and in the quality of the final forecast.

THE ANALYSIS OF RESIDUALS

As suggested earlier, the word residual is used in two different ways: as the remainder at each step of the decomposition process, and as the final, apparently unpatterned and therefore random and unforecastable "noise" component of a time series. Used in the first sense, our interest is in the

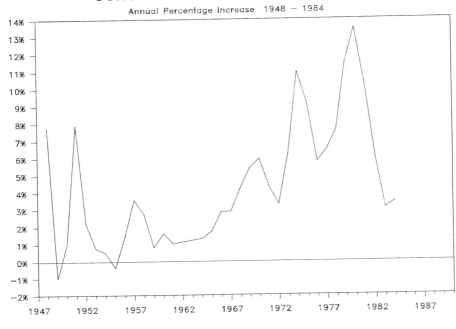

FIGURE 3-5a

Consumer price index, CPI(W): Annual percentage increase, 1948–1984 (*Source:* U.S. Department of Commerce, Bureau of Economic Analysis, *Survey of Current Business* and *Business Statistics* [biennial summary], various issues, 1950–1985)

residual as a new time series in which we look for patterns, just we did with the original. When we reach the point where we see no further patterns and wish to look on the residuals as a sort of statistical "noise," our approach changes; for the most part, we are no longer interested in specific residuals or the sequence in which they occurred. Instead, we look at the overall distribution of the residuals in terms of the average, the variability, and the shape or symmetry of the distribution.

Residuals should not be equated with forecast errors, although there is certainly a connection between the two. To the extent that the factors reflected in the residuals were unpredictable in the past, it is possible to assume that these same factors may be a source of forecast errors in the future. As we saw in Figure 3–5 and will see again, there are many different sources of forecast error, and to treat the distribution of residuals as *the*

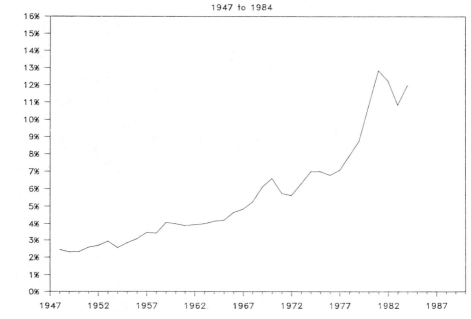

FIGURE 3-5b

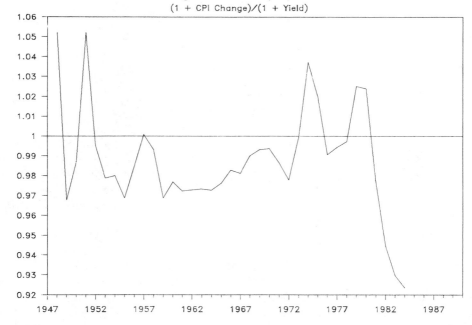

FIGURE 3-5c

Ratio of % Change CPI(W) to Bond Yield

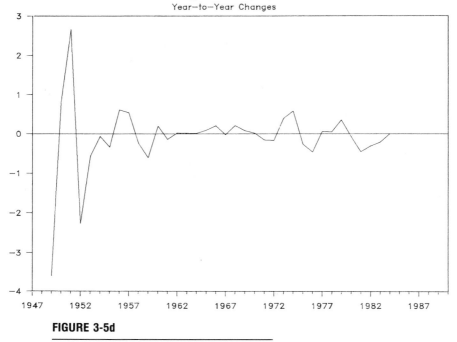

FIGURE 3-5d

Ratio of percent change CPI(W) to bond yield

forecast error distribution is to seriously overstate the probable accuracy of the forecasts that are developed from the analysis.

Residuals as a Time Series

At each stage in the analysis of a time series, as a component pattern has been tentatively identified, that pattern should be removed from the time series. This is usually done either by subtracting, taking the difference between the two series on a period-by-period basis, or by division, taking ratios. The differences or ratios are the temporary residuals, which are plotted as the new time series.

Figure 3–2e illustrated such a series of residuals. Although there was no apparent trend or cyclical pattern to the points plotted, the magnitude of the residuals (and thus the variability of the data) seemed to be increasing over time, with the larger residuals tending to the right side of the graph. As we will see, changing variability can cause problems in later analysis, and an adjustment for this would be needed. Detection of this

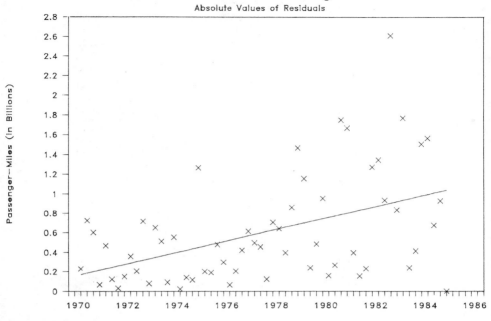

Airline Revenue Passenger—Miles
Absolute Values of Residuals

FIGURE 3-6

Airline revenue passenger-miles: Absolute values of residuals

type of problem can be aided by plotting the absolute values of the residuals as shown in Figure 3–6 (absolute values are the residuals ignoring the + or − signs). In this case, a trend line has been fitted to the absolute values of the residuals (using a technique to be discussed in Chapter 7) and shows clearly the pattern of increase.

Summary Descriptions and Residual Distributions

If the residual is the random component of the time series, its analysis must be based on summary, statistical measures and on observing and describing the frequency distribution of the residuals. In some cases we will want to compare the observed distribution to one of the standard theoretical distributions, such as the normal. Certainly we will want to identify any atypical values that might have been the result of particular nonroutine events, as, for example, severe weather conditions or a major international crisis. Such events do not routinely reoccur and may or may

TABLE 3-1

Factory Sales of Passenger Cars: United States, 1950 to 1985

Year	Passenger Factory (million cars)	First Differences
1950	6.67	NA
1951	5.34	−1.33
1952	4.32	−1.02
1953	6.12	1.80
1954	5.56	−0.56
1955	7.92	2.36
1956	5.82	−2.10
1957	6.11	0.29
1958	4.26	−1.85
1959	5.59	1.33
1960	6.68	1.09
1961	5.54	−1.14
1962	6.93	1.39
1963	7.64	0.71
1964	7.75	0.11
1965	9.31	1.56
1966	8.60	−0.71
1967	7.44	−1.16
1968	8.82	1.38
1969	8.22	−0.60
1970	6.55	−1.67
1971	8.58	2.03
1972	8.82	0.24
1973	9.66	0.84
1974	7.33	−2.33
1975	6.71	−0.62
1976	8.50	1.79
1977	9.20	0.70
1978	9.16	−0.04
1979	8.42	−0.74
1980	6.40	−2.02
1981	6.22	−0.18
1982	5.05	−1.17
1983	6.74	1.69
1984	7.62	0.88
1985	8.10^p	0.48

^{p}Preliminary

Source: U.S. Department of Commerce, Bureau of Economic Analysis, *Survey of Current Business*, various issues, 1952 to 1985.

not be predictable in the future. In any case, their effects should be noted and analyzed separately.

In the rest of this chapter and throughout the book where statistical analysis is necessary, the primary emphasis will be on techniques of what has come to be called *exploratory data analysis*. There are several reasons for this. First, many of these techniques are particularly suited to hand calculation and graphical analysis and are usable by the nontechnically oriented manager or planner, as well as by those with a more quantitative background or orientation. Second, they tend to be relatively insensitive to varying types of data and thus have the character of being all-purpose tools; techniques of this type are often referred to as being *robust* or *resistant*. Finally, they tend to be relatively less affected by the atypical data points or *outliers*, which are a frequent component of time series.

Since the use of these techniques in analyzing residuals can best be presented by example, the rest of this section will be based on the analysis of the time series "Factory Sales of Passenger Cars in the United States between 1950 and 1985." The data are shown in Table 3–1 and Figure 3–7. Notice that, because we are dealing with annual data, there is no seasonal pattern. There is, however, a suggestion of a slight upward trend, which should first be removed.

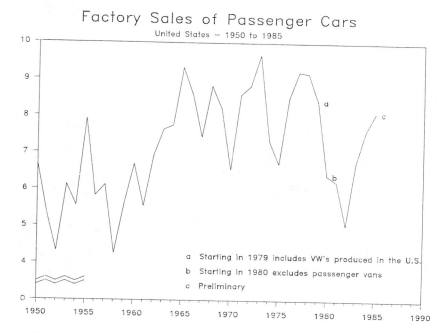

FIGURE 3-7

Factory sales of passenger cars: United States, 1950–1985 (*Source:* U.S. Department of Commerce, Bureau of Economic Analysis, *Survey of Current Business*, various issues, 1952–1985)

There are a number of different approaches to the analysis and removal of trends in time series, which will be explored in more detail in Chapter 4. One of the simplest and often most effective of these is to take the successive differences between the data values as shown in Table 3–1. These period-to-period changes are commonly referred to as *first differences*. For this example, the first differences are shown in Figure 3–8. It can be seen that the trend of the previous graph has been effectively removed. Since there are no obvious further patterns, we will consider these to be our residuals. A plot of the absolute values of the residuals (not shown here) would not show any systematic pattern of increase or decrease in the magnitudes of the residuals.

Stem-and-leaf Diagram.   As a first step in developing a statistical summary description of residuals (or of any set of numbers), it is useful to develop a distribution of the data values. When there are only a few values, this can be done by arranging them in an *array*, that is, in increasing or decreasing order. When a large number of data points is involved, they can

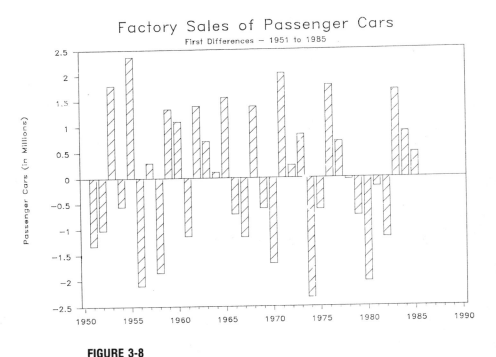

FIGURE 3-8

Factory sales of passenger cars: First differences, 1951–1985 be further summarized by grouping them into successive intervals and giving the frequency of values in each interval; this is called a *histogram*. The development of a histogram can be expedited by the use of a *stem-and-leaf diagram*. The basic form of this diagram is shown in Table 3–2a.

To develop a stem-and-leaf, start by finding the largest and the smallest number in the list of first differences in Table 3–1. In this case, the smallest value is −2.33 (in 1974) and the largest is 2.36 (in 1955). Of these two values, choose the largest in magnitude (ignoring + or − sign). Round this value to two (occasionally three) significant digits. In this case, the 2.36 would become 2.4. Similarly round the remaining data values. For example, the value for 1951 would become −1.3 and for 1954 −0.6.

Next, as shown, draw a vertical line and write the possible first digits to the left of the line. In this case the values are −2, −1, −0, +0, +1, and +2. These are the *stems*. Now, for the first data point (−1.3), write the second digit (3) to the right of the line next to the appropriate stem. Continue this until all the data points have been entered. These are the *leaves*. It is often convenient at this point to draw vertical dotted or dashed lines as shown to separate the "leaves" into groups of five to facilitate the following steps in the analysis.

In describing statistical distributions, it is helpful to calculate a few summary measures that identify, for the example, the location of the midpoint of the distribution and its width. The summary measures we will use to describe this distribution are called *position* measures. To calculate them, we need to identify the position or location of each number in the array. To the left of the stems, label a column "#" for "number" and write the cumulative counts of data points starting from both ends. When you reach the stem containing the middle value, write the actual frequency for that group and enclose it in parentheses as shown.

Notice that this diagram not only rearranges the data into (something close to) an array, but the lengths of the lists of "leaves" create horizontal bars giving a semigraphical picture of the distribution. This picture can sometimes be improved by increasing the number of stems. As a rule of thumb, a diagram with approximately 10 stems will usually give the best picture. In this case, however, we have only six. The number of stems can be doubled by listing each stem twice, followed by * or ● as shown in Table 3–2b. Leaves 0, 1, 2, 3, or 4 are placed next to the stem marked * while the remaining digits 5 through 9 are placed next to the stem marked ●. (Notice the bimodal appearance of the distribution. Would you have expected this from Figure 3–8?) The number of stems can also be increased by 5. This can be done as shown in Table 3–2c by subdividing the leaves for each stem into groups covering only two digits. In this case, 25 different groups are created. Visually, this seems to go too far in "flattening" the distribution. Notice, however, that, except for these differences in pictorial quality, the information in every case is the same.

TABLE 3-2

Factory Sales of Passenger Cars: Annual Changes in Sales (First Differences)

United States: 1951 to 1985
Alternative Stem-and-leaf Diagrams

a. Basic Display

#			
3	−2	130	
10	−1	30812	72
17	−0	67660	72
(8)	+0	37128	795
10	+1	83146	487
2	+2	40	

c. Expanded × 5

#			
1	−2	t	3
3	−2	*	10
4	−1	.	8
5	−1	s	7
	−1	f	
8	−1	t	322
10	−1	*	01
	−0	.	
15	−0	s	67667
	−0	f	
16	−0	t	2
17	−0	*	0
(1)	+0	*	1
17	+0	t	32
15	+0	f	5
14	+0	s	77
12	+0	.	89
10	+1	*	1
9	+1	t	3
8	+1	f	44
6	+1	s	67
4	+1	.	88
2	+2	*	0
	+2	t	
1	+2	f	4

b. Expanded × 2

#			
	−2	.	
3	−2	*	130
5	−1	.	87
10	−1	*	30122
15	−0	.	67667
17	−0	*	02
(3)	+0	*	312
15	+0	.	78795
10	+1	*	3144
6	+1	.	8687
2	+2	*	04
	+2	.	

* for 0, 1, 2, 3, or 4
. for 5, 6, 7, 8, or 9

* for 0 or 1
t for 2 or 3
f for 4 or 5
s for 6 or 7
. for 8 or 9

d. Reordered Stem-and-leaf Diagram

#			
	−2	.	
3	−2	*	310
5	−1	.	87
10	−1	*	32210
15	−0	.	77666
17	−0	*	20
(3)	+0	*	123
15	+0	.	57789
10	+1	*	1344
6	+1	.	6788
2	+2	*	04
	+2	.	

The data in Tables 3–2a, b, and c are not true arrays because the data values next to each stem are not completely ordered. If desired, as shown in Table 3–2d, the leaves in each row can now be reordered to complete the array. (Initially, you will find this a useful step. In time you will probably find it quicker to mentally rearrange them as necessary without actually writing them down a second time.)

Five-number Summary. From the stem-and-leaf diagram, we can now summarize the distribution with a small number of *summary statistics*. We will find five numbers to be particularly useful:

Median. This is the data value that separates the array into two equally sized groups.

Quartiles. These are values that further separate the upper and lower 25% of the distribution.

Extremes.The largest and smallest values in the distribution.

All these summary statistics can be read directly from the stem-and-leaf diagram.

To find the median, determine the total number of data points in the distribution. This is done by adding the number in the # column that is in parentheses to the cumulative counts on either side. For Table 3–2d, this is $17 + (3) + 15 = 35$. Call this number N. The *position* of the median is given by $(N + 1)/2$; here, $(35 + 1)/2 = 18$. The median is found by counting this number of values in from either end of the array. Counting from the top, there are 17 numbers in the first five groups, so the median (the eighteenth number) is the smallest value in the middle group, or $+0.1$.

To find the quartiles, take the position number of the median determined above (18), add 1, and divide by 2: $(18 + 1)/2 = 9\frac{1}{2}$. (If the position number of the median ends in $\frac{1}{2}$, use only the whole number part.) Count this distance in from either end; since the number ends in $\frac{1}{2}$, the quartiles are the average of the ninth and tenth values. Starting from the top, the ninth data point is -1.1 and the tenth is -1.0. The average of these two values is -1.05. Similarly, from the bottom it is between $+1.3$ and $+1.1$, or $+1.2$.

The extremes can be read directly from the stem-and-leaf diagram. Here they are -2.3 and $+2.4$.

These five values form the base of the five-number summary. Additional measures can now be derived from these five. These are shown in Table 3–3. Start by writing the five values in a row as shown. In a second row, write the successive differences between the numbers. In some applications we are interested in whether or not the distribution is symmetric or if it is skewed to one side. When the distribution is symmetric, the corre-

TABLE 3-3

Factory Sales of Passenger Cars: Annual Changes in Sales (First Differences)

United States: 1951 to 1985
Five-number Summary
Position of Summary Values

Number of observations			35	
Position of median		$(35 + 1)/2 = 18$		
Position of quartiles		$(18 + 1)/2 = 9\frac{1}{2}$		

Summary

	Smallest	Q_1	Median	Q_3	Largest
Values	− 2.3	−1.05	.1	1.2	2.4
Differences		1.15	1.15	1.1	1.2
Q spread (Qspd)			2.25		
Inner fences Q ± 1.5 Qspd	− 2.3	−4.43		4.58	2.4
Outer fences Q ± 3 Qspd		− 7.80		7.95	

sponding differences on opposite sides of the median should be approximately equal. For this example, this would seem to be the case.

In a third row, write the difference between the quartiles (the sum of the two central differences). Here $1.2 - (-1.05) = 2.25$. This is called the *interquartile range* or *Q spread* (Qspd). In later applications it will prove to be a useful measure of the spread or variability of the distribution.

We next need to develop a measure for identifying *outliers*, that is, data values that appear to be atypically large or small and are thus values that should be examined in more detail. Multiply the Qspd by 1.5 and add it to the third or high quartile and subtract it from the first or low quartile. Write these values in a fourth line as shown. For the fifth line, repeat this using 3 times Qspd. These values are called, respectively, the *inner fences* and the *outer fences*. Finally, find the smallest and largest data points just inside the inner fences; here these are also the extremes, −2.3 and +2.4. Write these beside the inner fences on line four. If there are any points between the inner and outer fences (there are none in this example), write them by the outer fences. If there are any points *outside* the outer fences, write them at the bottom.

As we shall see, points outside the outer fences are almost certainly outliers and should be marked for further study and analysis. Points between the inner and outer fences are possible outliers or atypical values and may be worth marking as such. Some authors suggest using 1 and 2 times Qspd rather than 1.5 and 3 as is done here. The effect of this is to mark a greater number of points as outliers or potential outliers. When N is small (say less than 25), this may be worthwhile in order not to take the chance of overlooking points worth this special study. We will examine this point in more detail shortly.

Box-and-whisker Diagram. The information in the five-number summary can be displayed graphically in what is called a box-and-whisker diagram. The distribution of the data is displayed as a box or bar, which can be drawn either horizontally or vertically, and is interpreted by comparing it to a scale drawn at the edge of the graph. For the residuals in this example, a box-and-whisker diagram is shown at the right side of Figure 3–9 (p. 76) along with a graph of the individual residuals.

To construct the box-and-whisker diagram, start by drawing lines at the median and the two quartiles as shown in the figure; connect these as shown to form the box (dashed lines for the median and quartiles have been drawn to facilitate comparison of the box and whiskers with the actual residuals). At the values corresponding to the points just inside the inner fences (in this example, -2.3 and $+2.4$), mark $\times$'s and connect them to the box with lines. These are the whiskers. Now, if there are any possible outliers (points between the inner and outer fences), mark these separately with symbols such as small black dots or (as in the next figure) with small diamonds; if there are points outside the outer fences, mark these with different symbols, such as large squares. In this example there are no points outside the inner fences so no outliers have been marked.

In Figure 3–10 (p. 77), the box-and-whisker diagram is shown next to a normal distribution. Comparing the two will suggest how the box-and-whisker diagram can be interpreted. First, notice that the center line of the box corresponds to the midpoint of the distribution, the median, while the width of the box covers the center 50% of the distribution. The box plus the whiskers covers the entire distribution except for any possible outliers. Notice that, depending on the setting of the inner fences, there is some chance that a few points will be incorrectly identified as outliers. Placing the inner fences at $\pm 1 \times$ Qspd means that, in a sample of 25 from a normal distribution, on the average one data point would be misidentified; in a sample of 50, there would be two. On the other hand, using $\pm 3 \times$ Qspd would mean that only one point in 500,000 would be incorrectly identified as an outlier.

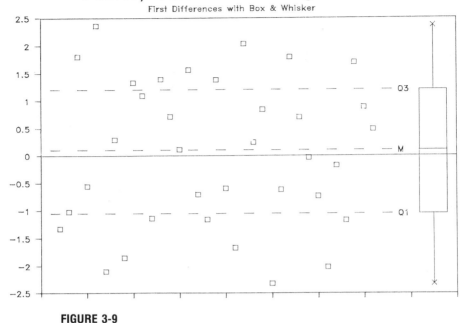

FIGURE 3-9

Factory sales of passenger cars: First differences with box-and-whisker diagram

---

SUMMARY

In this chapter we have blocked out a general approach to the analysis of single-variable (univariate) time series. It is based on an underlying assumption that a time series consists of a collection of separate patterns (trend, seasonal, cyclical) that can be decomposed and analyzed individually. While in many cases such an assumption would not seem unreasonable, it should be stressed that this is not the only possible approach or model that can be used; other methods of time-series analysis assume instead that some or all of the component patterns of a time series are conceptually interrelated in ways that make decomposition impossible. For example, it can be argued that economic cycles are phenomena that only exist because of an underlying pattern of economic growth or trend. In such a model, any separation of the trend from the cycles would seem completely inappropriate.

This chapter has argued that in analyzing patterns in time series there

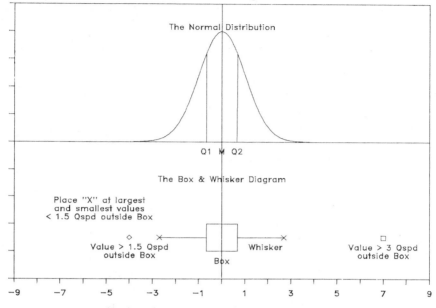

Outlier Identification
With Box and Whisker Diagrams

The Normal Distribution

Q1 M Q2

The Box & Whisker Diagram

Place "X" at largest
and smallest values
< 1.5 Qspd outside Box

◇ Value > 1.5 Qspd outside Box

Whisker

Box

□ Value > 3 Qspd outside Box

Number of Standard Deviations from Mean

For the Normal Distribution

Interval	Probability That a Point Lies Outside the Interval
Q ± 1 Qspd	0.043
Q ± 1.5 Qspd	0.007
Q ± 2 Qspd	0.0007
Q ± 3 Qspd	0.000002

FIGURE 3-10

Outlier identification with box-and-whisker diagram

are two major tools that the planner or forecaster will find particularly useful: the construction and interpretation of graphs and the analysis of residuals. Both of these tools will be used extensively in the remainder of the book. Building on these basic tools, in Chapter 4 we will begin to consider specific ways of analyzing the components of a time series: the trend, the seasonal, and the cyclical.

APPENDIX

A 1-2-3 Template for a Box-and-Whisker Diagram

Place the following labels in a protected column A and unprotected blanks in column B, rows 1 through 25, as indicated:

Median	B1
1st Quartile	B2
3rd Quartile	B3
Smallest value	B5
Largest value	B6
$(1 \times 1 < 1.5$ Qspd outside Q)	
Outliers	
$(1.5$ Qspd $< |X| < 3$ Qspd outside Q)	
O_1	B14
O_2	B15
O_3	B16
$(|X| > 3$Qspd outside Q)	
O_4	B20
O_5	B21
O_6	B22
Box label	B24
Vertical position of box label	B25

Data entered into these unprotected blanks will be automatically transferred to the following table, which should be in a protected part of the worksheet. Additional rows can be added if necessary for additional outliers. If this is done, additional rows should also be added to the following table.

Data Table for Box-and-Whisker Diagram

Graph Variables

Horizontal Position of Box X	*Box* B	*Fences* E	O_1 *to* O_3 C	O_4 *to* O_6 A	D	*Label*
2.7	+B1					
2.7	+B2					
3.3	+B2					(continued on next page)

Graph Variables, continued

Horizontal Position of Box X	Box B	Fences E	O_1 to O_3 C	O_4 to O_6 A	D	Label
3.3	+B3					
2.7	+B3					
2.7	+B1					
3.3	+B1					
3	+B2					
3	+B5	+B5				
3	+B3					
3	+B6	+B6				
3			+B14	+B20		
3			+B15	+B21		
3			+B16	+B22	+B25	+B24

Note: Assume that the data section of this table starts in Column A, Row 36.

To set up the graph, use /G and the following options, assuming that the data section of the table, as noted previously, starts in column A, row 36.

Graph Type: X–Y
Variables:

			Format:
X	A36..A52	Box location	
B	B36..B52	Box and whiskers	Lines
E	C36..C52	Fences	Symbols
C	D36..D52	O_1 through O_3	Symbols
A	E36..E52	O_4 through O_6	Symbols
D	F36..F52	Box label location	Neither

Locate data labels for variable D in G36..G52

Scale Options for Y Scale: Manual, Lower (0), Upper (6), Format (hidden)

Multiple boxes can be plotted by adding separate data-entry tables and sets of X variables to the data table.

Example

Figure 3A-1 shows a box-and-Whisker diagram for the following data:

Median	22		O_1	7
1st Quartile	19		O_2	9
3rd Quartile	25		O_3	36
Smallest value	12		($|X| > 3$Qspd outside Q)	
Largest value	30		O_4	45
($|X| < 1.5$ Qspd outside Q)			O_5	——
Outliers			O_6	——
(1.5 Qspd $< |X| < 3$ Qspd outside Q)		Box label	Box diagram	
		Vertical position of box label	3	

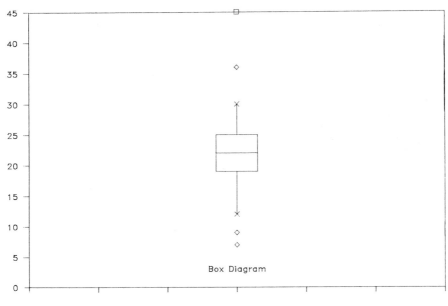

FIGURE 3A-1

Box diagram template example

READINGS

Graphing Time Series

Additional suggestions for the effective graphing of time series and other quantitative data can be found in

FREDERICK CROXTON ET AL., *Applied General Statistics*, 3rd ed., Englewood Cliffs, N.J., Prentice-Hall, 1967, Chapters 4 and 5.

JOHN W. TUKEY, *Exploratory Data Analysis*, Reading, Mass., Addison-Wesley, 1977, Chapter 5.

If you plan on doing much hand graphing, a wide range of different types of graph paper can be found in

JOHN S. CRAVER, *Graph Paper from Your Copier*, Tucson, Ariz., HP Books, 1980.

The Analysis of Residuals

The "classic" in this area is Tukey's *Exploratory Data Analysis,* cited previously. See Chapters 1 and 2. Other references that present or build on Tukey's work are

> FREDERICK HARTWIG, with Brian E. Dearing, *Exploratory Data Analysis,* Beverly Hills, Calif., Sage Publications, 1979, Chapter 2.
>
> PAUL F. VELLEMAN and DAVID C. HOAGLIN, *Applications, Basics and Computing of Exploratory Data Analysis,* Boston, Duxbury Press, 1981, Chapters 1 to 3.

Using Lotus 1-2-3

As in the appendix to this chapter, this book will give occasional hints on adapting the methods covered to use with the Lotus 1-2-3 spreadsheet program. Because this program has become so popular, a wide range of books is now available to help the user. One with some helpful hints on developing 1-2-3 graphics is

> DAVID C. RIER and EDMUND S. FINE, *Orchestrating 1-2-3®: Notes for Advanced Users,* Reading, Mass., Addison-Wesley, 1985.

For other hints, see also the users' magazine, *Lotus: Computing for Managers and Professionals.*

PROBLEMS

1. Select some time series on a subject in which you are interested. Possible sources are *Statistical Abstract of the United States, Survey of Current Business,* or *Business Conditions Digest.* All these are publications of the U.S. federal government. Present the data in graphical format using the appropriate graph paper and in appropriate format. Determine exactly how the data series was obtained, including any changes that may have taken place. Include this information in headnotes and/or footnotes as necessary. Include a source note describing exactly where you obtained the data.

2. For many years, various business publications such as *Business Week, Fortune,* and *Forbes* have published annual issues with tables summarizing corporate or industry performance for the previous year. Locate such a table in some past issue and present the information in stem-and-leaf and box-and-whisker diagrams. Discuss what, if any, information can be obtained from these diagrams that was not apparent in the original table.

3. Assume that it is the last week in December 1986. The G. E. Armstrong Company would like you to analyze their quarterly sales for the last 8 years and develop projections for the next year. You are given the following data:

Year	Quarter	Orders Received (000 units)	Year	Quarter	Orders Received (000 units)
1979	I	205	1983	I	515
	II	248		II	579
	III	188		III	561
	IV	202		IV	501
1980	I	197	1984	I	479
	II	269		II	674
	III	237		III	581
	IV	265		IV	617
1981	I	266	1985	I	748
	II	334		II	624
	III	316		III	862
	IV	346		IV	963
1982	I	390	1986	I	926
	II	406		II	935
	III	350		III	969
	IV	377		IV	1031

a. Plot the quarterly orders as a time series. Leave space on the right side for your projections through 1987. Use appropriate graph paper and format.

b. Calculate the changes in orders between successive quarters (first differences) and plot as a time series. Notice that the differences will be both above and below the base line at zero, so the base line and scale line will not be the same. Leave room on the right side for a box-and-whisker diagram.

c. Develop a stem-and-leaf diagram, a five-number summary, and a box-and-whisker diagram. Place the box-and-whisker diagram at the right of the graph developed in part b.

d. On the graph from part b, draw dashed or dotted lines at the median and quartiles. What patterns of change (if any) do you observe in these differences over time? (*Optional:* Draw a graph of the absolute values of the differences and compare with the graph in part b.)

e. Using the median first difference from part c, develop projections of orders for the four quarters of 1987 by adding this median difference to the actual orders for 1986 IV and then adding it again for each quarter projected. Plot on the graph drawn in part a using a dashed or dotted line. Interpret in words the meaning of this projection.

f. Using the quartiles of the first differences, develop two additional projections for the first quarter of 1987. Plot these on the graph in part a. Again, express in words your interpretation of these projections. What does this suggest about the possible accuracy of your projection from part e for the first quarter of 1987?

g. Suppose you wanted to develop a similar estimate of the accuracy of your projection for the fourth quarter of 1987. What additional problems might arise? Relate your answer to your verbal interpretations of the projections in parts e and f.

CHAPTER 4

Patterns
in Time Series

In this chapter we begin to consider techniques of searching for and analyzing various types of patterns in time series. The emphasis is on the use of graphs and the visual identification of the patterns most frequently seen in time-series data. In Chapters 6 through 9 and in Chapter 12 we will look at other approaches to pattern analysis as they arise in particular forecasting/planning situations. Whether considered visually or through a computerized procedure, what is considered in any specific application to be a "pattern" will depend on an underlying more-or-less formalized model or set of asssumptions that define that "pattern." In this chapter, our interest centers on describing apparent regularities in a time series without specifically considering either the underlying mathematical equation that might describe the observed regularity or the possible causes of the pattern observed. These issues will be topics for later chapters.

As we saw in Chapter 3, the three basic types of patterns that we will consider are trends and cyclical and seasonal fluctuations. We start by analyzing annual data because it has no seasonal component. This makes it easier to deal with the trend and cyclical fluctuations. Once we have introduced the tools that we will need for analyzing trends and cycles, we will turn our attention to data that do contain a seasonal component to see how the same basic procedures can be modified or adapted.

Major Points to be Noted

1. *The reasons why it is necessary to remove the trend component from a time series before analyzing other components and techniques of trend removal.*

2. *Smoothing as a way of separating and highlighting the cyclical component.*

3. *Alternative ways of dealing with seasonal patterns in time series.*

ANALYSIS OF TRENDS

Trends are systematic patterns of increase or decrease in a time series. The simplest way of describing a trend is as a function of time. The trend used in Figure 3–2b was of the form shown in Figure 4–1a (p. 86) and can be described by an equation of the form

$$Y_t = a + bt \tag{1}$$

where the subscript t refers to the time point corresponding to a specific Y value.[1] The advantage of this formulation is that it is relatively understandable and easy to use. All that is necessary is to substitute an appropriate value for t.[2] The difficulty with formulating a trend as a function of time is that it is hard to think of time itself as in any sense "causing" a particular value of Y. As we shall see in chapter 12, this will prove to be a problem when we begin to ask questions about whether a particular trend is or is not likely to continue for an extended period into the future.

---

[1]A procedure for actually fitting an equation of this type to empirical data is described in Chapter 7.

[2]Unfortunately, the forecaster can be carried away by the ease with which this can be done. In 1891, a Professor H. S. Pritchett fitted a cubic equation to the U.S. census data for the years 1790 to 1890 (a period of 110 years) and then used the equation to make population projections for 1900 through 2900 (a period of 1010 years).

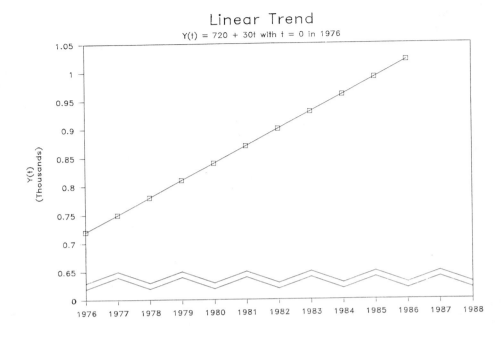

FIGURE 4-1a

Linear trend: $Y(t) = 720 + 30t$, with $t = 0$ in 1976

An alternative way of thinking about trends is as a pattern of change. In Figure 4–1b, instead of looking at Y_t directly, consider the pattern of changes (first differences) in Y, $(Y_t - Y_{t-1})$. It can be seen that

$$
\begin{array}{rcl}
Y_t & = & a + bt \\
Y_{t-1} & = & a + b(t - 1) \\
\hline
Y_t - Y_{t-1} & = & b
\end{array}
\qquad (2)
$$

That is, a trend that is linear when expressed as a function of time is equivalent to a pattern of constant period-to-period changes in the variable.

In practice, it is useful to think of trends sometimes as functions of time, sometimes as sequences of changes. In this chapter we limit our consideration to using differences or period-to-period changes as a way of removing the trend component from data. In Chapter 12 we return to the topic of trends and explore the relationship between these two alternative views and the use of trends in developing forecasts.

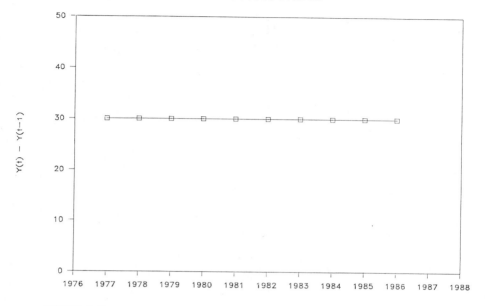

FIGURE 4-1b

First differences

Trend Removal Using Differences

We are interested in removing the trend component from a time series for two reasons. First, as we attempt to observe other patterns in the data, they usually tend to show up more clearly as fluctuations around a horizontal line than around a line that is sloping upward or downward. Also, at some point we will want to summarize the residuals as a statistical distribution where the mean of that distribution will be assumed to be constant. The variability of this distribution will then be interpreted as a measure of the unpatterned component of the time series. If the trend is not removed, it will erroneously contribute to this variability and make the residual distribution more difficult to interpret. When there is no trend in a time series, it is referred to as *stationary in the mean*.

A simple type of differencing was used in Chapter 3 to remove the trend from the data on "Factory Sales of Passenger Cars." In that example, the data showed a slight upward trend. When successive differences were taken, the upward slope in the original data was no longer apparent; the trend had been effectively removed. What if you are faced with a situation

TABLE 4-1

Passenger Car Registrations: United States, 1950 to 1983

Year	Millions of Cars	First Difference	Second Difference
1950	40.30	NA	NA
1951	42.70	2.40	NA
1952	43.80	1.10	−1.30
1953	46.40	2.60	1.50
1954	48.50	2.10	−0.50
1955	52.10	3.60	1.50
1956	54.20	2.10	−1.50
1957	55.90	1.70	−0.40
1958	56.90	1.00	−0.70
1959	59.60	2.70	1.70
1960	61.70	2.10	−0.60
1961	63.40	1.70	−0.40
1962	66.10	2.70	1.00
1963	69.00	2.90	0.20
1964	72.00	3.00	0.10
1965	75.20	3.20	0.20
1966	78.40	3.20	0.00
1967	80.40	2.00	−1.20
1968	83.60	3.20	1.20
1969	86.90	3.30	0.10
1970	89.20	2.30	−1.00
1971	92.70	3.50	1.20
1972	97.10	4.40	0.90
1973	102.00	4.90	0.50
1974	104.90	2.90	−2.00
1975	106.70	1.80	−1.10
1976	110.40	3.70	1.90
1977	112.30	1.90	−1.80
1978	116.60	4.30	2.40
1979	118.40	1.80	−2.50
1980	121.60	3.20	1.40
1981	123.50	1.90	−1.30
1982	123.70	0.20	−1.70
1983	125.40	1.70	1.50

Source: U.S. Department of Commerce, Bureau of the Census, *Statistical Abstract of the United States,* various issues.

where this procedure does not work? Table 4–1 and Figure 4–2a show the data for automobile registrations in the United States. Figure 4–2b (p. 90) shows the year-to-year changes (first differences). Notice that there is still a very clear upward trend in the first differences (at least until 1980).

One possible way of dealing with this problem is to simply think of the first differences as another time series with another trend and try the

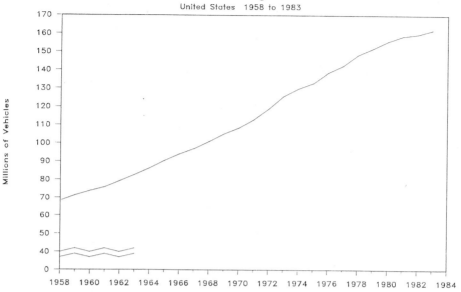

FIGURE 4-2a

Automobile registrations: United States, 1958–1983 (*Source:* U. S. Department of Commerce, Bureau of the Census, *Statistical Abstract of the United States,* various issues, 1958–1983)

another trend and try the same approach, taking differences in the differences, or *second differences*, as shown in Table 4–1. For this example, Figure 4–2c (p. 90) shows that the trend has been removed. If second differences do not remove a trend, then we can try third differences, or fourth, or fifth, or . . . ?

Transformations for Trend Removal

Several things are wrong with this technique of taking higher- and higher-order differences. One can be seen by examining Table 4–1. In taking first differences, one data point was lost; taking second differences removed a second. As each successive set of differences is taken, one additional data point is lost. If the time series is limited in length, this loss of data can begin to be a serious problem. Even worse, perhaps, taking higher-order differences is a technique that may not always work. Fortunately, there is an alternative approach. This is the use of a *data trans-*

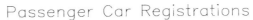
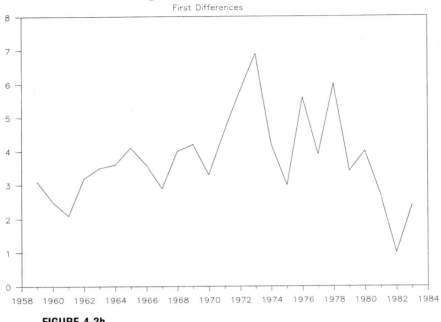

FIGURE 4-2b

First differences

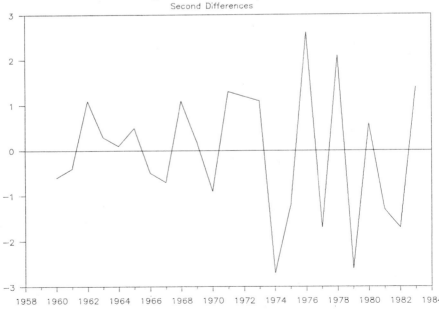

FIGURE 4-2c

Second differences

formation.[3] To see how this works, it will be helpful to start with one very commonly used transformation.

Trend for a Constant Rate of Growth. At the beginning of this discussion, we saw that taking first differences was equivalent to assuming a linear trend where the variable increased each period by (on the average) a constant *amount*. A frequently appropriate alternative is to assume that the variable increases at a constant *rate*, that is, by a constant period-to-period *percentage* or ratio. Equation (2) could also be written in the form

$$Y_t = Y_{t-1} + b \qquad (3)$$

If the variable were assumed to increase at a constant rate, then, rather than adding the constant, we would multiply

$$Y_t = Y_{t-1} \times (1 + g) \qquad (4)$$

where *g* is the constant rate of growth or increase.

The easiest way to remove this trend is to replace the differencing or subtraction of Table 4–1 ($Y_t - Y_{t-1}$) by division (Y_t / Y_{t-1}), as in Table 4–2 (p. 92). The result is shown in Figure 4–3a (p. 93); the strong upward trend is now gone but has been replaced by a downward trend—somehow we seem to have overshot. (We will return to this problem shortly.)

Log Transformation. As an alternative to the use of ratios, the data can be transformed to logarithms. With logarithms the operation of multiplication is replaced by addition. Thus, with the constant growth trend of equation (4) using logarithms (abbreviated either log or ln) gives the trend

$$\log Y_t = \log Y_{t-1} + \log (1 + g) \qquad (5)$$

which can be removed by taking first differences in the logs.

Transforming data to logarithms is not particularly difficult. At one time it was a bit inconvenient because it required special tables. Unless you used them frequently, remembering how to use those tables when they were needed was a problem. Now most hand calculators have a key that automatically changes numbers to logs.[4] It is also possible to buy

---

[3]As a rule of thumb, never go beyond taking second differences; if that does not work, immediately shift to using transformations.

[4]There are actually two different types of logarithms in frequent use: common logarithms, usually abbreviated log, and natural logarithms, abbreviated ln. Either can be used; some calculators have both, some have only natural logarithms. One advantage of natural logs is that, when the growth rate, *g*, is not too great, ln (1 + *g*) is approximately equal to *g*. To see this, compare the ratios with the log differences in Table 4–2.

TABLE 4-2

Passenger Car Registrations: United States, 1950 to 1983
Ratios and First Differences of Logs

Year	Millions of Cars	Ratios	Logs	Log First Difference
1950	40.30	NA	3.70	NA
1951	42.70	1.06	3.75	0.058
1952	43.80	1.03	3.78	0.025
1953	46.40	1.06	3.84	0.058
1954	48.50	1.05	3.88	0.044
1955	52.10	1.07	3.95	0.072
1956	54.20	1.04	3.99	0.040
1957	55.90	1.03	4.02	0.031
1958	56.90	1.02	4.04	0.018
1959	59.60	1.05	4.09	0.046
1960	61.70	1.04	4.12	0.035
1961	63.40	1.03	4.15	0.027
1962	66.10	1.04	4.19	0.042
1963	69.00	1.04	4.23	0.043
1964	72.00	1.04	4.28	0.043
1965	75.20	1.04	4.32	0.043
1966	78.40	1.04	4.36	0.042
1967	80.40	1.03	4.39	0.025
1968	83.60	1.04	4.43	0.039
1969	86.90	1.04	4.46	0.039
1970	89.20	1.03	4.49	0.026
1971	92.70	1.04	4.53	0.038
1972	97.10	1.05	4.58	0.046
1973	102.00	1.05	4.62	0.049
1974	104.90	1.03	4.65	0.028
1975	106.70	1.02	4.67	0.017
1976	110.40	1.03	4.70	0.034
1977	112.30	1.02	4.72	0.017
1978	116.60	1.04	4.76	0.038
1979	118.40	1.02	4.77	0.015
1980	121.60	1.03	4.80	0.027
1981	123.50	1.02	4.82	0.016
1982	123.70	1.00	4.82	0.002
1983	125.40	1.01	4.83	0.014

special graph papers that directly convert numbers to logs as they are plotted. (See Appendix A at the end of this chapter or the book by Craver cited at the end of Chapter 3.)

Table 4–2 gives the natural logs and log differences for automobile registrations. Figure 4–3b (p. 94) shows the natural logarithms of the data and Figure 4–3c (p. 94), the log differences. Notice the downward curvature in the graph of the logs in Figure 4–3b. Notice also the similarity between Figures 4–3a and c. Just as the upward curvature in the original data led to

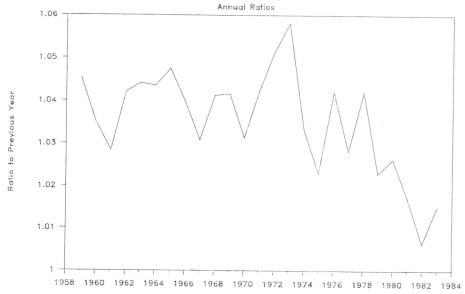

FIGURE 4-3a

Automobile registrations: Annual ratios

an upward slope in the first differences, so the downward curvature in the logs gives a downward slope in the ratios and in the first differences in the logs.

Other Transformations. A transformation is simply a mathematical function that changes the relative magnitudes of the numbers.[5]

Figure 4–4 (p. 95), for example, shows the function that relates numbers to their logs. It can be seen that this function curves downward. Since the original trend in Figure 4–3a curved upward, the effect of transforming the data to logs was a net "straightening" of the trend line compared to that of Figure 4–3b. Actually, as we saw, the curvature was in fact reversed, suggesting that the log gave too strong a correction. The question is, is there some transformation which would just balance the curvature in the original data? It turns out that there is.

It can be useful to think of a "ladder" of transformations of varying degrees of curvature as in Figure 4–5 (p. 96). We want to find a transforma-

[5]Some writers such as Tukey prefer the term "re-expression" to "transformation." For our purposes, the terms will be considered equivalent.

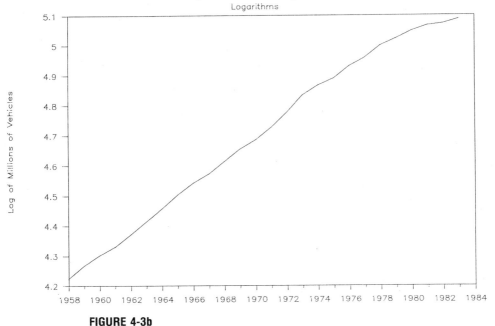

FIGURE 4-3b

Logarithms

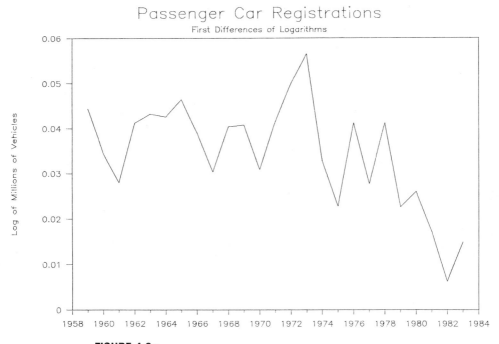

FIGURE 4-3c

First differences of logarithms

The Log Transformation

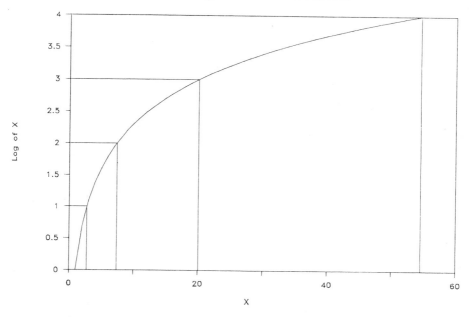

FIGURE 4-4

The log transformation

tion of appropriate curvature so that the trend in the transformed data becomes linear and thus the period-to-period differences (on the average) become constant or stationary. If the original trend curves upward, then we would use a transformation, such as the log, from the downward curving part of the ladder; if the original data are curving downward, then a transformation from the upper part of the ladder is appropriate.

In practice, we have two ways of selecting a transformation. In some cases there will be strong theoretical reasons for considering a particular function such as the log. As we shall see in Chapter 12, in many situations there can be structural reasons for expecting that a variable will grow at a constant rate. Alternatively, we can let our analysis of the data lead us to an appropriate transformation. It is this latter approach that we will consider here. This approach can have the danger that we may "tailor" the model to the data and begin to see "patterns" in what are only idiosyncrasies of the observed data, rather than true underlying and continuing movements. We will return to this problem in Chapter 9.

Data Transformations
Relative Curvatures

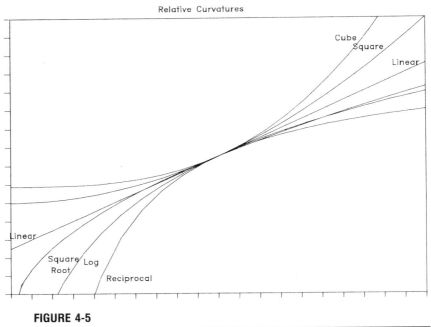

Cube
Square
Linear

Linear
Square
Root
Log
Reciprocal

FIGURE 4-5

Data transformations, relative curvatures

In this example, the original data curved upward (the first differences sloped upward); after trying logs, the trend curved downward (the first differences sloped downward), suggesting that we had overcorrected. In Figure 4–5 it can be seen that a transformation between the original data and the log is the square root. (The use of the transformation is shown in Table 4–3.) Figure 4–6a shows the plot of the square root of car registrations. It can be seen that the trend in the data now appears nearly linear and the first differences in the square roots appear to be horizontal, effectively removing the trend. Notice also, as shown by the box-and-whisker diagram of Figure 4–6b, that 1973 and 1982 are now clearly identifiable as outliers and should be the subject of a more detailed examination.

For the moment, don't try to make any literal sense out of the square root of an automobile. Remember that all we are trying to do is to find some mechanical device for removing the trend. We will see in Chapter 12 that an underlying rationale for the use of each of the transformations in the "ladder" can be developed.

Transformations can be used for purposes other than just trend removal. For example, in discussing the analysis of residuals in Chapter 3, it was noted that problems can arise when the variability or *spread* of the

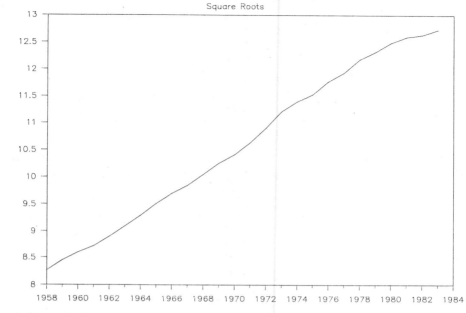

FIGURE 4-6a

Automobile registrations: Square roots

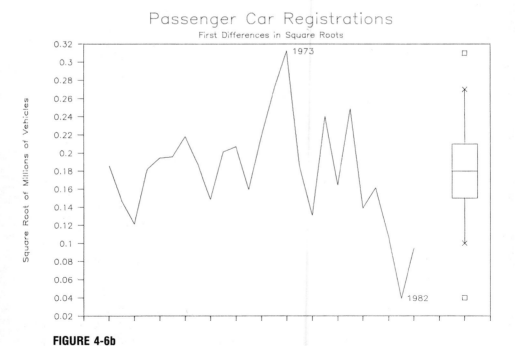

FIGURE 4-6b

First differences in square roots

TABLE 4-3

Passenger Car Registrations: United
States, 1950 to 1983
Square Roots and Differences

Year	Millions of Cars	Square Root	First Difference
1950	40.30	6.35	NA
1951	42.70	6.53	0.19
1952	43.80	6.62	0.08
1953	46.40	6.81	0.19
1954	48.50	6.96	0.15
1955	52.10	7.22	0.25
1956	54.20	7.36	0.14
1957	55.90	7.48	0.11
1958	56.90	7.54	0.07
1959	59.60	7.72	0.18
1960	61.70	7.85	0.13
1961	63.40	7.96	0.11
1962	66.10	8.13	0.17
1963	69.00	8.31	0.18
1964	72.00	8.49	0.18
1965	75.20	8.67	0.19
1966	78.40	8.85	0.18
1967	80.40	8.97	0.11
1968	83.60	9.14	0.18
1969	86.90	9.32	0.18
1970	89.20	9.44	0.12
1971	92.70	9.63	0.18
1972	97.10	9.85	0.23
1973	102.00	10.10	0.25
1974	104.90	10.24	0.14
1975	106.70	10.33	0.09
1976	110.40	10.51	0.18
1977	112.30	10.60	0.09
1978	116.60	10.80	0.20
1979	118.40	10.88	0.08
1980	121.60	11.03	0.15
1981	123.50	11.11	0.09
1982	123.70	11.12	0.01
1983	125.40	11.20	0.08

residuals appears to be changing over time. This problem can also usually be corrected by a suitable transformation of the data.

ANALYZING CYCLES

The term cycle as it is used in forecasting is perhaps something of a misnomer. Normally, when we think of cycles we think of regular oscillations, as when we talk about an alternating electrical current of 60 cycles per second. In forecasting, however, the term simply refers to fluctuations around some underlying trend, fluctuations that are, in most cases, very irregular.[6] In time-series analysis, components that are cyclical in the usual sense of the term are here referred to as seasonal.

Because the concept of a cycle as it is used here is so general, the primary problem in analyzing cycles is in deciding exactly which fluctuations are "cycles" and which are not. There are two basic approaches. When we have some underlying theory as a base, it may be possible to develop a specific model that can then be fitted to the data and tested. We will return to the modeling of cycles in Chapter 8. An alternative approach is to try to mechanically separate the cycles from the residual noise by some sort of mathematical filter, much as an electronic filter is used to separate a radio or television signal from any static that may be present.

This analogy with the noise or static filter in a radio is, in fact, a good one. Anyone who has listened to a poor radio knows how the noise can obscure and distort the music or other sound that you are listening to. If the radio signal is strong, the noise will be relatively unimportant; if the signal is weak or distant, it may not even be possible to identify the music being played although it may be possible to identify it as music rather than voices. The test of a good radio is how well it performs under these marginal conditions. In forecasting we are faced with exactly the same problem. When the pattern (signal) is strong, there is little problem in its identification and analysis; our concern is with designing filters that will be effective when the noise level is high and the pattern or signal is weak, as, for example, in the data on new car factory sales which we considered earlier. The difference is that in a radio we are concerned with physical filters; here our filters are mathematical and computational. Thus, although the term filter is sometimes used, a more common term is *smoothing*. Chapter 6 examines some filters with particular applicability to short-range forecasting. Here we are more concerned with the underlying concept and consider a more general approach to smoothing.

Smoothing with Moving Averages

The idea of the moving average can best be developed through an example. Table 4–4 (p. 100) shows a 10-period time series that is actually an artificial set of random numbers with an overall mean of 10.8, but with no other deliberate pattern. Also shown in the table is a moving average, which is based on a moving mean of groups of three observations.

Several things can be noted about this moving average. First, compared to the fluctuations in the original data the moving mean is much less

---

[6]Many forecasters would argue that, in analyzing cycles, we are in fact looking not at fluctuations "around" a trend, but at changes in the trend itself.

TABLE 4-4

Moving Groups of Three Observations

Period	Data	Three Period Groups			Moving Mean
		1st	2nd	3rd	
1	13	13			
2	6	6	6		11.33
3	15	15	15	15	10.30
4	10		10	10	14.00
5	17			17	11.33
6	7				10.00
7	6				9.00
8	14				10.67
9	12				11.33
10	8				

erratic; the process of averaging has reduced the magnitude of the random component. At the same time, it can be seen that using samples of only three data values did not do a complete job of averaging; some of the random noise remains.

Second, the process of smoothing spreads the effect of extremely large or small values over several periods. This can create a pattern that may resemble a cycle. Notice here that the moving mean in the last column seems to show a peak in period 4 and a trough in period 7 *even though the original data are only random numbers*. It would be possible of course to reduce this problem by increasing the size of the moving samples or groups to be averaged. The problem is that, as the group size increases, not only the random component is "smoothed"; any real cyclical patterns will tend to be flattened as well.

Finally, notice that it is not possible to calculate moving averages for the first or the last periods, which effectively reduces the length of the time series by two observations. Since most time series used in forecasting tend to be relatively short to begin with, such a loss can frequently be important. As we shall see shortly, techniques exist for estimating these end points, although they are not always completely effective.

The design of any moving-average filter or *smoother* must address three design considerations:

1. To smooth the residual noise and at the same time to have minimal impact on any patterns in the data.
2. To be relatively insensitive to outliers (unusually large or small values) that can create artificial cycles.
3. To deal with the shortening of the time series at the ends.

Design Characteristics of a Moving Average. In designing a moving average, four characteristics can be varied:

1. *Type of average.* The choice is usually between the arithmetic mean or the median, although other types of average can be used. In the preceding example, the arithmetic mean was used.

2. *Length of the average.* The number of periods included in each group. In the example the number was three.

3. *Weighted versus unweighted average.* In this example, each of the three numbers included in each mean was given the same weight or importance. In some cases heavier weights are given to some of the numbers in the average.

4. *Centered versus uncentered average.* In writing down the numbers in the column headed "moving mean," note that each value was centered on the same line as the middle of the three numbers in the average. Alternatively, it could have been aligned with one of the other two values.

In this example we used an *unweighted, centered,* moving *mean* of size *three*. We will now explore some other possibilities.

Smoothing with Medians

It is not at all uncommon to find outliers in the time series that arise in management and planning applications. Many different political, economic, social, and other events can cause relatively large temporary or permanent changes in a variable. Sales can be affected by the opening or closing of a sales outlet, by sales promotion activities, or by the introduction of new or changed products. Prices or costs can be changed by governmental acts or by changes in contracts. The actions of competitors can have effects.

Large, identifiable outliers should be adjusted as part of the initial editing process. In many cases, there will still be data points that might be outliers but that cannot be clearly identified or some that just slip through the initial editing. As with the measures used for summarizing residuals in Chapter 3, it is helpful to have smoothing techniques that are relatively insensitive to any outliers that may still be left in the data series.

In the last few years a class of *robust* smoothing procedures has been developed, which are particularly useful in these applications. These methods are based on the use of medians as averages and on the sequential use of several different smoothing procedures. Because this requires repeating a smoothing process several times, these methods for the most part are practical only in computer applications. Unfortunately, there are not as yet many median-based smoothing procedures available for microcomputers.[7] There is one procedure in this class that is suitable for hand calculation and that can be adapted for spreadsheet use. It will serve as an illustration of this approach and for many applications will be more than adequate as a tool for examining cyclical fluctuations.

Smoothing Process.   The basic steps in robust smoothing procedures tend to be similar. The approach used here is typical and illustrates some of the more common steps. In this example the smoothing process consists of four steps:

1. A moving median of 5 points, which will be labeled M5.
2. A moving median of 3 points (M3), which will be repeated until there are no further changes (M3R).
3. A weighted moving mean, which is called Hanning (H).
4. A procedure for extrapolating the first and last points so that the smoothed series is the same length as the original data.

As an optional fifth step, the entire process can be repeated using the residuals from the smoothed time series. The results of the two smoothing stages are then added together.

We will illustrate this procedure using the data of Table 4–4. The calculations are shown in Table 4–5 and should be followed by the reader in parallel with the description of the process that follows.

Taking a Moving Median of Five Points (M5)

---

1. Copy the first number in the data column into the first position in the M5 column.
2. Find the median of the first three numbers and enter it into the second position in the M5 column. (Here the first three data points are 13, 6, and 15, with a median of 13.)
3. Find the median of the first five numbers and enter it in the third position in the column. (These numbers are 13, 6, 15, 10, and 17, with a median of 13.)
4. Find the median of the second through the sixth points and enter it in the fourth position in the M5 column.

---

[7]One exception is the Statgraphics® program, which includes a number of techniques of exploratory data analysis useful in forecasting applications as well as the more traditional approaches.

Table 4-5

(a) Smoothing with Medians

Period	Data	M5	M3	M3R	H	End Adjust.	Smooth	Residual
1	13	13	13	13		14.50	13.00	0.00
2	6	13	13	13	13.00		13.00	−7.00
3	15	13	13	13	12.25		12.25	2.75
4	10	10	10	10	10.75		10.75	−0.75
5	17	10	10	10	10.00		10.00	7.00
6	7	10	10	10	10.00		10.00	−3.00
7	6	12	10	10	10.00		10.00	−4.00
8	14	8	12	10	9.50		9.50	4.50
9	12	12	8	8	8.50		8.50	3.50
10	8	8	8	8		6.50	8.00	0.00

(b) Resmoothing

Period	First Residual	M5	M3	M3R	Smooth	Final Smooth	Final Residual
1	0.00	0.00	0.00	0.00	0.00	13.00	0.00
2	−7.00	0.00	0.00	0.00	0.00	13.00	−7.00
3	2.75	0.00	0.00	0.00	−0.19	12.06	2.94
4	−0.75	−0.75	−0.75	−0.75	−0.56	10.19	−0.19
5	7.00	−0.75	−0.75	−0.75	−0.75	9.25	7.75
6	−3.00	−0.75	−0.75	−0.75	−0.56	9.44	−2.44
7	−4.00	3.50	0.00	0.00	−0.19	9.81	−3.81
8	4.50	0.00	3.50	0.00	0.00	9.50	4.50
9	3.50	3.50	0.00	0.00	0.00	8.50	3.50
10	0.00	0.00	0.00	0.00	0.00	8.00	0.00

5. Continue moving down the data column one line at a time, entering the medians of five points. This process can be aided by making a paper or cardboard mask as shown in Figure 4–7 (p. 104).

6. When you reach the next to the last position in the M5 column, notice that you can no longer take a median of 5. As at the beginning, find the median of the last three points and enter it in the next to the last position in the M5 column.

7. Copy the last number in the data column into the M5 column.

Taking a Repeated Moving Median of Three Points (M3R)

1. Repeat exactly the same process using the numbers in the M5 column rather than the original data and taking medians of three numbers

Period	Data	M5
1		13
2		13
3	15	13
4	10	13
5	17	10
6	7	
7	6	
8		
9		
10	8	

FIGURE 4-7

Data mask for calculating a moving median (M5)

rather than five. As before, the first number, 13, is copied into the M3 column. Next, the median of the first three numbers in the M5 column 13, 13, and 13) is entered in the second position, and the process is repeated to the bottom of the M3 column. As with M5, a cardboard mask that displays only three numbers at a time can be helpful.

2. The previous step should now be repeated a second time, except that the numbers in the M3 rather than those in the M5 column should be used. Notice that there is only one change between the M3 and the M3R columns: the 12 in the third position from the bottom is changed to a 10. In many cases there will be no changes. If changes do occur, the process should be repeated (this time using the numbers in the M3R column) until no additional changes are necessary.

Hanning (H)

1. Add together the first number in the M3R column, two times the second number, and the third number. Divide this total by 4 and enter in the second position in the H column.

2. Repeat this process as before to the bottom of the M3R column. The last position in the H column will be blank.

End-point Extrapolation

---

1. To determine the final smoothed value, start by finding three numbers:
    a. The number that was just entered in the next to the last position in the H column. (Here this is 8.50.)
    b. The last number in the M3R column, which should be the same as the last value in the column of the original data. (In this case it is 8.)
    c. The value that is shown in the column headed "End Adjust," and which is obtained by multiplying the value in the next to the last position in the H column by three and subtracting two times the preceding number ($3 \times 8.5 - 2 \times 9.5 = 6.5$).
2. Find the median of these three numbers. (Here the median of 6.5, 8, and 8.5 is 8.) Enter this in the last position in the H column.
3. To obtain the value for the first position, repeat the process using the numbers at the top of the table in reverse order. That is, use the first values in the H and M3R columns and calculate $3 \times 13 - 2 \times 12.25 = 14.5$.

Obtaining Residuals and Final Smoothing. When the time series being analyzed shows very distinct peaks and troughs, the smoothing process outlined here will tend to flatten these peaks and fill in the troughs. This will have the effect of reducing the apparent magnitude of the cyclical fluctuations. In such cases it can be helpful to calculate the residuals from this smoothed time series and repeat the smoothing process a second time. This is illustrated in Table 4–5b. There are four steps:

1. Determine the residuals by subtracting the smoothed time series from the original data.
2. Smooth the residuals using the approach previously described.
3. Add the results of this second smoothing to the first stage results to obtain the *final smooth*.
4. Obtain the final residuals by subtracting the final smooth from the original data.

The final smooth obtained by this method is compared to the simple three-period moving mean in Figure 4–8 (p. 106). Remember that the original data consist of 10 random numbers generated by a process with a theoretical mean of 10.8. In this case, median smoothing does not show the

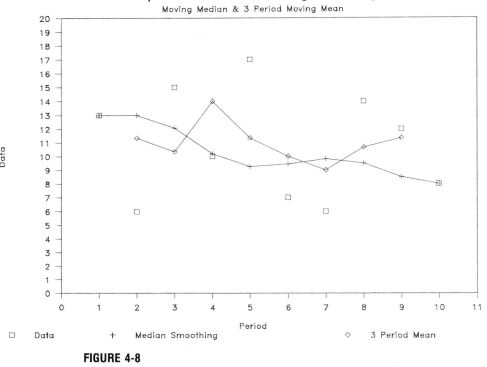

Comparison of Moving Averages
Moving Median & 3 Period Moving Mean

□ Data   + Median Smoothing   ◇ 3 Period Mean

FIGURE 4-8

Comparison of moving averages: Moving median and three-period moving mean

artificially induced "cycle" that appears in the moving mean. At the same time, because the first data value happens to be relatively large and the last relatively small, the overall effect is that of a nonexistent negative trend. The moral is, of course, that these methods are designed to be helpful—not infallible. In particular, the estimated end values in any smoothed time series should be interpreted with caution. Unfortunately, these are usually the points of most interest to the forecaster.

Smoothing First Differences. In the artificial data used in this example, there was no trend and no cyclical pattern. In a more realistic situation, there will be both. The question is: Should the data first be smoothed and the trend then removed or should the trend be first removed by differencing and the first differences then smoothed? The answer in many cases may be both. Two different but related pictures will be obtained and can be used together in analyzing the data.

For an example we can go back to Chapter 3, where we looked at the

TABLE 4-6

Factory Sales of Passenger Cars: United States, 1950 to 1984

Year	Sales (million cars)	(53RH)T Smooth	Residual	First Diff.	(53RH)T Smooth	Residual
1950	6.67	6.55	0.12			
1951	5.34	5.77	−0.42	−1.33	−1.14	−0.19
1952	4.32	5.37	−1.05	−1.02	−1.23	0.21
1953	6.12	5.48	0.64	1.80	−0.69	2.49
1954	5.56	5.71	−0.15	−0.56	−0.56	0.00
1955	7.92	5.82	2.10	2.36	−0.35	2.71
1956	5.82	5.82	0.00	−2.10	0.08	−2.18
1957	6.11	5.82	0.29	0.29	0.29	0.00
1958	4.26	5.75	−1.49	−1.85	0.29	−2.14
1959	5.59	5.60	−0.01	1.33	0.54	0.79
1960	6.68	5.80	0.88	1.09	1.04	0.05
1961	5.54	6.43	−0.89	−1.14	1.15	−2.28
1962	6.93	7.05	−0.12	1.39	0.86	0.53
1963	7.64	7.55	0.09	0.71	0.71	0.00
1964	7.75	7.84	−0.09	0.11	0.45	−0.34
1965	9.31	8.11	1.20	1.56	−0.08	1.64
1966	8.60	8.54	0.06	−0.71	−0.52	−0.19
1967	7.44	8.60	−1.16	−1.16	−0.81	−0.35
1968	8.82	8.29	0.53	1.38	−0.87	2.25
1969	8.22	8.24	−0.02	−0.60	−0.55	−0.05
1970	6.55	8.47	−1.92	−1.67	−0.02	−1.65
1971	8.58	8.58	0.00	2.03	0.24	1.79
1972	8.82	8.58	0.24	0.24	0.24	0.00
1973	9.66	8.56	1.10	0.84	0.24	0.60
1974	7.33	8.52	−1.19	−2.33	0.25	−2.58
1975	6.71	8.50	−1.79	−0.62	0.20	−0.82
1976	8.50	8.62	−0.12	1.79	0.07	1.72
1977	9.20	8.86	0.34	0.70	0.00	0.70
1978	9.16	8.96	0.20	−0.04	−0.04	0.00
1979	8.42	8.25	0.17	−0.74	−0.37	−0.37
1980	6.40	6.89	−0.49	−2.02	−0.94	−1.08
1981	6.22	6.22	0.00	−0.18	−0.95	0.77
1982	5.05	6.32	−1.27	−1.17	−0.17	−1.00
1983	6.74	6.76	−0.02	1.69	0.62	1.08
1984	7.62	7.62	0.01	0.88	0.88	0.00

time series on U.S. factory sales of automobiles. There first differences were used to remove the trend, and it seemed that there were no other obvious patterns in the data. Table 4–6 shows the results of applying the smoothing process just described to the auto sales data. As compared to the unsmoothed data, the picture as shown in Figure 4–9a (p. 108) is somewhat different. On the average, sales during the 1950s were relatively constant. During the first half of the 1960s, however, sales increased rapidly. (This was of course also the period in which the major part of the interstate highway

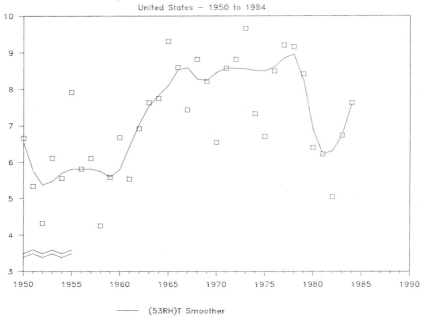

FIGURE 4-9a

Factory sales of passenger cars: United States, 1950–1984

system was constructed.) Following 1965, sales again leveled off, until the somewhat precipitous drop starting in 1979 and the recovery in 1981.

The smoothed first differences of Figure 4–9b show a different but complementary pattern. During the 1950s when sales appeared relatively constant, the smoothed differences were increasing. Such a pattern tends to precede an upturn. Similarly, in the early 1960s, although sales were rapidly increasing, the smoothed differences were declining, a precursor of a downturn. It is for this reason that it is sometimes argued that first differences are a *leading indicator*. That is, fluctuations in (smoothed) first differences tend to precede similar movements in the original time series. The extent to which this may or may not hold for a particular time series can be determined in many cases by the simultaneous consideration of these two smoothed graphs. You should note, however, the large variability in the residuals in both graphs, suggesting that the smoothed patterns should be interpreted cautiously.

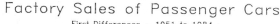

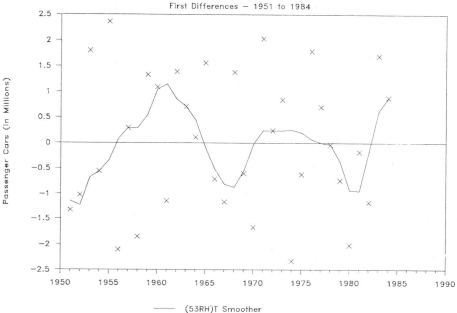

FIGURE 4-9b

First differences, 1951–1984

Other Forms of Robust Smoothing. This example has illustrated, with one minor exception, the major elements used in most robust smoothing procedures.[8] Individual methods differ primarily in how these elements are combined. To describe the different specific procedures, a simple notation is sometimes used. The order of a moving median is indicated by a number, H is used for Hanning, and R is used to indicate a repeated operation. T or the word twice is used to indicate that a step should be repeated two times. The method that has just been used would be specified as

(53RH) T　or　53RH, twice

Other possibilities and a comparison of some of the different smoothers can be found in the references at the end of the chapter.

Using the terms introduced earlier, the smoothing procedure used in this example could be described as a weighted, centered moving average

[8]The other component operation is called *splitting*, denoted by SS, and is discussed in the books by Tukey and by Velleman and Hoaglin cited at the end of the chapter.

based on a combination of medians and means. The length of the average depends on the number of times the M3 step is repeated and on whether the process is used once or twice, but it can be shown that 53RH is approximately an 11-period average, while (53RH) T covers approximately 21 periods, in both cases with the heaviest weighting at the center.

SEASONAL PATTERNS

Seasonal patterns are fluctuations that recur over specific calendar periods—a day, a week, a year. Most frequently, when the term seasonal is used by itself, it refers to annual fluctuations in either monthly or quarterly data. In general, the procedures used with monthly and quarterly data are the same. In forecasting applications, monthly data are probably more commonly used. The examples here will use quarterly data since it will reduce the number of data points that have to be used in the calculations. Modifications for monthly data will be noted as necessary. When weekly data are used, special problems arise because there is not a whole number of weeks in the year (there are 52 weeks plus 1 or 2 days). A method that can be used with weekly data is noted at the end of the chapter.

There are at least three different reasons why planners and managers may be interested in seasonal fluctuations in data. First, in many cases the seasonal is, after the trend, the most prominent component of the time series and tends to mask cyclical movements and cyclical turning points. This can be seen by comparing Figure 3–1 and Figure 3–2b. As a prelude to any further analysis, formal or informal, it is necessary to first remove the seasonal component. It is for this reason that most economic time series released by the federal government are reported as "seasonally adjusted" or "deseasonalized."

Second, from the standpoint of short-term (less than one year) planning of inventories, work force, or cash flow, seasonal movement usually is the largest element in period-to-period changes and thus the most important element in the forecast. An understanding of the seasonal changes that are likely to occur can be the most important factor in improving forecast accuracy.

Finally, an understanding of seasonal patterns can be an important element in longer-range planning. In searching for possible new products, many companies are particularly interested in products that have seasonal patterns different from those currently being produced or distributed. If a company manufactures lawn furniture, sales tend to be high in the spring and early summer, with production in the late winter and spring. Production and sales facilities may be relatively unused in the late summer and fall. It may be particularly desirable to consider products that can make use of these temporarily underutilized resources. Similarly, a multidivision company exploring new acquisitions may be particularly interested in candidate firms with counterseasonal needs for short-term working capital.

In this section we first examine a simple way of removing the seasonal component from data along with the trend removal. This can be useful when the forecaster is only interested in temporarily getting rid of the seasonal in order to better observe cyclical fluctuations. We then consider several methods of isolating the seasonal component for separate analysis. For a working example, we will use the data on passenger-miles carried by U.S. airlines previously presented in Chapter 3.

Taking Seasonal First Differences

A simple way of removing seasonal fluctuations is to calculate the change from the equivalent period in the preceding year, rather than from the immediately preceding quarter (or month). This can then be smoothed to isolate the cyclical component. In Table 4–7 (p. 112) and Figure 4–10a (p. 114), the results are shown and compared to the cyclical component as presented earlier in Figure 3–2d. The effect is to remove both the seasonal and the trend. If further differencing had been necessary to completely remove the trend, a regular difference between successive periods would have been used and not another seasonal difference. In all cases, all differencing should precede the smoothing operation.

Figure 4–10b shows an alternative approach, which will be considered next. Here the seasonal component was first removed using a seasonal index (a technique that will be discussed shortly) so that the cyclical component could be isolated by taking ordinary first differences and smoothing just as if there had been no seasonal pattern. It is again compared with the cycle as it was presented earlier. Comparing Figures 4–10a and b (p. 115), it can be seen that the patterns are quite similar. There is one very important difference. If turning points (peaks and troughs) are compared, those in Figure 4–10a tend to occur approximately two quarters after those of Figure 4–10b; both, however, tend to lead the turning points in the actual cycle. As discussed in the preceding section, first differences tend to be a leading indicator of cyclical movements in the actual data. Seasonal first differences, however, tend to have shorter lead times, a potential disadvantage in their use.

Studying the Seasonal Pattern

We will now turn our attention to situations where interest lies in the seasonal pattern itself. As an introduction to this, it may be useful to

TABLE 4-7

Scheduled Airline Passenger-miles Carried:
United States, 1970 III to 1985 II
Seasonal First Differences

Quarter	Billion Passenger- Miles	Seasonal 1st Diff.	Smooth	Residual
1970 I				
II				
III	38.59			
IV	30.12			
1971 I	29.76			
II	34.10			
III	38.86	0.27	0.34	−0.07
IV	33.08	2.96	2.80	0.16
1972 I	34.02	4.26	4.14	0.12
II	38.25	4.15	4.39	−0.24
III	43.22	4.36	4.21	0.15
IV	36.89	3.81	3.81	0.00
1973 I	36.49	2.47	3.36	−0.89
II	41.35	3.10	3.06	0.04
III	46.13	2.91	2.76	0.15
IV	38.00	1.11	2.29	−1.18
1974 I	38.46	1.97	1.70	0.27
II	42.39	1.04	0.84	0.20
III	44.96	−1.17	−0.44	−0.74
IV	37.10	−0.90	−1.36	0.46
1975 I	36.95	−1.51	−1.42	−0.09
II	40.00	−2.39	−0.55	−1.84
III	46.30	1.34	1.09	0.25
IV	39.55	2.45	2.70	−0.25
1976 I	40.88	3.93	3.69	0.24
II	45.54	5.54	3.98	1.56
III	50.06	3.76	3.66	0.10
IV	42.50	2.95	3.05	−0.10
1977 I	43.49	2.61	2.75	−0.14
II	47.75	2.21	2.99	−0.77
III	53.95	3.89	3.87	0.02
IV	48.04	5.54	5.19	0.35
1978 I	49.58	6.09	6.57	−0.47
II	56.05	8.30	7.94	0.36
III	65.21	11.26	8.83	2.43
IV	55.95	7.91	9.02	−1.11
1979 I	58.83	9.25	8.74	0.51
II	63.81	7.76	8.22	−0.46
III	73.40	8.19	7.23	0.96
IV	60.96	5.01	5.01	0.00
1980 I	60.62	1.79	2.38	−0.59
II	64.37	0.56	0.21	0.35
III	70.49	−2.91	−1.63	−1.28
IV	58.77	−2.19	−2.66	0.47
1981 I	56.19	−4.43	−2.87	−1.56
II	64.94	0.57	−2.37	2.93
III	68.68	−1.81	−1.16	−0.65
IV	58.60	−0.17	0.14	−0.32
1982 I	58.98	2.79	1.23	1.56
II	66.77	1.83	1.89	−0.06
III	71.10	2.42	2.17	0.26
IV	61.06	2.46	2.72	−0.26

TABLE 4-7, continued

Quarter	Billion Passenger- Miles	Seasonal 1st Diff.	Smooth	Residual
1983 I	64.98	6.00	3.69	2.31
II	70.73	3.96	4.34	−0.37
III	75.57	4.47	4.47	0.00
IV	65.83	4.77	4.55	0.22
1984 I	66.37	1.39	4.98	−3.59
II	76.55	5.82	5.84	−0.02
III	82.30	6.73	6.70	0.03
IV	72.99	7.16	7.16	0.00
1985 I	73.53	7.16	7.93	−0.77
II	86.08	9.53	9.47	0.06

consider a slightly different graphical way of looking at a time series, one that will tend to emphasize the seasonal pattern rather than the trend.

Seasonal Alignment Graph.   Figure 4–11 (p. 116) shows the data of Figure 3–1, except that the horizontal axis lists only the quarters (or months) and each year is plotted as a separate line on the graph. Notice that, to include the complete seasonal pattern, each line starts with the first quarter and ends with the first quarter of the following year. In this type of graph the seasonal becomes the dominant visual component. The trend can be seen in the gradual upward shift in the lines, while the cyclical appears as a change in the spacing of the lines. Notice the compression of the lines during the years 1972 to 1977 and 1979 to 1981 and the reversal in the ordering of the years in 1975 and 1981. Compare this to the appearance of the same periods as shown in Figure 3–2b.

Seasonal Ratios.   Looking at Figure 4–11, it can be seen that the pattern that is repeated each year consists of a relatively low first quarter, a strong summer peak, and a low fourth quarter (compare this to Figure 3–2a). This can be expressed numerically by ratios between what would be an average quarter with and without the seasonal component. Table 4–8 shows two possible ways in which this can be done.

In Table 4–8a, each quarter is averaged across all the years. To use similar data for all the techniques to be discussed, only the years between 1971 and 1984 were used for these averages. Thus the 14 first quarters between 1971 and 1984 averaged 48.26, while second quarters averaged 53.76. Overall the average quarter was 53.00. Seasonal ratios are obtained by dividing each average quarter by the overall average and multiplying by 100. For example, the first-quarter ratio is

$$\frac{48.26}{53.00} \times 100 = 91.06$$

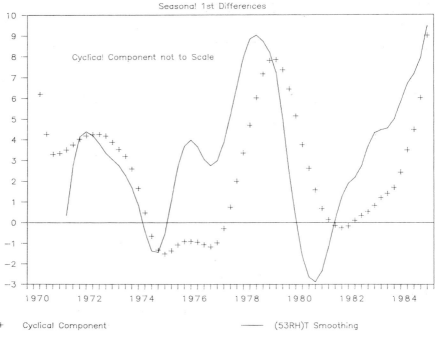

FIGURE 4-10a

Airline revenue passenger-miles: Seasonal first differences

This means that, on the average, first quarters were 8.94% below what would have been expected had there been no seasonal component.

   With this approach, a difficulty arises when there is a strong trend. By simply averaging the quarters, heaviest weight tends to be placed on the seasonal patterns in the years with the largest data values. When the trend is increasing, this may be desirable since the weight will be on the most recent years. When the trend is downward, the heavier weight will tend toward the oldest data. To make the weighting more uniform, an alternative approach can be used. As shown in Table 4–8b, seasonal ratios are calculated for each year separately. For the first quarter of 1971, the average for the year is 33.95 and the ratio is

$$\frac{29.76}{33.95} \times 100 = 87.66$$

The overall seasonal ratios are then obtained by averaging the ratios for each quarter. Since the numbers thus obtained will not always add up to

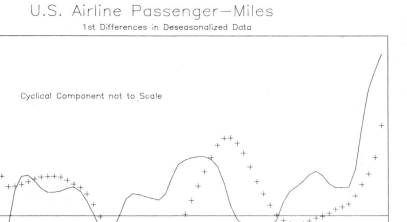

FIGURE 4-10b

First differences in deseasonalized data

400 (1200 for monthly data), it is common to adjust them so that they will. We show how this is done in the next section.

Seasonal Index

Both forms of seasonal ratios suffer from one additional problem. Looking again at Figure 4–11, it can be seen that the upward trend is not just between years; it exists within the years as well. This means that, with an upward trend, fourth quarters will tend to be high and first quarters low, not because of seasonal factors but because of the trend. If the trend changes, this pattern will change as well, even if there is no change in the actual seasonal component. One way of dealing with this problem is through the use of *seasonal relatives*.

To isolate the seasonal, without a trend effect, it is necessary to have a base line that changes continuously so that it reflects both trend and cyclical

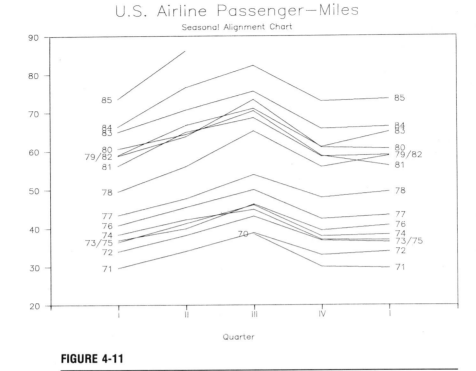

FIGURE 4-11

U. S. airline passenger-miles carried: Seasonal alignment chart

factors. One way of thinking about this is to consider the time-series values Y as consisting of the four components in the form

$$Y = T \times C \times S \times I \qquad (6)$$

where T refers to the trend, C to the cyclical, S to the seasonal, and I to the residual components.[9] The procedure used is to first isolate the T and C components as a time series ($T \times C$). If we then divide the original data by this *trend cycle*, we isolate the seasonal and residual components.

$$S \times I = \frac{Y}{T \times C} \qquad (7)$$

[9]As we are actually carrying out the calculations it would be more correct to write this as $Y = (T \times C) \times (S + I)$. The form given in equation (6) has, however, become more or less traditional.

TABLE 4-8

Scheduled Airline Passenger-miles Carried:
United States, 1970 III to 1985 II
Seasonal Ratios

(a) Ratios of Annual Averages to Overall Average

Quarter	I	II	III	IV	Average
1970	NA	NA	38.59	30.12	
1971	29.76	34.10	38.86	33.08	33.95
1972	34.02	38.25	43.22	36.89	38.10
1973	36.49	41.35	46.13	38.00	40.49
1974	38.46	42.39	44.96	37.10	40.73
1975	36.95	40.00	46.30	39.55	40.70
1976	40.88	45.54	50.06	42.50	44.75
1977	43.49	47.75	53.95	48.04	48.31
1978	49.58	56.05	65.21	55.95	56.70
1979	58.83	63.81	73.40	60.96	64.25
1980	60.62	64.37	70.49	58.77	63.56
1981	56.19	64.94	68.68	58.60	62.10
1982	58.98	66.77	71.10	61.06	64.48
1983	64.98	70.73	75.57	65.83	69.28
1984	66.37	76.55	82.30	72.99	74.55
1985	73.53	86.08	NA	NA	
					Overall
Average[a]	48.26	53.76	59.30	50.67	53.00
Ratio to overall	91.06	101.44	111.90	95.61	

[a]Averages based on 1971 through 1984

(b) Average of Annual Ratios

Quarter	I	II	III	IV
1971	87.66	100.44	114.46	97.44
1972	89.30	100.41	113.45	96.84
1973	90.12	102.12	113.92	93.84
1974	94.43	104.08	110.39	91.09
1975	90.79	98.28	113.76	97.17
1976	91.36	101.78	111.88	94.98
1977	90.03	98.85	111.68	99.45
1978	87.45	98.86	115.01	98.68
1979	91.56	99.32	114.24	94.88
1980	95.37	101.27	110.90	92.46
1981	90.48	104.57	110.59	94.36
1982	91.47	103.56	110.27	94.70
1983	93.80	102.10	109.08	95.02
1984	89.02	102.68	110.39	97.90
1985				
Average	90.92	101.31	112.15	95.63

These are referred to as *seasonal relatives*. Averaging these seasonal relatives removes the residual component, leaving only the seasonal.

This process is carried out in several steps, which we will consider in sequence.

Five-quarter Weighted Moving Mean. Averaging together four successive quarters (or 12 successive months) will remove the seasonal component because each period of the year is represented. The difficulty with such an average is that it centers between the original observations. For this reason it is more common to use a five-quarter (13 month) weighted moving average with weights of 1, 2, 2, 2, and 1. In Table 4–9 the first value in the moving-mean column is obtained by

$$\frac{1}{8} [38.59 + 2 \times (30.12 + 29.76 + 34.10) + 38.86] = 33.18$$

and similarly for the following values. Although five different quarters are represented, notice that each *type* of quarter is represented equally since there are two different first quarters, each having a weight of 1 while the other three quarters have weights of 2. This computation removes the seasonal and, to a large extent, the residual. The moving mean can therefore be thought of as consisting only of the trend and cyclical $(T \times C)$. Notice that in this smoothing the equivalent of 1 year of data is lost. It is possible to make end-point adjustments similar to those in the last section, but this is not usually done except in computerized versions (such as X-11 to be discussed later).

Seasonal Relatives. The smoothed time series now forms the base line for the seasonal, just as the annual averages did in our earlier approach. If the original data are divided by these smoothed values as shown in Table 4–9, what remains is the seasonal and the residuals $(S \times I)$, the

TABLE 4-9

Scheduled Airline Passenger-miles Carried:
United States, 1970 III to 1985 II
Seasonal Relatives

Quarter		Billion Passenger-miles	Five-Quarter Centered Average	Seasonal Relatives
1970	III	38.59	NA	NA
	IV	30.12	NA	NA
1971	I	29.76	33.18	89.70
	II	34.10	33.58	101.55

TABLE 4-9, continued

Quarter		Billion Passenger-miles	Five-Quarter Centered Average	Seasonal Relatives
	III	38.86	34.48	112.69
	IV	33.08	35.53	93.09
1972	I	34.02	36.60	92.96
	II	38.25	37.62	101.68
	III	43.22	38.40	112.54
	IV	36.89	39.10	94.35
1973	I	36.49	39.85	91.57
	II	41.35	40.35	102.47
	III	46.13	40.74	113.23
	IV	38.00	41.12	92.42
1974	I	38.46	41.10	93.58
	II	42.39	40.84	103.80
	III	44.96	40.54	110.91
	IV	37.10	40.05	92.63
1975	I	36.95	39.92	92.56
	II	40.00	40.39	99.03
	III	46.30	41.19	112.40
	IV	39.55	42.38	93.33
1976	I	40.88	43.54	93.90
	II	45.54	44.38	102.62
	III	50.06	45.07	111.07
	IV	42.50	45.67	93.05
1977	I	43.49	46.44	93.66
	II	47.75	47.62	100.28
	III	53.95	49.07	109.95
	IV	48.04	50.87	94.44
1978	I	49.58	53.31	93.00
	II	56.05	55.71	100.61
	III	65.21	57.85	112.72
	IV	55.95	59.98	93.28
1979	I	58.83	61.97	94.93
	II	63.81	63.62	100.29
	III	73.40	64.47	113.84
	IV	60.96	64.77	94.12
1980	1	60.62	64.47	94.02
	II	64.37	63.84	100.84
	III	70.49	63.01	111.87
	IV	58.77	62.53	93.99
1981	I	56.19	62.37	90.09
	II	64.94	62.12	104.53
	III	68.68	62.45	109.97
	IV	58.60	63.03	92.97
1982	I	58.98	63.56	92.79
	II	66.77	64.17	104.05
	III	71.10	65.23	109.00
	IV	61.06	66.47	91.86
1983	I	64.98	67.53	96.23
	II	70.73	68.68	102.98
	III	75.57	69.45	108.81
	IV	65.83	70.35	93.57
1984	I	66.37	71.92	92.28
	II	76.55	73.66	103.93
	III	82.30	75.45	109.08
	IV	72.99	77.53	94.14
1985	I	73.53		
	II	86.08		

seasonal relatives. The seasonal relative for the first quarter of 1971 is obtained by

$$\frac{29.76}{33.18} \times 100 = 89.70$$

and similarly for the other values.

The seasonal relatives are now rearranged in a slightly different format as shown in Table 4–10. As with the discussion of residuals in Chapter 3, the forecaster should be concerned with the possibility of outliers among the seasonal relatives. This can be rapidly checked by setting up a stem-and-leaf or box-and-whisker diagram for each quarter (or month) separately. For this example, the box-and-whisker diagrams are shown in Figure 4–12. For convenience in comparison, the diagrams are all shown in relation to the final seasonal index. In this case there do not appear to be any obvious outliers. (On the other hand, you might note the much smaller variability in the fourth-quarter seasonal relatives.)

While the median shown could now be used as the seasonal index, an alternative and slightly better approach is to use what is called a *trimmed mean*. In a trimmed mean, large and small observations are routinely

TABLE 4-10

Scheduled Airline Passenger-miles Carried:
United States, 1971 to 1984

Seasonal Relatives

Quarter	I	II	III	IV	
1971	89.70	101.55	112.69	93.09	
1972	92.96	101.68	112.54	94.35	
1973	91.57	102.47	113.23	92.42	
1974	93.58	103.80	110.91	92.63	
1975	92.56	99.03	112.40	93.33	
1976	93.90	102.62	111.07	93.05	
1977	93.66	100.28	109.95	94.44	
1978	93.00	100.61	112.72	93.28	
1979	94.93	100.29	113.84	94.12	
1980	94.02	100.84	111.87	93.99	
1981	90.09	104.53	109.97	92.97	
1982	92.79	104.05	109.00	91.96	
1983	96.23	102.98	108.81	93.57	
1984	92.28	103.93	109.08	94.14	
Maximum	96.23	104.53	113.84	94.44	
Minimum	89.70	99.03	108.81	91.96	
Trimmed					Totals
Mean	92.94	102.09	111.29	93.41	399.73
Index	93.01	102.16	111.35	93.48	400.00

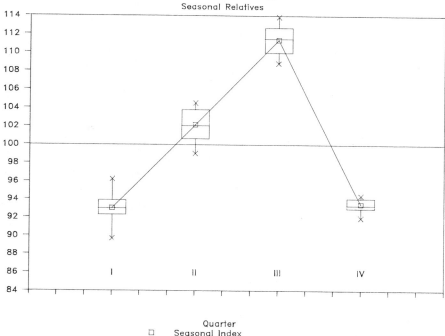

U.S. Airline Passenger—Miles
Seasonal Relatives

Quarter
□   Seasonal Index

FIGURE 4-12

U. S. airline passenger-miles: Seasonal relatives

dropped from the group before calculating the mean. For a 10% trimmed mean, the largest and smallest 10% are dropped. In Table 4–10 there are 14 observations for each quarter. Since 10% of this is approximately 1, the largest and smallest value should be dropped from the calculation. For the first quarter, these are the values 89.70 (first quarter of 1971) and 96.23 (first quarter of 1983). The arithmetic mean of the remaining 12 numbers is then found.

As a final step, the four index numbers must be adjusted to total 400 (1200 for monthly data) on the assumption that, if there were no seasonal, all the index values would be 100. The concept of the seasonal implies that seasonal movements above the base line should be exactly balanced by movements below so that the total, even with a seasonal pattern, should be 400.

The adjustment is made by summing the four (12 for monthly data) trimmed means. In this case the total is 399.73. The seasonal index is obtained by multiplying each mean by the ratio

$$\frac{400}{399.73}$$

as shown in the table.

Figure 4–13 compares the seasonal index to the seasonal ratios calculated previously; the patterns are quite similar. Because of the overall upward trend in the data, however, the seasonal ratio for the first quarter is substantially below the corresponding index value, while the ratio for the fourth quarter is above.

Changing Seasonals.   Seasonal patterns remain basically the same from one year to the next. Over time, they can slowly change. Rarely, large discontinuous changes may also occur. In the case of air passenger travel, it could be caused by changing attitudes toward when vacations are taken or by changing needs of business. In a time series of construction activity, it might be due to changes in construction technology that would extend the

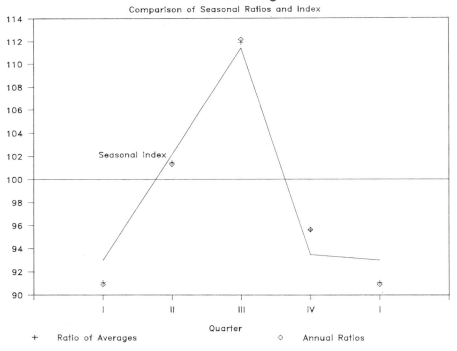

FIGURE 4-13

U. S. airline passenger-miles: Comparison of seasonal ratios and index construction season. If there is an indication that substantial changes are occurring or have occurred in the seasonal pattern, it may not be completely wise to use a seasonal index based solely on historical averages. It will be necessary to make adjustments for anticipated future changes in the index in order to adequately describe the seasonal pattern.

To decide whether adjustments for a changing seasonal should be considered, it can be helpful to plot the seasonal relatives for each quarter (or month) as a separate time series as in Figure 4–14. Although the changes in this example are not great, there does seem to be some indication that the relative level of activity in the third quarter is declining, with compensating increases in the other three quarters.

Deseasonalizing the Original Data. Although the seasonal index can often be usefully studied in itself, its main application is in removing seasonal fluctuations from data as a prelude to further analysis. This is done by simply dividing each observation by the corresponding seasonal index value and multiplying by 100. The resulting graph was shown in Figure 3–2b. Further analysis is then carried out as if a seasonal pattern did not exist.

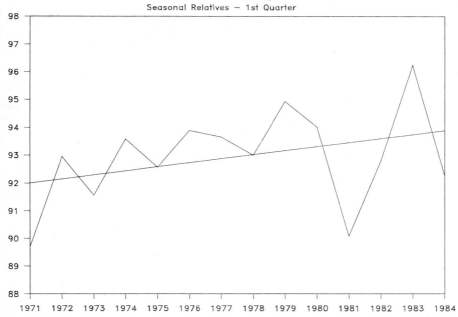

FIGURE 4-14a

U. S. airline passenger-miles: Seasonal relatives, first quarter

U.S. Airline Passenger—Miles

Seasonal Relatives — 2nd Quarter

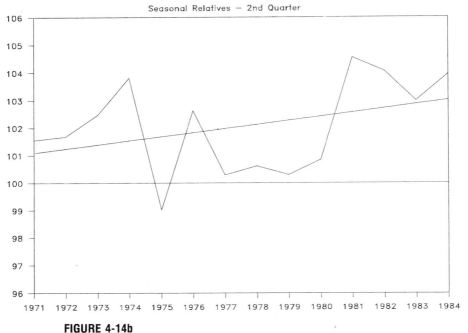

FIGURE 4-14b

Seasonal relatives, second quarter

U.S. Airline Passenger—Miles

Seasonal Relatives — 3rd Quarter

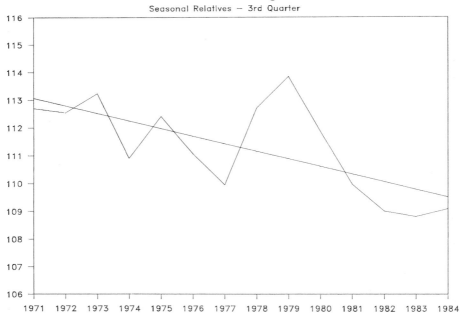

FIGURE 4-14c

Seasonal relatives, third quarter

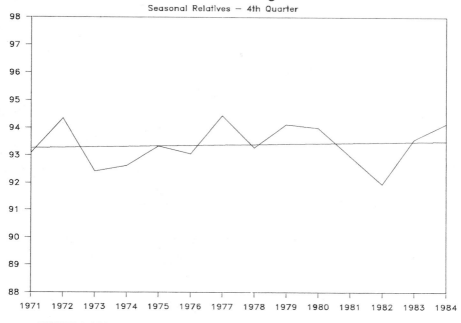

FIGURE 4-14d

Seasonal relatives, fourth quarter

Census X-11 Seasonal Adjustment Program. The approach described here is that used in a seasonal adjustment computer program developed by the U.S. Department of Commerce, Bureau of the Census, called X-11. This program is readily available and is included in many other time-series analysis and forecasting computer programs, including many of those available for microcomputers. It is also easy to adapt to any of the available spreadsheet programs. In addition to seasonal adjustment, X-11 includes procedures for trading-day adjustments, for adjusting for changing seasonals, and for smoothing of the seasonally adjusted data. For more information on this program, see the references at the end of the chapter.

THE DECOMPOSITION APPROACH TO ANALYSIS AND FORECASTING

Before moving on to some specific applications, it will be useful to summarize the basic steps in decomposing a time series as they have been developed in these two chapters. It will also be useful to distinguish between the steps in the *analysis* of a time series and those that should be followed in developing a projection or forecast.

To decompose a time series:

1. Check and correct any possible clerical and printing errors. Adjust for any changes in series definition.
2. Disaggregate the data into relatively homogeneous subseries.
3. Make preliminary adjustments as necessary for differences in the number of trading or working days, price changes, or other "nuisance" phenomena.
4. Unless working with annual data, make seasonal adjustments as necessary. In some cases this can be combined with step 5.
5. Remove the trend component from the data. Plot and examine the residuals for cyclical patterns and/or for outliers.
6. Look for possible reasons for any patterns or outliers observed in the data. Look for evidence that the patterns are or are not likely to persist in the future or that outliers are or are not likely to recur.

We will not be dealing specifically with forecasting until Chapter 6. It is worth noting, however, that forecasts are developed by simply reversing the decomposition procedure outlined here. Suppose a forecaster is asked to develop sales projections for a company for the next 3 years by months and goes through the following steps in the analysis:

1. Data checking and editing
2. Separation of the sales data into separate time series for each sales region
3. Trading-day adjustment
4. Adjustment of sales to constant dollars
5. Adjustment for changing numbers of customers in the region (a "per capita" correction)
6. Correction for the seasonal pattern, called deseasonalizing the data
7. Removal of the trend
8. Identification and evaluation of other patterns in the data

The development of the forecast would then reverse these steps:

1. Analysis and projection of the identified patterns
2. Analysis and projection of the trend; recombining of the trend projection with the projection in step 1

3. Analysis of the seasonal pattern and reseasonalizing the data

4. Analysis and projection of numbers of customers in each region; multiplication of this projection with that developed in step 3

5. Analysis and projection of price changes; conversion of the "constant dollar" projection in step 4 to actual dollars

6. Multiplication of the projection for each month by the number of trading days

7. Reaggregation of the projections for the regions into an overall sales projection for the company

SUMMARY

Chapters 3 and 4 have illustrated several of the basic types of tools that are available to the forecaster. In Parts III and IV we shift the focus back to planning. In each of these parts the first chapter develops some potential applications to provide a setting for the discussion of forecasting that will then follow.

APPENDIX A: USING SEMILOGARITHMIC GRAPH PAPER

Because it is now so easy to obtain logarithms with a hand calculator, the use of semilogarithmic graph paper in the analysis of time series has declined. It is still very frequently used in presenting time series when the forecaster wishes to emphasize differences in or changes in rates of growth but still wants to retain a meaningful Y scale[1]. It may be helpful therefore to discuss the construction and use of this type of scale and graph.

Semilogarithmic Graph Paper. This is a special type of graph paper that has one linear and one logarithmic scale. (On logarithmic graph paper, both scales are logarithmic.) An example of a logarithmic scale and of this type of paper is shown in Figure 4A-1. On the logarithmic (vertical) scale, equal intervals are associated with equal ratios rather than with equal differences, as on a linear scale. Notice that the distances between 2 and 4, 3 and 6, or 5 and the 1 above it are all equal. Notice also that the numbers marked alongside the scale are not logarithms; they are intended to represent the original numbers. In using a logarithmic scale, you plot the original data values, not the logs.

---

[1] If the log transform is used with a program such as 1-2-3®, the picture will be the same but the vertical scale will be in logs, not in the original units.

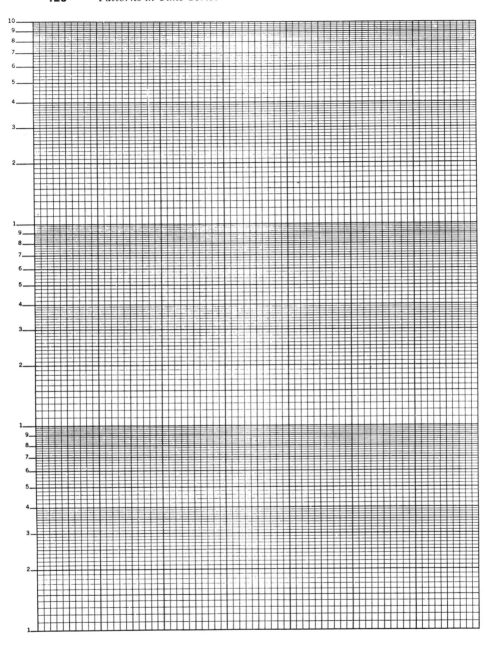

FIGURE 4A-1

Semilogarithmic graph paper, three cycles × 10 to the inch

The logarithmic scale as it appears on the graph paper starts at 1, goes through the sequence 2, 3, 4, and so on, and returns to 1. Each sequence is called a *cycle*. Semilogarithmic (and logarithmic) graph papers with one, two, or up to seven cycles are common. For most applications, three-cycle paper as shown here will prove most useful.

In setting up your scale line on the logarithmic scale, cycles must start and end at consecutive multiples of 10. A cycle can go from 1 to 10, 100 to 1000, 0.001 to 0.01, and so on. *No other renumbering of the scale is possible*. In contrast to what was said earlier about the linear scale, there is never a zero on a logarithmic scale.

The linear scale should be used as the (horizontal) time scale as in the usual time-series graph. Once the scales have been laid out, the data can be plotted in the usual way. Note, however, that the line spacing varies in the vertical direction, so care must be taken in plotting the data points.

Semilogarithmic graph paper is used to plot only the original data; it is not used for plotting differences since it is impossible to plot negative numbers.

Growth-rate Scale. On this type of graph, a time series increasing (or decreasing) at a constant rate, that is, by the same percent from one period to the next, appears as a straight line. Unlike straight lines on linear graphs, the rate of change cannot be determined directly from the slope of the trend line. It is possible, however, to add a separate growth-rate scale to the graph.

To construct a growth-rate scale as shown in Figure 4A-2, start at the 1 at the beginning of one of the cycles and plot a point. Imagine a trend growing at a constant rate, g, per period. One time period later, the trend would go from 1 to $(1 + g)$. A line going through these two points will have a slope corresponding to a growth rate of g. In Figure 4A-2, lines have been drawn for a number of different growth rates between 1% ($g = 0.01$) and 40% ($g = 0.40$). Figure 4A-3 shows the data on car registrations drawn on a semilog graph together with a growth-rate scale. By comparing the slope of the plotted data with these lines, the growth rate of the data can be estimated. In this example, the slope of the data seems closest to that for a 4% rate of increase ($g = 0.04$). Notice, however, that the trend line appears to be curving slightly downward, indicating that the rate is decreasing.[2]

When the spacing between successive years is small, it is too difficult to accurately draw a line through two points only one year apart. More accuracy can be obtained by using the *doubling rule*:

A variable growing at a constant percentage rate of r% per period will double in a number of periods approximately equal to $72/r$.

[2]Compare this to the results obtained in Figures 4-3b and c.

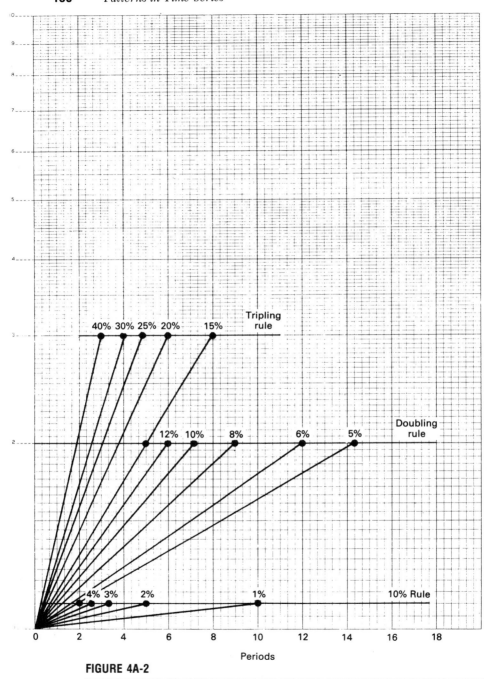

FIGURE 4A-2

The growth-rate scale

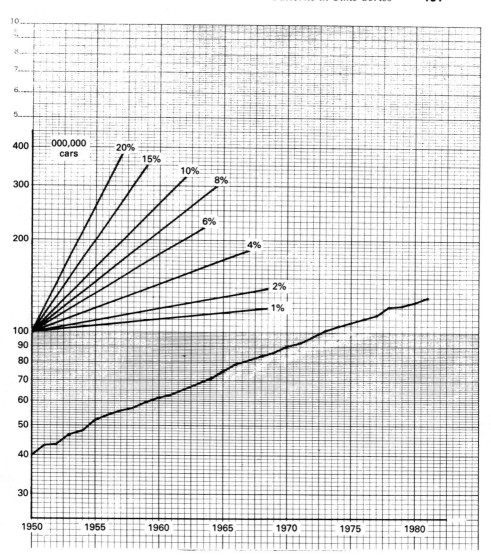

FIGURE 4A-3

Passenger car registrations: United States, 1950–1981

Thus a line starting from 1 and increasing at 6% per period will cross the horizontal line at 2 approximately 72/6 = 12 periods later (see Figure 4A-2).

For growth rates of less than 5%, a better rule is that the line at 1.1 will be crossed after 10/r periods (the *10% rule*), while for growth rates between 15% and 40% the horizontal line at 3 will be crossed after 120/r periods (a tripling rule).

APPENDIX B: 1-2-3 MACROS FOR MOVING AVERAGES

The calculation procedures of this chapter can all easily be adapted for use on a spreadsheet program such as 1-2-3. Transformations are obtained through use of the built-in functions. With 1-2-3, simple macros can be set up for most of the smoothing operations. Ideas on how to develop and use Macros can be found in Orchestrating 1-2-3 listed in the Readings.

Hanning

Assume that the results of the M3R operation are in cells E5 through E30. The first Hanning entry will be in cell F6 and can be obtained by the calculation +(E5 + 2*E6 + E7)/4. The copy command /C can then be used to obtain the rest of the Hanning column. A simple macro can be set up for the calculations. The five-quarter (12 month) centered moving average used in developing the seasonal relatives can be similarly obtained.

M3

The median of three consecutive numbers (in cells C5 through C70) can be obtained from the macro

@SUM (C5. .C7) − @MAX (C5. .C7) − @MIN (C5. .C7)

M5

We know of no simple macros for taking running medians of five consecutive numbers. If the data series is short, one possibility is to print out the data, find M5 by hand, and reenter M5. An alternative procedure, which is usually successful, is to replace M5 with a trimmed mean of the form

$+ (@SUM\ (B5.\ .B9) - @MAX\ (B5.\ .B9) - @MIN\ (B5.\ .B9))/3$

(Assume that the data are in column B.)

READINGS

Trends

This subject is covered in much more detail in Chapter 12. For now, two useful references are

C. W. J. GRANGER, *Forecasting in Business and Economics*, New York, Academic Press, 1980, Chapter 2.

JOHN W. TUKEY, *Exploratory Data Analysis*, Reading, Mass., Addison-Wesley, 1977, Chapter 5.

The projections for the U.S. population to the year 2900 mentioned in this chapter can be found in

H. S. PRICHETT, "A Formula for Predicting the Population of the United States," *Journal of the American Statistical Association*, vol. 12, no. 4 (June 1891), pp. 278–286.

It is perhaps unfair to pick on one author; there are many good (or bad) examples of this type of overenthusiastic trend projection. For what it's worth, Pritchett's forecast for 1980 was for 305 billion, compared to the actual census figure of 227 billion.

Transformations

As with many of the topics in this and other chapters, many of the ideas presented can be found in the book by Tukey cited previously. For more on this topic, see his Chapter 3. Also see

FREDERICK MOSTELLER and JOHN W. TUKEY, *Data Analysis and Regression*, Reading, Mass., Addison-Wesley, 1977, Chapters 5 and 6 and the Appendix.

Smoothing and Moving Averages

A discussion of some basic concepts of moving averages can be found in

> SPYROS MAKRIDAKIS, STEVEN C. WHEELWRIGHT, and VICTOR E. McGEE, *Forecasting: Methods and Applications*, 2nd ed., New York, Wiley, 1983, pp. 62–83.

Material on robust smoothing can be found in Tukey, Chapters 7 and 7+, and in

> PAUL F. VELLEMAN and DAVID C. HOAGLIN, *Applications, Basics and Computing of Exploratory Data Analysis*, Boston, Duxbury Press, 1981, Chapter 6.

Seasonal

A good coverage of the classical approach can be found in

> FREDERICK E. CROXTON, et al., *Applied General Statistics*, 3rd ed., Englewood Cliffs, N.J., Prentice-Hall, 1967.

A technique for calculating a seasonal index for weekly data can be found in the first (1939) edition of the same work.

Material on Census program X-11 can be found in Makridakis et al., cited previously, and in

> JULIUS SHISKIN et al., "A Summary of the X-11 Variant of the Census Method II Seasonal Adjustment Program," *Business Cycle Developments*, October 1964, pp. 57–71.

A discussion of one robust approach to seasonal adjustment can be found in

> HANS LEVENBACH and JAMES P. CLEARY,, *The Beginning Forecaster*, Belmont, Calif., Lifetime Learning Publications, 1981, Chapter 19.

1-2-3 Macros

There are many good books on how to use the 1-2-3 spreadsheet program that include sections on developing and using macros. Although it has not been discussed here in any detail, it is a device that can be invaluable in analyzing time series. The book referenced here is

DAVID C. RIER and EDMUND S. FINE, *Orchestrating 1-2-3, Reading, Mass., Addison-Wesley, 1985.*

PROBLEMS

1. You have been given the following sales data for a small company:

Sales in $000
Quarter

Year	I	II	III	IV
1979	220	224	265	248
1980	232	292	288	213
1981	249	245	156	142
1982	194	228	255	294
1983	360	483	446	596
1984	522	572	567	508
1985	486	538	519	558
1986	483	461	554	605

a. Plot these data.

b. Smooth using a 53RH smoother. Plot the data on the same graph.

c. Determine the residuals from the smooth. Plot and draw a box-and-whisker diagram for the residuals. Do you observe any patterns or outliers in the residuals?

d. Determine the absolute period-to-period changes in the smooth and in the residuals. Compare using box-and-whisker diagrams. What might be the implication of this comparison for a forecast for the first quarter of 1987?

e. Develop a box-and-whisker diagram for the absolute changes in the smooth over four quarters (e.g., the absolute value of the difference in the smooth between 1980 I and 1979 I). Draw a box-and-whisker diagram and compare to those in part d. What differences do you notice?

2. The following information was obtained from the *Survey of Current Business*.

Net New Orders: Durable Goods Industries and Producer's Price Index: Durable Goods, United States, 1970 to 1982

Year	New Orders (billions of $)	Price Index (1967 = 100)
1970	329.4	112.4
1971	359.4	117.0
1972	421.7	121.1
1973	514.7	127.9
1974	558.8	150.1
1975	506.0	165.8
1976	612.0	176.0
1977	717.5	188.1
1978	841.7	204.9
1979	952.2	226.9
1980	948.7	251.5
1981	999.3	269.8
1982	889.8	278.6
1983	1051.6	286.7
1984	1207.3	293.6

a. On standard graph paper, plot Net New Orders for 1970 to 1984. Describe in words the patterns observed.

b. Calculate first differences (year-to-year changes) in New Orders. Plot on a separate graph. Does the trend appear to have been removed?

c. Determine the median first difference. Assume a median change in New Orders from 1984 to 1985. Project New Orders for 1985.

d. Using the given price index, adjust the New Orders for price changes. Plot the adjusted series on the same graph as in part a. Discuss the differences you observe from the unadjusted series. Determine the median adjusted new orders.

e. On separate graphs plot the Price Index and first differences in the index. Does the trend appear to have been removed?

f. Transform the index in order to remove the trend and take first differences in the transformed index. Plot and try to determine if the trend has been removed.

g. Determine the median change in the transformed index. Assuming this median change holds between 1984 and 1985, project the price index for 1985.

h. Using the median adjusted new orders from part d, and the projected price index from part g, develop a projection of actual (unadjusted) New Orders for 1985. Is your answer the same as in part c? Discuss the possible reasons for any difference.

3. Using the data from Problem 2 on the Producer's Price Index for Durable Goods, develop stem-and-leaf and box-and-whisker diagrams for the first difference in the index and for the first difference in the reciprocal of the index. What are the implications of the two box-and-whisker diagrams for how you would evaluate projections of the index for the next two years?

4. The following data on U.S. beer production were obtained from various issues of the *Survey of Current Business*.

(in million btls)

Year	I	Quarter II	III	IV
1974	36.2	42.8	43.0	34.1
1975	36.1	44.6	44.1	35.7
1976	36.2	44.8	47.0	35.9
1977	39.7	49.7	44.5	36.6
1978	41.4	49.1	49.0	39.6
1979	44.2	50.1	48.4	40.6
1980	45.9	52.3	52.0	41.3
1981	44.6	55.2	55.2	41.7
1982	47.8	54.0	52.3	42.0
1983	46.1	52.2	52.5	41.4
1984	46.6	53.7	50.8	41.1

a. Plot these data and describe in words any patterns or irregularities that you observe.

b. Calculate and plot the seasonal first differences. Does it appear that this has removed the seasonal pattern? Does it appear that it has also removed the trend? If the answer to the latter is no, use a transformation and/or regular first difference to remove the trend. *Note:* Any transformation should be applied to the original data and not to the seasonal first difference.

c. Use your results in part b to obtain projections for the four quarters of 1985. Check your results against the information available in the *Survey of Current Business* and discuss any differences observed.

d. Develop a box-and-whisker diagram of the residuals in part b. Compare your "forecast errors" in part c against that summary. How do they compare?

e. You have been given the following seasonal index:

I	II	III	IV
94.55	110.57	108.75	86.13

Deseasonalize these data and plot. Remove the trend (if any) and develop and evaluate projections and residuals as in parts c and d.

f. Compare your projections to those developed in part c and to the actual production data. Discuss the possible reasons for any differences that you observe using the two sets of residuals.

5. This assignment is based on the data on U.S. beer production in Problem 4. For smoothing, use a 53RH smoother. Although it will take additional time, you may find it a useful exercise to repeat the process with (53RH) T in order to sharpen the cycles.

a. Smooth and plot the seasonal first differences of Problem 4b. Note any dissimilarities you observe with the unsmoothed differences.

b. Develop a box-and-whisker diagram of the residuals from the smooth. How does it compare to the corresponding box-and-whisker diagram from Problem 4?

c. Smooth the deseasonalized data from problem 4e. Compare with the preceding smoothed first differences. What differences do you observe, if any?

d. Set up comparable box-and-whisker diagrams for the four procedures (seasonal differences and deseasonalized; smoothed and unsmoothed). What differences do you note, if any?

e. Using the additional information from the smoothed data, discuss how you might modify your projections in Problems 4c and f.

CHAPTER 5

Operational Planning

As we look at the range of situations that face the planner and forecaster, it is helpful to distinguish between those where the forecaster has a strong sense of continuity between the past, present, and future and those where that sense of continuity is much weaker. In the former case, we look for patterns in the time-series data and project them in relatively straightforward ways. In the latter case, we may search the records of the past for analogies, but our confidence in applying these analogies to future situations is likely to be weaker and our interpretations of forecasts will be different.

As a practical matter, no forecasting situation is all one or all the other; each has some elements with strong apparent ties to the past and others that appear new. At the same time, in some situations the sense of continuity is very strong and can dominate our choice of forecasting method. A company that routinely develops one-month-ahead demand forecasts is usually willing to assume that next month will be more or less consistent with past experience. If there is a major change in the product or market, however (for example, the introduction of "New Coke" in 1985), the relevance of past sales in forecasting future demand will be much less clear.

To distinguish the effects of these two aspects of forecasting, planning situations where the sense of historical continuity is strong will be termed *operational*, while the others will be called *strategic*. Chapters 5 through 9 are concerned with the problems of forecasting for operational planning. Even here we will discover that different situations exist. When forecasting time horizons are short (less than one quarter), we can do little more than try to identify relevant patterns in the data and assume that the inertia that underlies most systems will allow us to project those patterns into the future. As the time horizon lengthens, this inertia becomes weaker and we must look to the underlying structure of the system as a basis for our forecasts.

Chapter 5 presents two different planning situations as a lead-in to the forecasting discussion that follows. Chapter 6 deals with forecasting methods that rely on system inertia. In Chapters 7 and 8, we examine some possible techniques for discovering and analyzing the underlying structure of a system. Finally, Chapter 9 explores the question of what makes a "good" forecast.

PLANNING MODELS

As used in this book, *operational* will refer to those activities within an organization that are on-going or that recur at reasonably short intervals. This includes the day-to-day management of inventories, production, distribution, work force, and cash flow, as well as the management of the acquisition and allocation of resources that tend to be planned on an annual or biennial cycle.

From the point of view of the forecaster, planning for operations has two distinctive and important characteristics. The first is a sense of historical continuity: the decisions being made involve similar elements and issues and are made under similar environmental conditions. Thus the records of the past can be assumed to be directly relevant, and techniques for analyzing time series, such as those discussed in the previous chapters, are clearly applicable. The second characteristic is that, because the underlying operational system and organization currently exist and because the types of decisions to be made have been made before, the structure of the problem is (or can be) studied and the specific forecasting needs of the planner identified.

In this chapter we explore the structure of some typical operational planning situations and the demands that they place on the forecaster. These are considered in two subgroupings: *activity planning*, which includes the short-range planning and scheduling of ongoing activities, and *aggregate resource planning*, which deals with longer-term and more aggregated issues of the acquisition and allocation of resources.

Major Points to be Noted

1. *The highly structured character of the activity planning model and the way it evolves directly from the payoff model in Chapter 2. This structure is the foundation for understanding the design of the automatic or semiautomatic forecasting/planning systems presented in Chapter 6.*

2. *The pro forma budgeting model as an example of the most common type of managerial planning model. The forecast requirements of this type of model are the central topic for Chapters 7 through 9.*

ACTIVITY PLANNING

As used here, activity planning refers to the planning and scheduling of specific short-term activities within the organization. This type of planning is done at a disaggregated or micro level and deals with specific products, specific inventory items, or the scheduling of specific machines or individuals. Time horizons tend to be short—one month or less. Planning for these activities is repetitive and routine. For all these reasons, procedures tend to be highly structured and quantitative and frequently oriented around formal models.

For these models the relevant external environment normally can be summarized in a single variable such as demand. As described in Chapter 1, uncertainty about this variable can be dealt with in a number of ways. In the case of scheduling activities, where it is the time required for the activity that is uncertain, extra time can be allowed. In setting production or inventory levels, safety stocks can be created. Often planning lead times can be shortened, increasing system flexibility. For example, a company uncertain of their need for spare parts can reduce the impact of this uncertainty by using air rather than surface shipment when obtaining parts.

It is the job of the forecaster to help reduce the environmental uncertainty through the analysis of, for example, past records of demand. As the techniques used by the forecaster become more complex (and it is hoped more accurate), they also become more costly. The manager and the forecaster must continually face the question of how much time and money should be put into forecasting as opposed to, say, simply carrying bigger safety stocks.

In this section we explore one particular activity planning model that has rather wide applicability. We consider, first, the specific roles that the forecast and measures of forecast uncertainty play in the planning model. Second, we explore the nature of the cost trade-off between forecasting and other methods of dealing with forecast uncertainty.

The Safety Stock Model

In short-term activity planning, one of the most common ways of dealing with environmental uncertainty is to carry extra inventory, to assign extra personnel, or to allow extra time for job completion. For example, a hotel newsstand, uncertain on a day-to-day basis of the demand for the *Wall Street Journal*, will probably routinely order extra copies because they would rather throw out a few unsold copies at the end of the day than not to have a copy if a customer wants one. How many extra copies they order depends on the relative costs of turning away a customer versus throwing out a paper and on their degree of uncertainty of the number of copies that customers might want.

A formalization of this situation has been referred to at various times as the Newsboy Problem, the Christmas Tree Problem, or the Safety Stock Model. We will discuss it here in the context of setting inventory or production levels. In fact, it is broadly applicable to many problems of worker-hour planning, job scheduling, or cash-flow planning.

Suppose that one item carried by our small-town hardware store is a well-known monthly magazine for people with home workshops. Assume that the wholesale price of the magazine is $0.50 and the retail price is $2.00. To keep the problem simple, assume further that the publisher does not accept returns, so any unsold copies are simply thrown out at the end of the month.[1] Gross profits from the sale of the magazine will depend on both the demand for the magazine and the number of copies that the store chooses to stock.

Suppose for the moment that the store starts a given month with 60 copies. Figure 5-1a shows gross profits as a function of demand. If no copies are demanded, they lose $30. The break-even point comes with a demand for 15 copies, while with a demand for 60 copies, profits reach $90.

---

[1] We are also assuming that there are no long-term effects from running out of copies, such as having disgruntled customers who will not return the following month.

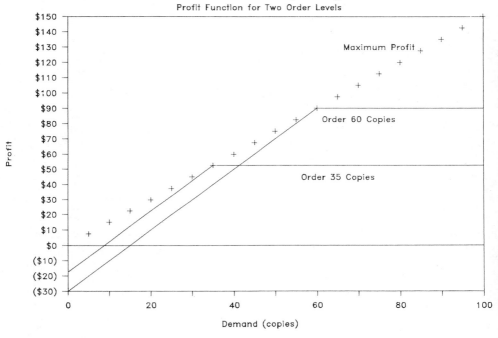

FIGURE 5-1a

Sales of a monthly magazine: Profit function for two order levels

Even if the demand is greater than 60, profits cannot exceed $90 because they have no more copies to sell.

Opportunity Costs. Suppose they could stock as many copies as they wished and could return the unsold copies. The "inventory" would always exactly match demand and they would make a profit of $1.50 per copy sold, giving the gross profits shown by the line of +'s. Since in this example no returns are possible, a specific stock level must be prechosen. For the action of stocking 60 copies, the opportunity costs will be the difference between these two lines, as shown in Figure 5-1b (p. 144).

In the example in Chapter 2 of choosing between two different production processes, separate opportunity cost functions were shown for each of the two possible actions. The same thing could be done here. There would be a separate function for each possible initial stock level, and each of these functions would have the same shape. Figure 5-1b also shows the profit and opportunity cost functions for an initial inventory of 35 copies. Notice that the same opportunity cost function results except that the zero

Sales of a Monthly Magazine

Opportunity Cost Functions

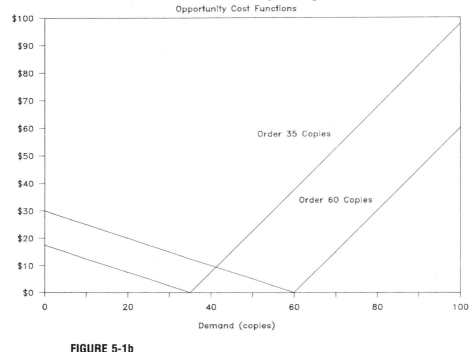

FIGURE 5-1b

Opportunity cost function

point is at 35 rather than 60. Similar opportunity cost functions could be drawn for every possible level of initial inventory by simply shifting the function so that the zero point would fall at the initial inventory.

An alternative way of thinking about this graph is that, if the demand is less than the number stocked, the opportunity cost is $0.50 times the number of copies that must be thrown away; if the demand is greater, the opportunity cost is the lost profit or $1.50 times the number of requests that cannot be filled.

The expected opportunity cost can be calculated as in Chapter 2 by multiplying for each possible level of demand the opportunity cost and the probability of that level of demand occurring, and summing over all possible levels of demand. For an order quantity of 60 copies, we would have

$$(-\$30) \times P \ (Y = 0) + (-\$28.50) \times P \ (Y = 1) + (-\$27.00) \times P \ (Y = 2) + \ \cdot \ \cdot \ \cdot$$

where P stands for probability and Y for demand, and where the sum is over all possible levels of demand.

For any order quantity A, this can be written in a general form.:

$$\text{Expected opportunity cost} = \sum_{Y=0}^{A} [\$0.50 \times (A - Y) \times P(Y)]$$
$$+ \sum_{Y=A+1}^{\infty} [\$1.50 \times (Y-A) \times P(Y)]$$

It can be shown that this cost is minimized when the marginal expected cost of ordering one more copy is just equal to the marginal cost of ordering one copy less:

$$\$0.50 \times F(A) = \$1.50 \times [1 - F(A)]$$

where $F(A) = \sum_{Y=0}^{A} [P(Y)]$

Solving this for $F(A)$ gives

$$F(A) = \frac{\$1.50}{\$0.50 + \$1.50} = 0.75$$

The optimal order quantity A occurs when 75% of the time the store has enough stock to satisfy demand and 25% of the time there is a stockout. Notice that the probabilities are in the same three-to-one ratio as the costs.

For the general case where C_1 is the cost of carrying or disposing of one unit of excess inventory and C_2 is the cost of not satisfying one customer, this becomes

$$C_1 F(A) = C_2 [1 - F(A)] \tag{1}$$

so that

$$F(A) = \frac{C_2}{C_1 + C_2} \tag{2}$$

or

$$F(A) = \frac{1}{\dfrac{C_1}{C_2} + 1} \tag{3}$$

In this second form it is not necessary to know the separate costs C_1 and C_2 but only their ratio.

The Cumulative Probability Distribution

$F(A)$ is the probability that demand Y is less than or equal to the quantity A and is called a *cumulative probability distribution*. An example is shown in Figure 5-2 (p. 146). If this distribution were available to the manager, the order quantity A could be found by first finding the appropriate

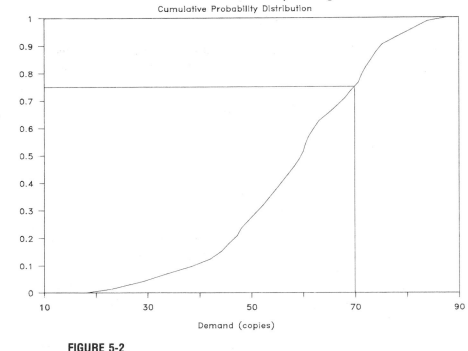

Demand for a Monthly Magazine

Cumulative Probability Distribution

Cumulative Probability

Demand (copies)

FIGURE 5-2

Demand for a monthly magazine: Cumulative probability distribution

value of $F(A)$ on the vertical axis (here 0.75) and then reading across and down as shown. The job of the forecaster is to supply this probability distribution.

Suppose that for the last three years, the owners of the hardware store have been ordering 60 copies each month and, at the same time, have been keeping track of the actual demand and of the "forecast errors" (thinking of the 60 copies as a sort of implicit forecast) as shown in Table 5-1 (p. 148).[2] A cumulative distribution of demand can be obtained by arranging the data in an increasing array as in Table 5-2 (p. 149) and plotting as shown in Figure 5-3.

In this graph, the horizontal axis gives the demands in increasing order. The vertical axis goes from zero to one. To obtain the vertical coordinates of the points, determine the number of points N to be plotted and imagine the vertical axis divided into N segments. The following line shows the division for $N = 5$.

[2]A major problem can arise in determining actual demand. When there are unsold copies, it is relatively easy, but when stockouts occur, a record is usually kept of sales but not of the number that could have been sold.

Demand for a Monthly Magazine

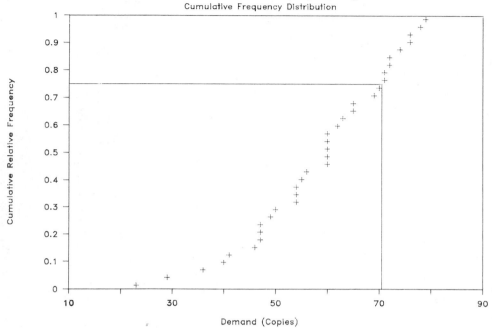

FIGURE 5-3

Demand for a monthly magazine: Cumulative frequency distribution

Now imagine each point plotted at the midpoint of a segment:

It can be seen that the coordinates of the points are given by

$$\frac{1}{10}, \quad \frac{3}{10}, \quad \frac{5}{10}, \quad \frac{7}{10}, \quad \text{and} \quad \frac{9}{10}.$$

The denominator is equal to $2 \times N$, and the numerators are the odd integers, 1, 3, 5, and so on. In general, the points are plotted at the values

$$\frac{1}{2N}, \quad \frac{3}{2N}, \quad \frac{5}{2N}, \quad \frac{7}{2N}, \quad \cdots \quad \frac{2N - 1}{2N} \tag{4}$$

Table 5-1

Demand for a Monthly Magazine, 1984 to 1986, with
Forecast Errors Based on a Constant Forecast of 60 Copies

	Month	Demand (copies)	Forecast Error
1984	Jan	65	5
	Feb	46	−14
	Mar	41	−19
	Apr	60	0
	May	62	2
	Jun	54	−6
	Jul	60	0
	Aug	55	−5
	Sep	23	−37
	Oct	71	11
	Nov	63	3
	Dec	72	12
1985	Jan	47	−13
	Feb	29	−31
	Mar	47	−13
	Apr	69	9
	May	36	−24
	Jun	54	−6
	Jul	60	0
	Aug	78	18
	Sep	56	−4
	Oct	60	0
	Nov	50	−10
	Dec	71	11
1986	Jan	76	16
	Feb	70	10
	Mar	60	0
	Apr	72	12
	May	76	16
	Jun	79	19
	Jul	47	−13
	Aug	49	−11
	Sep	65	5
	Oct	74	14
	Nov	40	−20
	Dec	54	−6
	Total	2091	−69
	Mean	58.1	−1.9

For the data of Table 5-1, $N = 36$, this gives the sequence

$$\frac{1}{72}, \frac{3}{72}, \frac{5}{72}, \frac{7}{72}, \frac{9}{72}, \ldots, \frac{69}{72}, \frac{71}{72}$$

as shown.

What has been plotted is not a probability distribution but rather an historical frequency distribution. If the store owner were willing to assume

Table 5-2

Demand for a Monthly Magazine, 1984 to 1986

Summary

#					
	1*				
	1.				
1	2*	3			
2	2.	9			
	3*				
3	3.	6			
5	4*	10		*Positions*	
10	4.	67779¦			
15	5*	45404¦		Number	36
16	5.	6		Median	18½
(7)	6*	02030¦00		Quartiles	9½
13	6.	595			
10	7*	12102¦4			
4	7.	8669			
	8*				

	Smallest	Q_1	*Median*	Q_3	*Largest*
Values	23	48	60	70.5	79
Differences		25	12	10.5	8.5
Q spread (Qspd)			22.5		

Other Statistics

Mean	58.1
Standard deviation	13.91
MAD (around mean)	11.2
Divided by 0.8	13.98
Qspd divided by 1.35	16.67

that demand in the future would be similar to that of the past, however, the frequency distribution could be treated as if it were a probability distribution.

To find the appropriate safety stock, enter the vertical axis of Figure 5-3 at 0.75 just as was done in Figure 5-2. Move horizontally to the plotted point closest to that horizontal line. In this case it is between the demands for 70 and 71 copies. Over the past 36 forecasts, 27 or 75% of the demands have been for 70 copies or less, while 9 or 25% have been for 71 copies or more.

Suppose that over that period of 36 months the owners had taken the "forecast" of 60 copies and had added a safety stock of 10 copies (an order quantity of 70 copies); 75% of the time there would have been enough to cover the demand and 25% of the time there would have been stockouts. As we shall see, this would have minimized the opportunity costs over the period. If it is

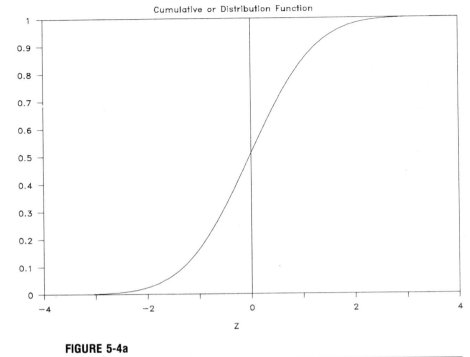

FIGURE 5-4a

Normal distribution: Cumulative or distribution function

believed that this pattern will continue, then it will be desirable in the future to order 70 rather than 60 copies, a safety stock of 10 copies.[3]

Theoretical Probability Distributions. One problem with the approach outlined so far is the technical or administrative one of maintaining these error distributions, not just for one product or activity but for all the products and/or raw materials stocked and for all the activities that must be planned. In a hardware store these might number in the hundreds, thousands, or more. To plot separate cumulative distributions for each would clearly be impractical.

Statisticians have studied many different theoretical probability distributions. The advantage of these is that they can be described by a relatively small number of parameters. One of the most common is the normal distribution whose cumulative distribution is shown in Figure 5-4a, but which is better known as the "bell-shaped curve" from the shape of its

---

[3]In this case, because 27 is exactly 75% of 36, either 70 or 71 copies gives the same average opportunity cost. This is not usually the case.

Normal Distribution

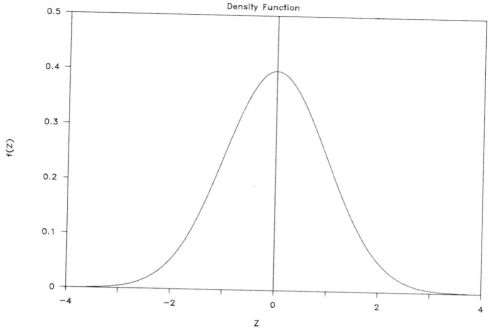

Density Function

FIGURE 5-4b

Density function

density function as shown in Figure 5-4b. This distribution requires only two numbers or *parameters* for its complete description, a mean (μ), which locates the center of the distribution, and a standard deviation (σ), which measures the spread or width of the distribution. If, in a given situation, it can be assumed that demand is approximately normally distributed, then, instead of keeping track of the entire cumulative distribution of demand, it is only necessary to determine its mean and standard deviation.

The question of whether it can be assumed that demand, in any particular case, is normally distributed is one that can only be answered by analyzing past demand. There are a number of possible tests. One of the simplest is the use of normal probability paper, as shown in Figure 5-5 (p. 152). To use this special graph paper, plot the cumulative distribution exactly as described for Figure 5-3 (note, however, that on probability paper the vertical scale goes from 0 to 100 rather than from 0 to 1, so all the vertical coordinates given previously must be multiplied by 100). If the forecast errors follow a normal distribution, the cumulative distribution should plot as an (approximately) straight line. Examination of Figure 5-5 suggests that the distribution is reasonably close to a normal, except in the

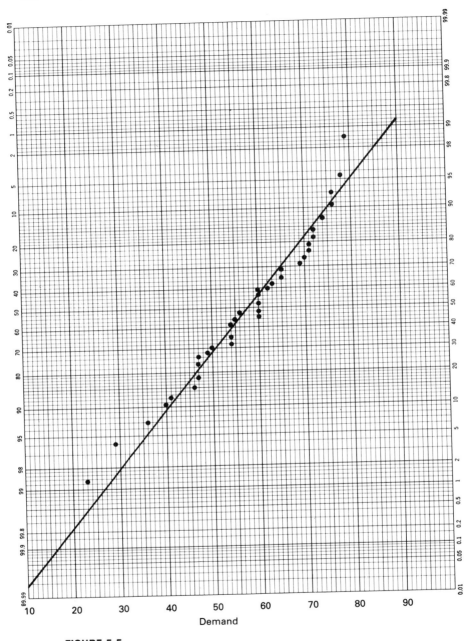

FIGURE 5-5

Demand for a monthly magazine: Cumulative frequency distribution on normal probability paper with fitted regression line

lower tail and at the extreme upper end of the upper tail.[4] Since we are primarily interested in the distribution near the line at 75%, this may not be much of a problem.

In general, minor deviations from a normal distribution have little effect on the overall results. In cases when it is very clear that use of this distribution would be inappropriate, two options exist: (1) to look for some alternative theoretical distribution or (2) to look for a data transformation, as discussed in Chapter 4, that would bring the distribution closer to the normal form. In practice, the latter option is the easier to use. Here we shall proceed as if the distribution were normal.

The Standardized Normal Distribution. The normal distribution depends on two parameters, a mean (μ) and a standard deviation (σ). If a normally distributed variable is transformed by subtracting the mean and dividing by the standard deviation, a variable is obtained that is still normally distributed but with a mean of zero and a standard deviation of one. This variable is usually given the symbol Z.

$$Z = \frac{Y - \text{mean}}{\text{standard deviation}} = \frac{Y - \mu}{\sigma} \tag{5}$$

If Z is given,

$$Y = \text{mean} + Z \times \text{standard deviation} = \mu + Z \times \sigma \tag{6}$$

The cumulative distribution for the Z distribution is shown in Figure 5-6 (p. 154) and Appendix Table A1. Notice that the Z value corresponding to $F(Z) = 0.75$ is 0.675.

To determine the required safety stock, it is necessary to obtain estimates of the mean and standard deviation of the forecast error distribution. There are several ways in which this can be done:

For the Mean

---

1. The *mean* of the observations of past demand. The mean is calculated by dividing the sum of the demands by the number of periods.

$$\bar{Y} = \frac{\Sigma Y}{N} \tag{7}$$

[4]To facilitate this examination, a straight line has been fitted to the points. The technique for doing this is discussed in Chapter 7.

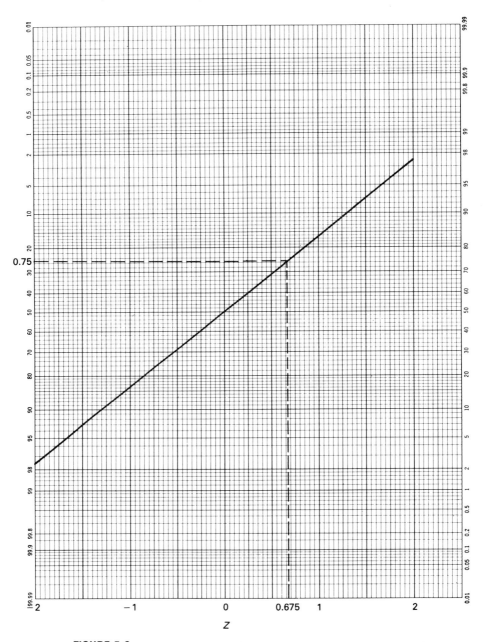

FIGURE 5-6

The standardized normal distribution: cumulative distribution on normal probability paper

From Table 5-1,

$$\frac{2091}{36} = 58.1$$

2. The *median* of the demands. From the five-number summary in Table 5-2, it can be seen that the median demand is 60 copies.

For the Standard Deviation

1. The *standard deviation* of past demand calculated from

$$S = \left[\frac{\Sigma Y^2 - \bar{Y}\Sigma Y}{N - 1} \right]^{\frac{1}{2}}$$

$$= \left[\frac{128227 - 58.1 \times 2091}{35} \right]^{\frac{1}{2}} \quad (8)$$

$$= 13.91$$

2. The *mean absolute deviation* of the historical observations. The standard deviation can be rather a nuisance to calculate if ΣY and ΣY^2 must be determined separately. With some calculators and computer programs, however, it only requires entering the data and pushing one button. An alternative that we will find useful in Chapter 6 is the mean absolute deviation (MAD) found by averaging the absolute values of the deviations of the demands from the overall mean (or sometimes the median). Absolute values are obtained by ignoring all minus signs, that is, treating all the deviations as if they were positive numbers.

$$MAD = \frac{\Sigma|Y - \bar{Y}|}{N} \quad (9)$$

For this example, MAD = 11.2. The standard deviation is approximately equal to the MAD divided by 0.8,

$$\frac{11.2}{0.8} = 13.98$$

3. *Interquartile Range (Qspd)*. Assuming that the underlying distribution is normal, the standard deviation is approximately equal to the Qspd in Table 5-2 divided by 1.35. Here

$$\frac{22.5}{1.35} = 16.67$$

4. *The Cumulative Distribution.* If a straight line is fitted to the probability plot of Figure 5-5 (using the graphical method described in Chapter 7), the standard deviation can be estimated from its slope. Find the values on the horizontal axis corresponding to the points where the line crosses horizontal lines at 10% and 90%. The difference between these two values divided by 2.56 gives still another estimate of the standard deviation.

$$\frac{76.5 - 41.5}{2.56} = 13.28$$

The different approaches suggested here for estimating the mean and standard deviation of a normal distribution lead to different numerical results because they are based on different characteristics of the distribution and are thus affected in different ways by any deviations from normality in the sample of forecast errors actually used. In this example, with the exception of the estimate based on the interquartile range, they are all quite close. As we shall see, even that difference in the estimate will not greatly affect the final decision.

Determining the Safety Stock

We have seen that the optimal order quantity from Figure 5-3 is 70 or 71 copies. By assuming that demand is normally distributed, it is possible to calculate the safety stock and order quantity from the estimates of the distribution mean and standard deviation. From Figure 5-6, it can be seen that the Z value corresponding to the cumulative probability of 0.75 is + 0.675. This value can be used to determine the desired safety stock and order quantity from the equations

$$\text{Safety stock} = Z \times \text{standard deviation}$$

and   (10)

$$\text{Order quantity} = \text{Forecast} + \text{safety stock}$$

Using the past mean demand as the forecast and the MAD to calculate the safety stock, this gives

$$\text{Safety stock} = (0.675) \times \frac{11.2}{0.8} = 9.45, \quad \text{or 10 copies}$$

and

$$\text{Order quantity} = 58.1 + 9.45 = 67.55, \quad \text{or 68 copies}$$

As shown in Table 5-3, using other estimates gives different results. For example, using the median and interquartile range gives a safety stock of 11 copies. The question we need to consider is how important are these differences.

Determining the Expected Opportunity Cost. Table 5-3 shows, for the 36 months, the actual total numbers of copies that would have been thrown out and the number of requests that would not have been satisfied for five different order quantities. In each case, multiplying the total number of unsold copies by $0.50 and the stockouts by $1.50 and dividing by 36 gives the average monthly opportunity cost over the 36 months. It can be

TABLE 5-3

Demand for a Monthly Magazine, 1984 to 1986
Various Calculations of Safety Stock and Order Quantity

Calculation of safety stock based on:
Mean and standard deviation:
Mean + 0.675 × standard deviation =
58.1 + 0.675 × 13.91 = 67.49
Mean and MAD:
Mean + 0.675 × MAD/0.8 =
58.1 + 0.675 × 13.98 = 67.55
Median and Qspd:
Median + 0.675 × Qspd/1.35 =
60 + 0.675 × 16.67 = 71.25

Constant Order of	Total Number Over	Short	Average Opportunity Cost
58	200	203	$11.24
60	232	163	10.01
68	417	60	8.29
70	468	39	8.13
72	524	23	8.24

seen that, with the actual order quantity of 60 copies, this averaged $10.01 per month.

Suppose that a safety stock of 10 copies had been carried (an order quantity of 70 copies); the opportunity cost would have been $8.13 per month, a decrease of $1.88. Notice that the opportunity cost does not vary greatly over the range of 68 to 72 copies but differs substantially from the case where *no* safety stock is used. Ordering the mean demand of 58 copies, the average opportunity cost would have been $11.24.

Instead of calculating the average monthly opportunity cost from the number of excess copies and stockouts as was done in Table 5-3, the expected opportunity cost for the optimal order quantity, assuming a normal distribution, can be estimated from the equation

$$\text{Expected opportunity cost} = (C_1 + C_2) \times \text{standard deviation} \times f(Z) \quad (11)$$

where $f(Z)$ is the height or ordinate of the normal density function shown in Figure 5-4 and Appendix, Table A1. It can be seen that $f(Z)$ is never greater than 0.4 and, for $Z = 0.675$, is approximately 0.32. This gives

$$\text{Expected opportunity cost} = (\$0.50 + \$1.50) \times 13.98 \times 0.32 = \$8.95$$

a value reasonably close to the $8.29 obtained by direct calculation.

The Value of a Better Forecast.   As we shall see in Chapter 6, forecasting methods for activity planning applications should be chosen with a concern for overall system efficiency and not just because a particular method appears to be the most accurate. This does not mean that accuracy is not relevant, and forecasters continually search for better ways of forecasting. The important question is, however, how much should be spent in additional time and resources for a given improvement in forecast accuracy? The expected opportunity cost can help to answer this. With the current forecasting system, this cost is approximately $8 to $9 per month. Clearly, this cost can never be reduced to zero; at best a 10% to 20% improvement (reduction in the standard deviation) might be expected. If any alternative forecasting system were to cost more than $1 to $1.50 more per month to develop and operate, it would be very unlikely that it would be worth consideration.

A BUDGETING MODEL

In addition to the detailed micro planning and scheduling of specific activities, operational planning is concerned with the macro allocation of resources to different activities, projects, and organizational units. While resource allocation must deal with all process inputs, worker-hours, plant and equipment, materials, and energy, these are usually converted to financial (dollar) variables to aid in aggregation and comparison. The resulting financial budgets normally are prepared for a 1- to 3-year period, with quarterly or semiannual updates. Since the preparation time for these budgets can take up to 2 years, it follows that the forecaster can be faced with relatively long forecast horizons.

Two problems complicate the job of the forecaster. First, resource allocation involves many different interrelated and uncertain variables, including demand, prices, wage rates, interest rates, and labor and capital availability. Second, in contrast to activity planning, where it is assumed that the environment is given and unaffected by any action of the manager, with the longer time horizons involved here, there are many things the manager can do to affect demand: prices can be raised or lowered, additional sales personnel hired, additional resources spent on advertising. It follows that forecasts must be conditional: *If* the price is increased by $X\%$, *then* demand is forecasted to be $\$Y$. In similar ways, actions can be taken to reduce costs.

We shall see in Chapter 7 how these problems affect our choice of forecasting techniques. To prepare for that consideration, it will be helpful to describe here one of the more common approaches to this type of planning, the pro forma budget.

The Pro Forma Budget

A *pro forma budget* is a complete set of accounting statements set up as they are expected to appear at various future points in time, assuming certain resource allocations and environmental events and trends. One common procedure is to start with the income statement as the basic planning model and from this develop pro forma balance sheets and other subsidiary schedules such as personnel and capital budgets. In this section we will look only at the pro forma income statement as it might be used in considering the effects of a proposed increase in the selling price of a product.

Table 5-4 (p. 160) shows an abbreviated version of a pro forma income statement as it might appear for a small company producing a single bulk chemical product. It can be seen that four variables in the model are likely to be affected by changes in the external environment: product demand, product returns, unit costs of goods sold, and other costs. As shown in the table, it is forecasted that demand will increase by 5% each quarter in 1987, that unit costs of goods sold will increase by 2.5%, and other costs by 3%. It is assumed that returns, discounts, and allowances will remain relatively stable at $\frac{1}{2}\%$ of sales and that productive capacity is adequate to

TABLE 5-4

Dreguld Company Pro Forma Income Statement for 1987 (assuming unit price of $4.00)

	Sales		Cost of Goods Sold		Sales, General, and Other Costs	
	% Increase	Units	% Increase	$/Unit	% Increase	$
1986 IV Actual	NA	123511	NA	$2.00	NA	$232,422
1987 Projected						
I	5.00%	129686	2.50%	$2.05	3.00%	$239,395
II	5.00%	136170	2.50%	$2.10	3.00%	$246,576
III	5.00%	142979	2.50%	$2.15	3.00%	$253,974
IV	5.00%	150128	2.50%	$2.21	3.00%	$261,593
	Total	558963			Total	$1,001,538

	1986 IV Actual	1987 Projected				Total
		I	II	III	IV	
Gross Sales	$494,042	$518,744	$544,682	$571,916	$600,511	$2,235,853
Discounts, Returns and Allowances	$2,470	$2,594	$2,723	$2,860	$3,003	$11,179
Net Sales	$491,572	$516,151	$541,958	$569,056	$597,509	$2,224,674
Cost of Goods Sold	$245,786	$264,527	$284,697	$306,406	$329,769	$1,185,399
Gross Profit	$245,786	$251,623	$257,261	$262,650	$267,740	$1,039,275
Sales, General, and Other Costs	$232,422	$239,395	$246,576	$253,974	$261,593	$1,001,538
Operating Income	$13,364	$12,229	$10,685	$8,677	$6,147	$37,737

cover demand (so that sales and demand will be the same). The table shows how these forecasts can be transformed into projections for operating profit for each of the four quarters.

Suppose that the manager is considering raising the unit price of the chemical. The forecaster will be required to develop demand forecasts, not only for the current price of $4.00 per unit, but for several hypothetical future prices as well. What is needed is a forecast of the future *relationship* between price and demand.

In addition, the manager needs some estimate of the probable accuracy of these forecasts. As with the activity planning example of the last section, this can be done by specifying a cumulative probability distribution for the forecast error. In budget planning this is somewhat more complex and often requires a dual approach. To deal with major uncertain events in the future environment, the forecaster may need to give several different forecasts using different assumptions about significant potential environmental events. For example, at the time of the first "oil crisis" in 1973, it was common to give several different forecasts of energy costs depending on different assumptions about future actions of OPEC or of the oil companies. These forecasts support the development of alternative pro forma budgets and contingency plans.

At the same time, the manager needs to deal with the uncertainty caused by the more general "random" errors in the forecasts. This is similar to the problem already considered in setting safety stocks. It is complicated by the multiple and interacting variables that are here necessary for the environmental description. Because the resulting computations can be quite complicated, it is common to use a simulation technique known as *risk analysis*.

Risk Analysis

Table 5-5 (p. 162) presents demand forecasts for each of three possible prices that could be charged for the chemical, the current price of $4.00 per unit and for price increases of $0.05 and $0.10 per unit. Notice that for both possible increases it is projected that there will be a substantial initial impact on the rate of increase of demand, as well as a lesser long-term impact. Forecasts are also given for the rates of increase in the two major cost elements.

If only the projected mean rates of increase are used, the pro forma budgets will give "most likely" projections of operating profit for each alternative price. These are shown in table 5-6 (p. 163). It appears that a $0.05 increase would lead to a substantial decrease in operating profit while a $0.10 increase would have a lesser impact. Since price seems to be a critical variable, it is important to know how these projections may be

TABLE 5-5

Dreguld Company: Sales and Cost Forecasts for 1987
Forecasts for Quarter-to-Quarter % Increases

Demand: Assuming Unit Selling Price of:

Quarter	$4.00 Mean (%)	$4.00 Standard Deviation (%)	$4.05 Mean (%)	$4.05 Standard Deviation (%)	$4.10 Mean (%)	$4.10 Standard Deviation (%)
I	5.00	0.40	3.50	0.60	2.00	0.70
II	5.00	0.50	4.00	0.70	3.00	0.80
III	5.00	0.60	4.50	0.80	3.50	0.90
IV	5.00	0.80	4.50	0.90	4.00	1.00

Cost of Goods Sold:

Quarter	Mean (%)	Standard Deviation (%)
I	2.50	0.30
II	2.50	0.40
III	2.50	0.50
IV	2.50	0.60

Sales, General, and Other Costs:

Quarter	Mean (%)	Standard Deviation (%)
I	3.00	0.30
II	3.00	0.40
III	3.00	0.50
IV	3.00	0.60

TABLE 5-6

Dreguld Company: Projected Operating Profits for 1987
for Three Alternative Unit Prices

Price/Unit	Projected Operating Profit
$4.00	$37,740
$4.05	$33,877
$4.10	$36,564

affected by possible errors in the forecasts. For this, some form of sensitivity analysis is necessary. When only a small number of major environmental variables is involved, the easiest approach may be to place upper and lower limits on the forecasts and to generate several different budgets using these limits in place of a single budget based only on the means or "most likely" forecasts. When a large number of forecasts is involved, all of which may be critical to the plan, an excessively large number of alternative budgets would have to be considered in connection with each proposed plan.

An alternative procedure that can be used in this case is that of simulation or *risk analysis*. For this, each point forecast (or at least the most important) is replaced by a probability distribution as in the previous safety stock example. These probability distributions are then used to (computer) generate a large number of different budgets, which are then summarized in frequency distributions for the desired performance measures (here operating profit).

The full procedure that would be used is beyond the scope of this book. We can develop a simple example by assuming that all the probability distributions are normal with the means and standard deviations shown in Table 5-5. We start by generating a random number between 0 and 1. This can be obtained from the table of random numbers that will be found in almost any statistics book. In this example, the simulations were run using the computer program Lotus 123, which can generate random numbers directly. Assume that the first number generated is 0.481. Just as in determining safety stocks, enter the graph of Figure 5-6 with this value on the vertical axis. Reading across to the right and down, you should obtain the Z value of -0.05. The first generated demand increase for a price of $4.00 is then

$$\text{Demand increase} = 5\% + (-0.05) \times 0.40\% = 4.98\%$$

and the generated demand for the first quarter of 1987 is

$$\text{Demand} = 123,511 \times (1 + 0.0498) = 129,662 \text{ units.}$$

In a similar way, unit costs of goods sold and other costs are generated. This information is used to develop the operating profit for the first quarter. This is repeated for each of the four quarters, noting that the means and standard deviations will change for each quarter because the forecasts become less accurate as the forecast horizon increases.

Figure 5-7 shows box-and-whisker diagrams for the probability distribution of total operating income for 50 simulation runs for each of the three possible prices, $4.00 per unit, $4.05 per unit, and $4.10 per unit. The pattern in the medians of the distributions is similar to that in the point forecasts developed earlier and shown again here as small boxes. The increase in profit between the prices of $4.05 and $4.10 does not appear, however.

What is of greater interest is the substantial lack of accuracy in the projections because of the basic lack of accuracy in the forecasts and because of the interactions among the potential errors in the different forecasts. Because the forecasts are for percent changes in demand, any error

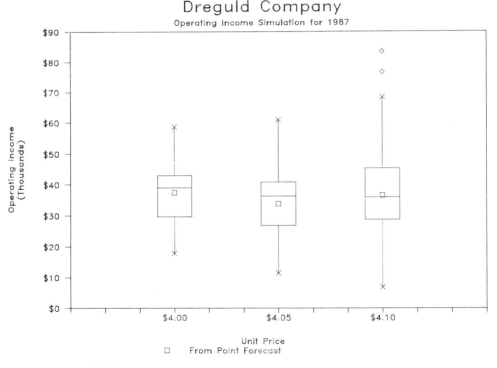

FIGURE 5-7

Dreguld company: Operating income simulation for 1987

in the forecast for the first quarter carries through all the remaining quarters. Because of this potential forecast inaccuracy, any decision to increase price should be treated cautiously and on grounds other than solely the possibility of a drop in operating income as shown in the comparison of the point projections.

OTHER OPERATIONAL PLANNING MODELS

In addition to the budget and inventory models described in this chapter, many other models are used in the planning of operations. These include simulation models of production processes, cash-flow models, models for work-force planning, models of distribution systems, linear programming resource allocation models, and many others designed for special applications. From the standpoint of the planner/manager, they share the characteristics of being highly structured and usually quantitative. For the forecaster, they all tend to have the common element of requiring not just "best guess" point forecasts but rather some form of probability distribution or of multiple forecasts.

In the following chapters we examine some of the different approaches to forecasting that are available for these applications and the factors that must be considered in choosing an appropriate approach.

READINGS

The Safety Stock Model

More detail on the use of safety stocks can be found in texts on operations management or management science. Two possibilities would be Levin and Kirkpatrick (Chapters 7 and 8), cited in the Readings for Chapter 2, and

> ARTHUR C. LAUFER, *Operations Management,* Cincinnati, South-Western, 1975, Chapters 16 and 17.

Pro Forma Budgets and Risk Analysis

For other introductions to risk analysis see

> ALAN J. ROWE, RICHARD O. MASON, and KARL DICKEL, *Strategic Management and Business Policy,* 2nd ed., Reading, Mass., Addison-Wesley, 1985, pp. 164–165.

JAMES B. BOULDEN, *Computer-Assisted Planning Systems,* New York, McGraw-Hill, 1976.

PROBLEMS

1. The order-processing department of a medium-sized mail-order firm wants your help in determining how many people to employ in the department during the next three months. They give you the following information:

   During the next three months the department work load is forecasted to average between 310 and 380 work hours per week.

   Each employee works 35 hours per week and can, if necessary, work up to an additional 8 hours per week in overtime.

   The cost per employee is $180 per week plus $6 per hour for overtime.

   a. Draw a graph of the labor costs for 9, 10, and 11 employees over the interval of 310 to 410 work hours per week of actual time required.

   b. On a different graph, show the opportunity cost curves over the same interval of possible work hours per week.

   c. Would you recommend using 9 or 10 employees? Why?

   d. How would this problem differ if this was a large company with 300 employees in the department.

2. Medstore, Inc., is a wholesale distributor of chemical and medical supplies to hospitals and laboratories. Inventory control is based on product groups. One group to be considered here consists of 50 chemical compounds, of which the following is typical.

   Compound X: Carrying cost per unit of excess inventory = $0.10 per two-week period and stockout cost (required rush order) = $10.00 per unit. Lead time on regular orders is two weeks. Average demand per two-week period is 60 units. Orders are placed every four weeks. The standard deviation of demand for a two-week period is 15.5 units and for a six-week period is 26.8 units. The company currently has 92 units on hand.

   a. What is the probability that the company will run out of compound X before the next order arrives? Assume that demand is normally distributed and use Figure 5-6 (or Appendix Table A1 if you prefer) to estimate the probability.

   b. What quantity should be ordered?

   c. A computer service bureau representative is suggesting that the firm should try a new demand-forecasting package that will cut the forecast errors in half. The cost of running this package once every four weeks for the 50 compounds in the group is estimated to be $200. Assume that the costs and standard deviations are the same for all the compounds in the group. Would you suggest shifting to the new forecasting approach? Discuss your reasons.

3. Merman Electronics, Inc., manufactures an automatic electronic switch used in various industrial safety devices. Their fiscal year goes from July 1 to June 30. They are now in the process of planning for fiscal year 1988. You are given the following anticipated income statement for 1987:

Net sales		
1,800,000 units @ $8.50		$15,300,000
Cost of goods sold		
Fixed costs	$1,000,000	
Labor at $4.00 per unit	7,164,000	
Material at $1.96 per unit	3,528,000	
Total		11,692,000
Operating revenue		3,608,000
General, sales, and administrative costs		
Fixed costs	730,000	
Variable costs at $0.93 per unit	1,674,000	
Total		2,404,000
Gross profit		$ 1,204,000

In 1988, fixed costs are forecasted to increase by 10%, production labor and overhead (G, S & A) costs by 7.5%, and the cost of production materials by 15%. Because of these increases, the company feels that it must increase the selling price of the unit and has developed two conditional forecasts: 2,000,000 units at $9 per unit and 2,500,000 units at $8.75 per unit.

  a. Develop pro forma income statements for 1988 for each of these forecasts and use these to decide on a price to charge in 1988.

  b. The person supplying the forecasts has indicated that the forecast for the price increase in production materials depends in part on international commodity prices and is very uncertain. Although a 15% increase is a reasonable guess and it would not be less than 12%, it could go as high as 40%. What effect would this uncertainty have on your answer in part a?

CHAPTER 6

Forecasting
by Smoothing

Chapter 4 introduced two different approaches to forecasting: forecasting by smoothing and forecasting by modeling. In *modeling*, historical records are used to develop a structural description or model of a time-series process that is then used to generate forecasts of future states of the environment. Examples that we have considered and that are applicable to forecasting would include the use of transformations and first differences in describing trends and the use of the seasonal index in analyzing seasonal patterns. In *smoothing*, the random noise is filtered from the time series, by some form of moving average, to expose the underlying patterns in the data. These patterns are then projected, either by judgment or by simple mechanical projection, to create the forecast. An example of this was the use in Chapter 4 of median smoothing to isolate the cyclical component of a time series.

These two approaches tend to find application in different situations. Modeling results in a specific structural description of the time series and can be used to describe interactions among time series. Since it results in a set of specific mathematical or logical equations or statements, it is possible to develop conditional forecasts and to make relatively long range projections. At the same time, it means that a specific model must be developed for each new situation and for each time series or set of time series to be considered. Smoothing, which is the subject of this chapter, is basically a mechanical approach that can be used with a wide range of different time series without the need to fit or adapt the procedure in any detailed way to each new application. It is, however, primarily a technique for analyzing single time series rather than interactions among time series. As with the cycle analysis of Chapter 4, it isolates patterns without developing any structural description of the underlying process that is generating the time series. This limits its use to applications requiring only short-range unconditional forecasts. Forecasting by smoothing is thus particularly applicable to the needs of activity planning, while modeling is appropriate for applications to resource planning and budgeting.

It should be noted that activity planning techniques are well suited to computer automation because of the high degree of structure and the repetitive nature of the decisions involved. The forecasting techniques discussed in this chapter are rarely used in hand calculations. They are so broadly applied and so well known that they cannot pass without discussion. We will not, however, go into all the possible variations on the basic approach nor will we discuss any of the specific computer-related problems of implementing planning models based on these methods.

Major Points to be Noted

1. *The basic concepts of exponential smoothing. Note particularly that the forecasts generated are relatively independent of the choice of the smoothing coefficient and start-up values.*

2. *The design characteristics of an automatic or semiautomatic forecasting and planning system and the way that exponential smoothing lends itself to this approach.*

3. *The extensions of the basic model, which can be used to improve the accuracy or the sensitivity of a forecasting system.*

EXPONENTIAL SMOOTHING

Exponential smoothing is a moving-average technique that has been used effectively for many years for short-range forecasting. Over that time many different variations on the basic approach have been developed. In this section we consider it in its original form: simple, first-order smoothing. In a later section, we examine some of the extensions that have been developed in order to see the great flexibility that is possible in applying this technique. In terms of the concepts introduced in Chapter 4, exponential smoothing can be thought of as an asymmetrically weighted, uncentered moving mean.

Alternative Forms of the Basic Model

The equation for simple, first-order exponential smoothing can be written in several different ways that are algebraically equivalent but that allow us to explore different aspects of the approach.

Simple Exponential Smoothing as a Constant Forecast.   It was suggested earlier that smoothing methods are model-free. This is not, strictly speaking, correct. Although these techniques tend to be effective over broad classes of time series and need relatively little tailoring to specific situations, their effectiveness does depend on the general characteristics of a particular series, such as whether the series has any distinctive trend or seasonal pattern. Simple exponential smoothing is most effective with data when these two components are weak or absent.

Imagine a time series that might reasonably be described as random noise around a more or less constant mean value. If that mean could be determined, then it would be possible to use the same forecast period after period, allowing for the random noise by an appropriate safety stock, as discussed in the last chapter. Unless, however, there were structural reasons for believing that the mean was really constant, it would be wise to take some precautions against possible shifts in that mean. One approach could be to adjust the constant forecast in the direction of any forecast error so that, if the errors become systematically positive or negative, the forecast would be adjusted upward or downward until the forecast errors again appeared to be random.

For a given time series, let the actual observation at time t be denoted by Y_t and the forecast developed at the end of period t by $\hat{Y}_t$. The new forecast is obtained by adding some fraction of the most recent forecast error to the previous forecast:

$$\hat{Y}_t = \hat{Y}_{t-1} + \alpha e_t \tag{1}$$

where

$$e_t = Y_t - \hat{Y}_{t-1} \tag{2}$$

For the forecast $\hat{Y}_t$, the subscript t refers to the period in which the forecast is developed. Because it is assumed that there is no trend or other systematic movement, the same forecast is used for all ensuing periods, and it is not necessary to identify the specific period for which the forecast is made. If the forecast in a given period is low, the forecast error e_t will be positive, and the forecast for the following period will be moved upward; if high, e_t will be negative and the shift will be downward. How much the forecast will be moved up or down will depend on the value of the coefficient α. As we shall see, useful values for α range from about 0.05 to 0.20.

Simple Exponential Smoothing as a Combination of Forcasts. A simple approach to forecasting often used in practice is to assume that the next period will be just the same as this one. This has come to be called a "naive" forecast. In contrast to the "constant" forecast, this type of forecast is continually changing and, almost certainly, will overreact to random movements in the time series. Indeed, these two approaches can be thought of as the extremes of stability versus volatility. It can be argued therefore that the correct forecast will often lie somewhere between the two. If equation (1) is multiplied and reorganized, we obtain

$$\hat{Y}_t = \alpha Y_t + (1 - \alpha)\hat{Y}_{t-1} \tag{3}$$

a weighted average of the last forecast and the last actual value. If α is close to 1, then most of the weight will be placed on the naive forecast; if it is near zero, the constant forecast will be emphasized.

Exponential Smoothing as a Weighted Moving Average. Although exponential smoothing was earlier described as a moving average, nothing in the discussion to this point would suggest this to be true. It is possible, however, to show that the actual calculation being performed is equivalent to a particular type of moving average.

In equation (3), the use of t to denote the time variable is arbitrary and can refer to any point in time; it would have been equally possible to write

$$\hat{Y}_{t-1} = \alpha Y_{t-1} + (1 - \alpha)\,\hat{Y}_{t-2} \tag{3a}$$

If this is substituted in equation (3) in place of $\hat{Y}_{t-1}$, we obtain

$$\begin{aligned} \hat{Y}_t = {} & \alpha Y_t + \alpha(1 - \alpha)Y_{t-1} \\ & + (1 - \alpha)^2 \hat{Y}_{t-2} \end{aligned} \tag{4}$$

The forecast is now related to the *two* previous observations.

Continuing this process eventually leads to the forecast as a weighted moving average of *all* previous values of Y in the form

$$\hat{Y}_t = \alpha Y_t + \alpha(1 - \alpha)Y_{t-1} + \alpha(1 - \alpha)^2 Y_{t-2}$$

$$+ \alpha(1 - \alpha)^3 Y_{t-3} + \alpha(1 - \alpha)^4 Y_{t-4} + \ldots \quad (5)$$

Notice that the weights are an exponentially (actually geometrically) decreasing series, hence the name "exponential smoothing." If α is small so that $(1 - \alpha)$ is close to 1, the weights tend to be relatively even over the past observations; if α is close to 1, almost all the weight is placed on the one or two most recent observations. By varying α it is possible to vary the relative importance of the recent versus the more historical, distant observations of Y.

Computational Form.   Although all these descriptions of simple exponential smoothing [equations (1), (3), and (5)] are mathematically the same, in practice, only equation (1) or (3) would be used in actual calculation. To see the procedure, we will go back to the problem of forecasting demand and setting order quantities as discussed in Chapter 5.

Suppose, to this point, the store owners have been using a constant sales forecast of 60 copies. It is now the end of December 1986, and, as usual, the December demand was forecasted to be 60 copies. Actual sales however were only 54 copies. It is now necessary to develop a forecast for January, and it has been decided to try using exponential smoothing with a smoothing coefficient α of 0.1. The new forecast will be

$$\text{New forecast} = 0.1 \times \text{last demand} + 0.9 \times \text{old forecast} \quad (6)$$

or

$$0.1 \times 54 + 0.9 \times 60 = 59 \text{ copies}$$

Because demand in December was less than that forecasted, the new forecast has been reduced. Notice that a major advantage of this approach when many routine forecasts are being made is that the data that must be stored from one month to the next are few; only the December forecast of 60 copies was needed. That can now be replaced in "storage" by the new forecast of 59 copies. If forecasts are needed for February and March, since it is assumed that there are no trends or other systematic patterns of change in demand, exactly the same forecast, 59 copies, will be used.

This simple, mechanical nature of exponential smoothing is at once its greatest strength and its greatest weakness. For very short range routine forecasting when little systematic change is anticipated, exponential smoothing allows the rapid and easy development of forecasts for large numbers of different activities and products. For longer-range forecasting, however, it ignores anything that could influence demand and thus gives only the most trivial straight-line projection.

DESIGNING A FORECASTING SYSTEM

To see how exponential smoothing can fit into a short-range routine planning process, let us continue to examine the magazine example of Chapter 5. Planning situations of this type exhibit several characteristics:

- The planning models are highly structured and quantitative.
- They will usually involve only a single environmental variable, such as the demand for a specific product or the anticipated level of a single activity (in a hospital, for example, it might be bed occupancy).
- The alternative actions to be considered are essentially reactive; demand is a "given" and the only question is how large an inventory will be needed to cover that demand.
- Because of the short planning horizon, the action taken will have no direct effect on the demand being forecasted (although it may have an effect on future demand). Forecasts are therefore unconditional.
- Because the forecasts are made routinely, the planner/manager normally is more interested in the long-term efficiency of the overall planning/forecasting process than in the accuracy of any single specific forecast.

All these characteristics tend to support the use of exponential smoothing.

Designing the Basic System

Again suppose that it is December 1986, but now you wish to develop an ongoing system for ordering the monthly magazine and not just a forecast for January. For purposes of designing and testing the system, the three years of monthly demand data from Chapter 5 are shown again in Figure 6-1 (p. 174). Since the data exhibit no strong trends or other patterns, simple exponential smoothing would seem to be a potentially useful forecasting tool. In designing the system, we need to consider three questions:

1. How should the smoothing coefficient α be chosen?
2. How is the forecasting system started up?
3. How is the system operated?

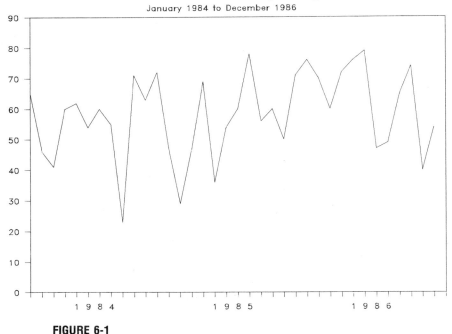

FIGURE 6-1

Demand for a monthly magazine, January 1984–December 1986

In exploring these issues, it will be necessary to have some way of evaluating system effectiveness. For this we will again use the concept of opportunity cost introduced in Chapter 5.

Assume as before that the magazines cost $0.50 and are sold for $2 so that $C_1 = \$0.50$ and $C_2 = \$1.50$. The safety stock should be set so stockouts occur no more than $C_1/(C_1 + C_2)$ or 25% of the time and there is sufficient stock $C_2/(C_1 + C_2)$ or 75% of the time.

In Table 6-1 the demands for the 3 years shown in Chapter 5 have been divided into two groups; the first four months of 1984 will be used to start up the system and the remaining 32 months, May 1984 through December 1986, will be used to test its operation. If you develop a stem-and-leaf diagram for those 32 months (you might do this for practice), you will see that the value that separates the upper 25% of the distribution (eight observations) is 71 copies. Following from the discussion of Chapter 5 and assuming that there are in fact no "forecastable" patterns in the data, the opportunity cost over those 32 months would have been minimized if a constant order quantity of 71 copies had been used. If you subtract this order quantity from each of the 32 demands, you will see that this would

TABLE 6-1

Simple Exponential Smoothing with Alpha = 0.10

Year and Month		Demand (copies)	Forecast	Forecast Error
1984	Jan	65		
	Feb	46		
	Mar	41		
	Apr	60		
1984	May	62	53.0	9.0
	Jun	54	53.9	0.1
	Jul	60	53.9	6.1
	Aug	55	54.5	0.5
	Sep	23	54.6	−31.6
	Oct	71	51.4	19.6
	Nov	63	53.4	9.6
	Dec	72	54.3	17.7
1985	Jan	47	56.1	−9.1
	Feb	29	55.2	−26.2
	Mar	47	52.6	−5.6
	Apr	69	52.0	17.0
	May	36	53.7	−17.7
	Jun	54	51.9	2.1
	Jul	60	52.1	7.9
	Aug	78	52.9	25.1
	Sep	56	55.4	0.6
	Oct	60	55.5	4.5
	Nov	50	55.9	−5.9
	Dec	71	55.4	15.6
1986	Jan	76	56.9	19.1
	Feb	70	58.8	11.2
	Mar	60	59.9	0.1
	Apr	72	59.9	12.1
	May	76	61.2	14.8
	Jun	79	62.6	16.4
	Jul	47	64.3	−17.3
	Aug	49	62.5	−13.5
	Sep	65	61.2	3.8
	Oct	74	61.6	12.4
	Nov	40	62.8	−22.8
	Dec	54	60.5	−6.5
1987	Jan		59.9	

have resulted in 423 excess copies and unfilled requests for 30 copies for an average monthly opportunity cost of $8.02. Unless it is possible to find and project patterns in the data that are not immediately apparent, no forecasting procedure would be able to improve on this, so it will form a useful base for evaluating our forecasts.[1]

---

[1]Remember that the specific numerical results in this example are, in part, an outcome of the particular data series used. This *type* of result, however, will be frequently observed.

Choosing α.   A number of optimization procedures used in management science can be applied to determining the best value of α. As a practical matter, one major reason for using exponential smoothing is that overall system efficiency should be relatively insensitive to the choice of α; if not, the univariate modeling methods to be discussed in Chapter 8 should be used. Generally, however, values of α between 0.05 and 0.20 tend to be appropriate for many different forecasting situations. When it is possible, as here, to have data that can be used for system testing, several different possible values of α can be tried to determine the sensitivity of the system to this choice. Figure 6-2 shows the average monthly opportunity cost as a function of α (we will see shortly how this was determined). It can be seen that, for α between 0.05 and 0.15, costs are relatively insensitive. On the other hand, as α approaches zero, costs increase rapidly. In this example, to keep calculations simple, a value of α = 0.1 will be used.

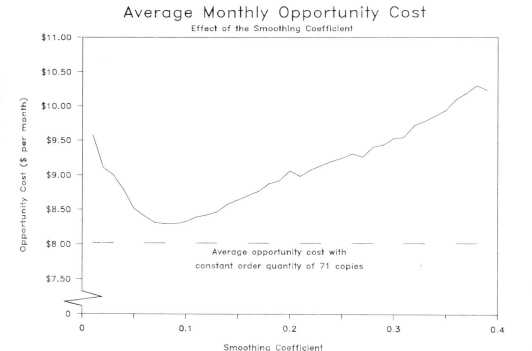

FIGURE 6-2

Average monthly opportunity cost: Effect of the smoothing coefficient

System Start-up.   The use of either equation (1) or (3) requires an initial forecast $\hat{Y}_0$ to start the process. Once this starting value is established, $\hat{Y}_1$ can be found from

$$\hat{Y}_1 = \alpha Y_1 + (1 - \alpha)\hat{Y}_0 \qquad (7)$$

and the succeeding forecasts similarly obtained. As the sequence of forecasts is generated, this initial value will have less and less weight and the forecasts will come to be more influenced by the actual pattern of demand. With α under 0.2, however, this initial value will continue to have a noticeable influence for a substantial period of time, and it is desirable to have it relatively close to the future average level of demand.

Table 6-1 illustrates how the process would work. To follow it systematically, assume that it is the end of April 1984. With a sheet of paper, cover all the data and forecasts starting with May 1984 so that the only information available is for the first four months. To start the system, the median of the first four observations, or 53, will be used for $\hat{Y}_0$.

The true average demand over the following 32 months will actually be 60 copies, so this starting value is slightly low. The effect of starting somewhat below the median value is not great as can be seen by examining the forecast errors in Figure 6-3 (p. 180). Although the forecast errors immediately following the start-up are all positive, they are relatively small and soon outweighed by the large negative error in September.

System Operation.   With α and the starting value chosen, the calculation of the ongoing sequence of forecasts and the forecast errors can be followed by moving your sheet of paper down so that each month in Table 6-2 is uncovered in sequence. The initial forecast developed in April is 53; actual demand in May is 62 for a forecast error of 9 copies. Adding 10% of this error ($\alpha = 0.10$) to the old forecast gives a new forecast of 53.9 [equation (1)]. Similar calculations can be followed through the rest of the table.

Setting Safety Stocks

As discussed in Chapter 5, this decision, the quantity to be ordered, requires more than just a "best-guess" point forecast. An estimate of the probable magnitude of the forecast error is needed to set an appropriate safety stock. One advantage of methods such as exponential smoothing is that this calculation can be part of the overall system design.

We need an estimate of the probability distribution of the forecast errors. If we assume that these are approximately normally distributed, this

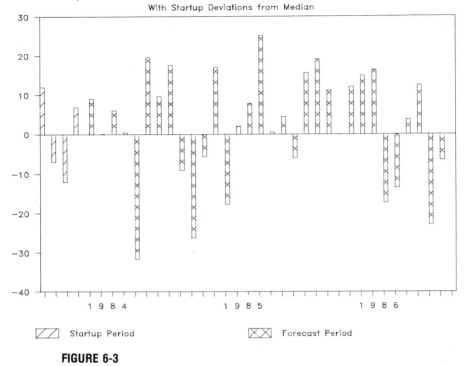

FIGURE 6-3

Exponential smoothing forecast errors, with start-up deviations from median

can be reduced to developing estimates of the mean and standard deviation of the error distribution. These can be calculated by the same exponential smoothing methods used in developing the forecast. The calculations are shown in Table 6-2. To follow the calculations, again start with only the data for the first four months showing, and uncover each ensuing month in sequence. In following the table notice that, for convenience in calculating the error, the forecast for October has been placed on the "October line," while the needed values of EBar and MAD, discussed next, are on the preceding line.

Estimating the Mean Error (EBar). The average error should be zero. In fact, this will rarely be true; during periods when changes are occurring in the time series, the average error can differ substantially from zero. Rather than design special procedures for such periods, we will simply routinely reestimate the mean error *(EBar)* by applying simple exponential smoothing to the forecast errors as shown in Table 6-2 (pp. 180–181).

The initial value of EBar as of April 1984 is assumed to be zero. The actual error for May 1984 is 9. Using an α of 0.1, the mean is revised to 0.9, as shown. At the end of June, the mean is again revised to $0.1 \times 0.1 + 0.9 \times 0.9 = 0.82$ and similarly as the error for each succeeding month is determined. It is not necessary to use the same smoothing coefficient for the forecast and for EBar as is done here, although it is often convenient to do so.

Estimating the Standard Deviation. The same procedure can be used in reestimating the standard deviation. Since calculating the standard deviation directly would involve the operations of both squaring and taking a square root, it is more convenient to determine the MAD and convert this to an estimate of the standard deviation as described in Chapter 5. This is done here by the same error smoothing except that the absolute value of the error is used rather than the error itself. The effect of using absolute values can be seen by comparing the two calculations for September 1984. The forecast error is, for the first time, negative. The calculation for EBar is

$$0.1(-31.6) + 0.9(1.26) = -2.02$$

The estimate of the MAD, however, uses the absolute value

$$0.1(+31.6) + 0.9(7.49) = 9.90$$

To set a starting value for the MAD, the mean absolute deviation around the median for the first four observations was used. Notice that the estimate appears initially to have been a bit low but seems to have stabilized in about six periods. It should be noted again that this calculation uses the absolute value of the *error* and not its deviation from the mean. If EBar is large, this will overstate the MAD. At the same time, it makes the calculation somewhat easier and does not have any important impact on the final calculation of the safety stock.

As noted in Chapter 5, the standard deviation is approximately equal to MAD/0.8. For September 1984, the estimate of the standard deviation would be $9.90/0.8 = 12.38$ and similarly for the following months.

Determining the Safety Stock. In Chapter 5, safety stocks were determined using the normal distribution with mean μ and standard deviation σ. Since EBar is an estimate of μ and MAD/0.8 is an estimate of σ, these values can be used in exactly the same way to determine the safety stock and the order quantity. For October 1984,

Safety stock $= -2.02 + 0.675 \ (9.90/0.8) = 6.3$ or 6 copies

TABLE 6-2

Simple Exponential Smoothing with Alpha = 0.10 with Safety Stocks and Order Quantities

Year and Month		Demand (copies)	Forecast	Error	EBar	MAD	Safety Stock	Order Quantity	Excess (−) or Stockout (+)
1984	Jan	65							
	Feb	46							
	Mar	41							
	Apr	60			0.00	9.50			
	May	62	53.0	9.0	0.90	9.45	8	61	1
	Jun	54	53.9	0.1	0.82	8.51	9	63	−9
	Jul	60	53.9	6.1	1.35	8.27	8	62	−2
	Aug	55	54.5	0.5	1.26	7.49	8	63	−8
	Sep	23	54.6	−31.6	−2.02	9.90	8	62	−39
	Oct	71	51.4	19.6	0.14	10.87	6	58	13
	Nov	63	53.4	9.6	1.09	10.75	9	63	0
	Dec	72	54.3	17.7	2.75	11.44	10	64	8
1985	Jan	47	56.1	−9.1	1.56	11.20	12	68	−21
	Feb	29	55.2	−26.2	−1.21	12.70	11	66	−37
	Mar	47	52.6	−5.6	−1.65	11.99	10	62	−15
	Apr	69	52.0	17.0	0.21	12.49	8	60	9
	May	36	53.7	−17.7	−1.58	13.01	11	64	−28
	Jun	54	51.9	2.1	−1.21	11.92	9	61	−7
	Jul	60	52.1	7.9	−0.31	11.51	9	61	−1

Year	Month							
	Aug	78	52.9	25.1	2.23	12.87	9	62	16
	Sep	56	55.4	0.6	2.06	11.64	13	69	-13
	Oct	60	55.5	4.5	2.31	10.92	12	67	-7
	Nov	50	55.9	-5.9	1.48	10.42	12	67	-17
	Dec	71	55.4	15.6	2.90	10.95	10	66	5
1986	Jan	76	56.9	19.1	4.52	11.76	12	69	7
	Feb	70	58.8	11.2	5.18	11.70	14	73	-3
	Mar	60	59.9	0.1	4.67	10.54	15	75	-15
	Apr	72	59.9	12.1	5.41	10.69	14	74	-2
	May	76	61.2	14.8	6.35	11.11	14	76	0
	Jun	79	62.6	16.4	7.35	11.63	16	78	1
	Jul	47	64.3	-17.3	4.89	12.20	17	81	-34
	Aug	49	62.5	-13.5	3.05	12.33	15	78	-29
	Sep	65	61.2	3.8	3.12	11.48	13	75	-10
	Oct	74	61.6	12.4	4.05	11.57	13	74	0
	Nov	40	62.8	-22.8	1.37	12.70	14	77	-37
	Dec	54	60.5	-6.5	0.58	12.08	12	73	-19
1987	Jan		59.9				11	71	

Number of Periods with Excess Inventory	21
Total Excess Inventory	353
Average	16.8
Number of Period with Stockouts	8
Total Stockouts	60
Average	7.5
Average Opportunity Costs	$8.33

and

$$\text{Order quantity} = \text{forecast} + \text{safety stock}$$
$$= 51.4 + 6.3 = 57.7 \text{ or } 58 \text{ copies}$$

Figure 6-4 shows the forecasts and order quantities over the 3-year period. Notice the upward trend in both the forecasts and the order quantities, which match a slight upward trend in the data. Also notice how the size of the safety stock (the distance between the forecast and order quantity lines) changes as the accuracy of the forecasts changes. Figure 6-4 also has a horizontal line for the constant order quantity of 71 copies discussed earlier. It can be seen that this quantity would have been too large for the first $1\frac{1}{2}$ years (too few stockouts) and too small for the latter half of the data. Finally, notice the response lag in the forecasts. The peak order quantity appears to occur several months after the demand itself has begun to drop.

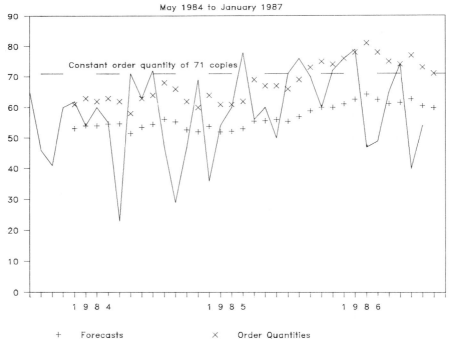

FIGURE 6-4

Forecasts and order quantities, May 1984–January 1987

Evaluating the Forecast Procedure. It is now possible to evaluate how the forecast procedure would have performed over the period of 32 months. Table 6-2 indicates the extent to which each forecast with its safety stock exceeded or fell short of the actual demand. As before, the average opportunity cost can be calculated and is here $8.33, and increase of $0.31 per month. Since the previous value was calculated using *all* the data and not one month at a time, this would suggest that there will be little value in any extensive search for a better forecasting system.

Ongoing Forecast Evaluation

There is another dimension to forecast evaluation. Forecasting systems of the type described here are designed to operate relatively automatically without intervention by the planner/manager. Under these conditions, if the underlying pattern of demand were to change in some major way so that the procedure was no longer adequate, it might be several months before the manager would discover that excessive or inadequate inventories were being carried. It is necessary to design into the system a procedure for ongoing forecast evaluation that will give warning of such changes. One such procedure is called *Trigg's tracking signal* and is based on the ratio between EBar and the MAD.

Consider again the way in which these two statistics were calculated in Table 6-2. As long as the process is operating adequately, there will be some negative forecast errors and some positive; EBar will remain close to zero, while the MAD, because all errors are treated as positive, will always be positive and larger than EBar. If systematic errors develop in the forecasts, they will be predominantly positive if the forecasts are too low or negative if they are too high. If all the forecast errors have the same sign (+ or −), the calculations for EBar and the MAD will (except for sign) become the same, and the ratio between EBar and MAD will begin to approach 1. Table 6-3 (p. 184) and Figure 6-5 (p. 186) show the tracking signal as applied to this example.

Even when the forecasting procedure is working well, the tracking signal does not remain exactly zero. The question for the system designer is: How large (ignoring sign) should the tracking signal be before we begin to suspect that the system may need to be changed? In this, the designer must balance two costs. If the system is generating inaccurate forecasts, then inventories and/or stockouts will be excessive resulting in higher costs. On the other hand, if the system is working properly, any time spent on redesign will be wasted.

Although a complete analysis of this problem is beyond the scope of this book, a general outline of the approach is possible. Suppose a system is

TABLE 6-3

Trigg's Tracking Signal using $\alpha = 0.10$ for EBar and MAD

Year and Month		Demand (copies)	Forecast	Error	EBar	MAD	Tracking Signal
1984	Jan	65					
	Feb	46					
	Mar	41					
	Apr	60			0.00	9.50	0.000
	May	62	53.0	9.0	0.90	9.45	0.095
	Jun	54	53.9	0.1	0.82	8.51	0.096
	Jul	60	53.9	6.1	1.35	8.27	0.163
	Aug	55	54.5	0.5	1.26	7.49	0.168
	Sep	23	54.6	−31.6	−2.02	9.90	−0.204
	Oct	71	51.4	19.6	0.14	10.87	0.013
	Nov	63	53.4	9.6	1.09	10.75	0.101
	Dec	72	54.3	17.7	2.75	11.44	0.240

184

TABLE 6-3, continued

Year and Month		Demand (copies)	Forecast	Error	EBar	MAD	Tracking Signal
1985	Jan	47	56.1	-9.1	1.56	11.20	0.139
	Feb	29	55.2	-26.2	-1.21	12.70	-0.096
	Mar	47	52.6	-5.6	-1.65	11.99	-0.138
	Apr	69	52.0	17.0	0.21	12.49	0.017
	May	36	53.7	-17.7	-1.58	13.01	-0.121
	Jun	54	51.9	2.1	-1.21	11.92	-0.102
	Jul	60	52.1	7.9	-0.31	11.51	-0.027
	Aug	78	52.9	25.1	2.23	12.87	0.173
	Sep	56	55.4	0.6	2.06	11.64	0.177
	Oct	60	55.5	4.5	2.31	10.92	0.211
	Nov	50	55.9	-5.9	1.48	10.42	0.142
	Dec	71	55.4	15.6	2.90	10.95	0.265
1986	Jan	76	56.9	19.1	4.52	11.76	0.384
	Feb	70	58.8	11.2	5.18	11.70	0.443
	Mar	60	59.9	0.1	4.67	10.54	0.443
	Apr	72	59.9	12.1	5.41	10.69	0.506
	May	76	61.2	14.8	6.35	11.11	0.572
	Jun	79	62.6	16.4	7.35	11.63	0.632
	Jul	47	64.3	-17.3	4.89	12.20	0.401
	Aug	49	62.5	-13.5	3.05	12.33	0.247
	Sep	65	61.2	3.8	3.12	11.48	0.272
	Oct	74	61.6	12.4	4.05	11.57	0.350
	Nov	40	62.8	-22.8	1.37	12.70	0.108
	Dec	54	60.5	-6.5	0.58	12.08	0.048
1987	Jan		59.9				

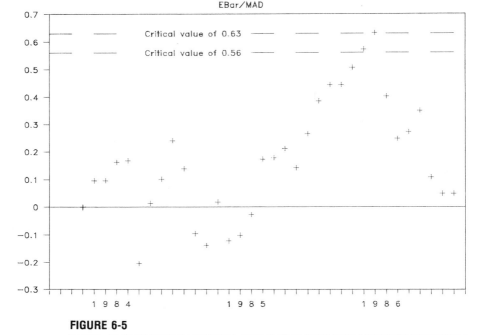

FIGURE 6-5

Trigg's tracking signal (EBar/MAD)

set for which it is known that the forecasting procedure is optimal (the forecast errors are a series of random normal variables). Over time, it would be possible to develop a cumulative frequency distribution of the tracking signal values generated just as we did with operating income in the budget simulation of Chapter 5. We could then determine those values that were exceeded only a small percent of the time. These are called *critical values*.

Table 6-4 was obtained by applying the tracking signal calculations to many different series of random numbers over 25 and 50 successive periods and observing the distribution of tracking signal values for different values of α. 25 periods would correspond to approximately 6 months for weekly data or 2 years for monthly data. The critical values shown are accurate to ± 0.02.

Suppose in our example the forecasting system designer decides to use a critical tracking signal value of 0.63. From Table 6-4 it can be seen that this value has one chance in four of being exceeded by chance over a period of about four years. Examination of the tracking signal for June 1986 in Table 6-3 suggests that this is just what has happened.

TABLE 6-4

Probability of Exceeding Specified Absolute Values of Trigg's Tracking Signal During Forecast Runs of 25 and 50 Periods

Probability of Exceeding Indicated Value	α for EBar and MAD							
	0.05		0.10		0.15		0.20	
	Periods in Run							
	25	50	25	50	25	50	25	50
	Absolute Values of Tracking Signal Critical Values							
0.50	0.27	0.36	0.50	0.56	0.63	0.69	0.72	0.80
0.25	0.36	0.42	0.57	0.63	0.70	0.75	0.79	0.84
0.20	0.37	0.44	0.58	0.66	0.71	0.77	0.80	0.86
0.15	0.40	0.46	0.61	0.67	0.73	0.79	0.83	0.87
0.10	0.43	0.48	0.64	0.69	0.76	0.82	0.85	0.89
0.05	0.48	0.51	0.69	0.73	0.80	0.85	0.90	0.92
0.02	0.53	0.54	0.74	0.77	0.84	0.88	0.94	0.95
0.01	0.57	0.56	0.78	0.79	0.88	0.92	0.96	0.98

187

The designer, of course, can reduce the chance of such a false alarm by using a larger critical value. At the same time, this will increase the chance that a real change in the system, should it occur, would go unnoticed.

OTHER FORMS OF EXPONENTIAL SMOOTHING

Simple exponential smoothing is designed for situations where there are no obvious dominant patterns in the data, such as a trend, seasonal pattern, or cyclical movement (which can appear in the short run very much like a trend). When a time series contains such patterns, simple exponential smoothing will pick them up but in a way that is damped and lagged. If this proves to be a problem, the exponential smoothing approach can be modified to include adjustments for these components. A number of different approaches are available. The one considered here is fairly typical. Others are noted at the end of the chapter.

Holt's Two-parameter Smoothing

The time series we have been considering in this chapter has what appears to be a very slight upward trend. This is probably the cause of the false alarm given by the tracking signal in Table 6-3. If it were to be decided, however, that this upward trend was real and therefore would continue, it might be wise to consider including it in the forecast.

Forecasting Model with Trend.   The model underlying this approach assumes that there is in the data a systematic tendency for the "average" to increase or decrease, and that this trend can be described in the short run by an equation of the form

$$\hat{Y}_t = b_{0t} + b_{1t}t \tag{8}$$

where b_{0t} is continually shifted so that t is set equal to zero in the current period. It is assumed that in the long run b_{1t} can also change, although relatively slowly. The forecasting model is

$$\hat{Y}_t(h) = b_{0t} + b_{1t}h \tag{9}$$

where the addition of the h to $\hat{Y}$ indicates that the forecast changes as the forecast horizon lengthens and refers to the number of periods in the future for which the forecast is made. The forecast for the next period becomes

$$\hat{Y}_t(1) = b_{0t} + b_{1t} \tag{10}$$

The method of simple exponential smoothing is used to determine the coefficients b_{0t} and b_{1t}.

Table 6-5 (p. 190) illustrates the procedure. In this example a smoothing coefficient of $\alpha = 0.1$ has been used for smoothing b_{0t} and a coefficient of 0.05 (referred to as β) has been used for b_{1t}. To start the system, we need initial estimates b_{00} and b_{10}. As in the previous case, all that are needed are reasonable values since the smoothing process will, over time, modify them as necessary. In Table 6-5 a very simple process is used:

b_{0t} for April is the median of the demands for the four months, January through April (53 copies).

b_{0t} for the May forecast is obtained by simple exponential smoothing using the difference $60 - 53$ as the error.

$$0.9 \times 53 + 0.1 \times 60 = 53.7$$

b_{1t} for the May forecast is obtained by taking the difference between these two values

$$53.7 - 53.0 = 0.7$$

The b_{0t} and b_{1t} values to be used for June are now obtained in sequence. First combine the previous b_{0t} with the actual demand for May:

$$0.1(62) + 0.9(53.7 + 0.7) = 55.2$$

Notice that the old b_{0t} was based on April and had to be updated by adding one trend increment b_{1t} to shift it to May. Next obtain the new value of b_{1t} by combining the old b_{1t} with the difference between the last two values of b_{0t}. Frequently, it is desirable when making projections only one or two periods ahead to allow b_{1t} to be slightly more or less responsive to changes in the data than is b_{0t}. In this example a slightly smaller value (0.05) is used for b_{1t}.

$$0.05(55.2 - 53.7) + 0.95(0.7) = 0.7.$$

The forecast for June is now obtained by adding the values of b_{0t} and b_{1t}.

$$\hat{Y}_6 = 55.2 + 0.7 = 55.9$$

The forecast error, EBar, MAD, and the tracking signal are obtained and used just as before. The average opportunity cost over the period is $8.13 compared with the $8.33 calculated earlier for simple exponential smoothing, a saving of $0.20 per month. Such a minimal saving is unlikely to justify the cost of the additional calculation and data storage required.

TABLE 6-5

Holt Second Order Smoothing with $\alpha = 0.10$ and $\beta = 0.05$

Year and Month		Demand (copies)	$b_{0,t-1}$	$b_{1,t-1}$	Forecast	Forecast Error	Tracking Signal
1984	Jan	65					
	Feb	46					
	Mar	41					
	Apr	60	53.0				0.000
	May	62	53.7	0.7	54.4	7.6	0.082
	Jun	54	55.2	0.7	55.9	−1.9	0.058
	Jul	60	55.7	0.7	56.4	3.6	0.099
	Aug	55	56.8	0.7	57.5	−2.5	0.062
	Sep	23	57.3	0.7	58.0	−35.0	−0.300
	Oct	71	54.5	0.6	55.1	15.9	−0.109
	Nov	63	56.7	0.6	57.3	5.7	−0.048
	Dec	72	57.9	0.7	58.5	13.5	0.085

TABLE 6-5, continued

Year and Month		Demand (copies)	$b_{0,t-1}$	$b_{1,t-1}$	Forecast	Forecast Error	Tracking Signal
1985	Jan	47	59.9	0.7	60.6	-13.6	-0.050
	Feb	29	59.3	0.7	59.9	-30.9	-0.278
	Mar	47	56.8	0.5	57.3	-10.3	-0.336
	Apr	69	56.3	0.5	56.8	12.1	-0.207
	May	36	58.0	0.5	58.5	-22.5	-0.338
	Jun	54	56.3	0.4	56.7	-2.7	-0.352
	Jul	60	56.4	0.4	56.8	3.2	-0.315
	Aug	78	57.1	0.4	57.5	20.5	-0.099
	Sep	56	59.6	0.5	60.1	-4.1	-0.131
	Oct	60	59.7	0.5	60.2	-0.2	-0.132
	Nov	50	60.2	0.5	60.6	-10.6	-0.220
	Dec	71	59.6	0.4	60.0	11.0	-0.093
1986	Jan	76	61.1	0.5	61.6	14.4	0.051
	Feb	70	63.1	0.6	63.6	6.4	0.108
	Mar	60	64.3	0.6	64.9	-4.9	0.054
	Apr	72	64.4	0.6	64.9	7.1	0.123
	May	76	65.6	0.6	66.3	9.7	0.212
	Jun	79	67.2	0.7	67.9	11.1	0.301
	Jul	47	69.0	0.7	69.7	-22.7	0.035
	Aug	49	67.4	0.6	68.0	-19.0	-0.131
	Sep	65	66.1	0.5	66.6	-1.6	-0.144
	Oct	74	66.5	0.5	67.0	7.0	-0.067
	Nov	40	67.7	0.5	68.2	-28.2	-0.282
	Dec	54	65.4	0.4	65.8	-11.8	-0.351
1987	Jan		64.6	0.3	64.9		

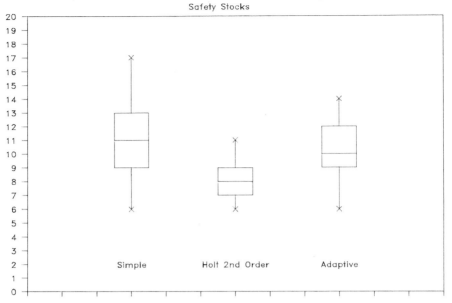

Comparison of Three Smoothing Methods
Safety Stocks

FIGURE 6-6

Comparison of three smoothing methods: Safety stocks

Figures 6-6, 6-7, and 6-8 examine the differences between the two methods in more detail (along with another method to be considered shortly). Use of the Holt method reduced substantially the size and variability of the safety stock carried (Figure 6-6). The number of stockouts decreased by one, and the average size of a stockout by one also (Figure 6-7). Months with excess inventories increased by two with a slight decline in the average size. Overall this suggests that the Holt method was only slightly more responsive to changes in demand than simple smoothing. Figure 6-8 (p. 194) compares the performance of the tracking signal. The upward drift in the signal observed with simple exponential smoothing is no longer evident.

Even if the Holt method were clearly preferable, it must be stressed again that its use is not costless. Now two numbers b_{0t} and b_{1t} must be stored, rather than just one, and the computations are increased. The question that must be raised in each case is whether the reduction in opportunity costs is enought to warrant its use.

A similar approach used when the data show a strong seasonal pattern is called the *Winter's method*. It adds to the Holt method a seasonal index that is updated each period in a manner similar to that used here for b_{1t}. It

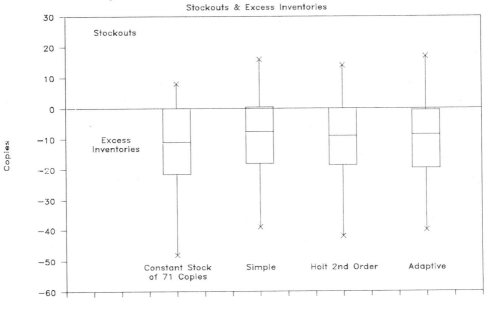

FIGURE 6-7

Comparison of three smoothing methods: Stockouts and excess inventories

is covered in detail in the sources noted at the end of the chapter. With the Winter's method, as with some other seasonal methods in common use, data storage requirements begin to become quite large. Here, for example, it would be necessary to continuously store estimates of b_{0t}, b_{1t}, and 12 monthly seasonal index factors.

Adaptive Methods

In the initial description of the exponential smoothing coefficient, it was noted that, when the underlying process was stable, small values of α (0.05 to 0.20) were most effective. If the underlying process is changing, however, a small value of α tends to be underresponsive, so changes in the forecasts tend to lag behind the changes in demand.

A variety of methods is available that are designed to adapt the smoothing coefficient or coefficients so that they remain small during periods when the time series is stable, but automatically become larger if it appears that the underlying system is undergoing some major change.

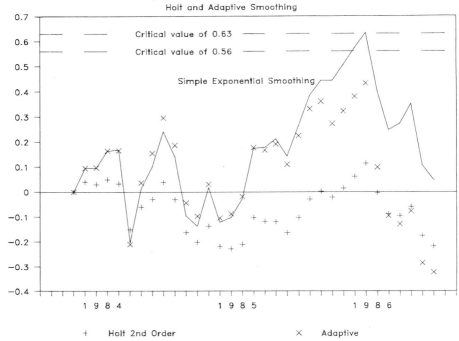

FIGURE 6-8

Trigg's tracking signal: Holt and adaptive smoothing

One simple approach makes use of the fact that the tracking signal exhibits a similar pattern: it is near 0 when the forecasting procedure is working well but begins to approach 1 if the forecast procedure is not under control. In this adaptive approach, the absolute value of the tracking signal is used as the smoothing coefficient α. Table 6-6 shows the calculation procedure; the comparison with simple and Holt exponential smoothing is shown in Figures 6-6, 6-7, and 6-8. It can be seen that safety stocks are less variable than with simple exponential smoothing although in other ways the two methods give similar results. Examination of the tracking signal in Figure 6-8 indicates that the adaptive approach responded somewhat better to the apparent upturn in early 1986. Its overall performance, however, was actually worse than that of simple exponential smoothing. The average opportunity cost was $9.20, an increase of $0.87 per month. This should not be taken as a criticism of the basic idea; it is simply a result of the particular data used in this example. At the same time, it is one more indication that, as a rule of thumb, simple methods should be chosen in

TABLE 6-6

Adaptive Smoothing

Year and Month		Demand (copies)	Adaptive Forecast	Forecast Error	Tracking Signal
1984	Jan	65			
	Feb	46			
	Mar	41			
	Apr	60			
	May	62	53.0	9.0	0.10
	Jun	54	53.9	0.1	0.10
	Jul	60	53.9	6.1	0.16
	Aug	55	54.9	0.1	0.17
	Sep	23	54.9	−31.9	−0.21
	Oct	71	48.2	22.8	0.04
	Nov	63	49.0	14.0	0.15
	Dec	72	51.2	20.8	0.30
1985	Jan	47	57.3	−10.3	0.19
	Feb	29	55.4	−26.4	−0.04
	Mar	47	54.3	−7.3	−0.10
	Apr	69	53.5	15.5	0.03
	May	36	54.0	−18.0	−0.10
	Jun	54	52.1	1.9	−0.09
	Jul	60	52.3	7.7	−0.02
	Aug	78	52.4	25.6	0.18
	Sep	56	56.9	−0.9	0.17
	Oct	60	56.8	3.2	0.19
	Nov	50	57.4	−7.4	0.11
	Dec	71	56.6	14.4	0.22
1986	Jan	76	59.8	16.2	0.33
	Feb	70	65.2	4.8	0.36
	Mar	60	66.9	−6.9	0.27
	Apr	72	65.0	7.0	0.32
	May	76	67.3	8.7	0.38
	Jun	79	70.6	8.4	0.43
	Jul	47	74.2	−27.2	0.10
	Aug	49	71.6	−22.6	−0.10
	Sep	65	69.4	−4.4	−0.13
	Oct	74	68.8	5.2	−0.08
	Nov	40	69.2	−29.2	−0.28
	Dec	54	60.9	−6.9	−0.32
			58.7		

preference to those that are more complex unless it is clear that the simple methods are not adequate.

Other Adaptive Methods. In some cases, instead of continuously changing α, it is changed to a larger value only when the tracking signal is out of control and is then changed back to the smaller value after a fixed number of periods, somewhat like shifting in and out of overdrive on a car.

Other approaches use a weighted moving average (but not exponentially weighted), with the weights determined from the pattern of forecast errors in the immediate past. As is the case with many of these approaches, data storage and the complexity of calculations increase rapidly; it is necessary to be very careful that the costs of the more complex methods do not exceed their benefits.

SUMMARY

This chapter has dealt with essentially "model-free" methods of forecasting that have their major applications in short-range planning and scheduling of specific activities. Their central advantage is not so much forecast accuracy, but rather overall system efficiency. In many cases this includes the possibility of completely automating or computerizing the system.

As planning horizons become longer, as planning models become more complex and interactive, as the opportunity costs of the forecast errors become greater, smoothing and adaptive methods begin to lose their advantages. It is necessary to turn to approaches involving the more formal analysis and modeling of the structure of the environment. This will be the subject of Chapters 7 and 8.

READINGS

Exponential Smoothing

Exponential smoothing is one of the most used and most written about forms of forecasting. Material on this approach can be found in almost any forecasting text and in many books on operations management and management science. The following references give more extensive treatment of the topics introduced here, as well as coverage of additional adaptive and smoothing procedures.

WARREN GILCHRIST, *Statistical Forecasting*, London, Wiley, 1976.

CHARLES W. GROSS and ROBIN T. PETERSON, *Business Forecasting*, 2nd ed., Boston, Houghton Mifflin, 1983.

SPYROS MAKRIDAKIS, STEVEN C. WHEELWRIGHT, and VICTOR E. MCGEE, *Forecasting: Methods and Applications*, 2nd ed., New York, Wiley, 1983.

NICK T. THOMOPOULOS, *Applied Forecasting Methods,* Englewood Cliffs, N.J., Prentice-Hall, 1980.

Anyone who is particularly interested in this topic should be familiar with one of the classics.

ROBERT G. BROWN, *Smoothing, Forecasting, and Prediction of Discrete Time Series,* Englewood Cliffs, N.J., Prentice-Hall, 1963.

Exponential smoothing is also the basis for many of the standard computer and calculator forecasting packages. As one example, the *Business Decisions Module* for the Texas Instruments TI 58/59 programmable calculators is based on the Winter's method noted earlier. Almost all the available personal computer forecasting software include some form of exponential smoothing as one of the options.

PROBLEMS

1. A company manufactures electronic signaling equipment used to monitor hospital patients. They have a policy of filling orders within two days even though this means that they have to carry inventories of a large number of different models. In fact, if a particular model is out of stock when an order is received, enough units to fill the order are custom assembled. Since this usually has to be done on overtime, it has been calculated that it adds 25% to the basic cost of the unit. If too many units are produced in a given month, they are carried in inventory. It has been calculated that this adds 2% to the unit cost.

   a. For one particular model, at the end of March the end of month inventory was 27 units. The forecast for April was for 212 units with an EBar of 2.7 and a MAD of 24.3. Determine the production order for April.

   b. Actual April demand was for 240 units. Assume that the forecast was developed using simple exponential smoothing with $\alpha = 0.1$. Use this information to update the forecast and MAD and to determine the production order for May.

   c. The research department has suggested using a different approach to forecasting, which they feel would reduce the MAD by 25%. Discuss how you would evaluate this suggestion. Assume that the average cost of manufacturing a unit is $50.

2. The Proxtor Company produces a variety of industrial chemicals. Among them is a cleaning compound made by blending a special active agent with an inert base and abrasives. The active agent is

prepared for them by another company. For storage reasons, the Proxtor Company tries to limit the amount of this agent on hand to a one-week supply. They have an arrangement with the supplier to make a delivery every Monday morning based on an order that they phone in on Friday. Excess inventory carried over into the next week is believed to add to the cost an average of $0.02 per week per pound carried over. If the company runs out during the week, they have to special order, which costs them an additional $0.135 per week per pound of shortage. Usage for the last 10 weeks has been:

Week	Usage (lb)	Week	Usage (lb)
1	5999	6	6555
2	5928	7	6690
3	6016	8	6648
4	6193	9	6538
5	6379	10	5943

a. On probability paper, graph a cumulative distribution of demand. Does demand appear to be normally distributed?

b. Based on the distribution in part a and the costs given, determine the safety stock that should have been carried and the average opportunity cost. Does this give any indication of how much you might be willing to spend to develop a forecasting system? Discuss.

c. Using the information given, show how you would set up and run a forecasting/ordering system. Use an initial forecast of 6000 and an initial MAD of 250. Use an α of 0.1.

d. Graph and analyze the forecast errors for the 10 weeks. Do you observe any patterns in the errors?

e. Show how you would set up and operate a forecast control system using the Trigg tracking signal.

f. At the end of week 10 there are 127 lb on hand. How much should be ordered?

g. For the system developed in part c, calculate the average opportunity cost. Compare your results to those obtained in part b.

3. For the data in Chapter 4 on factory sales of passenger cars (Table 4-6) or on scheduled airline passenger-miles carried (Table 4-7), smooth the data using simple exponential smoothing and compare your results to those obtained with the (53RH)T smoothing method. Present your comparison graphically and in words.

CHAPTER 7

The Basics
of Modeling

We have seen that operational planning frequently makes extensive use of formal quantitative models either in the form of single mathematical equations, as in the case of safety stock determination, or as systems of equations, as in pro forma budgets. To the extent that factors in the external environment enter as elements in these equations, the planner must have forecasts.

In the very short term planning situations that we have referred to as activity planning, the external environment enters in a relatively simple way: it is given. This does not mean that it is known. Rather it means that the planner accepts the external environment as a factor that cannot be influenced or changed and plans in a reactive way to make the best decisions possible *given* that environment and its uncertainty. As we saw in the last chapter, this leads to forecasts that are simple, single-variable, unconditional projections for which smoothing techniques are ideally suited.

Planning for the longer-range acquisition and allocation of resources is a different matter. It is not just that the decisions are "bigger," involving larger financial risks. The entire structure of the planning system is different and requires a different approach. There are several reasons for this:

1. Planning models are multivariate and multiequation and include many different interrelated environmental variables. The forecaster must be sure the forecasts of the different environmental variables are internally consistent.

2. Planning time horizons are longer; actions taken by the manager can affect the external environment and thus the forecast. Forecasts will be conditional of the form: *If $X* are spent on advertising, *then* sales will be *Y* units.

3. Longer forecast horizons allow the use of leading indicators. Changes in one environmental variable may be preceded by changes in another. For example, changes in demand for a product sold in an industrial market can be preceded by changes in customer's sales or levels of activity. When planning time horizons are short, there may be no time to take advantage of the information in a leading indicator even if it were available. With longer planning horizons, such information takes on special value.

4. Because of the complexities of the model, the range of environmental factors that must be considered is greater. Because of the longer time horizons, the range of possible or probable environmental changes is increased. Looking one month ahead, demand for a specific product may change, but the underlying economic and social factors affecting that demand, such as the general level of employment or consumer tastes, can usually be expected to remain essentially the same. This need not and usually will not be true when the forecast horizon is six months to several years.

For these reasons, simple projection models tend to be of limited use. In developing a pro forma budget, for example, there are minor cost elements that do not have much impact on the overall model but for which some forecast is still necessary. For these, simple projection methods are still adequate. For the environmental variables that are central to the model, this is not true and a different approach is needed.

Major Points to be Noted

1. *The different techniques of fitting a model to data.*
2. *The measures and statistical tests that can be used to determine the adequacy of that fit.*
3. *The extension of this approach to models with more than one independent variable.*

MODELS AND MODELING

Planning models of the type being considered here consist of sets of mathematical equations. Without going into detail on the nature and construction of the models, it will be helpful to note some characteristics of the equations that are of special interest to the forecaster. First, from the point of view of structure, planning model equations can be classified as one of four types:

1. Definitions
2. Institutional relationships
3. Theory-based relationships
4. Empirically developed relationships

Definitions are equations that establish or interpret concepts within the overall model or that act to establish the units in which variables are expressed. As a practical matter, the large majority of relationships within any planning model tend to be definitions. For example, in Chapter 5, the relationship

Gross profit = net sales − cost of goods sold

was of this type; that is, it identified the specific operation necessary to obtain a number that was called "gross profit." Definitions tend to be of little interest to the forecaster except as they specify the level of aggregation of the specific units that must be used in forecast development.

Institutional relationships are defined by law, custom, or contract. In the pro forma income statement of Chapter 5, if we had carried the example further to include the calculation of corporate taxes due and contribution to retained earnings, it would have been necessary to make use of the federal corporate tax rate tables, an institutional relationship. Similarly, in calculating the cost of goods sold, the wage rates and possible overtime payments to be used might have been specified in a union contract—another institutional relationship. The forecasting of possible changes in institutional relationships is often of major concern to the planner. It is not an issue that can be addressed by the methods of this chapter, but it will be relevant to the methods discussed in Chapter 11.

Theory-based relationships most frequently arise in describing physical systems where the underlying structure of the process is well known. In determining cost of goods sold, it is necessary to convert the concept "number of units produced" into specific costs—of raw materials, of labor, and of equipment. The *structure* of the relationships needed for these conversions may be known, and yet it may still be necessary to forecast the values of the specific numbers to be inserted into the equations. Often these values tend to be relatively fixed so that we speak of "estimating" rather than of forecasting them. In some cases, as for example when production technologies are changing, it may become a problem for the forecaster.

Empirically developed relationships are of most interest to the forecaster. When we talk about the external environment, we are usually focusing on economic, social, and political issues where little is known about the structure of the relationships. The forecaster is faced with a fourfold question: Is there a relationship among the specified variables? What is the structural form of that relationship (assuming that it exists)? What are the appropriate values for the coefficients? and, finally, How sure can we be that the relationship is not just a historical artifact and that it will, in fact, continue to exist in a similar form in the future?

A second distinction of importance to the forecaster relates to the different uses of model equations that can:

- describe the internal structure of the organization;
- deal with the structure of the external environment;
- deal with interactions between the external environment and the internal structure of the organization.

In the type of operational planning considered here, the most important external environments are the economic, the political, and the social. For the planner/forecaster, it is useful to distinguish between the general structure of these external environments and the structure of the specific interfaces or forums where the organization interacts with its external environment. In the area of economics, for example, it is helpful to distinguish among the analysis and forecasting of the general economic environment common to all organizations (the general price levels, the overall levels of economic activity in the country or region, the levels of unemployment, interest rates and money supply), the forecasting of conditions in specific markets (for labor, financial capital, raw materials, the sale of finished products), and the forecasting of events and changes in the various nonmarket forums, such as interactions with government regulatory agencies, where the organization operates and where actions of the organization can directly or indirectly influence conditions in the markets or decisions of the agencies.

For forecasting general environmental conditions, the planner can make use of outside organizations and consultants that specialize in such forecasting; for forecasts of events and trends in specific markets and interaction forums, the planner/forecaster must look to internal resources and systems.

ANALYZING RELATIONSHIPS

In working with empirically based relationships, a distinction must be made between causal and covariant relationships. Ideally, we would like to develop models that describe the actual causal structure of the system that we are studying. More often than not this is not possible, either because the structure is unknown or because the data necessary for the practical implementation of the model are unobtainable. A good example of this is the use of an equation involving calendar time to describe a trend. In an equation such as

$$Y_t = a + bt \tag{1}$$

which is commonly used to model a linear trend, there is no intent to suggest that time in the form of the variable t *causes* the variable Y. Rather it will have been noticed that, for whatever reason, Y has been increasing (or decreasing) over time by more-or-less constant increments b and, in the absence of any reason to the contrary, the forecaster decides to assume that this pattern will continue. Contrast this to an equation that attempts to relate the sale of automobile tires to new car sales, numbers of cars currently registered, and total miles driven. In this latter case, it can be argued that all these variables should have a direct causal link to the demand for tires.

Other useful distinctions are between relationships that involve only a single variable as opposed to multivariate relationships and between relationships that are expressed in a single equation and those that require a system of equations. In this chapter we are primarily concerned with single-equation bivariate and multivariate relationships.

Exploratory Versus Confirmatory Data Analysis

In recent years a distinction has developed between the exploratory and confirmatory uses of statistics in data analysis. This distinction has important ramifications for the forecaster. In confirmatory analysis, the model is developed independently of the data from knowledge of the underlying structure of the system or by analogy with similar situations observed in the past. For example, it is known that many populations grow at a constant rate (for reasons that will be developed in Chapter 12). A forecaster projecting the future population of an area might therefore propose using the constant growth-rate model

$$Y_t = A(1 + r)^t \tag{2}$$

as described in Chapter 4. The forecaster would still need to estimate the coefficients A and r and confirm whether or not the model was, in fact, an adequate representation of the data.

On the other hand, a forecaster modeling the relationship between the demand for a product, its price, and consumer disposable income might believe that such a relationship existed but have little or no idea of the form of that relationship. In this latter case, it would be necessary to use the data to explore and guide the development of the relationship model.

This chapter is concerned solely with problems of fitting and testing a prespecified model, that is, with confirmatory data analysis. Chapters 8 and 9 then look at some elementary aspects of the exploratory use of data.

Linear Models

Throughout the following chapters we will be referring to the fitting of linear models. It is important to note that this does not mean that we are only interested in fitting straight lines. The term *linear* refers to the *coefficients* of the model, not the *variables*. Thus

$$Y_t = a + b_1(X_{1t}^2) + b_2\ \frac{X_{2t}}{X_{1t}} \tag{3}$$

is a linear equation because the coefficients a, b_1, and b_2 are multiplied by the terms 1, (X_{1t}^2), and X_{2t} / X_{1t} and summed. By contrast, the equations

$$Y_t = Ab^t \tag{4a}$$

and

$$Y_t = At^b \tag{4b}$$

are not because the coefficient b enters in one case raised to a power and in the other case as an exponent.[1]

In equation (3), X_{1t} and X_{2t} are the independent *variables* and X_{1t}^2 and X_{2t}/X_{1t} are the *carriers* of the linear model.[2]

TECHNIQUES FOR FITTING MODELS

It will be useful to start by examining two techniques for fitting and checking simple linear relationships involving just two variables, *least squares* and *median fit*. Later we will see how these can be applied in more complex situations. We must start by deciding which is to be considered the independent variable X and which the dependent Y. In most cases the forecaster will consider the variable that is to be forecasted as the dependent and the other(s) as independent. In some models the choice will be based on assumptions about the direction of causation; in other cases the choice will depend on which variables occur earlier in time or for which data can be independently obtained.

To develop these two techniques, we will use cross-sectional data, that is, data collected at one point in time, to avoid some of the particular problems that arise in analyzing relationships among time series. We will return to problems of times series and forecasting in Chapter 8.

Imagine a chain of medium-sized clothing stores located in 11 cities throughout the Midwest. Although some planning decisions are made centrally, historically, most operating decisions have been left in the hands of the local managers. A central budgeting model is now being developed. As an input to this model, it is decided to look at the effect of local sales promotion expenditures on sales growth. The data for the 11 stores for 1986 are shown in Table 7-1 (p. 206).

Scatter Diagram

A primary tool in searching for and confirming relationships between two variables is the *scatter diagram*, a simple two-dimensional plot of the data points being analyzed. Figure 7-1 (p. 207) shows the scatter diagram for the data of Table 7-1; each point relates to a specific store. It can be seen that there is a general tendency for the pattern of points to slope upward to the right, suggesting that stores that spent more on sales promo-

[1]On the other hand, both of these equations can be "made" linear by using the log transform discussed in Chapter 4.

[2]See Mosteller and Tukey, pg. 267ff

TABLE 7–1

Sales and Sales Promotion Expenditures for Eleven Clothing
Stores, Arranged in Increasing Order of Amounts Spent on Sales
Promotion

Store Location	Sales Promotion Expenditures X (% of gross sales)	Sales Increase Y (%)
A	0.26	9.58
B	0.64	10.83
C	1.07	10.67
D	1.22	14.33
E	1.41	0.17
F	1.82	8.42
G	2.03	12.33
H	2.68	18.25
J	4.23	23.58
K	5.03	19.75
M	5.08	21.17

tion also had greater increases in sales. It needs to be stressed, however, that *covariation* in a scatter diagram says nothing about causation. Here, for example, stores that in 1985 (correctly) forecasted increases in demand and thus greater revenues were perhaps willing to spend more on sales promotion so that the true direction of causation was actually from the "dependent" variable of (expected) sales increase to the "independent" one of sales promotion expenditures.

Fitting a Linear Equation

The intent of modeling is to express the relationship that appears in the scatter diagram by a mathematical equation. As with the decomposition of a time series discussed in Chapter 3, we are interested in separating the observed variability in the dependent variable (change in sales) into two parts, a pattern of *covariation* between the independent variable and sales promotion and the *residual* or random noise that arises from other factors not yet identified.

$$\text{Observed change in sales} = \text{pattern} + \text{noise} \qquad (5)$$

or, in symbols,

$$Y_i = \hat{Y}_i + e_i \qquad (6)$$

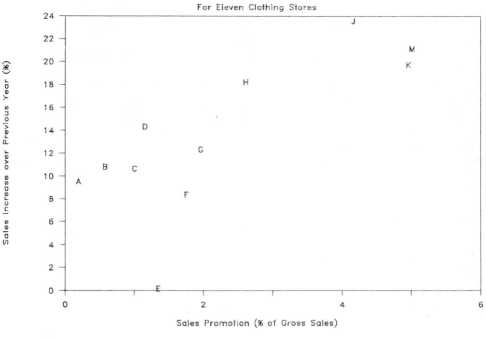

FIGURE 7-1

Sales increases and sales promotion for eleven clothing stores

where the subscript i refers to a specific store. In this section we start by assuming that the pattern can be expressed by a linear equation of the form

$$\hat{Y}_i = a + bX_i \qquad (7)$$

In fitting this model to the data, we would like to include as much of the variation in Y as possible in the pattern part $\hat{Y}$ and keep the residual e as small as possible.

Least-squares Fitting

Least squares is the single most used approach in the statistical modeling of data; it is used in most computer-based statistical and forecasting programs and is also built into many hand calculators. Because of this, it can be used by the planner/manager for simple desk-top analyses, as well as by the technical analyst in the development of large-scale computer models.

The idea underlying this method is that the residuals e can be made small and the patterned component $\hat{Y}$ large by *minimizing* the sum of the *squares* of the residuals, Σe_i^2, where $e_i = Y_i - \hat{Y}_i$. It is called for this reason, least squares.

For the equation

$$\hat{Y} = a + bX \tag{8}$$

this leads to equations for a and b of

$$b = \frac{\Sigma XY - \overline{Y}\Sigma X}{\Sigma X^2 - \overline{X}\Sigma X} \tag{9}$$

and

$$a = \overline{Y} - b\overline{X} \tag{10}$$

The details of the calculations can be seen in Table 7-2. This gives the equation

$$\hat{Y} = 6.61 + 3.00X \tag{11}$$

Residuals are obtained by subtracting $\hat{Y}$ from Y as shown in the table and can then be used in measuring the degree of fit of the model. The least-squares line is shown in Figure 7-2a (p. 210), with the residuals e shown by the vertical lines connecting the individual points to the fitted line. Figure 7-2b (p. 211) compares the variability of the original data with that of the

TABLE 7–2

Least-squares Calculations

Sums and Sums of Squares		*Least-squares Results*	
$\Sigma X =$	25.47	Constant (a)	6.61
$\Sigma X^2 =$	7165.6698	Slope (b)	3.00
$\Sigma Y =$	149.08	Standard error	
$\Sigma Y^2 =$	244931.4000	of estimate	4.60
$\Sigma XY =$	434.4550	R^2	0.58
		F value	4.92
		Critical (0.05) value	4.26
		No. of observations	11
		Degrees of freedom	9

residuals. With the exception of store E, the individual points seem reasonably close to the line and the variability of the residuals substantially less than that of the original observations. Notice that store E appears as an outlier in the residuals but not in the original data.

Fitting Relationships with Medians

Least squares suffers from a number of problems of particular concern to the forecaster and planner. At a mechanical level, if the planner/manager does not have either a computer or suitable calculator handy, hand calculation for the least-squares approach is not particularly convenient. Far more important, because forecasters must often work with rather limited amounts of data, least squares, because it is based on the *squares* of the residuals, is very sensitive to outliers. Here, because of the inclusion of store E, the line has been shifted downward and there has been a substantial effect on the slope of the line as well.

To deal with the effects of outliers on the fitting of relationship models, a number of techniques termed *robust* or *resistant* have been developed. The majority of these require substantial amounts of calculation and are only now becoming available in microcomputer or calculator form. One such method, however, is easily adapted to hand calculation and has the added advantage that it can be fitted graphically to a plotted scatter diagram.[3] This can be a particular advantage when making rough estimates of relationships. The approach is called the *median fit*.

Graphical Fitting. We will find it useful to start with the direct fitting of a line to a graph and will then develop the computational equivalent of that graphical procedure.

Start by separating the points on the scatter diagram into three groups based on the X variable as shown by the vertical lines in Figure 7-3a (p. 212). The sizes of these groups should be as nearly equal as possible, and the groups of the largest and smallest X values should be the same size. Here there are 11 points, so the end groups contain 4 points each and the middle group 3. If there had been only 10 points, the end groups would have had 3 points and the middle group 4; with 9 or 12 points, all the groups would have been equal in size.

Next find the median of the four smallest X values (the group to the left) and draw a short vertical line as shown. For the same group of points, find the median of the Y values and draw a horizontal line to form a small cross. Repeat the process for the rightmost group. Notice that, with an

---

[3]In Chapter 5, the standard deviation was estimated by fitting a line to the cumulative frequency distribution as plotted on probability paper. Because the vertical scale was not linear, the graphical approach was particularly convenient.

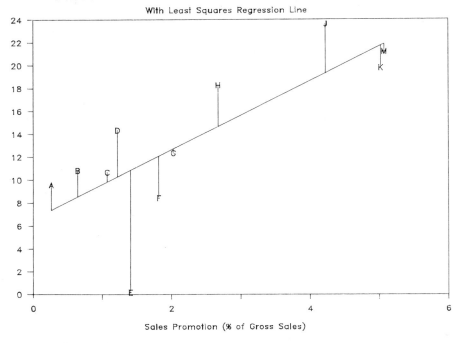

Sales Increases and Sales Promotion
With Least Squares Regression Line

Sales Increase over Previous Year (%)

Sales Promotion (% of Gross Sales)

FIGURE 7-2a

Sales increases and sales promotion with least-squares regression line

even number of points, the medians lie halfway between the middle two X or Y values.

Now, as in Figure 7-3b (p. 213), lay a straightedge across the two crosses as shown by the dashed line (it is helpful if the straightedge is transparent). Notice that 5 points lie above the line and 6 below. Move the straightedge parallel to the line through the two crosses until there are 5 points on each side of the line and one point (the median point) exactly on the line. Draw in this line as shown; this is the *median fit* line.

Computing the Median Fit.   Table 7-3 (p. 214) gives the computational equivalent of this graphical procedure. First, the data for the 11 stores should be rearranged so that the X values are in increasing order. Next, horizontal lines are drawn that separate the data into three groups, just as on the graph of Figure 7-3a.

The medians of the X and Y values for the top and bottom groups are determined and the slope b obtained by

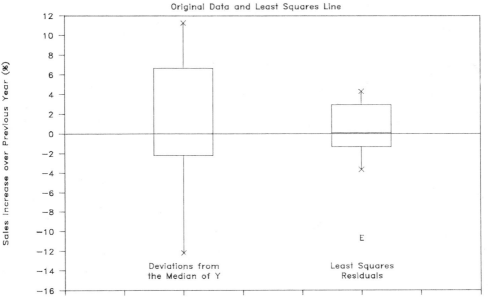

FIGURE 7-2b

Comparison of residuals

$$b = \frac{\text{median } Y \text{ for bottom group } - \text{ median } Y \text{ for top group}}{\text{median } X \text{ for bottom group } - \text{ median } X \text{ for top group}}$$

(12)

$$= \frac{(19.75 + 21.17)/2 - (10.67 + 10.83)/2}{(4.23 + 5.03)/2 - (0.64 + 1.07)/2}$$

$$= 2.56$$

From each value of Y, b times the corresponding X is subtracted and the median of these values determined. This median, 8.11, is the intercept a. This value of a is then subtracted from the last column to obtain the residuals shown.

Figure 7-4 (p. 215) shows box-and-whisker diagrams for the residuals for both the median and the least-squares fits, as well as the original Y data. As might be expected from the previous discussion, the median least-squares residual is greater than zero to compensate for the low outlier. Also, the shapes of the two residual distributions are quite different. Because the least-squares approach is sensitive to the larger residuals, the overall range of residuals is smaller than for the median fit. At the same time, the "box" or central 50% of the residuals is clearly wider.

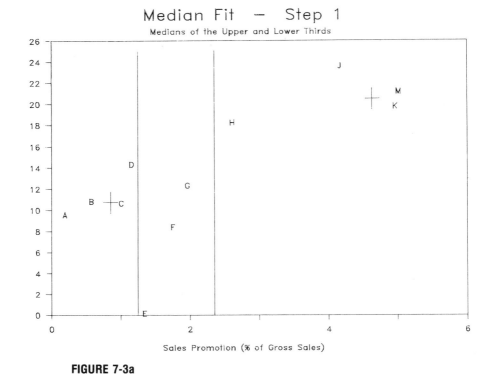

FIGURE 7-3a

Step 1: Medians of the upper and lower thirds

Other Robust Techniques.   One easy way of dealing with outliers is to simply discard them. Table 7-4 (p. 215) gives the *a* and *b* values for four different fitting procedures: least squares and median fit, with and without the inclusion of store E. Figure 7-4 (p. 215) shows the residuals. Notice that the median fit is much less affected by the inclusion of store E. With store E omitted, however, the two procedures give basically similar results.

A rule of thumb that is often suggested is to initially try both approaches. If there is little difference between the two, then use the least-squares method because of its convenience. If the two approaches give substantially different results, then either omit the outliers or use some robust method of fitting.[4]

Although the median-fit approach can be very useful for the quick estimation of relationship models, more effective robust methods are in-

---

[4]In either case the outliers should not be completely discarded but should be the subject of a separate study to determine why they are outliers.

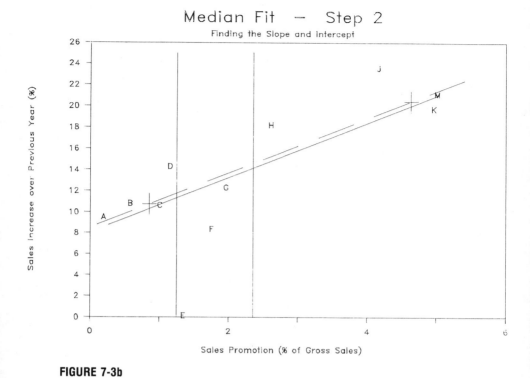

FIGURE 7-3b

Step 2: Finding the slope and intercept

creasingly becoming available. These generally involve the use of weighted averages; the data points on the scatter diagram are given weights inversely related to their distances from the fitted line. Points close to the line are given high weights; outliers are included, but with small weights, so that their influence on the fit of the line is small. The problem with these methods is that the line must first be fitted to determine the weights and the weights then used to refit the line. Because this process must be repeated several times, the use of a computer is essential.

MODEL FIT: MEASURES AND TESTS

Central to the process of modeling are the measures that enable the user to evaluate the degree to which a given model fits or identifies patterns in data. In confirmatory analysis, we start by assuming a particular model and that the residuals are random and follow a specified probability distribution

TABLE 7-3

Median-fit Computation

Store	Sales Promotion Expenditures (% of gross sales) X	Sales Increase (%) Y	Medians X_M	Medians Y_M	$Y - bX$	Residual
A	0.26	9.58			8.92	0.81
B	0.64	10.83			9.18	1.07
C	1.07	10.67	0.86	10.75	7.92	-0.19
D	1.22	14.33			11.20	3.09
E	1.41	0.17			-3.46	-11.57
F	1.82	8.42			3.74	-4.37
G	2.03	12.33			7.12	-0.99
H	2.68	18.25			11.37	3.26
J	4.23	23.58			12.72	4.60
K	5.03	19.75	4.63	20.46	6.82	-1.29
M	5.08	21.17			8.11	0.00

$b = (20.46 - 10.75) / (4.63 - 0.86) = 2.576$

$a = 8.11$

214

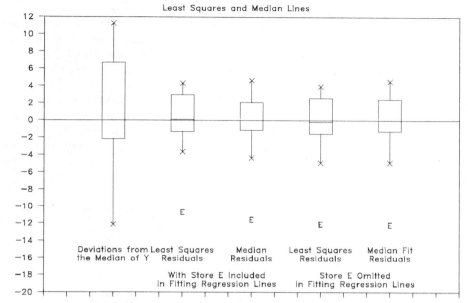

FIGURE 7-4

Comparison of residuals: Least squares and median lines

TABLE 7–4

Intercepts and Slopes for Four Fitting Procedures

Least Squares	*Median Fit*
With store E included	With store E included
$Y_i = 6.61 + 3.00X_i$	$Y_i = 8.11 + 2.58X_i$
With store E omitted	With store E omitted
$Y_i = 8.56 + 2.63X_i$	$-Y_i = 8.99 + 2.40X_i$

(usually normal). It is then necessary to have measures that can test, formally or informally, the correctness of these assumptions.

In exploratory analysis, which will be discussed in Chapter 8, we start with very simple models and, by examining the available data, gradually develop models that we hope will more accurately describe the process of interest. In this, a number of questions arise: How well does a particular tentative model fit the data? Does some alternative model fit better? Will a particular modification improve the model? How much improvement? Answers to these questions also require measures of model fit.

Interpretation of any measures must be done cautiously. In exploratory model development, it is very easy to *overfit*. Overfitting means to develop a model that not only describes underlying persistent patterns (of potential use to the forecaster), but also includes idiosyncracies unique to the specific data set analyzed, which are not likely to recur. Measures of model fit can help in deciding whether an improvement in the model is large enough to be treated seriously or whether it is only a relatively insignificant mechanical improvement. They are *not* directed toward the more fundamental question of whether the relationship under study might not be simply an artifact of the data and the forecaster's analysis. We turn to this question in Chapter 9.

Finally, measures of model fit are of only limited value in dealing with the forecaster's most critical question: How accurate is a particular model likely to be in predicting the future? This also is an issue for Chapter 9.

Degrees of Freedom

Forecasters almost never have as much data as they would like for model development because the process of modeling actually "uses up" the data. A major cause of overfitting is, in fact, the development of model complexity beyond that which can be supported by the available data.

As an example, suppose that, instead of 11, we only had 2 stores A and F. If we were to try to fit the previous equation, we could the use the values of X and Y for those stores from Table 7-1 and solve simultaneously the two equations

$$9.58 = a + 0.26b$$

$$8.42 = a + 1.82b \tag{13}$$

to obtain $a = 9.77$ and $b = -0.744$ even if no relationship of any kind existed between the two variables. As more and more complex models are fitted to the data, it is important for the model builder to keep track of what might be called the "effective remaining sample," but which is more commonly referred to as *degrees of freedom*.

In the simple confirmatory analysis considered here, the degrees of freedom are obtained by subtracting from the original sample size the number of unidentified coefficients estimated from the data. In this example, data exist for 11 stores, less the 2 coefficients a and b, leaving an effective sample size or degrees of freedom of 9.

Although seldom treated explicitly, a similar problem exists in exploratory analysis. With data for 11 stores, were we to try 11 different models and choose the "best," we would use up our sample just as thoroughly as if we had tried to fit a model with 11 different coefficients.

In time-series analysis, another problem exists as well. By original sample size, we mean the number of original *independent* observations. In this example, presumably we could increase the sample size to 131 observations by simply using monthly rather than annual sales and sales promotion data. Because sales and sales promotion in successive months for a given store would not be independent, although some increase in the effective sample size might result, it would not be 12 times as large.

Graphical Checks

Least-squares analysis and the confirmatory tests we will discuss shortly are most commonly based on assumptions that the residuals are normally distributed with a standard deviation whose magnitude is not changing over time and is not related to the X or independent variables. It is also assumed that there are no outliers to distort the fit of the model. While formal tests of these assumptions are available, simple graphical checks can be helpful. In this chapter we have already used the box-and-whisker diagram in observing the effects of the different modeling approaches on the residuals, in identifying a possible outlier, and in seeing the effects of omitting that outlier from the analysis. Similarly, in Chapter 3 we considered the use of time-series plots of the residuals and the absolute values of the residuals in observing possible changes over time. In Chapter 8 we consider additional residual plots that can be used in model evaluation.

Least-squares-based Measures and Tests

Standard Error of Estimate. Just as the standard deviation

$$S_y = \left(\frac{[\Sigma Y^2 - \overline{Y}\Sigma Y]}{n-1}\right)^{\frac{1}{2}} \tag{14}$$

is used to measure the variability of a single variable Y, so the standard deviation of the residuals e can be used as a simple measure of variability of the residuals and thus of model fit. This measure is called the *standard error of estimate* and is given by

$$S_e = \left(\frac{\Sigma e^2}{degrees\ of\ freedom}\right)^{\frac{1}{2}} \tag{15}$$

Here

$$S_e = \left(\frac{190.42}{9}\right)^{\frac{1}{2}} = 4.60 \tag{16}$$

One aim of modeling is to make the standard error of estimate as small as possible. Note, however, that increasing the complexity of the model affects the degrees of freedom, so it is actually possible to "improve" the model only to have the standard error increase.

As with all the measures we are considering here, the usefulness of the measure depends on the appropriateness of the underlying assumptions. As we saw earlier, the method of least squares minimizes a sum of squared residuals Σe^2, where all the residuals are weighted equally. If there are outliers or if the residuals are changing systematically as in the airline passenger-miles carried example of Chapter 3, the results will be dominated by the larger (and presumably poorer) residuals. In the same way, the standard error of estimate will reflect the influence of the larger residuals in a disproportionate way.

Coefficient of Determination.   The standard error of estimate cannot be easily used to make comparisons between situations involving different dependent variables because it is expressed in the units of the dependent variable. An alternative unitless number is the coefficient of determination, sometimes referred to as *R squared*.

This measure can be interpreted as the proportion of the original variance (the square of the standard deviation) that can be associated with the model. Presumably, the greater this proportion, the more of the original variance that has been "explained" by the model and therefore the better the model.

Ignoring for the moment the degrees of freedom, the original variance of the Y variable was

$$\Sigma Y^2 - \overline{Y}\Sigma Y = 2478.73 - (13.55)(149.08) = 458.70 \tag{17}$$

By fitting the model, this was reduced to $\Sigma e^2 = 190.42$. The proportional reduction was

$$R^2 = \frac{458.70 - 190.42}{458.70} = 0.58 \tag{18}$$

a 58% reduction in the variance as a result of fitting the model.

F Test.   An important question in confirmatory analysis is: Could the results observed (the fit of the model) have been obtained solely by chance? Although a complete discussion of the question of statistical significance is beyond the scope of this chapter, an outline of the argument can be developed.

We start by assuming that the hypothesized relationship (here $Y_t = a + bX_t$) does *not* exist. Based on that assumption, a test statistic and its probability distribution are developed. A value for the test statistic is calculated for the fitted model. If the value obtained seems inconsistent with the assumption of *no* relationship, we decide that there is probable cause for believing that the relationship does exist.

In model fitting, the most common test is based on the *F* statistic obtained by

$$F = \frac{R^2}{1 - R^2} \frac{n - k}{k} \tag{19}$$

where *n* is the original sample size, *k* is the number of coefficients in the model, and $n - k$ is the degrees of freedom. Here

$$F = \frac{0.58}{1 - 0.58} \frac{9}{2} = 4.92 \tag{20}$$

Appendix Table A2 gives the values of *F* that should be exceeded no more than one time in twenty (0.05) if, in fact, no relationship of the form modeled exists. For this example, that value is 4.26. Since the value calculated in equation (20) is greater than this, we can conclude that there is a reasonable chance that a relationship as modeled actually exists.

MULTIPLE REGRESSION

The least-squares method of fitting can easily be extended to models with more than one independent variable. The actual calculations are beyond the scope of this chapter and, in any case, would never be carried out by hand; microcomputer versions are readily available.

Suppose that, for the previous example, 3 years of sales data were available for each of the 11 stores, as shown in Table 7-5 (p. 220). To allow for the possibility of a trend in sales apart from any changes in sales promotion expenditure, it is decided to use a model of the form

$$Y_t = a + b_1 X_{1t} + b_2 X_{2t} + e_t \tag{21}$$

where X_{1t} is a time trend with values 1 in 1984, 2 in 1985, and 3 in 1986, and X_{2t} is sales promotion expenditure as before. The results are shown in the table. The fitted equation is

$$\hat{Y}_t = 6.13 + 3.69X_{1t} + 2.95X_{2t} \tag{22}$$

It can be seen that the fit is apparently poorer than before. The standard error of estimate has increased to 8.80 and R^2 has decreased to 0.37. The *F* statistic, however, has increased due to the increase in the effective sample size. Examination of Figure 7-5 suggests a reason for this result. While overall the relationship appears much as before, there now appear to be four distinct outliers, B3, K3, M2, and M3.

Testing Individual Coefficients

When fitting models with two or more independent variables, it is useful to test each *b* coefficient separately for significance. Table 7-5 gives, for each coefficient, its associated standard error. For each, the ratio be-

TABLE 7–5

(a) Multiple Regression Analysis

Year	Store Location and Year	Sales Increases $Y(\%)$	Year $X1$	Sales Promotion Expenditures: $X2$ (% of gross sales)
1984	A1	9.58	1	0.26
	B1	10.83	1	0.64
	C1	10.67	1	1.07
	D1	14.33	1	1.22
	E1	0.17	1	1.41
	F1	8.42	1	1.82
	G1	12.33	1	2.03
	H1	18.25	1	2.68
	J1	23.58	1	4.23
	K1	19.75	1	5.03
	M1	21.17	1	5.08
1985	A2	4.98	2	0.63
	B2	12.23	2	1.23
	C2	0.07	2	0.09
	D2	20.53	2	3.17
	E2	16.40	2	0.88
	F2	14.62	2	1.52
	G2	4.93	2	1.42
	H2	16.45	2	5.30
	J2	16.18	2	3.02
	K2	22.35	2	4.72
	[a]M2	39.77	2	5.37
1986	A3	− 0.82	3	0.48
	[a]B3	26.83	3	0.34
	C3	17.87	3	1.03
	D3	17.53	3	1.67
	E3	19.00	3	2.23
	F3	14.82	3	1.22
	G3	1.13	3	0.68
	H3	16.25	3	4.55
	J3	22.78	3	6.47
	[a]K3	37.35	3	3.52
	[a]M3	45.57	3	2.60

[a]Probable Outliers

(continued on next page)

Table 7-5 (Continued)

(b) Least-squares results

		Standard Error	*t* Value	*Critical (P = 0.05) Value*
Constant (*a*)	1.92			
Slopes				
Time (*b*₁)	3.25	1.87	1.74	2.042
Sales				
Promotion (*b*₂)	3.33	0.86	3.88	
Standard error				
of estimate	8.76			
*R*²	0.37			
F value	5.96			2.92
No. of observations	33			
Degrees of freedom	30			

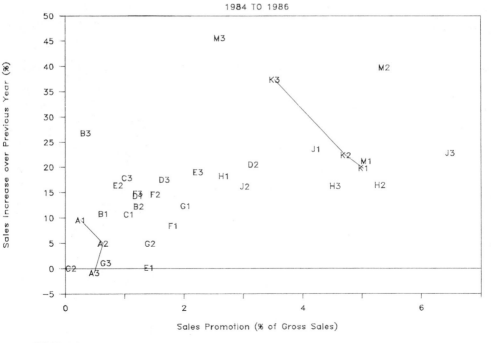

FIGURE 7-5

Sales increases and sales promotion, 1984–1986

tween the coefficient and its standard error gives a test statistic referred to as t. The probability distribution of t is given in Appendix Table A3. With 30 degrees of freedom, the critical value of t (similar to the critical F value just discussed) is 2.042. It can be seen that b_2 with a t value of 3.88 is significant and should be kept in the model, while b_1 has a t value of only 1.74 and could be dropped.

The reason for this can be seen in Figure 7-5. The sequences of points for stores A and K have been connected and appear to have quite different time trends. For store A, sales promotion has remained relatively constant while the sales increases have decreased. For store K, sales promotion expenditures have decreased while sales have actually increased. The reader may wish to similarly connect the point sequences for the other nine stores. It will be seen that no two stores have similar trend patterns.

SUMMARY

This chapter has introduced a few simple techniques for fitting and evaluating relationship models. Chapter 8 explores some of the special problems that can arise in applying these methods in the study of time series and develops an exploratory approach to modeling. Chapter 9 looks at problems of model evaluation as they relate directly to the problems of forecasting.

READINGS

Techniques for Analyzing Relationships

Techniques for fitting models by the method of least squares are covered in almost all statistics and forecasting texts. A good introduction can be found in

> SPYROS MAKRIDAKIS, STEVEN C. WHEELWRIGHT, and VICTOR E. McGEE, *Forecasting: Methods and Applications*, 2nd ed., New York, Wiley, 1983, Part 3.

Useful texts at a more advanced level would include

> DALE G. BAILS and LARRY C. PEPPERS, *Business Fluctuations*, Englewood Cliffs, N.J., Prentice-Hall, 1982.
> ROBERT S. PINDYCK and DANIEL L. RUBINFELD, *Econometric Models and Economic Forecasts*, New York, McGraw-Hill, 1976.

Simple and multiple regression procedures based on least squares are widely available in microcomputer software packages. These range from the "bare-bones" procedures, such as the one now included in Lotus 1-2-3 Release 2 and used here, to advanced packages often combined with other statistical or econometric programs for time series analysis and forecasting.

Material on median fitting can be found in

> DONALD R. MCNEIL, *Interactive Data Analysis*, New York, Wiley, 1977, Chapter 3.

> PAUL F. VELLEMAN and DAVID C. HOAGLIN, *Applications, Basics, and Computing of Exploratory Data Analysis*, Boston, Duxbury Press, 1981, Chapter 5.

If you wish to pursue the topic of robust methods further, good introductory discussions can be found in

> HANS LEVENBACH and JAMES P. CLEARY, *The Beginning Forecaster*, Belmont, Calif., Lifetime Learning, 1981, Chapter 17.

> FREDERICK MOSTELLER and JOHN W. TUKEY, *Data Analysis and Regression*, Reading, Mass., Addison-Wesley, 1977, Chapter 14.

A procedure for identifying and rejecting outliers, based on least squares and suggested as an alternative to robust regression, is developed as part of the STATGRAPHICS® program developed by STSC, Inc., Rockville, Md. This package also includes a wide variety of other models for time-series analysis and forecasting.

PROBLEMS

1. You have been given the following deseasonalized quarterly sales data:

Sales in Thousands of Dollars

1982	I	178	1985	I	293
	II	190		II	313
	III	217		III	327
	IV	209		IV	332
1983	I	214	1986	I	344
	II	221		II	351
	III	219		III	351
	IV	234		IV	354
1984	I	242			
	II	249			
	III	271			
	IV	278			

a. Plot the sales data and fit a linear trend.

b. Plot the residuals and analyze using a box-and-whisker plot. Mark any outliers for future reference.

c. Using this trend, develop a projection for the first quarter of 1987.

d. Develop a scatter diagram of the residuals by plotting each residual (starting with the second quarter of 1982) against the residual for the preceding quarter. Fit a linear relationship to this scatter diagram and determine the residuals from this relationship. Compare against the residuals from part b.

e. Use this information to develop a new projection for the first quarter of 1987. How does it compare with your projection in part c?

f. For the original data, remove the trend by differencing. Again, develop a box-and-whisker diagram of the residuals and a projection for the first quarter of 1987. How do these compare to your earlier results?

2. You have been asked to develop projections for the Consumer Price Index through 1990 and have the following data:

Year	CPI(W)	% Change
1962	90.6	1.12%
1963	91.7	1.21%
1964	92.9	1.31%
1965	94.5	1.72%
1966	97.2	2.86%
1967	100.0	2.88%
1968	104.2	4.20%
1969	109.8	5.37%
1970	116.3	5.92%
1971	121.3	4.30%
1972	125.3	3.30%
1973	133.1	6.23%
1974	147.7	10.97%
1975	161.2	9.14%
1976	170.5	5.77%
1977	181.5	6.45%
1978	195.3	7.60%
1979	217.7	11.47%
1980	247.0	13.46%
1981	272.3	10.24%
1982	288.6	5.99%
1983	297.4	3.05%
1984	307.6	3.43%

a. For the percent change in the index, fit a trend line using the method of least squares.

b. Repeat part a using the median-fit method. Compare coefficients obtained by the two methods.

c. Find the residuals for each method and compare by graphing the residuals and using box-and-whisker diagrams.

d. Using each line, develop projections for 1985 through 1990 for both the percent change and the index. For the latter you will need to successively multiply $(1 + \%$ change$)$ by the index value for the preceding year. Compare your results.

e. Discuss the implications of your results for the use of the least-squares method.

3. Repeat Problem 2, using CPI(W) and an appropriate transformation to make the trend linear. How do your results compare to those obtained in Problem 2?

4. Using the median-fit method, fit a line to the data of Table 7-5. Set up a box-and-whisker diagram for the residuals from that line. Compare the slope coefficient to that obtained by least squares and shown in the table. Discuss the implications of your results.

CHAPTER 8

Exploratory
Methods
in Modeling

Chapter 7 outlined a number of procedures for fitting and testing relationships where the form of the relationship could be specified in advance. In the physical sciences and in engineering, there often exists a substantial body of theory that makes this approach to modeling practical. In the social sciences and in management applications, the issue is more difficult. We may have good reason to believe that *some* relationship exists and yet be unsure as to its form. For the example of Chapter 7, we may be convinced that money spent on sales promotion will affect sales and at the same time have no idea whether that impact:

- is linear in the sense that each additional dollar spent has the same impact as the first,

- has a threshhold value so that some minimum amount must be spent before there is any impact,

- occurs immediately or only after some time delay,
- is the same for all stores or depends on the characteristics of the local population.

The model of the form $Y = a + bX$ that was used may be an adequate approximation to the true relationship or it may be completely misleading.

A common procedure is to try a large number of different models and choose the one that appears to give the best fit. Indeed, computer methods exist that can sift rapidly through all the members of some prespecified set of possible models and select the one that gives, for example, the largest F value. This still leaves unanswered the question of how to establish the prespecified model set to be used in the search.

In this chapter, we first consider briefly a model set that is frequently used in univariate (and sometimes in multivariate) modeling and see how it can be used in developing a forecasting model. Then we turn our attention to multivariate modeling and to some of the problems that can complicate the modeling process when dealing with time series. Finally, we introduce a guided approach to multivariate modeling that uses systematic graphical evaluation of model residuals as a way of uncovering underlying model structure.

Important: In exploratory model development, no matter what approach is used, *never* use the same data to develop and to test the model. Exploratory procedures cannot distinguish the "true" underlying structure of a relationship from transient idiosyncracies in the data that may appear "significant" but that are of no value in forecasting. As we will see in Chapter 9, even when data are limited, part of the available data should always be put aside for confirmatory testing.

Major Points to be Noted

1. *Univariate models as an alternative to the smoothing methods discussed in Chapter 6.*
2. *The use of correlograms for detecting time-lagged relationships, that is, relationships involving prior values of a variable.*
3. *The use of connected scatter diagrams to observe the effects of trends and cyclical patterns in time series.*
4. *The use in modeling of residual plots and guided regression as a way of sequentially exploring the importance of different independent variables.*

UNIVARIATE MODELING

In Chapters 3 and 4, with our use of time-series decomposition, we began to explore how univariate or single-variable *models* could be used in time-series analysis and forecasting. The seasonal index and the use of differencing to remove the trend were forms of univariate models. It was only in the analysis of the cyclical component that we shifted our attention to the alternative approach of *smoothing* and the use of moving averages. In this section we again consider the cyclical component and some ways of modeling rather than just smoothing it.

Interest in economic forecasting dates from the latter half of the nineteenth century. During this period the possibility of analyzing and forecasting major economic fluctuations or cycles first came to be of general interest to economists. This led to the use of decomposition procedures to isolate the cyclical component. Early attempts at modeling economic cycles borrowed heavily from the physical sciences, particularly in the use of sine and cosine waves. The first analyses of economic cycles were based on models of the form

$$Y_t = \Sigma\{a_i \sin[\theta_i(t + g_i)]\} + e_t \tag{1}$$

that is, on sums of sine waves of different amplitudes a_i, of different frequencies θ_i, and with different starting points in time g_i. Such a model, however, proved less successful in economics than in the physical sciences, and interest shifted to other alternatives. Two models in particular showed promise, autoregression and moving averages. These were shown to have the ability to generate cyclical movements that were very similar to those obtained using sines or cosines but that could be more easily related to economic concepts. Figure 8–1 shows three different time series generated from the same set of random numbers. The first is a simple sine wave plus random numbers e_t. The second and third are autoregressive and moving-average models generated from the same values of e_t. The specific equations are given in Table 8–1 (p. 230).

The autoregressive model made use of the least-squares fitting procedure already discussed, except that the independent variable(s) were simply lagged values of the dependent variable.

$$Y_t = b_0 + b_1Y_{t-1} + b_2Y_{t-2} + \cdots + e_t \tag{2}$$

It was known that such a model (called a difference equation) could generate cycles similar to those observed in economic data and, as already seen in Figure 8–1, was an alternative to the sine-wave model.

Three Artificial Time Series
Generated From the Same Random Numbers

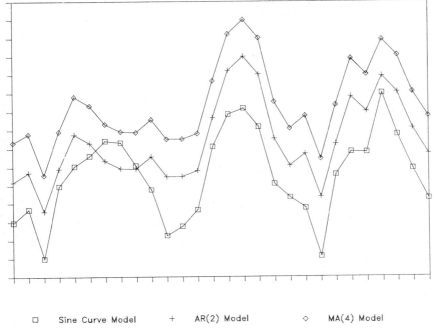

□   Sine Curve Model   +   AR(2) Model   ◇   MA(4) Model

FIGURE 8-1

Three artificial time series generated from the same random numbers

At about the same time, it was also discovered that cycles could be generated by taking moving averages of numbers that were, in themselves, random and without pattern:

$$Y_t = b_0 + e_t + b_1 e_{t-1} + b_2 e_{t-2} + \cdots \tag{3}$$

Notice this is a different use of the term moving average than that of Chapter 4. There it referred to a procedure for smoothing data; here it is a structural element of a model.

Although these were clearly an improvement over the earlier sine-wave models, univariate approaches were still based on empirically observed covariance rather than on theoretical notions of causation.[1] The interest of economists therefore began to shift to the study of multivariate and multiple-equation models as a way of describing economic phenomena.

[1] In contrast to the physical sciences where difference-equation models can be developed from known underlying theoretical physical principles.

TABLE 8–1

Three Alternative Univariate Time-series Models as Shown in Figure 8–1

Sine-curve Model

$$Y_t = 2 \sin \left\{ \frac{2\pi}{9}(t-5) \right\} + e_t$$

Autoregressive [AR(2)] Model

$$Y_t = 0.866\, Y_{t-1} - 0.25 Y_{t-2} + e_t$$

Moving-average [MA (4)] Model

$$Y_t = e_t + 0.866 e_{t-1} + 0.5 e_{t-2} + 0.2165 e_{t-3} + 0.0625 e_{t-4}$$

In the 1970s, interest in univariate modeling was revived by George Box of the University of Wisconsin and the late Gwilym Jenkins of London University. Making use of the electronic computing power not available a century earlier, they combined three separate univariate models, the autoregressive (AR), differencing (I)[2], and moving average (MA), into one that is now referred to as the *ARIMA model*. Equally important, they began an extensive study of the characteristics of this model and developed procedures for determining the appropriate form of the model and for fitting it to empirical data. Although limited to relatively short range forecasting, the ARIMA procedure has now become an important approach to univariate time-series analysis.

Basic Types of ARIMA Forecasting Models

In describing the different types of ARIMA models, it is common to refer to the *order* of the model rather than to the number of independent variables. A first-order autoregressive model denoted AR(1) would be, in its forecasting form,

$$\hat{Y}_t(1) = a + bY_t \tag{4}$$

where, as in Chapter 6, $\hat{Y}_t(1)$ refers to a one-period-ahead forecast made at the end of period t. An AR(2) model would be

$$\hat{Y}_t(1) = a + b_0 Y_t + b_1 Y_{t-1} \tag{5}$$

[2]I stands for integration, another term for summation and the inverse of differencing.

The simple first difference used in Chapters 3 and 4 would be an I(1) model

$$\hat{Y}_t(1) = a + Y_t \tag{6}$$

while the second difference model introduced in Chapter 4 would be denoted as an I(2) model. MA models, in forecasting, make use of past forecast errors, so an MA(1) model would have the form

$$\hat{Y}_t(1) = a + b(Y_t - \hat{Y}_{t-1}(1)) \tag{7}$$

These basic models can be combined in more complex ways. For example, the simple exponential smoothing model of Chapter 6,

$$\hat{Y}_t(1) = \hat{Y}_{t-1} + \alpha(Y_t - \hat{Y}_{t-1}(1)) \tag{8}$$

can also be written in the form

$$\hat{Y}_t(1) = Y_t + b(Y_t - \hat{Y}_{t-1}(1)) \tag{9}$$

an IMA(1, 1) model. Similarly, the Holt model turns out to be based on an IMA(2, 2) model. It is important to note that, although the underlying structures are the same, exponential smoothing methods are not ARIMA models. In the former case, no attempt is made to formally model the underlying structure or estimate "optimal" coefficients. Adaptive forms of exponential smoothing where the coefficients change over time have no direct ARIMA equivalents.

ARIMA Model Identification. An important element of the contribution of Box and Jenkins to univariate modeling was the development of procedures to assist in the identification of the type and order of an ARIMA model appropriate to a particular time series. This is done by studying a graph called a *correlogram*.

In Chapter 7, the coefficient of determination R^2 was introduced as a measure of the strength of a relationship between variables. When only two variables are involved, the square root of the coefficient of determination is called the *coefficient of correlation* and is given the symbol r. When r is used to measure the strength of a relationship between a variable and a lagged value of the same variable, it is called an *autocorrelation coefficient*. Thus the correlation of Y_t with its immediately preceding value Y_{t-1} would be given by[3]

$$r_1 = \frac{\Sigma(Y_t - \hat{Y})(Y_{t-1} - \hat{Y})}{\Sigma(Y_t - \hat{Y})^2} \tag{10}$$

[3]There are several different ways of calculating the autocorrelation coefficient, which give slightly different numerical values. The form used here is the simplest version.

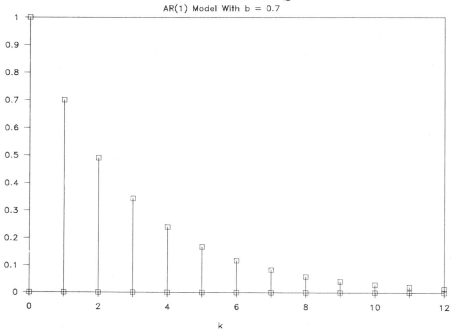

Theoretical Correlogram
AR(1) Model With $b = 0.7$

FIGURE 8-2a

Theoretical correlogram: AR(1) model with $b = 0.7$

and the general term for a lag of k periods would be

$$r_k = \frac{\Sigma(Y_t - \hat{Y})(Y_{t-k} - \hat{Y})}{\Sigma(Y_t - \hat{Y})^2} \qquad (11)$$

Notice that r_0 is automatically equal to 1.

A graph of the values of r_k for different values of k is called a *correlogram*. It is possible to show that each of the basic types of ARIMA models has its own distinctive correlogram, as shown in Figure 8–2. The AR(1) model (Figure 8–2a) can be shown to have the values

$$r_k = b^k \qquad (12)$$

where b is the slope coefficient in the AR(1) model. The MA(1) correlogram (Figure 8–2b) consists of a value of r_1 equal to b with all others equal to zero. Finally, the correlogram for models with an I component (Figure 8–2c) consists of values of r that tend to stay close to 1.

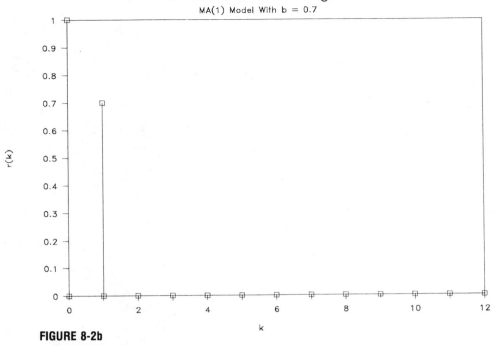

FIGURE 8-2b

Theoretical correlogram: MA(1) model with b $= 0.7$

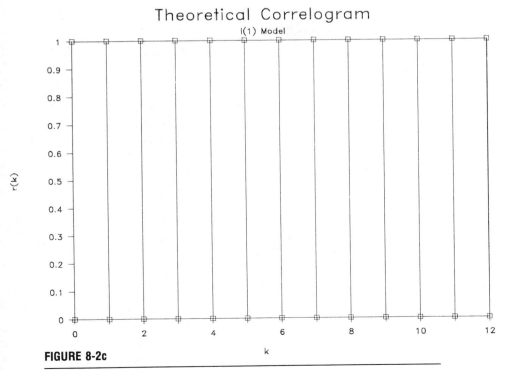

FIGURE 8-2c

Theoretical correlogram: I(1) model

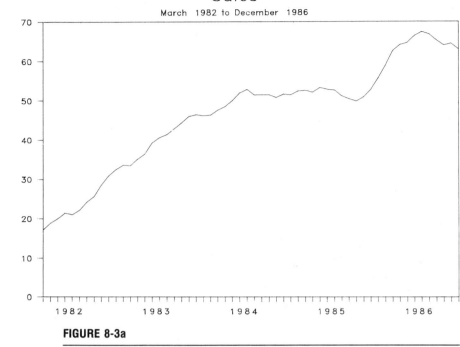

FIGURE 8-3a

Sales, March 1982–December 1986.

An Example. Figures 8–3a and b show a time series covering 58 consecutive periods with its correlogram. Notice that the values of r tend to remain large as k increases, suggesting the need to take a first difference. Figures 8–3c and d (p. 236) show the first differences with their correlogram. Figure 8–3d also shows the theoretical correlogram for an AR(1) model with $b = 0.6$. Notice that, for the first five values of k, the actual and theoretical correlograms are quite similar, suggesting that an AR(1) model with a coefficient of 0.6 might be an appropriate model. Fitting this model to the data gives the residuals shown in Figure 8– 3e (p. 236) and correlogram shown in Figure 8–3f (p. 236). Since these do not appear to show any additional patterns, the model is identified as an ARI(1, 1).[4]

---

[4]r_6 appears somewhat larger than the others. Although it is not large enough here to be significant, with monthly data, large values of r_k for $k = 2, 3, 4, 6,$ and 12 are often indicative of a seasonal pattern in the data.

Correlogram for Original Data

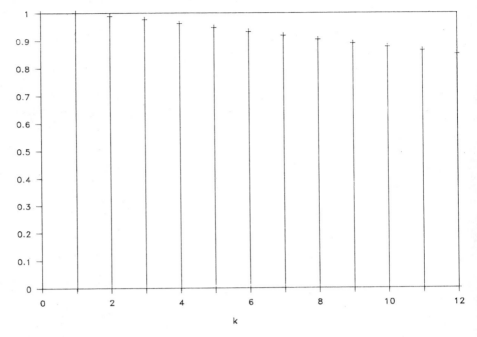

FIGURE 8-3b

Correlogram for original data

Multivariate ARIMA Models

This concept of structural modeling can be extended to problems involving interrelationships among several different time series, although the theoretical and computational issues involved will not be developed here. Univariate modeling is inherently short range and thus limited to situations similar to those discussed in Chapter 6. The same is not necessarily true for multivariate models, although they do suffer from the same problem of being only descriptions of empirically observed structure rather than attempts to model an underlying causal mechanism. Both univariate and multivariate ARIMA models have one major limitation: their effective use requires large amounts of data, which in practical planning situations may not always be available.

MULTIVARIATE MODELING

Univariate models have their main value in short-range unconditional forecasting. The longer-range forecasting used in aggregate resource planning

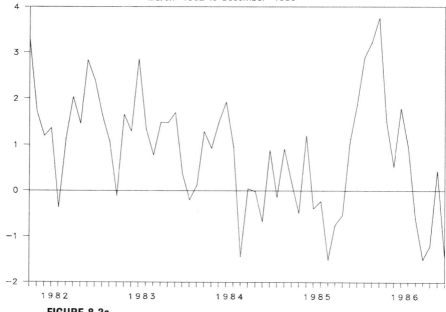

FIGURE 8-3c

Month to month change in sales

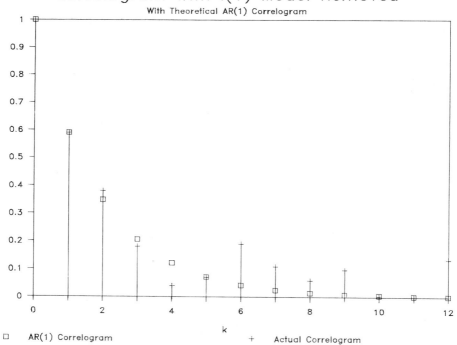

FIGURE 8-3d

Correlogram with I(1) model removed with theoretical AR(1) correlogram

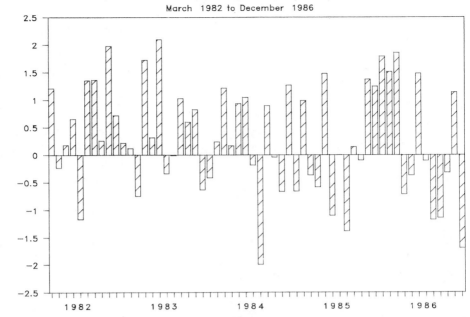

FIGURE 8-3e

Residuals from ARI (1,1) model, March 1982 to December 1986

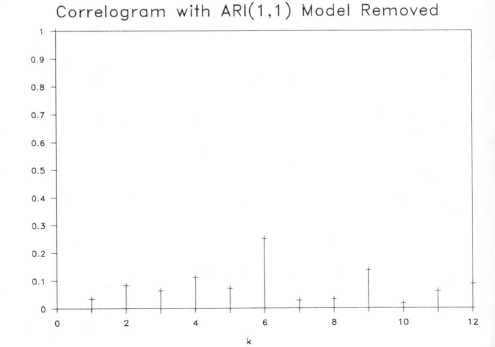

FIGURE 8-3f

Correlogram with ARI (1,1) model removed

requires some form of multivariate modeling. The dependent variables in these models are those for which forecasts are needed: demand, activity levels, and costs and prices. The independent variables are of three types:

1. Variables that are under the control of the manager and that will have an effect on the external environment being forecasted. Examples would be the prices to be charged for products, expenditure levels on sales promotion, or amounts of sales effort to be budgeted. While in short-range forecasting there is not sufficient time within the forecasting horizon for any action of the manager to significantly affect the environment, this is not true as the forecasting/planning horizon increases. In fact, a major element in this type of planning is the development of sequences of actions that will have a positive impact on the environment.

2. External variables that are more easily forecasted than the specific environmental variable of interest to the planner. Here we would include those variables that were previously referred to as leading indicators. As a simple example, public school enrollments are in part affected by the numbers of children born six years before. In educational planning, births are a leading indicator of school enrollments. In some cases, a variable may not be a leading indicator but may be easier to forecast or available in a more accurate form. Many general economic variables, such as price levels or levels of economic activity, are forecast by external government agencies or consulting firms. No small company could devote the resources necessary for this type of forecasting. Use of these, however, can frequently improve the company's sales forecasts.

3. External variables relevant to contingency planning. Proposed government legislation could be expected to have a major impact on a company's operations. If the passage of the legislation is uncertain, the company might want to develop contingency plans in case it is passed. For this, it would be necessary to develop a model forecasting the probable impact of the legislation assuming that it is passed.

In this section we explore some of the problems facing the forecaster in the exploratory development of multivariate forecasting models. The emphasis is on determining an appropriate structural form for the model and in dealing with some of the special problems that arise when we use time-series data. We will not discuss specific statistical techniques of model fitting; descriptions of these are available in other sources.

Special Problems in Modeling Time Series

Problems of modeling relationships among time series are of two types: (1) those that arise from the uncertain delay times between causes and effects, and (2) those arising because time series consist of multiple components that affect a relationship in different ways. As an example of the latter, consider the problem of a forecaster for a brewing company who is asked by management to determine the relationship between temperature and beer consumption. What is really being asked? Certainly, beer consumption and temperature have similar seasonal patterns: both increase in the summer. Beer consumption also has shown an upward trend and there appears to be a long-term upward trend in temperature. In either case, we might ask, Is it the warmer temperatures that are "causing" the increases in consumption?

More important, are these the relationships that the forecaster is being asked to study? Probably not. It is more likely that the real question is, If July in a particular year is warmer than the average July, will beer consumption also be above the average? This is a question of the relationship between residuals. Similarly, a manufacturer of automobiles might be interested in the relationship between unemployment and the demand for new cars as a relationship between cyclical changes.

In this type of analysis, the problem for the forecaster is one of *masking*. If a relationship between two variables is studied without first asking which components are relevant, any strong patterns in the data tend to hide weaker ones, and relationships (real or spurious) between the strong patterns contaminate the ones we wish to study. In most time series, the dominant patterns are the trend and the seasonal, while the forecaster is usually interested in studying relationships among cyclical patterns and residuals. Seasonal effects in many cases can be dealt with by deseasonalizing the data.[5] Our interest therefore focuses on the need to remove or reduce the masking effect of the trend. The study of relationships among seasonal patterns and among trends is considered at later points in the book.

Trend Contamination and the Use of Connected Scatters.   Many elementary statistics texts stress the problems that can arise from spurious relationships in statistical modeling. Many of the examples cited involve attempts to study relationships among time series with dominant trends. It has been reported, for example, that there is an apparent correlation between the salaries of church ministers in New England and the price of rum in Puerto Rico. It arises because both time series have risen over time with the general price level, and not from any implication that New England ministers are directly or indirectly in the rum business. In the same way, any two price or wage rate time series would show a long-run tendency to move together. Because of this we will not be able to use the modeling techniques of this chapter to study relationships among trends; time series in which the trends are dominant will always show apparent relationships. We return to this issue in Chapter 12.

[5]In some cases the nature of the relationship itself may change from one seasonal period to the next. In such cases, simply deseasonalizing the data will not be sufficient.

Even when our primary interest is in fluctuations around the trend or cycles, any trends in the data will distort the patterns we wish to study. As a first step in dealing with this, it is helpful to start by plotting a scatter diagram as discussed in Chapter 7, connecting the points in the scatter diagram in sequence forming what is called a *connected scatter diagram*. Figure 8–4a shows a scatter diagram between the production index for the printing and publishing industry and average hours per week worked in that industry for the years 1947 to 1984. As might be expected, there seems to be a strong relationship between the two variables, as shown by the fitted line. Indeed, if you were told that in some future year the production index was expected to reach 220, you would probably feel relatively confident in projecting this line to forecast that employment should average around 32.2 million hours per week: $17.05 + 0.0689(220) = 32.2$.

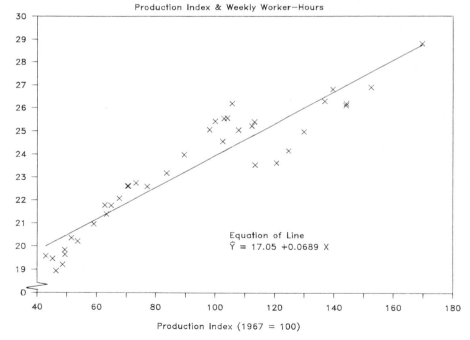

Printing & Publishing Industry
Production Index & Weekly Worker–Hours

Equation of Line
$\hat{Y} = 17.05 + 0.0689\ X$

Production Index (1967 = 100)

FIGURE 8-4a

Printing and publishing industry: Production index and weekly worker-hours (*Source:* U. S. Department of Commerce, Bureau of Economic Analysis; *Survey of Current Business,* various issues, 1950–1985)

Figure 8–4b shows the same data as a connected scatter diagram. It can be seen that the data actually consists of at least three distinct periods, a long period of relatively uninterrupted increase in both variables between 1947 and 1969, a period of substantial employment decline from 1969 to 1975, and a new period of increase thereafter. The period of decline can be clearly tied to a major technological innovation, the replacement of the linotype machine and hot-metal type casting with photocomposition and the introduction of computers. Table 8–2 (p. 244) compares three models that differ only in the period used for fitting (shown in Figures 8–4a and c, p. 242). Note particularly the differences in the slopes. Suppose the projection based on a production index of 220 is made using only the data since 1976. The new forecast would be for 33.8 million hours per week, a substantially larger figure: $12.31 + 0.0975(220) = 33.8$. Finally, there seems to have been another technological shift in 1981. The question for the long-range forecaster, which we return to in Chapter 12, is, Will there be further changes and, if so, when?

One way of dealing with this problem for shorter-range analysis and projection is to remove the trend from the data before plotting the scatter diagram. There are two ways that this can be done: (1) by taking first (or

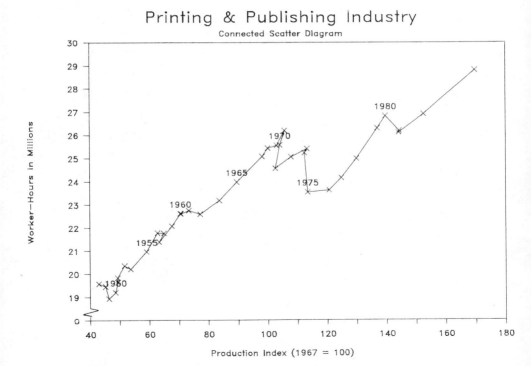

FIGURE 8-4b

Connected scatter diagram

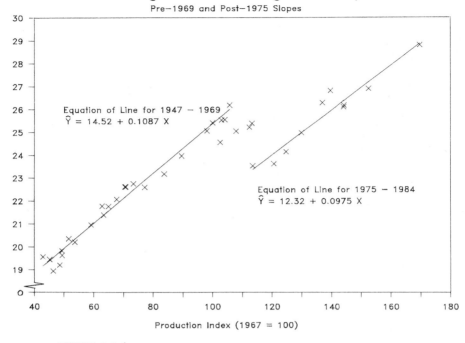

Printing & Publishing Industry
Pre−1969 and Post−1975 Slopes

Equation of Line for 1947 − 1969
$\hat{Y} = 14.52 + 0.1087\ X$

Equation of Line for 1975 − 1984
$\hat{Y} = 12.32 + 0.0975\ X$

Worker−Hours in Millions

Production Index (1967 = 100)

FIGURE 8-4c

Pre-1969 and Post-1975 slopes

higher-order) differences as discussed in Chapter 4, or (2) by fitting trend lines to the two series and then using the deviations from the trends in the scatter diagram. In any given situation, one or the other may prove the better approach. There is usually no obvious theoretical reason for preferring one or the other, however, so it is wise to try both. The use of the first approach is shown here and the second in the next example.

Table 8–3 (p. 248) and Figure 8–4d show the development of a model relating changes (first differences) in production with changes in employment. As expected, positive increases in production tend to be related to similar changes in employment. Although the relationship is perhaps not as visually impressive as that in Figure 8–4a and the R^2 is certainly smaller, it is a more realistic assessment of the magnitude of future forecasting errors. Notice that, except for the three outlier years of 1975, 1976, and 1981, the year-to-year changes both before and after 1975 seem to follow a similar pattern.[6] This suggests that, for short- to medium-term forecasting, a fore-

---

[6]In fitting the line in Table 8–3, the differences for the years 1975, 1976, 1981, and 1984 were omitted. The first three can clearly be seen to be outliers; the last corresponds to an unusually large one-year increase in the Production Index that would have dominated the model fit.

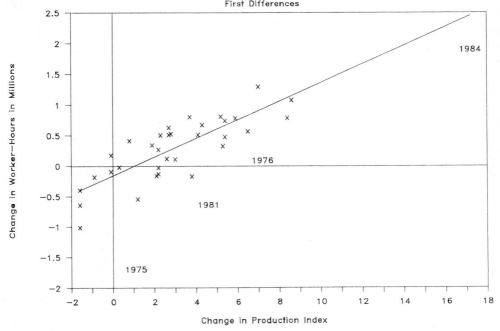

FIGURE 8-4d

First differences

cast model could be based on first differences. As shown by the outliers and by the period between 1969 and 1975, discontinuous changes can occur rapidly, so any projection of this model would have to be combined with a study of the reasons for the outliers and a monitoring of the environment for similar future changes.

Time Delays and Cyclical Movements. When analyzing the cyclical component of a time series, time delays in the relationship can cause problems in identifying the form of the model. The following example is deliberately artificial so that the issues involved do not become confused by other problems that can arise in analyzing oscillations in time series.

Figure 8–5a (p. 245) shows the scatter diagram for two artificial time series generated by the equations

$$X_t = 10\,(1.01)^t\,\sin\!\left(\frac{\phi_t}{7} + 0.15\right) + 15 \tag{13}$$

and

$$Y_t = 25X_{t-2} + 25 + e_t \tag{14}$$

__ __ ____ ____ __

244   *Exploratory Methods in Modeling*

where e_t is random noise that is normally distributed with a mean of zero and a standard deviation of 25. In most cases, this random component would be considerably larger and the cyclical component would have a much less regular appearance. This would make the observation and interpretation of the pattern more difficult, but the basic approach would be the same.

TABLE 8-2

(a) Printing and Publishing Industry Production Index and Average Weekly Hours Worked

Year	Production Index (1967 = 100)	Average Hours Worked per Week (in millions)
1947	42.90	19.58
1948	45.10	19.46
1949	46.30	18.93
1950	48.50	19.22
1951	49.30	19.64
1952	49.20	19.84
1953	51.50	20.36
1954	53.60	20.21
1955	59.00	20.97
1956	62.70	21.78
1957	64.90	21.77
1958	63.30	21.39
1959	67.60	22.08
1960	70.40	22.62
1961	70.70	22.61
1962	73.30	22.75
1963	77.10	22.60
1964	83.60	23.18
1965	89.50	23.97
1966	98.10	25.06
1967	100.00	25.42
1968	103.00	25.55
1969	105.70	26.19
1970	104.10	25.56
1971	102.50	24.56
1972	107.90	25.05
1973	113.20	25.39
1974	112.30	25.23
1975	113.40	23.53
1976	120.60	23.63
1977	124.70	24.15
1978	129.90	24.98
1979	136.90	26.29
1980	139.60	26.81
1981	144.20	26.18
1982	144.10	26.10
1983	152.50	26.90
1984	169.70	28.80

Source: U.S. Department of Commerce, Bureau of Economic Analysis, *Survey of Current Business*, various issues.

Table 8-2, continued

(b) Least-squares Results

	1947–1984	1947–1969	1975–1984
Constant (a)	17.05	14.52	12.32
Slope (b)	0.0689	0.1087	0.0975
Standard error of estimate	0.91	0.32	0.46
R^2	0.88	0.98	0.93
F Value	25.33	514.5	53.14
Critical value ($P = 0.05$)	3.26	3.47	4.46
No. of observations	38	23	10
Degrees of freedom	36	21	8

Scatter Diagram for Two Sine Curves

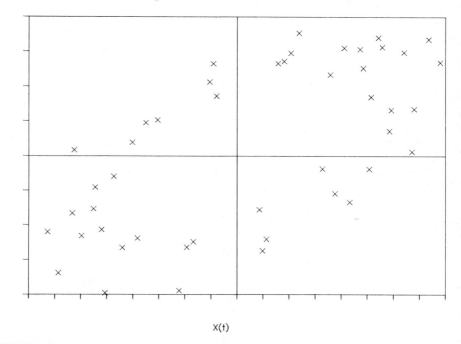

X(t)

FIGURE 8-5a

Scatter diagram for two sine curves

Connected Scatter for Two Sine Curves

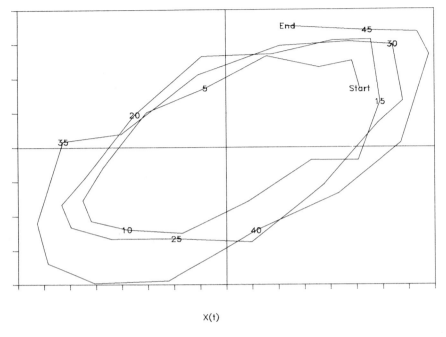

Y(t)

X(t)

FIGURE 8-5b

Connected scatter diagram for two sine curves

The scatter diagram appears to show a relatively weak relationship between the two variables. The only unusual element is the rather strange "hole" in the middle.[7] When the points of the scatter are connected as in Figure 8–5b, a definite pattern emerges; the points are circling counterclockwise. To follow this pattern, find a point on the graph where X reaches a maximum or a minimum; as one example, locate the point on the graph-that is farthest to the left. Now count the number of periods in a counterclockwise direction until the Y variable reaches a maximum or a minimum; here it is 2 periods later. Do the same for the other maximums and minimums for X. You should find two turns where the count is 3, three where it is 2, and one where it is 1. There would therefore seem to be a lag that averages about 2 periods between the peaks and troughs in X and those in Y. Now, as in Figure 8–5c, consider the relationship between Y_t and X_{t-2}. As might be expected from equation (14), there is a very strong linear relationship between the variables.

[7]If the random component was larger, this "hole" would not be apparent.

Scatter Diagram For Two Sine Curves
Y Variable Lagged By Two Periods

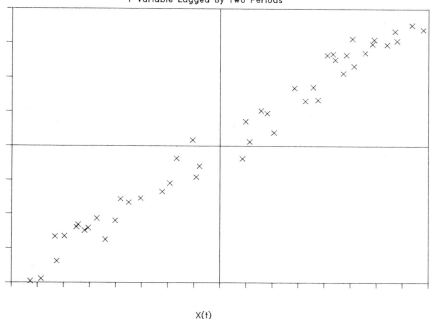

FIGURE 8-5c

Y variable lagged by two periods

A Note on Relationships between Seasonal Patterns. To say that a particular variable is a "cause" of a seasonal pattern is to suggest that it is a factor in one month or quarter being higher or lower than the others. For example, we argue that Christmas and the holiday period are the reason why retail sales show a peak in November and December. One way that this can be analyzed is to consider each seasonal period as a separate time series for analysis. Thus, for forecasting retail sales, it might be necessary to have separate models for each month (or in some cases each week) of the year. This can become rather time consuming and will not be pursued any further here.

GUIDED REGRESSION

Whenever possible, the structure of a model should be based on whatever underlying theory is available. In many cases, such theory is either not available or is incomplete or ambiguous. It becomes necessary to use the available data in an exploratory way to develop the forecasting model. A very powerful approach, which will briefly be outlined here, is *guided regression*, a procedure proposed originally by Mosteller and Tukey.

In exploratory model development, two critical issues face the forecaster: (1) What independent variables should be included in the model and (2) what should be the form of the model? In dealing with these issues, the forecaster must recognize that any modeling will be limited by the

Table 8-3

(a) Printing and Publishing Industry Production Index and Average Weekly Hours Worked: Year-to-year Changes (First Differences)

Year	Index First Difference (1967 = 100)	Hours Worked First Difference (in millions)
1947		
1948	2.20	−0.11
1949	1.20	−0.53
1950	2.20	0.28
1951	0.80	0.43
1952	−0.10	0.19
1953	2.30	0.52
1954	2.10	−0.15
1955	5.40	0.75
1956	3.70	0.82
1957	2.20	−0.01
1958	−1.60	−0.38
1959	4.30	0.69
1960	2.80	0.54
1961	0.30	0.00
1962	2.60	0.14
1963	3.80	−0.15
1964	6.50	0.58
1965	5.90	0.79
1966	8.60	1.09
1967	1.90	0.36
1968	3.00	0.13
1969	2.70	0.64
1970	−1.60	−0.63
1971	−1.60	−1.00
1972	5.40	0.49
1973	5.30	0.34
1974	−0.90	−0.16
1975[a]	1.10	−1.70
1976[a]	7.20	0.09
1977	4.10	0.52
1978	5.20	0.83
1979	7.00	1.31
1980	2.70	0.52
1981[a]	4.60	−0.64
1982	−0.10	−0.07
1983	8.40	0.80
1984[a]	17.20	1.90

[a]Years omitted from least-squares calculations.

Table 8-3 (Continued)

(b) Printing and Publishing Industry Production Index and Average Weekly Hours Worked: Year-to-Year Changes (First Differences)

Constant (a)	-0.15
Slope (b)	0.15
Standard error of estimate	0.30
R^2	0.66
F Value	30.09
Critical value $(P = 0.05)$	3.31
No. of observations	33
Degrees of freedom	31

amount of data that are available and the problem of *degrees of freedom* discussed in Chapter 7. Thus pains must be taken to keep the model as simple as possible; only the most important variables should be included and structural complexities should be kept to a minimum.

Choosing Variables

Mosteller and Tukey suggest that potential independent variables should be classified into three groups:

1. *Key variables.* A small number of variables (not more than six) that will almost certainly be included in any final model, either because of their known importance or because they are variables that must be under the control of the manager.

2. *Promising variables.* Additional variables (not more than 12) that the forecaster feels are important enough to at least consider in some detail.

3. *Miscellaneous variables.* Mosteller and Tukey refer to these as the "haystack." These are the marginal variables that would be considered only if time, resources, and data permit.

As a practical matter, forecasters routinely suffer from a lack of sufficient data. Rarely will it be possible to go beyond consideration of a few key variables. This means that the forecaster should be extremely careful in any initial variable classification and selection.

Knowing the correct variables to include in the model can be of limited value unless the forecaster can also determine the structural form of that model. Suppose the forecaster is sure that the dependent variable Y is related to two independent variables X_1 and X_2. The relationship could still take many different forms. For example,

$$Y = b_0 + b_1 X_1 + b_2 X_2 + e$$

$$Y = b_0 + b_1 X_1{}^2 + b_2 \frac{X_2}{X_1} + e \tag{15}$$

or

$$\text{Log } Y = b_0 + b_1 \text{ Log } X_1 + \frac{b_2}{X_2} + e$$

would all relate the variables but in very different ways, using different carriers. Unfortunately, many of the exploratory procedures that have been proposed are limited to the first case of Y as a simple linear combination of the X's,

$$Y = b_0 + b_1 X_1 + b_2 X_2 + e \tag{16}$$

and concentrate solely on variable selection, rather than trying alternative model forms. The advantage of the Mosteller–Tukey approach is that it carefully examines one X variable at a time, making appropriate adjustments to the model structure in an incremental fashion.

Dummy Variables. In many cases the forecaster may need or wish to combine qualitatively different data sets in the same model. In the example of Chapter 7, some of the stores may be located in downtown city areas while others are in suburban shopping malls, and the forecaster may believe that location has an important effect on the relationship between sales promotion and sales. It would of course be possible to construct two different models but, with only 11 stores in all, this could be difficult. An alternative approach is to introduce into the model a *dummy* or 0–1 variable.

Assume that the basic model is, as before,

$$Y = b_0 + b_1 X_1 + e \tag{17}$$

where X_1 is the amount spent on sales promotion and Y is the sales increase. Suppose that the forecaster believes that the slope b_1 is likely to depend on whether the store is downtown or in a shopping mall. Define a new variable X_2 as 0 for downtown stores and 1 for stores in suburban malls. The model becomes

$$Y = b_0 + b_1 X_1 + b_2 X_1 X_2 + e \tag{18a}$$

Notice that this model reduces to

$$Y = b_0 + b_1 X_1 + e \tag{18b}$$

for downtown stores and

$$Y = b_0 + (b_1 + b_2)X_1 + e \qquad (18c)$$

for stores in malls. At the same time, only one value of b_0 is required, and the residuals are combined in determining the standard error of estimate, as discussed in Chapter 7. Instead of having two separate models, each with only a small number of degrees of freedom, here the degrees of freedom are combined for a total of 8.

Note that a dummy variable can *only* take on the values of 0 and 1. Suppose in this example that there were three categories of stores: downtown, shopping mall, and other city (not downtown). It would be necessary to define *two* dummy variables with the following values:

Location	X_2	X_3
Downtown	0	0
Suburban	1	0
Other city	0	1

Searching for Model Structure

Once the list of variables has been developed, the key variables should be introduced into the model one at a time, starting with the most important. As we shall see in the example, if one of the key variables is a time trend, this should always be dealt with first.

As each independent variable is brought into the model, the residuals should be closely examined for nonlinearity and other clues to model structure. In this the residuals and their absolute values should be plotted as functions of:

Chronological time (a time series)

Each of the independent variables already in the model

The predicted value of the dependent variable, which, at this point, is a function of all the independent variables already in the model

In the example that follows, this was done. For simplicity, however, only a few of the more useful residual plots are actually shown.

As each new variable is brought into the model, it must first be adjusted for the independent variables already in the model. For example, suppose that you are fitting a model with a dependent variable Y and two key variables X_1 and X_2. As a first step, you have obtained the model

$$\hat{Y} = f_1(X_1) \qquad (19)$$

and residuals

$$e_Y = Y - \hat{Y} \tag{20}$$

To now add the second key variable X_2, you must first fit a model to X_2 and X_1:

$$\hat{X}_2 = f_2(X_1) \tag{21}$$

with residuals

$$e_{x_2} = X_2 - \hat{X}_2 \tag{22}$$

The next stage of the model search will then examine the relationship between the two sets of *residuals:*

$$\hat{e}_y = f_3(e_{x_2}) \tag{23}$$

In the case of the following example, note that *both* the Y and X variables must be corrected for time trends before proceeding to the next step in the analysis.

An Example

As you may guess, this process can rapidly become unmanageable for hand calculation and will require the use of a computer. Here we examine a very simple example that is limited to outlining the basic approach and illustrating some of the issues introduced earlier.

The example is similar to the one previously considered, a relationship between a measure of the activity level of an organization and the associated need for personnel. Here we examine the relationship between the number of active ships in the U.S. Navy and naval military personnel for the years 1951 to 1984. The data are shown in Table 8–4. We first fit a simple linear model to the two variables and then compare it to a model fitted in a sequential, guided way.

It should be noted that robust fitting methods (such as the median fit discussed earlier) can be particularly useful in exploratory modeling because of the likelihood of having to deal with nonlinearities and outliers in the data. To keep the example as simple as possible, least-squares methods have been used throughout.

Simple Regression.   Figure 8–6a (p. 255) shows a scatter diagram for the two variables and the least-squares relationship line

$$\hat{Y} = 366.1 + 0.351\,X \tag{24}$$

Overall the fit appears reasonably good, except that the data points seem to be much more variable around the line on the right side of the graph. The overall value of R^2 for the 34 years is 0.854.

Table 8-4

(a) U.S. Naval Ships in Active Service and Active Naval Personnel, 1951 to 1984

Year	Personnel (000)	Ships
1951	736.7	1102
1952	824.3	1129
1953	794.4	1129
1954	725.7	1113
1955	660.7	1030
1956	669.9	973
1957	677.1	967
1958	641.0	891
1959	626.3	860
1960	618.0	812
1961	627.1	819
1962	666.4	900
1963	664.6	916
1964	667.6	917
1965	671.4	936
1966	745.2	947
1967	751.6	973
1968	765.4	976
1969	775.9	926
1970	692.7	769
1971	623.0	702
1972	588.1	654
1973	564.5	584
1974	545.9	512
1975	535.1	496
1976	524.7	476
1977	529.9	464
1978	530.2	453
1979	521.9	468
1980	527.2	473
1981	540.2	482
1982	553.0	513
1983	560.3	506
1984	572.2	526

Source: U.S. Department of Commerce, Bureau of the Census, *Statistical Abstract of the United States*, various issues.

(continued on next page)

254   *Exploratory Methods in Modeling*

Table 8-4, continued

(b) Least-squares regression results

		Standard Error	t Value	Critical (P = 0.05) Value
Constant (a)	304.44			
Slopes				
Trend (t)	1.912	0.645	2.96	2.04
Ships (b₁)	0.368	0.033	9.84	
Wartime Correction (b₂)	73.75	7.047	10.46	
Standard error of estimate	12.295			
R²	0.983			
F value	426.98			2.69
No. of observations	34			
Degrees of freedom	30			

The nature of the underlying problem begins to be apparent in Figure 8–6b (p. 256), which shows the connected scatter, and Figure 8–6c (p. 256), which shows the residuals plotted as a function of time. The residuals are *not* random as assumed by the usual least-squares line fit but show a clear cyclical pattern. Equally important, the magnitudes of the residuals since 1971 are much smaller than during the previous period and cover a completely different range of X values. We would seem to have unwittingly lumped at least two different situations into one model.[8]

A Guided Regression.   The guided approach to modeling starts with the identification of the key variables and the order in which they should be considered. Whenever one of these is chronological time, it should be considered first. Here, three such variables are suggested:

- Time effect (trend and/or cycle)
- Number of active ships
- Difference between wartime and peacetime conditions

The second step is to find the relationship between the first X variable (time) and Y. Figure 8–6d (p. 257) shows the residuals from the trend

[8]The author first ran across this example in 1971. At that time, initial examination of the scatter diagram and simple regression model suggested that there was *no* relationship between the number of ships and personnel.

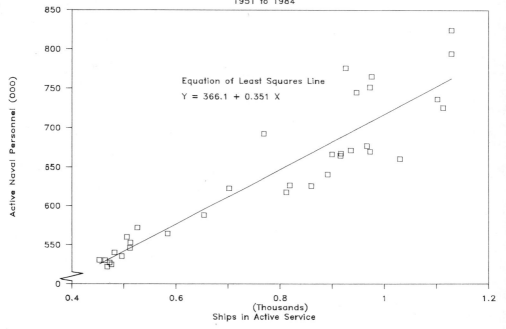

FIGURE 8-6a

U. S. Navy ships and naval personnel, 1951–1984 (*Source:* U. S. Department of Commerce, Bureau of the Census, *Statistical Abstract of the United States,* various issues, 1952–1985)

(755−6.645t) plotted as a function of time. Previously, it was suggested that the residuals should be plotted as functions of time, X, and $\hat{Y}$. In this simple example these would all be the same graph as shown here.

Figure 8–6d also shows the two relevant wartime periods. It can be seen that the "cycle" really consists of two wartime personnel increases, two postwar reductions in force, and a third buildup starting in 1980.

The next step is to introduce the second X variable, number of ships, into the model. Since the Y variable has been adjusted for the time trend, the second X variable must be adjusted as well. Figure 8–6e (p. 258) shows the residuals from the trend (1154−21.568t). In this example, the same type of linear trend was fitted to both variables. This need not be generally true. In some cases, first differences may be used for one variable and a linear trend for the other. Sometimes it will be useful to use data transformations as described in Chapter 4.

U.S. Navy Ships & Naval Personnel

Connected Scatter

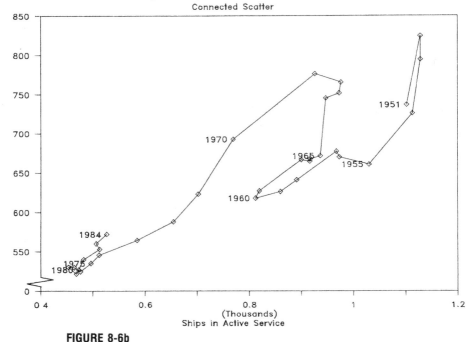

FIGURE 8-6b

Connected scatter

U.S. Navy — Active Naval Personnel

Residuals from Line Y = 366.1 + 0.351 X

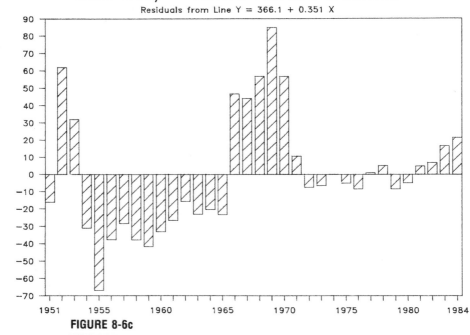

FIGURE 8-6c

Residuals from line Y = 366.1 + 0.351X

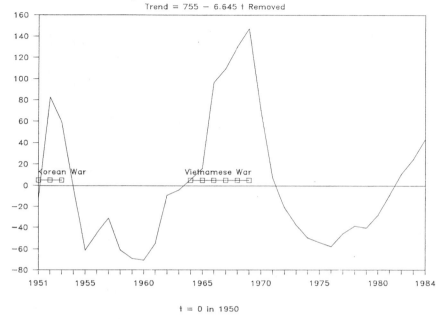

FIGURE 8-6d

Trend = 755 − 6.645, t removed

Figure 8–6f (p. 259) shows the scatter diagram for the two sets of residuals. Individual data points have been identified by the last two digits for each year. Two separate groups of data points are now clear. One group consists of the war years 1952 to 53 and 1966 to 70, and the other of the remaining years.[9]

Figure 8–6f also shows the least-squares line fitted to only the lower left group of data points, and Figure 8–6g (p. 259) shows the residuals for *all* the points from that line. Notice in Figure 8–6f that the two groups of points appear to have similar slopes and to differ only in level. This suggests that a simple additive "wartime" correction may be adequate. Figure

[9]The Korean War started in July 1950; the fighting ended in July 1953. The Vietnamese War is usually dated from the Bay of Tonkin Resolution of August 7, 1964. U.S. forces reached a peak in April 1969, and the final evacuation occurred in April 1975. Thus, in both cases, the first full year of the war (1951 and 1965) is not in the upper right group. 1970, however, is included. Also note that 1955 is a potential outlier in the other direction.

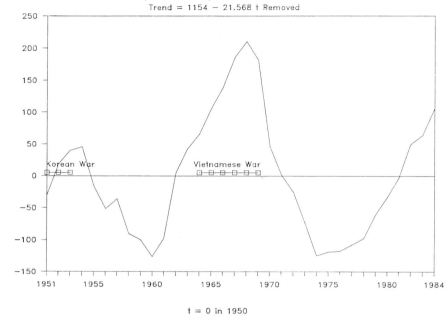

U.S. Navy — Ships in Active Service

Trend = 1154 − 21.568 t Removed

t = 0 in 1950

FIGURE 8-6e

8–6g also tends to isolate 1955 as a possible outlier year, which should be considered separately.

Using a dummy 0–1 variable for the 7 years in the upper group gives the final model:

$$\hat{Y}_t = 304.44 + 1.912t + 0.368X_{2,t} + 73.45X_{3,t} \qquad (25)$$

with the final residuals shown in Figure 8–6h (p. 260). Figure 8–6i (p. 260) compares the original deviations from the median of the Y variable with the residuals from the simple linear and final models as fitted. The final R^2 is 0.983, as compared to 0.854 for the simple linear regression model; other summary statistics are shown in Table 8–4b. The final model seems to do an excellent job of describing the movements of the last 34 years. One critical question remains unanswered: To what extent is the model shown "real" in the sense that the structure shown can be expected to persist into the and to what extent is it an artifact of the perhaps unique events of the period covered? Have we only a descriptive rather than a predictive model? This is a question to which we return in Chapter 9.

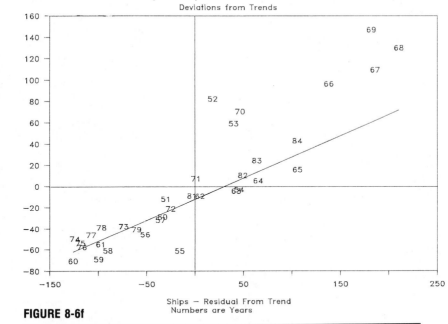

FIGURE 8-6f

Deviations from trends

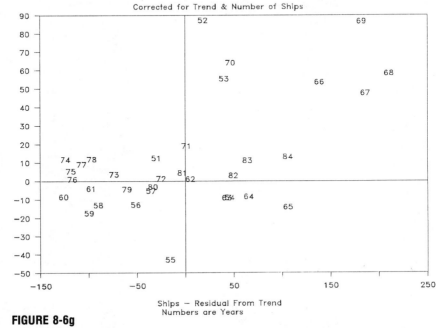

FIGURE 8-6g

Corrected for trend and number of ships

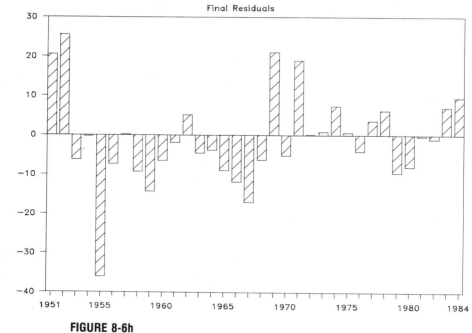

FIGURE 8-6h

Final residuals

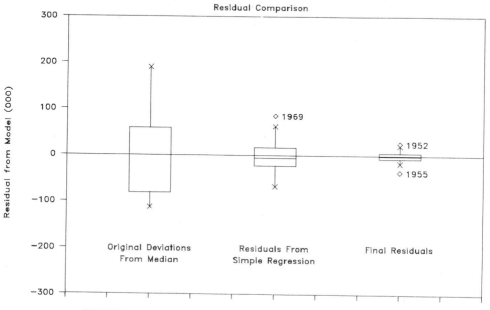

FIGURE 8-6i

Residual comparison

SUMMARY

Rarely in time-series analysis and forecasting will we be fortunate enough to be faced with the classical situation of knowing the true underlying structure of the problem we wish to model and of having more than enough data so that we need not be concerned with problems of limited degrees of freedom. In the usual case, we are faced with ambiguous structure and insufficient data. It becomes critical to make as effective use as possible of what we have. This chapter has introduced a few of the exploratory techniques available to the forecaster for this process.

READINGS

Univariate Modeling

The original book on ARIMA modeling is still one of the best:

GEORGE E. P. BOX AND GWILYM JENKINS, *Time Series Analysis, Forecasting, and Control*, rev. ed., San Francisco, Holden-Day, 1976.

Other good presentations are

MAKRIDAKIS, WHEELWRIGHT, and McGEE, cited in the Readings for Chapter 7.

CHARLES R. NELSON, *Applied Time Series Analysis for Managerial Forecasting*, San Francisco, Holden-Day, 1973.

RICHARD McCLEARY and RICHARD A. HAY, JR., *Applied Time Series Analysis for the Social Sciences*, Beverly Hills, Calif., Sage, 1980.

Guided Regression

The ideas presented in this section have been adapted from

FREDERICK MOSTELLER and JOHN W. TUKEY, *Data Analysis and Regression*, Reading, Mass., Addison-Wesley, 1977, Chapters 12 through 16.

PROBLEMS

1. One of the smaller national U.S. airlines has asked for your help in developing a model to forecast total revenue passenger-miles for their company on a quarterly basis. This is to be used as one of the inputs into their budget and financial planning. Assume that the company has a three-quarter lead time on budget planning and the budget period is 2 years. This means that the model will be used to forecast up to 11 quarters into the future.

   a. Discuss the general form of the model that you would propose, including any preliminary data modifications or adjustments that you would expect to have to make to your data.

   b. Develop lists of key, promising, and miscellaneous variables to be used in developing the model. For the key variables, discuss how and why they would be included in the model. For all the variables, indicate where you would be able to obtain the necessary data and why you classified it as you did.

2. Comstock Industries, Inc., believes that sales in one of their divisions should be related to capacity utilization in an industry that is a major user of that division's product. They have given you the past 3 years of quarterly data, as follows:

Quarter		Sales ($000,000)	Customers' % Utilization of Capacity
1984	I	696	57
	II	668	48
	III	730	54
	IV	804	62

Quarter		Sales ($000,000)	Customers' % Utilization of Capacity
1985	I	980	87
	II	1048	94
	III	990	80
	IV	950	69
1986	I	874	52
	II	978	65
	III	1040	71
	IV	1102	77

a. Plot these data and fit a linear relationship of sales to capacity utilization. Determine and interpret the slope of the line fitted.

b. Using the methods of guided regression discussed in the chapter, analyze the data. Compare the slope coefficient obtained with that in part a. Are they the same or different? Discuss the reasons for any differences in the models noted.

3. Pat Marshall is the manager of a South Dakota branch of Philpott Stores, a nationwide chain of apparel stores. The corporate office has developed a monthly economic newsletter that is sent to all store managers. The newsletter includes a monthly market potential index for each region that has been developed by the corporate economist. At this point, Pat is not quite sure how to use this index in planning.

Shown next is the market potential index for the Upper Midwest for the last year, together with the sales for Pat's store. Both have been seasonally adjusted.

Month	Sales ($000)	Market Potential Index
January	230	110
February	230	116
March	240	118
April	240	112
May	220	98
June	180	80
July	130	72
August	100	72
September	90	80
October	100	94
November	130	104
December	150	108

a. Determine whether or not you think a relationship exists between the two variables and, if so, the form of the relationship.

b. The market potential index for January is forecasted to be 102. The January seasonal index for the store is 84. Develop a sales projection for the store for January.

CHAPTER 9

Forecast

Evaluation

Behind all the forecaster's efforts in modeling the environment lie continuing questions: How well will the model work when it is actually used for forecasting and planning? How accurate will the forecasts be? Are there ways that the model or the forecast could still be improved? Would they be worth the additional cost? These questions are fundamentally different from those that face the research modeler concerned with models as a way of learning how the environment operates or with the quantitative historian interested in describing patterns of the past. In this chapter we look at forecast evaluation from the viewpoint of both the forecaster and the forecast user, the planner or manager.

In previous chapters we implicitly treated the past residuals as the measure of future forecast accuracy. This is only partially correct; the residuals are, at best, a measure of how well the model fits or describes the data of the past; they do not answer the question of how well the model will fit the data of the future. Statisticians make a distinction between sampling and nonsampling errors. Residuals are a measure of sampling errors, random deviations from the model fitted. For the forecaster the real source of forecast error lies in the nonsampling errors, in problems such as having the wrong model or incorrect input data.

The forecasting and planning process is being considered here as part of an ongoing operational planning and management system. Forecasts, in this context, are normally not a one-time affair; they are developed on a regular basis to deal with questions whose form changes only slowly. Having developed forecasts, there will be a need to develop a system for monitoring the accuracy of the forecasts and for modifying the plans and decisions to reflect the changes in the forecasts.

In a practical sense, forecasts must always be evaluated before the outcome of the event forecasted is known. By the time it is known whether a particular forecast is or is not correct, it will be too late for this knowledge to be of any direct value to the planner or manager. At the same time, when a forecast is part of some ongoing forecasting system, knowledge of how forecasts have performed in the past can be a useful input in evaluating future performance. It is necessary to distinguish between ex ante evaluation, which is carried out as the forecast is being developed and before the actual accuracy of the forecast is known, and ex post evaluation, performed after the variable or event forecasted has occurred and is known.

It is important also to make a distinction between a quantitative evaluation of the accuracy of a forecast, that is, of how close the forecast came to describing the event or outcome forecasted and the qualitative evaluation of a forecast. Qualitative evaluation is directed toward questions, not of accuracy itself, but of whether or not the correct model was chosen, of events that were not included in the forecast but that turned out to be reasons for forecast error, of assumptions that were made and turned out to be incorrect. That is, it deals with the nonstatistical aspects of forecast evaluation.

Major Points to be Noted

1. *The similarities but also the differences between ex post and ex ante forecast evaluation. In ongoing forecasting systems, the way that ex post evaluation of the error in the last forecast should lead into the ex ante evaluation of the next forecast or forecasts that must be made.*
2. *The interrelationships between the quantitative and qualitative aspects of forecast evaluation.*

EX POST QUANTITATIVE EVALUATION

We have already seen one technique of ex post quantitative evaluation in the Trigg tracking signal of Chapter 6. This technique is specifically designed to be part of an automated forecasting system. It is a control device much like a smoke alarm, designed to go off when there is a potential problem. Like a smoke alarm, while it indicates the existence of a fire, it does not necessarily give any information on what kind of fire or where. In this section we look at evaluation methods that have diagnostic ability as well. Two specific techniques are described: the CUSUM graph and the P–R diagram.

CUSUM Graph

The CUSUM is a *CUmulative SUM* of forecast errors. In this, it is similar to the use of the tracking signal. It differs in that, instead of a single cumulative sum (or average) of all past errors, several different sums are calculated and evaluated. As we shall see, this can aid the forecaster, not only in detecting a problem, but in determining when the problem may have first occurred.

Table 9-1 shows monthly revenue forecasts for a company as they might be developed as part of the annual budgeting process. In this case they consist of a trend projected to increase at a rate of 5% per month and a seasonal index. Suppose that the planner wants to set up a control proce-

TABLE 9-1

Monthly Revenue Forecasts

	Month	*Trend* *(5% per year)*	*Seasonal* *Index*	*Revenue* *Forecast*
1986	Jan	$500,000	76.98	$384,900
	Feb	505,000	108.68	548,834
	Mar	510,050	135.85	692,903
	Apr	515,151	99.62	513,193
	May	520,302	86.04	447,668
	Jun	525,505	72.45	380,728
	Jul	530,760	54.34	288,415
	Aug	536,068	40.75	218,448
	Sep	541,428	67.92	367,738
	Oct	546,843	163.02	891,463
	Nov	552,311	199.25	1,100,480
	Dec	557,834	95.09	530,444

dure so that, if the forecasts are or become less accurate than anticipated, a warning will be given. Certainly the individual forecast errors can and should be checked on a monthly basis. Sometimes, however, a situation can arise where the errors are small and not individually a problem, but are, at the same time, systematically high or low. Although individual errors stay within acceptable limits, by the end of the year the cumulative error turns out to be excessive. It is for early detection of this problem that the CUSUM is designed.

Table 9-2 shows the actual monthly revenues and forecast errors. For convenience, this is shown for the entire year. In the discussion that follows, imagine that it is being created one line at a time at the end of each month. (It may be useful to put a ruler over the table so that you cannot see the months that have not yet occurred.) The data are fictitious, generated by a process where for the first four months, the forecasts would be correct on the average but with an error standard deviation of $20,000. Starting in May, the forecasts for each month were given a downward bias of $10,000.

The fifth column of Table 9-2 is labeled $j = 2$. These numbers are the sums of pairs of successive errors. Thus the first entry is the sum of the forecast errors for January and February: $9715 + (-25,835) = -16,120$. The second entry is the sum of $-25,835$ and $35,314$, and so down the column. The next column, labeled $j = 3$, contains sums of three consecutive errors. It is most easily obtained by adding the most recent error to the previous total in the $j = 2$ column. Thus, the first entry is obtained by adding the forecast error for March: $35,314$ to $-16,120$ from the $j = 2$ column for February. The remainder of the columns are obtained in a similar way. Notice that there are delays in obtaining these totals, so the CUSUM for $j = 6$ does not start until June.

Control limits can be set for each CUSUM. One suggested procedure is to use limits of

$$\pm ks (d + j) \tag{1}$$

where s is the anticipated standard deviation of the forecast errors, j is the number of consecutive errors summed, and k and d are design characteristics of the control procedure. The appearance of the control limits is shown graphically in Figure 9-1 (p. 270). It can be seen that the effect of changing d is to shift the limits for the CUSUMs equally. A large value of d means that the procedure is less likely to incorrectly indicate a problem. At the same time, it is slower to detect substantive changes when they do occur. Changing k (with a corresponding change in d) changes the slope of the limits. A small value of k means that the system is relatively less sensitive to a single large error (positive or negative), while it is more sensitive to a cumulative sum of several small errors all in the same direction. A large

TABLE 9-2

Forecast Errors and CUSUMs (in dollars)

Month	Revenue Forecast	Actual Revenue	Forecast Error	Number of Periods (j)					Error Sum
				2	3	4	5	6	
1986:									
Jan	384,900	394,615	9,715						9,715
Feb	548,834	522,999	-25,835	-16,120					-16,120
Mar	692,903	728,217	35,314	9,479	19,194				19,194
Apr	513,193	510,583	-2,610	32,704	6,869	16,584			16,584
May[a]	447,668	433,583	-14,085	-16,695	18,619	-7,216	2,499		2,499
Jun	380,728	358,122	-22,606	-36,691	-39,302	-3,988	-29,823	-20,108	-20,108
Jul	288,415	275,713	-12,702	-35,308	-49,393	-52,004	-16,690	-42,525	-32,810
Aug	218,448	193,419	-25,029	-37,731	-60,337[b]	-74,422[b]	-77,032[b]	-41,718	-57,838
Sep	367,738	335,412	-32,326	-57,355[b]	-70,057[b]	-92,663[b]	-106,748[b]	-109,358[b]	-90,164
Oct	891,463	886,049	-5,414	-37,740	-62,769[b]	-75,471[b]	-98,077[b]	-112,162[b]	-95,579
Nov	1,100,480	1,131,147	30,667	25,253	-7,073	-32,102	-44,804	-67,410	-64,911
Dec	530,444	473,420	-57,024[b]	-26,357	-31,771	-64,097[b]	-89,126[b]	-101,828[b]	-121,936
Critical Values:			±36,000	±44,000	±52,000	±60,000	±68,000	±76,000	

$k = 0.4$

$d = 3.5$

$s = \$20,000$

[a]Bias of $+\$10,000$ introduced into the forecast.

[b]Exceeds the critical value.

Control Limits For CUSUM Graph
Limits In Units of Variable Controlled

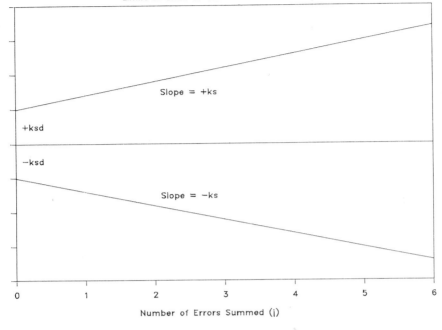

FIGURE 9-1

Control limits for CUSUM graph: Limits in units of variable controlled

value of k conversely is more sensitive to the individual errors. Three k, d, pairs that are frequently effective are

k	d
0.4	3.5
0.4	6.0
0.25	8.0

For this example we will use $k = 0.4$ and $d = 3.5$ and assume that the forecast error standard deviation has been (correctly) estimated to be $20,000. In Table 9-2, the first point "out of control" occurs in August (remember that a deliberate bias of $10,000 was introduced into the forecasts starting in May). The forecast errors in May, June, and July were negative, but none were individually or collectively large enough to indicate any problem. With the occurrence of a fourth negative error in August, the CUSUMs for $j = 3, 4$, and

5 all exceed their respective limits. If there were any question, this signal is reinforced by the CUSUMs for September.

In addition to indicating the existence of a (possible) problem, the CUSUMs give an indication of when the problem may have started. Generally, this will have been approximately j periods earlier. Here the August CUSUMs for $j = 3$, 4, and 5 simultaneously exceeded the control limits, indicating that the change probably occurred 3 to 5 months earlier. In this case we know that it occurred three periods previously in May.

The CUSUMs can also be set up as a graphical control procedure. The last column in Table 9-2 also gives the cumulative sum of all the forecast errors starting with that for January. These are plotted in Figure 9-2. In setting up this graph for hand data entry, you should leave plenty of space at the top and bottom because, over time, the sums can become large and either positive or negative. On a computer graph, of course, this is not a problem since the scales will be shifted automatically.

To develop graphical control limits, prepare a cardboard mask as shown in Figure 9-3 (p. 272) using the desired values of k, d, and the

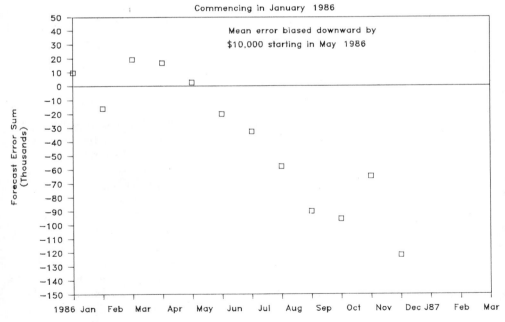

FIGURE 9-2

Cumulative sum of forecast errors, commencing in January 1986

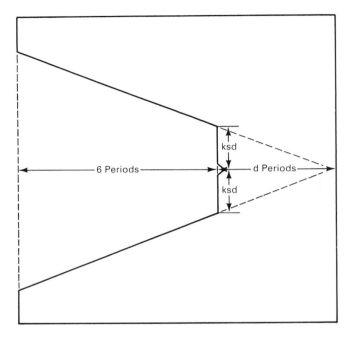

FIGURE 9-3

CUSUM mask

anticipated error standard deviation s. The width of the cardboard should be at least $(d + 6)$ time units. A small notch should be cut as shown to aid in aligning the mask with the most recent data point. At the end of each month, the latest forecast error is added to the previous total and plotted. The cardboard mask is then laid on the graph as shown in Figure 9-4. The notch should be on the most recent plotted point. As long as all previous plotted points are visible, the forecasts are assumed to be in control. If any points are hidden by the card, a potential problem is indicated. In Figure 9-4, the mask is shown as it would be placed in July. At this point all the previously plotted sums are visible, although the one for May is close to the upper limit. A similar picture for August would show the points for April, May, and June all hidden by the cardboard mask, indicating that the forecasts were out to control. CUSUM computer programs are available that automatically create and overlay an appropriate mask. It is also possible to set up the mask using a Lotus 1-2-3 macro as with the Box and Whiskers diagram of Chapter 3.

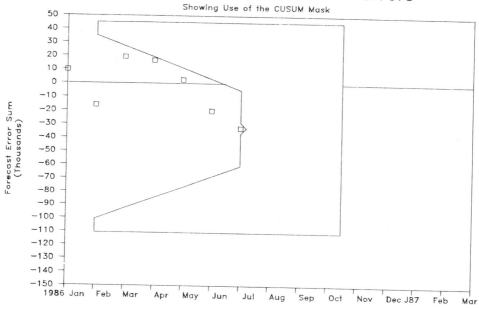

FIGURE 9-4

Cumulative sum of forecast errors, showing use of CUSUM mask

The P–R Diagram

The CUSUM graph can be used both for forecast control and for preliminary diagnosis if problems arise. The P–R (prediction–realization) diagram is primarily a diagnostic tool. It is intended to identify types of problems that can arise in forecasting and in some cases to suggest possible forecast improvements.

This diagnostic technique makes use of a plot of actual (A) versus predicted (P) (forecasted) changes in the variable. Table 9-3a (p. 274) shows a (hypothetical) company's actual and forecasted quarterly sales for the last three years. The column labeled A gives the quarter to quarter changes (first differences). The P column gives the forecasted change (*not* the change in the forecast).

$$A_t = Y_t - Y_{t-1}$$

$$P_t = \hat{Y}_{t-1}(1) - Y_{t-1}$$

(2)

TABLE 9-3

(a) Actual and Predicted Changes in Sales

				Changes		
Quarter		Forecast	Actual Sales	Actual A	Predicted P	Forecast Error
1984	I	NA	522	NA	NA	
	II	568	572	50	46	4
	III	575	567	−5	3	−8
	IV	557	508	−59	−10	−49
1985	I	487	486	−22	−21	−1
	II	495	538	52	9	43
	III	575	519	−19	37	−56
	IV	557	558	39	38	1
1986	I	563	483	−75	5	−80
	II	481	461	−22	−2	−20
	III	520	554	93	59	34
	IV	575	605	51	21	30

(b) U Statistics

	Actual Change A	Predicted Change P
Mean	7.55	16.82
Standard deviation	50.28	24.12
Correlation (r)	0.7058	
U Components		
Mean	85.98	
Variance	684.33	
Correlation	713.69	
Mean-square error (MSE)	1484.00	
U_M (%)	5.79%	
U_S (%)	46.11%	
U_C (%)	48.09%	
	100.00%	

To follow the calculation of A and P, start with data for the forecast and actual sales for the second quarter of 1984 in Table 9-3a. From equation (2) it can be seen that, to determine A and P, it is necessary to have the actual sales for the previous period, in this case the first quarter of 1984. P is the predicted change or the difference between the forecast and the previous actual sales: $568 - 522 = 46$. A is the actual change or $572 - 522 = 50$.

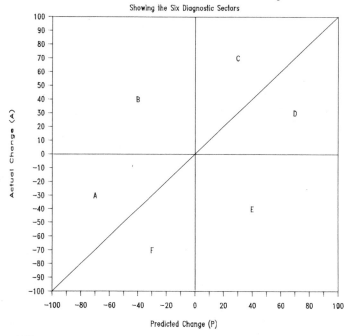

Prediction–Realization or P–R Diagram

Showing the Six Diagnostic Sectors

FIGURE 9-5

Prediction-realization or P-R diagram showing the six diagnostic sectors

Notice that the forecast error e_t for any period t can be calculated as either the difference $Y_t - \hat{Y}_{t-1}$ (1) or the difference $A_t - P_t$.

The format for the P–R diagram is shown in Figure 9-5. A is plotted on the vertical scale and P on the horizontal.[1] Exactly the same units should be used for both scales. A line marking the points where $A = P$, called the *line of perfect forecasts,* is drawn as shown. This line together with the two axes divides the graph into six segments. Points falling into the different segments indicate different types of forecast error:

Sectors A, B, and C indicate overforecasts of the level of the variable.

Sectors D, E, and F indicate underforecasts of the level.

Sectors A and D indicate overforecasts of the change.

[1]The use of the P–R diagram was originally suggested by Theil, who placed P on the vertical axis and A on the horizontal. They have been reversed here to simplify a later calculation.

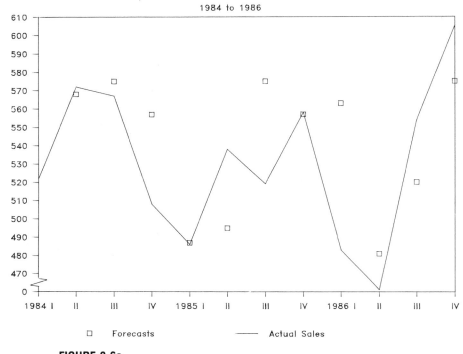

Quarterly Sales and Sales Forecasts
1984 to 1986

FIGURE 9-6a

Quarterly sales and sales forecasts 1984–1986

Sectors C and F indicate underforecasts of the change.

Sectors B and E indicate that the change was in the opposite direction to that forecasted.[2]

Figure 9-6 shows the P-R diagram for the data of Table 9-3 as well as the graph of the actual and forecasted demand. Notice that, of the 11 plotted points, two are very close to the line of perfect forecasts. Six are clearly underforecasts of changes. Five of the 11 points lie below the line of perfect forecasts and four are above, suggesting that, on the average, the forecasts of the level of the variable have tended to be correct. Finally, the

---

[2]Thiel (1971), who developed this technique, referred to these as *turning point errors*. In economic forecasting, this term can also refer to errors in forecasting the *timing* of cyclical changes (or turning points) in economic activity. This is not the sense in which Thiel uses the term, although errors in forecasting the timing of economic peaks and troughs will result in turning point errors on the P–R diagram.

Quarterly Sales And Sales Forecasts

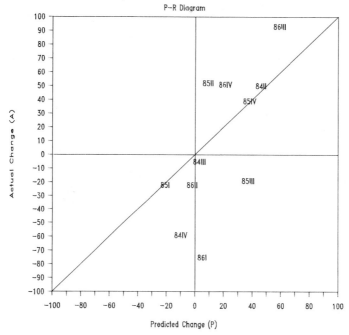

FIGURE 9-6b

P-R diagram

scatter of the points suggests that the correlation between the predicted and actual changes has been postive but low.

U Statistics. Supplementary measures related to the P–R diagram can be calculated to assist in the evaluation. These involve the decomposition of a measure of forecast accuracy, the *mean-square error*, defined as the average squared forecast error:

$$\text{MSE} = \frac{1}{N}\Sigma e_t^2 = \frac{1}{N}\Sigma\,(A_t - P_t)^2 \tag{3}$$

where N is the number of points plotted on the P–R diagram. Notice that this is similar to the MAD of Chapter 5, except that squares of the errors are used rather than their absolute values.

The MSE can be separated algebraically into three components

$$\text{MSE} = (\bar{A} - \bar{P})^2 + (S_A - S_P)^2 + 2S_A\,S_P\,(1 - r) \tag{4}$$

where $\bar{A}$ and $\bar{P}$ are the means of the A's and P's, S_A and S_P are the standard deviations, and r is the coefficient of correlation between A and P. The coefficient of correlation is the square root of the coefficient of determination discussed earlier.

$$\bar{A} = \Sigma \frac{A_t}{N}, \qquad \bar{P} = \Sigma \frac{P_t}{N}$$

$$S_A = \left(\frac{\Sigma A_t^2 - \bar{A} \, \Sigma A_t}{N} \right)^{1/2}$$

$$S_P = \left(\frac{\Sigma P_t^2 - \bar{P} \, \Sigma P_t}{N} \right)^{1/2}$$

$$r = \frac{\Sigma A_t P_t - \bar{A} \, \Sigma P_t}{N S_A S_P}$$

(5)

Dividing both sides of equation (4) by the MSE and multiplying by 100, the percentages of the total MSE associated with each component can be calculated. These are called the U statistics.

$$U_M = \frac{100 \, (\bar{A} - \bar{P})^2}{\text{MSE}}$$

(6a)

$$U_S = \frac{100 \, (S_A - S_P)^2}{\text{MSE}}$$

(6b)

$$U_C = \frac{100 \, [2 \, S_A \, S_P \, (1 - r)]}{\text{MSE}}$$

(6c)

Each component indicates a different type of forecast error as illustrated in Figures 9-7a through f (pp. 279–284). Each of these pairs of graphs shows the sales data from Table 9-3 but with different sets of forecasts.

U_M.   When, on the average, the points tend to lie above or below the line of perfect forecasts, $\bar{A} \neq \bar{P}$ and the first term in equation (1) will not be equal to zero. Figures 9-7a and b show the time series graph and P–R diagram for a situation where the forecasts are all exactly 10 units too low. A and P have equal standard deviations, so $S_A = S_P$ and, since A and P are perfectly correlated, $r = 1$. $U_M = 100$ and the other two components equal zero. The forecast error is entirely the result of a systematic upward bias.

U_S.   Forecasts can be correct on the average but still not reflect the changes that are occurring. A television weather reporter each evening, summer and winter, predicts that the temperature the following day will be 60° (or whatever the annual average is for the area). At the end of the year, it can be claimed that "on the average" the forecasts have been completely accurate. As a practical matter, they have been worthless. Simi-

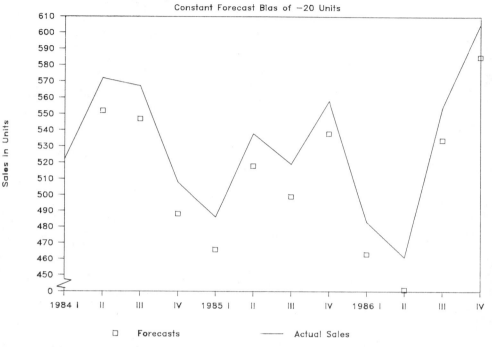

Quarterly Sales and Sales Forecasts
Constant Forecast Bias of −20 Units

☐ Forecasts   ——— Actual Sales

FIGURE 9-7a

Quarterly sales and sales forecasts, constant forecast bias of −20 units

larly, a company that always forecasts next year's sales as 15% greater than this year's may, in some long run sense, turn out to have been very accurate. For planning current operations, however, the forecasts may give little guidance. If forecasts are to adequately reflect short-term changes in sales (or the variable forecasted), there should be as much variability in the predicted changes as in the actual; S_A should equal S_P.[3]

Figures 9-7c and d illustrate a situation where forecasts are correct on the average but where the forecasted change is always the same, so $S_P = 0$ and $U_S = 100$. Notice in Figure 9-7c that a forecast of constant change is not the same as a constant forecast. The pattern of forecasts is almost exactly the same as the actual data but lagged one period.

[3]This is not exactly correct. Unless the forecast and actual changes are perfectly correlated ($r = 1$), ideally S_A should be slightly larger than S_P.

Prediction — Realization Diagram

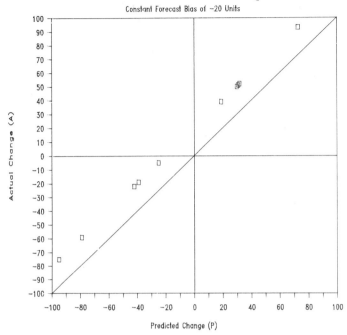

Constant Forecast Bias of −20 Units

FIGURE 9-7b

P-R diagram, constant forecast bias of −20 units

U_C.   Because of random and unpredictable factors, it will never be possible to exactly forecast a future event or variable and r will always be less than 1. (The case where forecasts are negatively correlated with actual changes is possible but rare. Most of these forecasters have hopefully by now found alternative lines of work.) Figures 9-7e and f show the case where the first two components U_M and U_S are zero but the forecasted changes have little relationship to the actual changes (in this example, $r =$ 0.164). All the forecast error is related to this lack of correlation and $U_C =$ 100.

In practice, forecast errors are combinations of all three components. Table 9-3b shows the calculation of the U statistics for the data of Table 9-3a and Figure 9-6. As suggested by our earlier inspection of Figure 9-6b, the bias (difference) in the means is small $(7.55-16.82 = -9.27)$ and contributes only 5.79% to the MSE. The major sources of forecast error are in underforecasts of changes (46.11%) and in lack of correlation (48.09%).

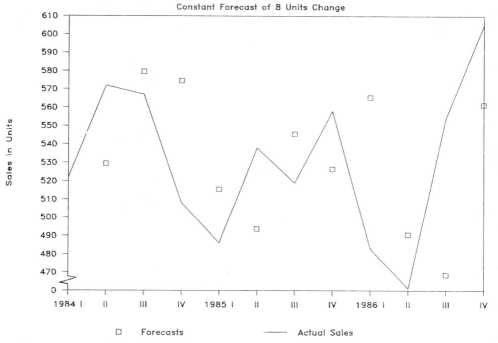

FIGURE 9-7c

Constant forecast of 8 units change

Forecast Adjustments.   Little can be done about a lack of correlation between P and A except to search for better forecasting models or procedures. In cases where the first two components, U_M and U_S, are large, it may be possible to improve the forecasts with a simple mechanical adjustment by fitting a linear relationship to the variables P and A. Table 9-4a (p. 285) and Figure 9-8 (p. 286) show the calculation of a linear relationship between P and A using the method of medians.[4] The resulting relationship can be written in the form

$$P^* = a + bP \tag{7}$$

That is, given a forecasted change P, it should be multiplied by a factor b to increase or decrease its S_P, and an amount a should be added to correct for forecast bias. As shown in Figure 9-8, P is entered on the horizontal axis and P^*, the corrected forecast, is obtained from the vertical. Table 9-4b (p. 285) and Figure 9-9 (p. 287) show the effect of these corrections on past

[4]As noted earlier, A is placed on the vertical axis to simplify fitting this relationship graphically.

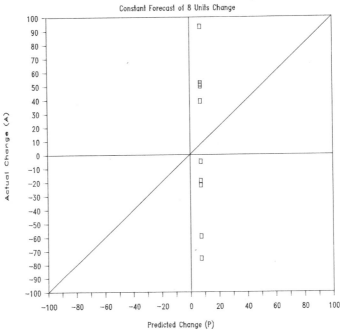

Prediction — Realization Diagram

FIGURE 9-7d

Prediction-realization diagram

forecasts. Comparison of the box-and-whisker diagrams in Figure 9-9 suggests that the correction would have had mixed results. While the middle 50% of the forecasts (the box) is smaller, some of the forecasts were, in fact, less accurate. In any case, for these past forecasts it is too late to make any adjustments. On the other hand, if conditions remain relatively unchanged, a similar adjustment might improve future forecasts.

EX POST QUALITATIVE EVALUATION

In addition to an ex post quantitative determination of the accuracy of the past forecasts, future forecasts and modeling can be aided by reviewing the appropriateness of the assumptions underlying the model and forecast and by searching for variables that were not included in the model but that, in retrospect, could have improved the forecast. Such an evaluation can involve some quantitative measures but is primarily concerned with qualitative considerations. The evaluation should cover three major areas: (1)

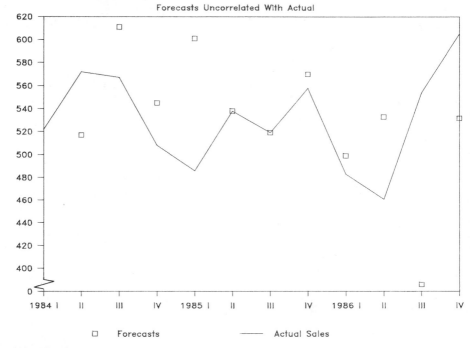

FIGURE 9-7e

Forecasts uncorrelated with actual sales

model specification errors, (2) errors in the independent variables, and (3) effects of omitted factors.

Model Specification Errors

Unless there was a clear theoretical basis for the selection of the form of the forecasting model, it was probably chosen largely because of its apparent fit to historical data. There is always the question of whether the model in fact reflects some stable underlying structure or whether it instead simply describes a temporary, transient state. An ex ante evaluation of the residuals from the model fitted cannot really deal with this issue; a purely quantitative ex post analysis of the magnitudes of the past forecast errors may not always help either.

A detailed study of each forecast error can be of great value. This is especially true when the forecaster had to apply the model to situations that were novel or different. A simple illustration is that of model extrapolation.

Extrapolation means using the model with values of the independent

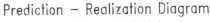

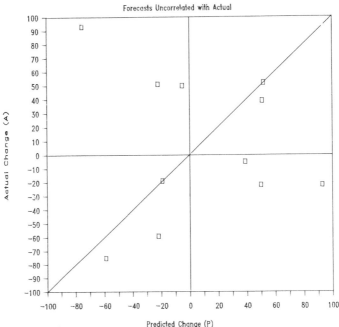

FIGURE 9-7f

P-R diagram, forecasts uncorrelated with actual

variables outside the historical range of the data that were used to develop and fit the model. Although most elementary statistics texts include a warning against extrapolation, for the forecaster it is inevitable. For example, a model that includes a time trend such as $\hat{Y}_t = a + bt$ can only be used by extrapolating to future values of t. This does not mean that extrapolation is not without real and substantial dangers. Figure 9-10 (p. 288) shows hypothetical data generated by a nonlinear relationship between the variables X and Y as shown by the dashed line. Because a random component has been added, the curvature is not readily apparent in the data (shown by the squares). Empirically, a linear model (the solid line) would seem appropriate. As long as future forecasts are based on values of X within the historic range of 1 to 12, it makes little difference that the "wrong" model has been used. Suppose, however, that a forecast requires use of an X value of 17. There will be the potential for a large error in the forecast. On the bright side, if model performance is carefully monitored, such a situation can give additional information about the structure of the system that will not be available as long as X remains within its historic

TABLE 9-4

(a) Corrected Predictions Using a Median-fit Correction Line

Predicted Change P	Actual Change A	A − bP	Corrected Prediction P*
NA	NA		
−21	−22	7.09	−42.74
−10	−59	−45.15	−27.50
−2	−22	−19.23	−16.42
3	−5	−9.16	−9.49
5	−75	−81.93	−6.72
9	52	39.53	−1.18
21	51	21.91	15.45
37	−19	−70.26	37.61
38	39	−13.65	39.00
46	50	−13.73	50.08
59	93	11.26	68.09

For median-fit line: $b = 1.39$
$$a = -13.65$$

(b) U Statistics

	Actual Change A	Predicted Change P	Corrected Prediction P*
Mean	7.55	16.82	9.65
Standard deviation	50.28	24.12	33.42
Correlation (r)		0.705821	0.7058
U components			
Mean		85.98	4.45
Variance		684.33	284.37
Correlation		713.69	988.76
Mean-square error (MSE)		1484.00	1277.58
U_M (%)		5.79%	0.35%
U_S (%)		46.11%	22.26%
U_C (%)		48.09%	77.39%
		100.00%	100.00%

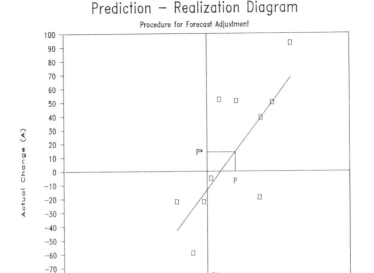

FIGURE 9-8

P-R diagram: Procedure for forecast adjustment

range. Careful study and use of that information can help to improve the forecasting model.

Errors in the Independent Variables

Since models are fitted using existing data, the necessary values of the independent variables are known. When the forecast is developed, it is necessary to use anticipated or forecasted values for these variables. To the extent that these forecast values prove incorrect, the forecasts are in error even if the underlying model is correct. In such a situation, ex post forecast errors should be calculated in two ways: (1) as they actually occurred, and (2) from forecasts recalculated using corrected values for the independent variables. The difference will be the error component due to errors in the

Comparison of Forecast Errors

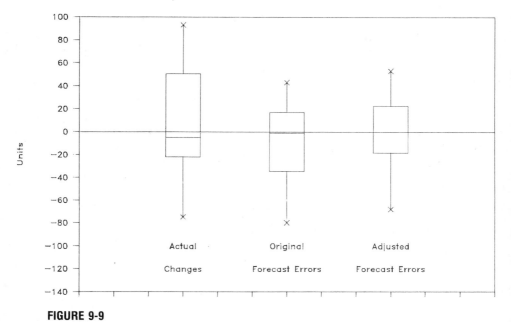

FIGURE 9-9

Comparison of forecast errors

independent variables. In this way the evaluation of the model can be treated as a separate issue from that of the accuracy of the inputs.

Omitted Factors

Just as situations where it is necessary to use extrapolated values for independent variables can add to our knowledge of system structure, unexpectedly large positive or negative forecast errors (outliers) can be helpful and should be carefully analyzed. In most cases, outliers arise because of changes in variables that were not included in the model. This does not always mean that such variables should be included in future forecasts. Many years ago there was a heavy snowstorm in Boston, Massachusetts on Palm Sunday. The effects of the storm were felt well into the following week. The usual pre-Easter peak in retail clothing sales never materialized. A very large forecast error was caused by a factor that we can be sure had not been included in any "model" used by the clothing store forecasters. By the same token, it is unlikely that it was included in future models. It

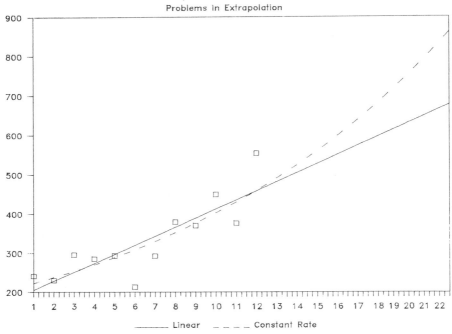

FIGURE 9-10

Model specification error, problems in extrapolation

was an unpredictable external factor and unlikely to become a regular occurrence. In any other cases, an analysis of outliers will give useful insights into the structure of the model and its sensitivity to additional independent variables, which the forecaster can then consider formally including in future models.

EX ANTE QUANTITATIVE EVALUATION

We saw in Chapter 5 that, for operational planning, it is necessary to implicitly or explicitly think of the future forecast error as a probability distribution. The purpose of an ex ante quantitative evaluation is to estimate that distribution. As discussed earlier, a distinction must be made between the sampling errors that can be estimated from the residuals from the fitted model and the nonsampling errors that arise from model misspecification, errors in the independent variables, and omitted factors. Our concern here is with the estimation of the effects of the nonsampling errors on the forecast error probability distribution.

Specification Errors

Models always fit the data used in model development better than any other. Because of this inevitable "overfitting," a better estimate of the probable magnitudes of the forecast errors can be obtained by splitting the data into two parts, one part for model development and one for error estimation. There are a number of ways in which this can be done; one simple approach is illustrated here.

In Chapter 8, a guided approach to model development was illustrated using data on U.S. naval ships and naval personnel. The model developed seemed to describe past changes in personnel well. The critical question for the planner is, will it continue to perform as well in the future? In trying to answer this question, the analysis of Chapter 8 is here repeated using a split-sample approach. Table 9-5a (p. 290) shows the data used previously split into two parts, the years 1951 to 1970 and the years 1971 to 1984. 1971 was chosen as the breakpoint because it falls within the transition period ending the Vietnamese War and beginning the postwar reduction in forces. If a model can be fitted to the earlier years that effectively forecasts the later period, our confidence in our ability to model the underlying structure will be increased. The analysis followed the guided regression procedure described in Chapter 8 and will not be developed here.

The resulting least-squares model is shown in Table 9-5b (p. 291) and compared to the previous model in Table 9-5c (p. 292). In comparison with the model developed earlier, the coefficient of the variable Number of Ships is smaller and the Wartime factor is larger; there is no time trend. The R^2 is slightly smaller. The F value is smaller but still well above the critical value.

This model was next applied to both periods, 1951 to 1970 and 1971 to 1984. The residuals are shown in Figure 9-11 (p. 293) and the P–R diagram in Figure 9-12 (p. 294). Both substantiate the fit of the model to the 20-year period from 1951 to 1970. When the model is applied to the test data, however, the picture appears quite different. Beginning almost immediately in 1972, there appears a large and relatively constant downward bias in the forecasts, indicating that the postwar cutback in the number of ships was not matched by the expected cutback in personnel.

This result illustrates an issue of critical importance to the forecaster. We tend to think of sample size as equivalent to the number of data points used in fitting the model. Here we had 20 years of data and thus a sample of size 20. Looked at another way, the critical element in forecasting personnel after 1970 is the nature and magnitude of the postwar reductions. In

TABLE 9-5

(a) U.S. Navy Ships in Active Service and Active Naval Personnel, 1951 to 1984: Split Data Analysis

Year	Ships	Personnel (000)	Forecast (000)	A	P	Forecast Error
Data used for model development						
1951	1102	736.7	717.9	87.6	76.5	11.1
1952	1129	824.3	813.2	-29.9	-11.1	-18.8
1953	1129	794.4	813.2	-68.7	-73.0	4.3
1954	1113	725.7	721.4	-65.0	-31.2	-33.8
1955	1030	660.7	694.5	9.2	15.2	-6.0
1956	973	669.9	675.9	7.2	4.1	3.1
1957	967	677.1	674.0	-36.1	-27.9	-8.2
1958	891	641.0	649.2	-14.7	-1.8	-12.9
1959	860	626.3	639.2	-8.3	-2.8	-5.5
1960	812	618.0	623.5	9.1	7.8	1.3
1961	819	627.1	625.8	39.3	25.1	14.2
1962	900	666.4	652.2	-1.8	-9.0	7.2
1963	916	664.6	657.4	3.0	-6.9	9.9
1964	917	667.6	657.7	3.8	-3.7	7.5
1965	936	671.4	663.9	73.8	82.6	-8.8
1966	947	745.2	754.0	6.4	17.2	-10.8
1967	973	751.6	762.4	13.8	11.8	2.0
1968	976	765.4	763.4	10.5	-18.2	28.7
1969	926	775.9	747.2	-83.2	-79.8	-3.4
1970	769	692.7	696.1			
Data used for model testing						
1971	702	623.0	587.8	-69.7	-104.9	35.2
1972	654	588.1	572.2	-34.9	-50.8	15.9
1973	584	564.5	549.4	-23.6	-38.7	15.1
1974	512	545.9	526.0	-18.6	-38.5	19.9

Table 9-5 (continued)

Year	Ships	Personnel (000)	Forecast (000)	A	P	Forecast Error
1975	496	535.1	520.8	-10.8	-25.1	14.3
1976	476	524.7	514.3	-10.4	-20.8	10.4
1977	464	529.9	510.4	5.2	-14.3	19.5
1978	453	530.2	506.8	0.3	-23.1	23.4
1979	468	521.9	511.7	-8.3	-18.5	10.2
1980	473	527.2	513.3	5.3	-8.6	13.9
1981	482	540.2	516.2	13.0	-11.0	24.0
1982	513	553.0	526.3	12.8	-13.9	26.7
1983	506	560.3	524.0	7.3	-29.0	36.3
1984	526	572.2	530.5	11.9	-29.8	41.7

(b) Split Data Analysis, Least-squares Regression Results

		Standard Error	t Value	Critical (P = 0.05) Value
Constant (a)	359.4			
Slopes				
Ships (b_1)	0.325	0.033	9.84	2.11
Wartime Correction (b_2)	86.538	7.067	12.25	
Standard error of estimate	14.844			
R^2	0.946			
F value	99.27			3.20
No. of observations	20			
Degrees of freedom	17			

(continued on next page)

TABLE 9-5 (Continued)

(c) Comparison of Three Models

	Split Data 1951 to 1970	All Data, 1951 to 1984	
		With Trend	Without Trend
Constant (a)	359.4	304.4	400.2
Slopes			
Trend (t)		1.912	
Standard error		.645	
t Value		2.965	
Ships (b_1)	0.325	0.368	0.285
Standard error	0.033	0.030	0.011
t Value	9.84	12.30	24.99
Wartime Correction (b_2)	86.5	73.7	85.5
Standard error	7.067	7.047	6.514
t Value	12.25	10.46	13.13
R^2	0.946	0.983	0.978
F value	99.27	426.98	452.65
Degrees of freedom	17	30	31

292

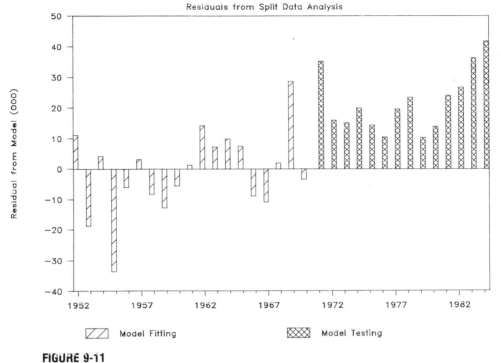

FIGURE 9-11

U. S. Navy—active naval personnel, residuals from split data analysis

forecasting this, we in fact have only a sample of 1. The only postwar period included in this data is that following the Korean War. Looked at in that way, the model may have done a very good job of forecasting since the bias was only approximately 20,000 persons out of a total of approximately 550,000, or 3.6%.

This analysis can be carried a bit further. Table 9-5c compares the coefficients for three models, the split data analysis and models with and without trend fitted to all 34 years of the data from Chapter 8. Notice that when the trend term is omitted the two sets of coefficients are quite similar. The t value for the trend coefficient has, throughout the analysis, been such that the inclusion or exclusion of this term would be a matter of individual judgment.

How should this analysis affect our evaluation of the forecasting model? Overall, the results should be considered to be encouraging. On the other hand, we saw that a major external event (the ending of a war) could have an immediate and large effect on the magnitudes of the forecast

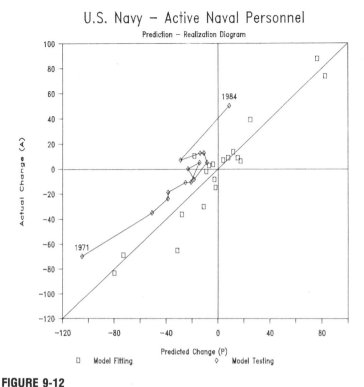

FIGURE 9-12

U. S. Navy—active naval personnel, P-R diagram

errors. This would suggest that the model can be used with some confidence, but with sensitivity to forces in the environment that may not be adequately reflected in the model or in the data used to develop it.

Hidden Extrapolation

As we saw in Figure 9-10, errors in model specification can be amplified greatly when it is necessary to use values of the independent variables that lie outside historical ranges. Ex ante analysis should be particularly sensitive to the possible effects of extrapolation on future forecast error. In this, the forecaster needs to be particularly sensitive to what might be called *hidden extrapolation*.

Hidden extrapolation can occur when the pattern of the independent variables changes, even though each variable by itself may lie within its own historical range. For example, imagine a company that over several years has been increasing the size of the sales force and advertising expenditures both by between 5% and 25% per year. Also suppose that the increases have always been approximately the same for the two variables (within 1% to 2%). Now suppose that next year it is proposed to increase advertising expenditures by 18%, but increase the size of the sales force by only 6%. In fact, the historical data give no information about the effect of this on sales; even though each variable separately lies within its past range, the proposed combination of the two is completely new.[5]

Figure 9-13 (p. 296) shows the problem graphically. Along the band shown in the horizontal plane by the bases of the vertical lines, a relationship between increases in the independent variables and in sales can be determined from the historical data.[6] Outside this band there is no information on whether the relationship is linear or nonlinear or even on the slope of the relationship plane. As an extreme case, imagine that advertising has no effect on sales so that all the increases are due solely to the increases in the size of the sales force. Increasing advertising expenditures by 18% would be irrelevant; only the 6% increase in sales force would have any effect on sales. In practice, of course, the situation would rarely be this extreme. The problem remains, however; if there is any substantial change in the pattern of the independent variables, errors because of model misspecification should be anticipated.

Errors in the Independent Variables

Errors in input data and input forecasts used in the model can be a major source of final forecast error. It can be anticipated in several ways. An ideal solution would be to always use independent variables that "lead" the variable to be forecasted. In this way the input variables would be known and not an additional source of error. As a practical matter, this possibility seldom occurs and becomes more unlikely as the forecast horizon increases.

In some cases an input variable is obtained from forecasts developed in a consistent way or from a consistent source. In such cases it may be useful to construct the model in terms of the available forecast of the variable, rather than the variable itself. For example, suppose a company has a sales forecasting model that includes the independent variable U.S.

---

[5]This problem is very closely related to (although not the same as) the problem of *multicollinearity,* which arises in the statistical fitting of multivariate models. See Pindyck and Rubinfeld (1976) pp. 66–69.

[6]In practice, when two variables are this closely related, only one of the two would actually be included in the model. The problem would remain, although in a different way—that of an "omitted factor."

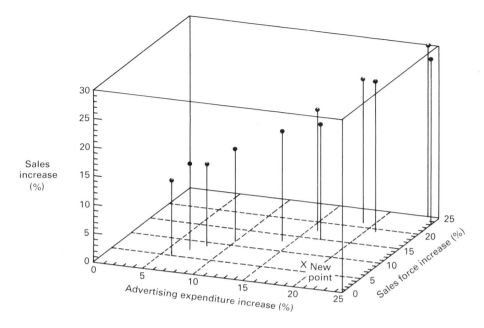

FIGURE 9-13

Hidden extrapolation

Disposable Income. In implementing the model, this variable might be replaced by a forecast regularly obtained from one of the well-known econometric forecasting services. A possible approach would be to construct the model using not disposable income, but rather its forecast.

For most situations a more practical approach to estimating the effects of input variable errors is simulation. The approach is similar to that discussed in Chapter 5 as risk analysis. Having developed a model using input variables whose future values are uncertain, those variables are replaced with their probability distributions, and the final forecast error distribution is obtained by a Monte Carlo type of simulation in the same way that the distribution of operating income was obtained in the example of Chapter 5.

Estimating the Effects of Omitted Factors

In some cases it is possible to develop contingency adjustments for specific factors that could have an impact on the forecasts. The Wartime constant in the Navy personnel model is an illustration. Corrections for strikes, extreme weather, and similar events are other possibilities. In many cases, however, the structured historical data needed for this are not available. In such cases it is necessary to develop the estimates by subjective or judgmental methods. This is discussed in more detail in Chapter 11.

EX ANTE QUALITATIVE EVALUATION

This aspect of forecast evaluation becomes particularly important in the following chapters with the consideration of long-range forecasting and strategic planning. Discussion is therefore postponed until Chapter 12. One aspect of particular importance here is the question of developing and using multiple models. In most forecasting situations it is possible to develop several different models for the same variable. For example, trends can be removed by fitting a trend line or by differencing. The trend can be linear or a logarithmic transformation can be used. Specific input variables may or may not be included. A common question is, Which model should be used? The answer is, All of them. As noted in the readings, techniques exist for combining different models into a single forecast. More important, to the extent that models give dissimilar forecasts, the planner is alerted to additional sources of possible forecast error for which some form of contingency planning may be necessary. The converse is not necessarily true. The fact that all the models give similar results may only indicate that they have all been constructed by the same person or persons with the same subjective biases. Unfortunately, it too often seems to be a human failing to confuse agreement with accuracy.

SUMMARY

A question of central concern to both the forecaster and the planner/manager is that of the quality of the forecast or of the procedure used to obtain the forecast. The manager is primarily interested in ex ante evaluation, that is, how good or how accurate the forecast is likely to be. The forecaster is also interested in ex post evaluation as a way of improving future forecasts. Even for the manager, the past performance of a forecasting method can be an indication of how well it will perform in the future. In this chapter, we have limited discussion to those aspects of forecast evaluation that are normally of concern or interest to the planner/manager, as well as the technical analyst and forecaster. Technical issues of concern primarily to the forecaster are treated in detail in some of the following references.

READINGS

The CUSUM Graph

An extended coverage of the CUSUM approach can be found in

C. S. VAN DOBBEN DE BRUYN, *Cumulative Sum Tests: Theory and Practice*, London, Charles Griffin & Co., 1968.

Other material can be found in

P. J. HARRISON and O. L. DAVIS, "The Use of CUSUM Techniques for the Control of Routine Forecasts of Product Demand," *Operational Research Quarterly*, vol. 12 (1964), pp. 325–333.

WARREN GILCHRIST, *Statistical Forecasting*, London, Wiley, 1976, pp. 252–254.

The Statgraphics® program noted in Chapter 7 includes a graphical CUSUM procedure that automatically overlays a mask on the graph. The technique used to design the mask is slightly different from the one outlined here.

The P–R Diagram

The P–R diagram was originally proposed by Theil. A good description can be found in

HENRI THEIL, *Applied Economic Forecasting*, Amsterdam, North-Holland, 1971, Chapter 2.

Split-sample Validation

Additional material can be found in

CHARLES W. GROSS and ROBIN T. PETERSON, *Business Forecasting*, 2nd ed., Boston, Houghton Mifflin, 1983, Chapter 10.

J. SCOTT ARMSTRONG, *Long-Range Forecasting*, New York, Wiley, 1978, pp. 309–319.

FREDERICK MOSTELLER and JOHN W. TUKEY, *Data Analysis and Regression*, Reading, Mass., Addison-Wesley, 1977, pp. 36–41.

Simulation

For a discussion of the use of simulation in forecasting, see

ROBERT S. PINDYCK and DANIEL L. RUBINFELD, *Econometric Models and Economic Forecasts*, New York, McGraw-Hill, 1976, Chapters 10–12.

Combining Forecasts

An introduction to this topic can be found in

C. W. J. GRANGER, *Forecasting in Business and Economics*, New York, Academic Press, 1980, Chapter 8.

An additional bibliography can be found in

DEREK W. BUNN, "Statistical Efficiency in the Linear Combination of Forecasts," *International Journal of Forecasting*, vol. 1, no. 2 (1985), pp. 151–164.

Forecast Evaluation

For other views on this subject, see Granger (Chapter 8) and J. Scott Armstrong (Part 3), both cited previously. For the perspective of an economist, see

WILLIAM F. BUTLER et al., eds., *Methods and Techniques of Business Forecasting*, Englewood Cliffs, N.J., Prentice-Hall, 1974, Part 6.

PROBLEMS

1. The Trekun Company uses sales force estimates that are collected monthly as a basis for forecasting the dollar volume of sales for the following month. Each month by the fifteenth, all sales personnel must submit estimates of their sales for the following month to the sales office managers, who then consolidate this information and send it to the vice-president of sales. This person in turn totals these estimates and makes final adjustments as necessary. The final forecast is then used as a basis for short-range-production and cash-flow planning.

You have been given the following information covering the past two years on the forecasts as developed by the VP Sales and actual monthly sales (000 omitted):

Month	1985 Actual	1985 Forecast	1986 Actual	1986 Forecast
Jan	221	213	423	411
Feb	209	219	369	410
Mar	264	246	504	480
Apr	239	280	476	507
May	280	326	590	560
Jun	319	332	599	603
Jul	327	337	658	615
Aug	302	359	561	624
Sep	367	363	596	627
Oct	357	383	588	625
Nov	374	406	638	635
Dec	426	411	597	619

   a. Using the 1985 data only, estimate the standard deviation of the forecast errors. Base your estimate on the Qspd of the errors, as discussed in Chapter 4.

   b. Using this estimate of the standard deviation, set up a CUSUM table and graph with $d = 6$ and $k = 0.3$. Analyze the forecast errors for both 1985 and 1986. Discuss your results.

2.   a. Using the data from Problem 1, develop a P–R diagram and U statistics for the 1985 data. Interpret your results.

   b. Using only the 1985 data, develop an equation for P^* and apply the correction to the data for both 1985 and 1986.

   c. Develop separate P–R diagrams for 1986 using P for one and P^* for the other. Compare and interpret your results.

3. Compare the approaches used in Problems 1 and 2. What do you think would be the advantages and disadvantages of each?

4. The Ephring Manufacturing Company makes a wide variety of laboratory and testing equipment for industry and research activities such as universities. A program has just been started to improve budget planning. As part of this, they are exploring alternative approaches to sales forecasting. As an initial test, they have chosen one of their more established products, a testing device used in the brewing industry, for which they have 6 years of data.

Initial study suggests that there is a relationship between sales of this device and the output of the brewing industry as measured in millions of barrels of beer produced per quarter. The data are shown in

TABLE P9-4

Instrument Sales and Sales Forecasts, 1979 to 1984

	Quarter	Beer Production (million bbl)	Instrument Sales ($000)	Sales Forecast ($000)
1979	I	44.2	$369	$414
	II	50.1	376	380
	III	48.4	402	381
	IV	40.6	377	408
1980	I	45.9	427	445
	II	52.3	417	413
	III	52.0	404	438
	IV	41.3	430	422
1981	I	44.6	472	421
	II	55.2	441	457
	III	55.2	466	488
	IV	41.7	463	429
1982	I	47.8	508	479
	II	54.0	466	439
	III	52.3	496	443
	IV	42.0	509	435
1983	I	46.1	551	448
	II	52.2	504	412
	III	52.5	540	446
	IV	41.4	531	424
1984	I	46.6	577	457
	II	53.7	561	435
	III	50.8	580	419
	IV	41.1	555	418

Table P9-4. It was decided to use the data from 1979 to 1982 to fit the model and then use the remaining eight quarters for testing the model.

The first model, using seasonally adjusted data, was:
Sales (in dollars) = 16,186 * beer production (in millions of barrels) − 379,652.

a. Forecasts and actual sales by quarters are shown in the table. Using these data, develop graphs of the model residuals (as discussed in Chapter 8) and a prediction/realization (P–R) diagram.

b. For the years 1979 to 1982 and 1983 to 1984, calculate and interpret the U statistics.

c. In evaluating the potential of this model for forecasting, what other factors should be considered?

d. After further analysis, it was finally decided to use a different forecasting model based on cumulative sales to date and industry capacity, as well as production and sales of the previous quarter. This model is not shown here. Why do you think this model might have been chosen?

Experience with this model through 1985 and 1986 has been favorable. It is now the second quarter of 1987 and the budgeting cycle for the calendar year 1988 is in progress. You are in charge of developing a budget proposal for consideration by the top management of the firm and have been given the following projections. 1988 I, $629,000; II, $665,000; III, $646,000; IV, $630,000.

  e. What factors would you want to consider in an ex ante evaluation of these projections? What additional information would you need for planning purposes?

  f In 1988, as feedback is obtained on the accuracy of these projections, you would like to be prepared to evaluate the forecasts as a way of improving future forecasts. What information will you need and what techniques of ex post evaluation will you use?

5. In time-series analysis, unlike other types of statistical analysis, not all data points are created equal. In the text example of the relationship between U.S. Navy ships and personnel, a model was fitted to the years 1951 through 1970 using least squares. Using the data of Table 9-5, use least squares to fit the same model to the years 1951 through 1971. Discuss possible reasons for differences observed in the two resulting models.

6. For the years 1951 through 1971, also fit the relationship using the median-fit technique. Compare your results. Now use the median-fit technique on the period 1951 through 1970. Do the differences appear the same?

CHAPTER 10

Strategic Programs and Projects

In Part III we looked at planning and forecasting in situations where it was possible to build on a strong sense of continuity between past, present, and future. This would occur, for example, where we were concerned with servicing the demand for a specific product with a well-established customer base and forecasts were obtained by analyzing historic time series. We would look for patterns and relationships, and project these patterns into the future. We would be able to use our knowledge of past forecast errors as a way of estimating the probable magnitude of future forecast errors and to use this information in incorporating forecast uncertainty into the planning process.

Now, we shift our attention to situations where that sense of continuity is much weaker and patterns and relationships of the past are less clearly relevant in planning for the future. As we shall see, forecasts and evaluations of forecasts must be developed by drawing analogies between the present and what appear to be similar situations in the past and by the subjective interpretation of historical information, rather than by completely objective and possibly mechanical data analysis and projection.

In fact, no planning or forecasting problem is ever completely a matter of mechanical projection or solely one of subjective analysis; in the real world, all planning combines, in varying degrees, elements of both. To emphasize the differences, however, Chapter 5 focused on examples that depended primarily on the formal projection of historic patterns; in Chapter 10, we examine two types of planning situations which arise most often when historical continuity is lacking.

ORGANIZATIONAL CHANGE

Change in organizations is implemented through broad strategic programs that integrate and coordinate the individual activities of many different organizational subunits. These programs in turn are made up of smaller projects that are designed to accomplish specific components of the program. In both cases the emphasis is on dealing with new situations and new activities so that the applicability of past experience and historical records is usually limited. This, in turn, severely restricts the usefulness of many of the forecasting techniques considered in previous chapters and requires a different sense of the meaning of forecasting. To set the stage for our exploration of these new issues, we examine two simple planning situations where planners typically must deal with this lack of relevant history.

The first is strategic program planning. Organizations have, implicitly or explicitly, a basic sense of long-run direction or mission that is shared, or at least understood, by the members of the organization. Strategic planning is designed to translate this sense of mission into an explicit organizational strategy and to develop specific programs for implementing that strategy. In the example to be developed here, we will not attempt to deal with all the complexities of that process but limit ourselves to the problem of dealing with the uncertainty about the future that must be faced in choosing a specific program to implement.

The second situation is that of project planning as it might occur in developing a new product, opening a new plant, entering a new market, or acquiring another company. It is tied to the first in that strategic programs are implemented through series of specific projects; it differs in that projects, as compared to programs, are developed at a much more detailed level, are shorter term, and are more quantitative.

Chapters 11 and 12 introduce forecasting procedures that are particularly relevant for (although not limited to) these applications. A fundamental problem is the lack of an adequate historical data base and the need to rely on human judgment in developing forecasts. Chapter 11 explores procedures for collecting and combining subjective opinions as an input to planning and forecasting. Equally important, in strategic planning the forecast needs are long range and multivariate. To the extent that historical quantitative data are available, they may be helpful, but new problems arise in the interpretation and projection of these data. Chapter 12 expands on the discussion of trends begun in Chapter 4 and considers some issues in long-range trend projection as it relates to long-range forecasting. Also, Chapter 12 looks at the way in which the multivariate character of strategic planning affects our approach to forecasting and how the different quantitative and qualitative forecast elements are put together and used in what have come to be called *scenarios*.

Major Points to be Noted

1. *The differences between operational and strategic planning; the use of outcome and payoff tables in guiding the process of creating and evaluating alternative strategies.*

2. *The use of scenarios as a way of describing alternative states of the external environment and alternative outcomes.*

3. *The uses of probability distributions in strategic program and project scheduling. It should be noted that the issues raised in Chapter 5 in the use of pro forma budgets are still appropriate here.*

STRATEGIC PLANNING

In Chapter 2 we followed a young couple through a series of decisions as they considered and then purchased a small-town hardware store. Although the example is relatively simple, the process outlined is common to all organizations, large and small. Six distinct stages in this planning process were identified. Of these, two are the subject of strategic planning:

1. The formulation of a statement of organizational direction or mission and the expressing of this mission through strategic objectives and policies.

2. The translation of the strategic objectives and policies into strategic plans for existing business operating units and into programs for strategic change.

Developing the Mission Statement

The mission of an organization cannot simply be described in financial terms. It is a function of the personal goals and desires of the internal stakeholders—the active owners, managers, and key employees, the resources available to the organization, and the forces active in the external environment. Because the internal stakeholders will never have individual desires that are completely in agreement, the process of developing a sense of mission or direction for the overall organization will be a political or negotiated one as the various stakeholder groups attempt to reconcile their different points of view. In the case of our hypothetical hardware store, a wide variety of options is potentially open: to continue to run a farm-based hardware store, to expand into the outdoor recreation business, to expand into the sale of art and handicraft such as pottery, hand weaving, and similar products. The two owners probably have somewhat different ideas as to the future they would like to see. One may love boating and fishing and dream of someday operating a marina; the other may hope that the store and town will become a center for artists and craftspeople and the store a sort of local gallery.

If the store is in the center of the town, expansion in some of these tourist-related areas may attract similar businesses so that the development of their store will be only part of a broader change in the entire downtown area. Current merchants and residents may or may not be in favor of such change. The proposed recreation area, if developed, will affect the practicality of expanding into tourist-related fields. The overall state of the economy and the availability of financial capital will be critical. The extent to which the current business remains profitable will affect their ability to attract new capital and thus their ability to expand.

The skills of the owners will have a strong impact on the areas in which they are able to expand. The size and location of the current store will have an effect. Do they have room to expand? Can they acquire lake or river frontage for a marina?

Whether or not the chosen direction or mission is ever actually put in writing, development of a sense of direction requires discussion among the stakeholders. Assumptions about future events and trends will be part of these discussions. It is the job of the forecaster to help develop these assumptions. The use of these forecasts or assumptions is essentially political, a basis for a negotiated agreement on future direction. The primary criterion of a "good" forecast will not be solely ex post accuracy. The assumptions made may prove to be correct, but by the time the accuracy of the forecast is known it will no longer be important because it will be too late to make the necessary corrections or adjustments. The more important criterion is that the forecast be plausible. This does not mean that the sole purpose of the forecast is to help someone "win" the argument (although it can have this effect); the primary purpose is to give everyone involved a common view of the future that they can believe in and work toward. An equally important aspect of these forecasts is that they direct our attention to potential environmental threats that could jeopardize success and to possible opportunities that could be pursued to advantage.

Strategic Objectives

To implement this overall sense of direction, it is necessary that the broad statement of mission be expanded into sets of strategic objectives.[1] These are statements of required accomplishments if the mission is to be achieved. In this example, one objective might be to continue to run the existing business profitably. Another might be to expand into the recreational boating and fishing business. A third objective might be to work toward convincing others in the area of the desirability of turning the town into a recreation and tourist center in order to create a more favorable environment for the boating business.

Compared to the overall statement of mission, strategic objectives are quite specific. At the same time, the time frame tends to be flexible, the precise details of how the objectives are to be achieved are not included, and formal quantitative measures of success are not specified. These are developed as the strategic programs are developed and as tactical objectives are set for evaluating the performance of the programs and business units.

Strategic Programs and Operating Businesses

Each strategic objective must be assigned for accomplishment to one or more organizational units. It is useful to make a distinction between organizational units whose charter or mandate is primarily concerned with ongoing operational activities and those units intended to deal with the implementation of major changes in the direction of the organization. In this example, the current hardware store will need to continue to be operated profitably if only to supply the capital necessary to move into the other areas. As in Chapter 5, this means that budgets must be developed and ongoing activities and inventories maintained. Tactical objectives must be set and measures of performance developed to assure the success of that business.

By contrast, the objective of developing a recreational business could be implemented in two different ways. If the current plan is only to have

---

[1]Some writers prefer the word "goals" to "objectives." In this discussion, no distinction is made between the two terms.

this as an adjunct to the existing hardware store, it might be set up as an additional activity within the hardware store. In that case it would probably take the form of a relatively limited project and could be managed as part of the current business. If, on the other hand, the intention is to eventually develop a major recreation business consisting of a marina and campground, with recreational boat sales and service and equipment rental, a simple addition to the present store may or may not be the right way to start. What may be needed is a longer-range developmental program. Although the same people may be involved, it will probably be conceptualized as a separate business unit rather than as a part of the existing store.

In this case the program could include a number of separate but interrelated projects. In this example, one project might be directed toward funding, financing, and acquiring the land necessary for the future marina/campground development. There might be another project for the start-up of a boat sales and service business, possibly at a different location. A third project within the overall program might be the store addition discussed earlier. Each project would require separate, detailed tactical objectives. At the same time, all would be directed toward the same strategic objective, the development of a recreational boating business.

Strategic Planning Scenarios

Strategic planning, whether at the level of developing the mission statement or of creating business and program strategies, involves assumptions about the future external environment. These assumptions need to cover the entire environmental range—economic, political, social, technological, and natural factors. Time horizons can be long; the development of a large recreational business from the base of a small-town hardware store can take many years. There is little point to arguing whether forecasting is possible over these long time horizons; decisions have to be made. To support these decisions, assumptions about the future are needed. It makes little difference whether they are called forecasts or by some other name, the problem is the same.[2] At one time it was common to use the term "planning assumptions." Now the usual term has come to be "scenario."

A *scenario* (or set of planning assumptions) is a set of statements about a possible future state of the environment and of the events and other changes that will lead to that future state. These statements are both qualitative and quantitative and cover the full range of factors necessary for

---

[2] In this book we have chosen to use "forecasts" and "forecasting" as general terms covering all the different approaches because, as we shall see in the following chapters, many of the techniques used in scenario development tend to have applications in other forecasting and planning situations as well.

the development of the required plans. It must be stressed that the issue is not whether it is possible to foresee the outcomes for all these factors. Assumptions will be made one way or another; the issue is whether the assumptions are explicit and collectively agreed upon or implicit and different for each person involved.

A scenario consists of statements about events and trends. An *event* is something that can be identified as happening at a particular time and is described by indicating *what* happens, *when* it happens, and *where*. Ideally, it should also describe *how*, that is, the other events and factors that will lead up to the event. Its description may involve some quantitative elements but is for the most part expressed qualitatively.

A *trend* is a pattern of change over time, almost always in some quantitative variable. As the term is used here, trends can include not only the trend component of a time series, as discussed in Chapter 3, but also long-term cyclical movements and systematic changes (trends) in seasonal patterns.

The scenario that combines these events and trends can be thought of as a sort of "short story," except that the literary format of the latter is replaced by a high degree of structure and terseness. Table 10-1 (p. 310) shows an abbreviated outline of the assumption topics that might be included in a scenario to be used in planning for the future of the hardware store of our example.

Even in this short list, several important characteristics of planning assumptions can be noted. First, the necessary assumptions cover far more than just economic or market conditions. For convenience, the assumptions have been grouped into five categories: economic, political, social, technological, and natural (sometimes called ecological). Further subdivision would be possible: social, for example, includes demographic and cultural as well as social variables; technological covers both product (materials) and process (standards); natural includes both inputs or raw materials and pollution effects. At the same time, the assignment of assumptions to categories is, to a degree, arbitrary. Taxation is both an economic and a political variable; water pollution is as much a technological and political as a natural factor.

Assumptions are not independent. Changes in property taxes and in family conditions affect the extent of ownership of second homes. Changes in the pattern of industrial development in the area affect water quality. It follows that, beyond developing assumptions for each of the individual trends and events, it is necessary to assure ourselves that the overall pattern of the assumptions is internally consistent.

Uncertainty and Multiple Scenarios. Strategic evaluation of any program or business involves three different elements:

1. Comparison with the mission and the strategic objectives. Will it accomplish the desired results?

TABLE 10–1

Environmental Scenario Outline for a Hardware Store in Southern Wisconsin

Economic

1. Rate of growth or decline in the area dairy economy:
   a. Demand for dairy products
   b. Total output of dairy products
   c. Number, size, and types of farms
   d. Prices and operating costs
2. Regional urban unemployment rate
3. Interest rates and availability of long-term capital
4. Price and availability of motor fuel
5. Industrial development in nonurban parts of the region

Political

1. Construction of federal dam and recreational area
2. Federal and state licensing and taxation of recreational boating
3. State and federal income tax changes
4. Changes in state and local property taxes
5. State expenditures on tourism and tourist industry support
6. Changes in government safety regulations
7. Community government support for recreation and tourism
8. State and federal dairy farm support
9. State and local support of nonurban industrial development

Social

1. Regional demographic change
2. Distribution of population by marital status and family size
3. Distribution of primary residence by urban, suburban, and rural
4. Ownership of second homes
5. Changes in use of four-day work week
6. Changes in preferences for different types of vacations
7. Changes in structure of family versus corporate farming

Technological

1. Changes in materials and technology for boat construction and repair
2. Changes in standards and standardization within the boating industry
3. Changes in design and construction of farm equipment
4. Changes in farm chemical use
5. Changes in construction technology and practices

Natural

1. Changes in rainfall and water levels in rivers and lakes
2. Changes in water quality and effects on fish populations
3. Changes in air and water quality and effects on dairy farming

2. Comparison between the required and the available resources. Is it feasible?

3. Evaluation of the sensitivity of the program or business to differences between the environmental assumptions and the actual environmental conditions that will evolve. What will be the possible outcomes and consequences if the assumptions prove to be incorrect?

The forecaster (and this chapter) is primarily concerned with the third aspect of evaluation. As we shall see, this involves the development and use of several different sets of environmental assumptions which have come to be referred to as *multiple scenarios* or *alternative futures*.

For our purposes, sensitivity testing will be viewed primarily as a rational, analytic process. The approach is similar to the use of the *outcome table* as described in Chapter 2. Here, however, the emphasis is on the creation of new strategic programs rather than on choosing from a prespecified set of specific actions and on evaluating program sensitivity rather than on making an "optimal" choice of an action. The general structure of the process, as it might be developed for the hardware store, is outlined in Table 10-2 (p. 312).

In Table 10-2a, possible program components are identified. In this example, the list includes current businesses (P_1), expansion possibilities (P_2 and P_3), and new business opportunities (P_4, P_5, and P_6). In Table 10-2b, several possible scenario themes are suggested, chosen to reflect different sets of environmental assumptions and to test the strengths and weaknesses of the potential program components. Unlike the actions and environmental states of the examples introduced in Chapters 2 and 5, neither of these lists is final or all-inclusive. They will be augmented as the process of developing a strategic program unfolds.

Environmental scenarios should consider only factors that are not affected by the company's choice of strategy. For example, the actions that a competitor might take if the store were to expand into the sale of bulk chemicals (P_2) should be thought of as part of the outcome of that program component and not be included in the environmental scenario (although the general structure of local competition might be). For each combination of a strategy element and an environmental scenario, it is necessary to develop a detailed description of the anticipated outcome. To distinguish these from the environmental scenarios, they are referred to as *outcome scenarios*. As can be seen in Table 10-2c, with six possible program components and four environmental scenarios, 24 possible outcomes will need to be evaluated. For example, for the assumption of a weak rural economy scenario (T_4), the long-term viability of the basic business (P_1) would be evaluated as outcome O_{14}. A major limitation on the number of environmental scenarios that can be considered is the extent to which it also expands the number of outcome scenarios that must be evaluated.

TABLE 10–2

Strategic Planning for a Hardware Store in Southern Wisconsin

(a) List of Possible Strategic Program Components

P_1 Maintenance and improvement of the basic general hardware business

P_2 Expansion of the farm hardware business to sales of heavy farm equipment and sales of bulk chemicals

P_3 Expansion of fishing and hunting lines to other recreational and tourism supplies

P_4 Development of a recreational boating business, including boat sales and operation of a marina

P_5 Development of a dealership in country antiques

P_6 Development of a dealership in art and handicraft

(b) List of Alternative Environmental Scenario Themes

T_1 A strong agricultural and dairy economy, but with little expansion of industry into rural areas of the region

T_2 Weak and declining agricultural economy, but expansion of industrial development with strong support from all levels of government

T_3 Decline of the local dairy-based economy, but a major increase in tourism based on regional development of water resources and strong government support of the tourism industry

T_4 Generally weak and variable economy in the Upper Midwest affecting both urban and rural regions

(c) Outcome Table Framework

Strategic Program Components	Alternative Environmental Scenario Themes			
	T_1	T_2	T_3	T_4
P_1	O_{11}	O_{12}	O_{13}	O_{14}
P_2	O_{21}	O_{22}	O_{23}	O_{24}
P_3	O_{31}	O_{32}	O_{33}	O_{34}
P_4	O_{41}	O_{42}	O_{43}	O_{44}
P_5	O_{51}	O_{52}	O_{53}	O_{54}
P_6	O_{61}	O_{62}	O_{63}	O_{64}

Development of Environmental Scenarios. The job of the forecaster is to develop and interpret the environmental scenarios necessary for this evaluation. Several questions must be addressed:

How many scenarios should be developed?

What should be the themes of the scenarios?

What elements should be included in each scenario?

What should be the form of each scenario?

The answers to these questions depend on how the scenarios are in fact to be used. Although here we are emphasizing the rational/analytic aspects of the process, in most cases, strategy development cannot be treated solely in this way; the issues are too important and complex. In practice, scenarios are used by management as inputs to a much more complex organizational and political decision and planning process. The nature and number of the scenario(s) is as much a function of the needs and desires of the managers involved as of the forecaster's desires for analytical correctness and completeness.

How Many Scenarios? For many managers, especially those who are only beginning to use a formal approach to planning, there may be difficulties in dealing with more than one set of environmental assumptions. The forecaster will be asked to develop a single "most likely" forecast. The danger of using only one scenario is that the resulting strategy is likely to be "tailored" to fit those specific assumptions and may be overly sensitive to deviations from them.

The alternative is to develop and consider several different sets of assumptions or *multiple scenarios*. The number depends primarily on the desires of the managers. The simplest procedure is to create two. These should both appear to be highly likely and, at the same time, equally plausible. They are sometimes referred to as "deadly enemy" scenarios. This approach has the desirable effect of forcing the manager(s) to recognize the real uncertainty that they face. Its limitation is the difficulty of capturing all the different threats and opportunities in only two alternative futures. At the other extreme, most people have difficulty in simultaneously considering more than perhaps three or four different scenarios. A useful approach is to start with two to four scenarios that focus on what appear to be the most pressing and immediate threats in the external environment. As the process of strategy development proceeds and managers explore new strategic programs, new relevant scenarios can be added. In many cases the forecaster may develop and explore 10 to 15 different scenarios, even though these will not all be presented simultaneously to management.

What Themes? With one scenario, it will be expected to be a "most likely" set of assumptions and should reflect the best judgment of the forecaster. Indeed, this is the difficulty with this approach, because even the most likely scenario of the most skillful forecaster usually turns out to be very wrong in some significant ways and to omit some elements that, in retrospect, turn out to have been critical.

With two or more scenarios, each should be plausible, but none should appear to dominate the others. With three, there is an unfortunate tendency to think of one as the "most likely" and the other two as the "most optimistic" and "most pessimistic." The difficulty with this is twofold. In such a situation there is a strong tendency to ignore all but the "most likely" and return to a de facto consideration of one scenario. Also, it is not always clear, given the complexity of the planning process, exactly what is meant by "most optimistic" or "most pessimistic." Scenarios in which everything goes wrong or every aspect exceeds expectations are rarely plausible. A more useful approach with multiple scenarios is to construct each around a significant theme based on the occurrence of a critical event or events or the dominance of certain trends chosen from a list such as that of Table 10-1. In Table 10-2b, four themes were suggested, each emphasizing certain key factors from Table 10-1. The intent should be to develop scenarios illustrative of the full range of possibilities, rather than to be overly concerned with minor variations on what is currently assumed to be "likely." This is more easily said than done. Experience has shown that one of the hardest challenges facing the forecaster is to separate issues of scenario internal consistency and plausibility from those of what the forecaster personally believes to be "likely."

What Elements?   The specific elements that should be included depend on the particular businesses and strategic programs being evaluated. This is one reason why the forecaster should be prepared to develop additional scenarios as the planning process proceeds. The initial list, as in Table 10-2b, should be as broad as possible, but clearly cannot include every possible aspect of the environment. Of necessity it will strongly reflect the manager's initial perceptions of the elements with the potentially greatest impact on the strategic options open to the firm. As the planning process proceeds and new types of options are considered, the content of the scenarios needs to be changed as well.

In choosing elements it is important to distinguish between environmental factors that are truly external and beyond even the indirect influence of the manager and those that the manager can affect. As indicated earlier, the latter should be included in the outcome scenario rather than in the environmental scenario. Suppose in a nearby town there is a farm equipment dealer who also sells boats. If our couple decides to enter the recreational boating business, it will undoubtedly provoke some response from that dealer. That response, however, is part of a particular strategic outcome and would not occur if the couple pursued a different strategy. The dealer's response is therefore not part of the general external environment.

What Form?   Scenarios are not short stories. They should be as brief as possible. A format consisting of short statements of the component assumptions arranged by major topic areas is frequently used. Such a scenario could be supplemented by appropriate graphs and tables if desired. When multiple scenarios are used, it is helpful to have them all in the same format. If the first scenario makes an assumption about the size and composition of the local population, all the others should have an assumption covering the same elements at the same place. While frequently it is useful to arrange the material in outline form, some managers feel more comfortable with a more informal structure similar to a briefing report. If the outline form is used, it is helpful to start with a short abstract that summarizes the basic theme of the scenario.

The forecaster will also find it useful to develop a *range table* that lists all the common elements of the scenarios in a column and the alternative themes in the caption. Table 10-3 (p. 316) shows a small part of such a table. A complete range table would include all four scenarios from Table 10-2b and all the elements of Table 10-1. The body of the table would then list and compare the different assumptions made under each theme. The intent is to avoid making the same or overly similar assumptions for a particular element across all the scenarios considered.

Using Scenarios in Planning

To this point we have been considering the various factors that the planner/manager must focus on in developing strategic programs, with particular emphasis on the issues involved in creating the necessary forecasts or scenarios. Although a full discussion of the use of these concepts in the planning process is beyond the scope of this book, it will be useful to end this section by summarizing the remaining steps.

The next stage starts with a list of potential strategic program components (P_i) and scenario themes (T_j). For each combination of these, detailed outcome scenarios (O_{ij}) must be developed. This is not a simple task. It is relatively easy to surmise that scenario T_1 (strong agricultural economy) will be favorable for program components P_1 (the current business) and P_2 (farm equipment and chemicals), but to work out the precise details of this relationship is a much more complicated process. It is necessary to take each assumption for each element of Table 10-1 and for the given theme scenario and interpret it in the context of the current position of the store, the particular program component, and the other assumptions. For a small business, of necessity, these will have to be based on rough calculations and guesses, while for a larger business it may be possible to develop and apply a variety of computer planning models.

The next step is to combine the program components into strategic programs. As in Table 10-4a (p. 314), three possible programs might be:

1. To concentrate on the agricultural hardware business (P_1 plus P_2)
2. To expand into the recreation business (P_1, P_3, and P_4)
3. To expand into art, handicrafts, and antiques (P_1, P_5, and P_6)

TABLE 10–3

Partial Range Table for Scenario Themes for Hardware Store Strategic Planning

Scenario Element	Scenario Theme	
	T_1: Strong Agriculture	T_2: Industrial Development
Economic		
1. Rate of growth/decline in area dairy economy		
a. Demand for dairy products	Average increase for all products: 2.5% per year	For all products: less than 1% per year
	For specialty products such as cheese: 6% per year	
b. Total output of dairy products	Local output increases at same rate as national demand	Shift of production to the southwest U.S.; local output declines at 1% per year
c. Number, size, and types of farms	Decline in number since 1980 levels off and stays constant at 1984 level	Number of farms decreases by 5% per year
	Average size and type (primarily dairy) unchanged	Size of remaining farms increases slightly (2% per year); increased specialization; total number of people employed decreases by 2.5% per year
d. Prices and operating costs	Fluid milk support price drops to $11.50 per cwt (hundred pounds) and then increases at rate of inflation	Support price drops to $10 per cwt and remains at that level
	Parity index rises to 75 by 1988 and then remains steady	Parity index drops to and remains at 50.

TABLE 10–4

(a) Strategic Payoff Table for a Hardware Store in Southern Wisconsin

Alternative Strategic Programs	Program Components	Alternative Environmental Scenario Themes			
		T_1	T_2	T_3	T_4
S_1	P_1 and P_2	65	30	50	20
S_2	P_1, P_3, and P_4	55	75	100	5
S_3	P_1, P_5, and P_6	50	65	80	0

(b) Opportunity Cost Table

Alternative Strategic Programs	Program Components	Alternative Environmental Scenario Themes			
		T_1	T_2	T_3	T_4
S_1	P_1 and P_2	0	45	50	0
S_2	P_1, P_3, and P_4	10	0	0	15
S_3	P_1, P_5, and P_6	15	10	20	20

The choice of the specific program to implement can be aided, as in Chapter 5, by creating a payoff table. The problem is that the relative desirability of the different outcomes in cases such as this can rarely be captured by simply computing discounted present values of future potential earnings; the evaluations must reflect all the personal goals and objectives of the various stakeholders. One approach might be to ask the store owners to choose the outcomes that they perceive to be best and worst (here S_2 with T_3 and S_3 with T_4) and arbitrarily give these values of 100 and 0, respectively. The owners could then be asked to subjectively place the other outcomes between these two extremes. Here, for example, S_2 with T_4 is considered to be almost as bad as the worst outcome (a value of 5), while S_3 with T_1, is halfway between the best and worst (a value of 50).

Clearly, four scenarios cannot, even approximately, cover all the future possibilities, so expected payoffs will have little meaning. Min-max type of evaluations, on the other hand, may be helpful. Table 10–4b shows the opportunity costs for the three strategies being considered.[3] It can be seen that, under two of the scenarios, S_1 would be the preferred option. At the same time, under T_2 or T_3, this program would be relatively undesirable. Overall, S_2 would seem to be the best choice because it is, in every case, better than S_3, the best for two scenarios, and in no case extremely poor. The question that the forecaster must consider is whether or not

---

[3] See Chapter 2 for a discussion of opportunity costs.

there may be still another scenario T_5 in which S_2 would face some potentially serious threats that the store owners should consider or some additional program that would be less sensitive to the scenario differences.

The forecaster needs to recognize the interactive nature of this process. Based on the evaluation, new or modified strategic programs are developed. The forecaster then needs to develop new scenario themes and elements that point up the strengths and weaknesses of these programs. This may then lead to new program modifications, which will require new scenarios. In this, the job of the forecaster is not to attempt to foresee *the* future, but to develop alternative plausible futures that will provide adequate tests of the uncertainties and risks in the various strategic options.

PROJECT PLANNING

Operations planning as discussed in Chapter 5 involves the scheduling and coordinating of repetitive or recurrent activities. Project planning involves the scheduling and coordinating of new and changing activities. Since the structure of an operational system is set, operations planning tends to focus on aggregate questions of the acquisition and allocation of resources. Project planning is concerned with this, but must also deal with the timing considerations of the scheduling and coordination of specific component subprojects and activities as these change over the life of the project. From the viewpoint of the forecaster, probably the most important difference is that, in operations planning, the ongoing nature of the activities generate historical data that can be used as a basis for developing the necessary forecasts. Such a record is rarely available in project planning.

PERT/CPM Scheduling

Aggregate resource planning for projects makes use of pro forma budgets just as in operations planning. The major differences are that the structure of the budget is much more variable and, of particular interest to the forecaster, there may be few or no similar previous project budgets that can be used as a model. When similar budgets do exist (as, for example, with construction projects), there will still be enough differences so that forecasts must be developed by searching the past for similar or analogous situations, rather than by a simple, mechanical projection of historical patterns.

The additional element that must be considered in the planning of developmental projects is the timing of the component activities. Many techniques are used for this. Because we are primarily interested in exploring the problems that this type of planning poses for the forecaster, we will limit our review to one of the better known approaches, PERT/CPM.

The current use of PERT/CPM has evolved out of two different techniques developed in the 1950s. PERT (Program Evaluation and Review Technique) was created by the U.S. Navy as a way of coordinating the work of over 10,000 different government offices and outside contractors during the development of the Polaris missile. At roughly the same time, CPM (Critical-Path Method) was developed by engineers at Du Pont as a means of planning, scheduling, and controlling the construction of new plants. Although developed independently, the basic structure and approach of the two were the same and eventually were combined into a single technique, PERT/CPM.

Events and Activities.   The central concept of PERT/CPM in project planning involves identification of the component *activities* that make up the project and the sequence in which these activities need to occur. *Events* are defined as either starting or ending points of activities. Depending on the intended use of the analysis, the level of aggregation used in defining activities can vary. For example, imagine a company planning to build a new assembly plant and install new automated equipment. At the corporate level, the interest is as much in coordinating the necessary financial, legal, and political factors as in the actual construction and might consider "order and install new equipment" as one component of the overall project. At an engineering level, however, this aggregate activity would have to be broken down into, perhaps, 50 to 100 separate subactivities.

As a general rule, the level of aggregation must be detailed enough so that there can be no confusion over the starting or ending events. In this example, suppose that new personnel must be trained to operate the equipment. Training must be completed by the time the new equipment is installed, but cannot start until the specific equipment to be used is selected and ordered. The event "start training" would occur in the middle of an activity "order and install new equipment," so this activity would have to be separated into two parts: "order new equipment" and "install new equipment."

The PERT Chart.   Ordering relationships among activities can be shown graphically as in Figure 10–1 (p. 320). In this preliminary example, three activities have been identified. These are represented by the three line segments. The starting and ending events are shown by small numbered circles. Thus event 1 is defined as "start to order new equipment" and event 2 is "new equipment ordered." These events are separated by the activity (1–2), "order new equipment." The ending event, "new equipment ordered," is also the starting event for the two next activities, "receive and install new equipment" (2–3) and "train personnel" (2–4).

Dummy Activities. Suppose that the next activities in the project that must be accomplished are "test the new system and layout" (3–5) and "develop and test operating procedures" (4–6). The latter must be preceded by both the activities (2–3) and (2–4). This is shown in the diagram by introducing what is called a "dummy activity" (3–4) indicated by the dotted line in Figure 10–2. No actual activity is associated with this line. It is solely a device to show that both events 3 and 4 must precede the start of the actual activity (4–6). Note that the sequence of events is always from the lower to the higher number so that the sense of the dummy activity is to require event 3 to precede activity (4–6), and not event 4 to precede activity (3–5).

A Planning Example. To discuss the general issues of planning and forecasting, we will continue the example of the young couple who have decided to buy a small-town hardware store. Let us suppose that they are

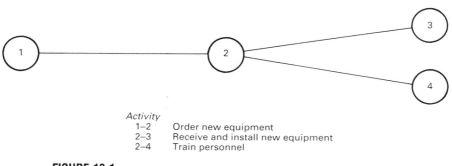

Activity
1–2   Order new equipment
2–3   Receive and install new equipment
2–4   Train personnel

FIGURE 10-1

Activities and events

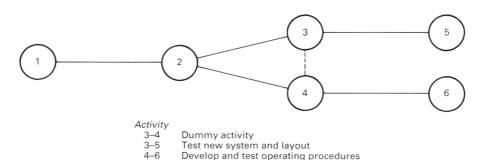

Activity
3–4   Dummy activity
3–5   Test new system and layout
4–6   Develop and test operating procedures

FIGURE 10-2

Dummy activities

now planning to add a department that will sell to the tourist and vacation markets. They anticipate that this will include equipment and supplies for camping, boating, and fishing, as well as souvenirs, gifts, handicrafts, and similar items. Selling sports-related clothing is also a possibility. At the same time, they intend to maintain the current hardware business, which is much more utilitarian and directed toward the needs of farmers and small contractors. Because the businesses will be so different, they are planning to build an addition to the current store with a separate entrance and parking lot. Table 10–5 lists the activities to be accomplished together with the number of months that they forecast each will take. Figure 10–3 (p. 322) shows the corresponding PERT chart. The dotted line connecting events 5 and 6 is again a dummy activity indicating that the completion of the building shell (event 5) must precede the start of fittings installation (event 6), even though there is no specific activity connecting the two.

Critical Path. By adding together the anticipated times along each set of connected activities, the total time required to reach each event and for the project as a whole can be determined. These cumulative times are shown in Table 10–6 (p. 323) and next to each event circle in Figure 10–4 (p. 322). At each event, one or more activities determine the earliest time that the event can be reached. From event 2 to event 4 there are two paths: (2–3) plus (3–4) and (2–4). The first will take 2 + 3 = 5 months, whereas (2–4) will take only 4.5 months. It is the longer of these two times that determines when the event will be reached. The activities (2–3) and (3–4) that make up this time are said to be on the *critical path*. Examination of Figure 10–4 and Table 10–6 shows that the events in the sequence

TABLE 10–5

Planning for a Store Addition: Activities and Times

Number	Activity	Time in Months
1–2	Develop preliminary plans and budgets	5
2–3	Develop detailed store plans	2
2–4	Obtain financing	4.5
2–8	Develop new personal skills and knowledge	12
3–4	Develop construction plans	3
3–8	Prepare and commence advertising	3
4–5	Construct building shell	4
4–6	Order and obtain fittings and equipment	5
4–7	Order and obtain supplies and inventories	9
5–6	Dummy activity	0
5–8	Complete external construction	2
6–7	Install fittings and equipment	3
7–8	Final preparations and staffing	2

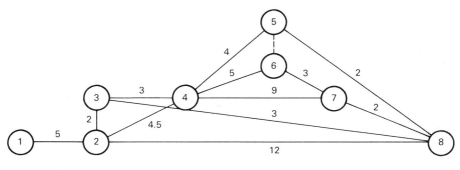

FIGURE 10-3

Planning for a store addition: PERT chart and activity times

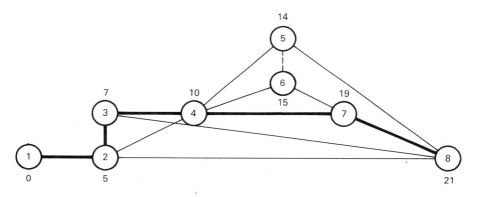

FIGURE 10-4

The critical path

(1–2), (2–3), (3–4), (4–7), and (7–8) form the critical path for this project; it is shown in the figure by the heavy line. It can be seen that the earliest that event 8 (and thus the project) can be realized is at the end of month 21.

To determine the time slack for events not on the critical path, the times on the PERT chart can be accumulated in reverse order, starting from the ending event, as in the column labeled Latest Time in Table 10–6. This can be translated into critical times for each event. In this example, suppose that the owners want to have the new addition opened by March 1990 in order to be ready for the spring fishing season. This corresponds to month 21 in the table. Working backward, it can be seen that event 7 must be completed no later than month 19 (January 1990). Similar calculations can be made for the other events. The events must occur by these specific times as shown in the table if the opening is to occur on schedule. Because

TABLE 10–6

Events and the Critical Path

Event	Earliest Time (in months)	Latest Time (in months)	Required Date	Slack
1	0	0	6/88	0
2	5	5	11/88	0
3	7	7	1/89	0
4	10	10	4/89	0
5	14	16	10/89	2
6	15	16	10/89	1
7	19	19	1/90	0
8	21	21	3/90	0

of the dummy activity, event 6 cannot occur earlier than event 5. If this dummy activity had not been included, it would have appeared (incorrectly) that event 5 could be delayed until month 19.

Time Slack for Activities. Events that are not on the critical path can be delayed without delaying the overall project, and thus the preceding activities can also be stretched or deferred. Activity (5–8), for example, requires 2 months. Since it is predicted that event 5 will be completed by month 14 and event 8 will not be reached until month 21, there are 7 months available for that activity and $7-2 = 5$ months *slack*. Even if activity (5–8) takes longer than expected, it is unlikely that it will delay the overall project. Notice, however, that this calculation assumes that all preceding events occur on schedule. If preceding events are delayed, the available slack will be reduced.

Table 10–7 (p. 324) shows the calculation of the time slack for each activity based on the earliest and latest times for each event from Table 10–6. Each activity must be completed within a *window* given by the difference between the earliest time for the preceding event and the latest time for the event following $(C-B)$. For activity (2–4), this is between month 5 and month 10, a window of 5 months. Since this activity is expected to take only 4.5 months (A), there is 0.5 months excess time or slack available $[(C-B)-A]$. For activities on the critical path, the window is the same as the anticipated time.

Uncertainty in Project Planning

Some projects consist of activities that are in themselves routine, although they may be put together in a package unique to the specific project. This occurs for example in construction where it normally is possi-

TABLE 10–7

Slack in Individual Activities

Activity	Expected Time (A)	Earliest Time for Preceding Event (B)	Latest Time for Following Event (C)	Slack (C−B) − A
1–2	5	0	5	0
2–3	2	5	7	0
2–4	4.5	5	10	0.5
2–8	12	5	21	4
3–4	3	7	10	0
4–5	4	10	16	2
4–6	5	10	16	1
4–7	9	10	19	0
4–8	3	10	21	8
5–6	0	14	16	2
5–8	2	14	21	5
6–7	3	15	19	1
7–8	2	19	21	0

ble, on the basis of past experience, to predict relatively closely how long it will take to dig a foundation or to complete a brick wall. A given building may require some new combination of the basic elements but, once the appropriate PERT chart is constructed, determining the time necessary to complete the project is relatively simple. In other cases, as for example in the development of a technologically new product or planning an entry into a new market, the activities themselves may be new and unique. Forecasting how long each will take will be much more difficult and uncertain.

This time uncertainty affects project planning in two different ways. If the activity or activities that are of uncertain duration lie on the critical path, it makes the overall project completion time uncertain as well. It is also possible for the critical path to change if an activity not on the initial critical path becomes critical by taking longer than expected and exceeding the available "window." In Figure 10–4, the activity "obtain financing" (2–4) is not on the critical path. At the same time, it has only two weeks slack and, with any delay greater than this, it will move to the critical path and begin to have an effect on the ending date of the overall project.

In using the PERT chart, the planner must be concerned not only with the probability that the overall project will be delayed or will be completed early, but also with the probabilities that particular activities will or will not be on the critical path and thus require additional management attention. It follows that the forecaster will be called on for two types of forecasts: (1) "best guess" predictions of the activity times and (2) estimates of the related time probability distributions. When the activities are routine, as in construction, and historical records exist, the problem becomes similar to those considered in Chapters 5 through 8. More frequently, the activities are similar to but not precisely the same as previous activities. It is necessary for the times to be predicted and the probability distributions estimated by drawing analogies with similar situations in the past. The recognizing of situations that are, in fact, analogous requires a good deal of subjective judgment, a topic explored in Chapter 11.

Use of Probabilities in Project Planning

To illustrate how uncertainty in estimating activity times can influence the planning process, Table 10–8 (p. 326) assumes that the time estimates or forecasts given earlier are really only expected or average times and adds estimates of the forecast standard deviations. We consider in Chapter 11 how these standard deviations might be obtained. As before, the expected total time is the sum of the forecasted times along the critical path.[4] The standard deviation of this sum can be shown to be the square root of the sum of the squares of the standard deviations. Here the expected time is

$$5 + 2 + 3 + 9 + 2 = 21 \text{ months}$$

and the standard deviation

$$(0.3^2 + 0.7^2 + 0.3^2 + 0.5^2 + 0.2^2)^{1/2} = 0.98 \text{ months}$$

If the individual time probability distributions are reasonably symmetric and have similar standard deviations, we can approximate the probability distribution of the sum by a normal distribution.[5]

Suppose that you are interested in determining the probability that the actual sum of these times is greater than 23 months. As discussed earlier in Chapter 5, the corresponding Z value is

$$Z = \frac{23 - 21}{0.98} = 2.04$$

From Figure 5–6 or Appendix Table A1, the probability that this value of Z will be exceeded can be seen to be approximately 0.02.

It should be noted again that this assumes that the critical path remains the same. If the times along the critical path are shorter than expected or if other, currently noncritical, times increase, this may not be

---

[4]As long as the critical path does not change.

[5]Given the many problems associated with the use of subjective probabilities, not much will be lost in any case by assuming normality.

TABLE 10-8

Activity Uncertainty and the Critical Path

Activity	Expected Time	Standard Deviation	Slack	Probability of Being on Critical Path[a]
1–2	5	0.3	CP[b]	—
2–3	2	0.7	CP	—
2–4	4.5	0.9	0.5	0.29
2–8	12	0.0	4.0	0.00
3–4	3	0.3	CP	—
3–8	3	0.0	11.0	0.00
4–5	4	0.3	2.0	0.00
4–6	5	0.7	1.0	0.08
4–7	9	0.5	CP	—
5–6	0	0.0	2.0	0.00
5–8	2	0.2	5.0	0.00
6–7	3	0.5	1.0	0.02
7–8	2	0.2	CP	—

[a]For activities not currently on the critical path
[b]Activity is on the critical path

true, and simply combining the times and standard deviations along the critical path tends to overstate the probability that the project will be completed within the indicated time. An alternative and more exact approach would be the use of simulation similar to that discussed in connection with risk analysis in Chapter 5. Whether the additional precision is worth the extra analysis depends in part on the number of other activities that are not on but are "close" to the critical path.

The question of whether other activities are likely to become part of the critical path depends on their expected time slacks and their probability distributions. Table 10–8 gives the probabilities that each activity not currently on the critical path could become part of that path by taking more time than expected. It can be seen that the only activity that might be of concern is (2–4), "obtain financing." Such an activity should probably be added to the list with those on the critical path as objects of special management attention and monitoring.

SUMMARY

Developmental or project planning, here represented by the PERT/CPM model, shares with operational planning the characteristics of being highly structured, quantitative, and analytic. The problems facing the forecaster arise primarily because of the lack of an adequate historical base for developing forecasts. The forecaster must rely much more heavily on techniques for eliciting people's subjective analyses and judgments.

Strategic program planning also suffers from this lack of an adequate forecasting data base. In addition, it is much less structured, is more qualitative and multidimensional, and is used in a process in which the analytic must be combined with and support political and organizational aspects of the planning process. To the extent that the relevant future can be described in quantitative terms, techniques of modeling and trend projection may be helpful. At best, however, these can only be a partial answer to the problems facing the forecaster and planner.

In the next two chapters we explore the various types of techniques that may be helpful to the forecaster in these situations.

READINGS

Strategic Planning

A good general discussion of the process of strategic planning and decision making can be found in

GEORGE A. STEINER , *Strategic Planning: What Every Manager Must Know,* New York, Free Press, 1979.

Many of the current textbooks in strategic management also have good general coverage. Two examples would be

JOHN A. PEARCE II and RICHARD B. ROBINSON, JR., *Strategic Management: Strategy Formulation and Implementation,* 2nd ed., Homewood, Ill., Irwin, 1985.

ARTHUR A. THOMPSON, JR., and A. J. STRICKLAND III, *Strategic Management: Concepts and Cases,* 3rd ed., Plano, Tex., Business Publications, 1984.

Scenario Development and Use

The following are now somewhat old but are still excellent introductions to some of the basic ideas of scenario development. Bright in particular has had substantial impact on the way the material has been presented in this chapter.

JAMES R. BRIGHT, *Practical Technological Forecasting: Concepts and Exercises,* Austin, Tex., Industrial Management Center, 1978, Chapter 11.

René D. Zentner, "Scenarios in Forecasting," *Chemical and Engineering News,* Oct. 6, 1975, pp. 22–24, 29–34.

Rochelle O' Connor, *Planning under Uncertainty: Multiple Scenarios and Contingency Planning,* New York, Conference Board, 1978.

An alternative and very interesting approach can be found in

Roy Amara and Andrew J. Lipinski, *Business Planning for an Uncertain Future: Scenarios and Strategies,* Elmsford, N.Y., Pergamon Press, 1983.

The following reference gives a good discussion of an approach to creating outcome scenarios, although the emphasis is almost entirely on economic and financial factors.

John Chandler and Paul Cockle, *Techniques of Scenario Planning,* London, McGraw-Hill, 1982.

Journals that frequently have articles on the development and use of scenarios as well as on other aspects of strategic planning are:

Futures
Long-Range Planning
Managerial Planning
The Planning Review
Technological Forecasting and Social Change

Project Planning

Material on project scheduling can be found in most texts on operations management. For example, see

Roger G. Schroeder, *Operations Management,* 2nd ed., New York, McGraw-Hill, 1985, Chapter 12.

Three books that deal with broader issues of project planning are

Clifford F. Gray, *Essentials of Project Management,* Princeton, N.J., Petrocelli, 1981.

Jack R. Meredith and Samuel J. Mantel, Jr., *Project Planning: A Managerial Approach,* New York, Wiley, 1985.

David I. Cleland and William R. King, *Systems Analysis and Project Planning,* 3rd ed., New York, McGraw-Hill, 1983.

PROBLEMS

1. Otto Standfeld is owner and president of the Standfeld Manufacturing Company. The company was formed in 1980 to manufacture and market a computer-controlled process monitoring device with application in the pharmaceutical industry. Industry acceptance of the device has been good and sales and profits have both been high. There appears to be another large and unexplored market in certain food-processing applications as well as sales potential remaining in the pharmaceutical field. At the same time, Mr. Standfeld is becoming concerned with the possibility of competition from larger firms, which would reduce prices and profit margins, and with the possibility of new developments in the rapidly changing chemical and electronics fields, which would make the monitoring device obsolete. The company is in the process of developing operating budgets for the coming year and finds that it will have access to approximately $1 million in funds that can be used in R&D or marketing, invested in new plant or equipment, invested in securities, or taken out in dividends.

   a. List some strategic program components open to the company that Mr. Standfeld might consider.

   b. What are some of the environmental factors that should be considered?

   c. Describe some scenario themes that could be used in evaluating the program components.

   d. Show how you would develop outcome and payoff tables for this problem. Discuss how you would develop and evaluate the outcome scenarios.

   e. From Chapter 4, what are possible criteria for selecting a specific strategic program? What are the implications of each for the types of scenarios that you would need?

2. You are director of planning for a regional intercity bus company covering all or parts of six states. Currently, your major activities are passenger service and small package delivery between major cities and smaller communities within your service area. Your buses are of varying ages and sizes, although, on the average, they are both older and smaller than those of a national carrier such as Greyhound.

   a. Develop some possible strategic options that might be open to your company and the planning time horizons that would be required.

   b. Outline three scenario themes that might be used in evaluating these options. Indicate why you chose these three rather than others that might have been considered. Give each scenario a short but descriptive title.

Complete the following steps for *one* of your themes.

  c. Prepare a summary or abstract of approximately 200 words for your scenario.

  d. Identify the principle topic areas that you would include in your scenario.

  e. For each topic area, identify the relevant events and trends. Choose specific values for each and set these up in the form of a range table. Assume that your other scenario themes would form the following columns of the table.

  f. Using the values from part e, develop a scenario based on your theme and develop a specific strategic program for your company.

  g. Suppose your scenario turns out to be incorrect. Discuss the impact that this might have on your proposed strategic program.

3. Carl Schmitt is one of three associate editors on a medium-sized city newspaper. He is 50 years old and married. His wife is a high school teacher. All their children are grown and have left home. He has a chance to buy a weekly newspaper in a rural and resort area about 500 miles from where he is now living. While he has always dreamed of owning his own newspaper, he is hesitant about giving up his present position, particularly since the present editor will be retiring in about 5 years and, presumably, one of the three associate editors will be selected to replace him. Carl has asked your advice. Discuss how alternative scenarios could be used in this process.

4. Martha Murray is the administrator of a community hospital and medical clinic in a city with a population of just under 8000 located in the southwestern United States. In addition to the city, they supply services to the surrounding smaller communities, farms, and ranches. The hospital board is comprised of local community and agricultural leaders, the president of a local manufacturing firm, and the administrator of a much larger hospital in another state. The board has indicated to Ms. Murray that they would like an analysis of how well the hospital and clinic are meeting current community needs and a long-range plan for future development. They feel that any development would almost certainly involve some sort of fund-raising activities. It has been 15 years since their last major fund drive and they would like to plan so that, if a drive is set up for 1989, another would not be needed until at least 2000.

Martha Murray has asked for your help in this planning and in developing some alternative environmental scenarios.

a. What general topic areas would you want to include in these scenarios? What are some of the specific events and trends that might be included in each area?

b. Explain the difference between an event and a trend. Using one of your proposed topic areas, give examples to illustrate this difference.

c. Using the topic areas from part a, give an example of a possible scenario.

d. What is a range table? How would it be useful in this situation? Discuss how you would choose the values for the variables in the range table.

e. Assume that you have developed several alternative scenarios. Discuss how they could be used in planning for the future development of the clinic and hospital.

5. You live in a small city. The local Chamber of Commerce has decided to hold a week-long festival to attract tourists and aid local businesses. You have been chosen to chair the event. The plans include a parade, day and evening entertainment, and other activities that might attract people from outside the area. No particular theme has been chosen for the event although several have been suggested. Discuss how you would develop and use a PERT chart for planning this event. What problems might arise in trying to forecast the amount of time, money, and other resources necessary to prepare for the festival?

6. You are given a PERT scheduling model consisting of the following activities:

Activity	Expected Time (days)	Standard Deviation
1–2	15	1
1–3	13	1
1–4	14	2.5
2–4	Dummy activity	
2–6	8	3
3–4	Dummy activity	
3–7	19	5
4–5	12	2
5–6	Dummy activity	
5–7	12	2
6–7	13	2

a. Develop a PERT chart and find the critical path. What is the expected completion time?

b. What problems might arise if you wanted to place some sort of upper limit on the completion time?

CHAPTER 11

The Use of Judgment in Forecasting

Studies comparing forecasts based on human judgment and expertise with those developed by more formal analytical techniques have generally favored the objective techniques. On the other hand, in many situations the nature of the problem or the lack of structured historical records make human judgment and subjective analysis the only possible approach.

When forecasts cannot be simply extrapolated from the past but must instead be developed by a process of analogy, objective methods of analysis may be of limited value. A particular activity in a research project may be similar to things that have been done in the past, but not to the extent that the time necessary for its completion can be estimated by any simple historical average. In the same way, many of the elements in a scenario for strategic planning may have historical analogies that can be used for forecasting, but not in a form for which statistical analysis is appropriate. It follows that planning situations of the types discussed in Chapter 10 will depend heavily on subjective forecasting.

Even in situations where the final forecast is generated through the use of an objective model, the development and use of that model will require judgmental inputs at many stages of the process. Anything that can be done to improve these subjective inputs will potentially enhance the value of the forecast. Procedures for operational planning and forecasting in Part III emphasized objective models and forecasts, yet many elements of judgment remained. Some of the most obvious were:

- The choice of the model or models to be used in developing the forecast

- The choice of the variables to be included in the model, of the historical time period to be used for developing the model, and of the sources to be used in obtaining the necessary data

- Estimates of the possible impact of events and factors not included in the formal model, of any necessary modifications to the forecast, and/ or of the potential effects on forecast accuracy

- Estimates of the value of putting additional time and effort into trying to develop better forecasts or forecasting models, including estimates of the probability that a better model can be developed

- Ex ante tests of the reasonableness of the objective model developed, including judgmental checks of the signs and magnitudes of the coefficients of any regression models developed.

The guided regression approach outlined in Chapter 8 is a good example of the way that objective and subjective techniques can be combined in modeling.

In many situations there is another important reason for including subjective forecasts in the planning process, that of motivation. In sales planning, the line between a sales *forecast* and a sales *goal* is not always clear, since sales can depend as much on the efforts of the sales force as on the environment. In project planning, the time necessary to complete an activity will be greatly affected by the commitment of the people involved. Similarly, the long-run success of a strategic program can be compromised because of lack of managerial support. In such cases it may be desirable to explicitly base some elements of a forecast on executive, employee, or sales force judgment as a way of building commitment. Although such uses of forecasting are not unrelated to the issues to be dealt with here, they are not strictly speaking a subject for this chapter.

As a rule, given a choice between using an objective model or using subjective judgment in forecasting, it is safest to assume that the objective procedure will be at least as good and usually better unless a good deal is known about the track record of the subjective forecaster. This caution can be carried to extremes. There are forecasters so committed to objective models that, in the absence of an objective approach, they would decline to give any forecast and argue that forecasting is impossible. At the same time, the planner/manager must make decisions for which forecasts are required. In such a situation, it is senseless to say that forecasting is impossible; the only question, given the circumstances, is how it can best be done and by whom. Techniques exist for aiding human judgment and creativity, although a complete discussion of the topic would be well beyond the scope of this book. Here we limit ourselves to exploring some of the issues involved and taking a look at a few simple procedures that can be used to obtain judgmental forecast inputs.

Major Points to be Noted

1. *Some of the possible reasons why subjective forecasts may be poor.*
2. *The different approaches that have been suggested for the subjective estimation of probabilities and probability distributions.*
3. *The combining of individual opinion into group opinion as a way of improving forecasts, the limitations and dangers as well as the strengths.*

THE LIMITATIONS OF JUDGMENT

Many writers have explored the accuracy of subjective methods in forecasting and the possible reasons for errors in judgment which can affect that accuracy. As might be expected, the majority of these studies have used relatively short range forecasts and situations where objective forecasting methods were available as a basis for comparison. It is also not surprising that much of the original work was in the field of psychology.

One of the earliest studies was a book by Meehl, *Clinical vs. Statistical Prediction*, written in 1954. It examined the differences between clinical panels and statistical models in diagnosing various mental states and conditions. Statistical models showed a clear superiority in predicting treatment success. In his book, Meehl made an important distinction between data collection and data combination and concluded that, in many cases, clinical (subjective) observation could be an important source of data, but that statistical (objective) methods of data analysis were always to be preferred to judgmental procedures. Meehl noted in passing that this was in direct contrast to the attitudes of most clinicians, who preferred hard (objective) data but wanted to use personal judgment in interpreting that data.

A critical problem in any use of objective forecasting methods is deciding when and to what extent the forecaster should override the output of the objective model to adjust for information not in the model. Meehl refers to this as the "broken leg" situation and poses the following example: Suppose that a professor is known to always go to the movies on Wednesday evenings (clearly a 1954 example). If it is Wednesday, you would be justified in predicting that the professor will be found at the movies. If, however, you also knew that the professor had just broken his leg while leaving the house, you would almost certainly override that forecast.

The problem is that most situations are not as clear as the "broken leg" example of Meehl. Harris (1963) compared the performance of a computer model to judgments by sportswriters in predicting the outcomes of college football games. As part of the study, the man who created the computer model was asked to review its output each week and make what he felt to be necessary adjustments. Although the differences were not great, he did not do as well in his adjusted predictions as did his own unadjusted model.

This issue is particularly relevant to economic and sales forecasting where formal statistical models are routinely developed but are subject to forecaster and manager review and modification before use, and when it is likely that those modifications will be of more psychological than practical benefit. One way of dealing with this problem is to have managers (and others involved) develop independent subjective forecasts, which are then combined with the objective forecasts using an objective regression model. Note that this assumes that the forecasting is done *routinely* so that sufficient data exist and excludes modifications needed in clear "broken leg" situations. A second possibility is to routinely "feed back" to managers the effects of their forecast modifications using techniques such as the P–R diagram of Chapter 9.

A more telling limitation on the use of judgmental forecasting (where objective methods are available) is reported by Mabert (1976). In a situation involving routine sales forecasting in a manufacturing firm, three types of objective procedures (two types of exponential smoothing and an ARIMA model) were compared with the procedure actually used by the company, which was based on sales-force judgmental forecasts. Although the objective approaches were more accurate, the differences were not great. The real differences were in the amounts of time necessary to develop the forecasts. The company procedure required 103 work-hours of effort and 27 days to produce the final forecast as compared to an average of 13.6 work-hours and 2.2 days for the objective models.[1]

---

[1]Note, however, that this comparison again excludes any "broken leg" information and any motivational value that may arise from requesting input from the sales force and from managers.

To balance this negative evaluation of subjective methods, Murphy and Brown (1984) studied the performance of professional weather forecasters against objective models in making short-range weather projections. In some cases the professionals outperformed the models. This article discusses some of the issues of separating the evaluation of the performance of the forecasters from that of the objective models, which are available to them in making their projections. Armstrong (1983) summarizes five previous studies which tend to show that, in making year-ahead forecasts of earnings, managers outperform both technical analysts and formal models. He suggests also a number of cautions that should be observed in interpreting these results. Finally, it needs to be stressed that objective methods are useful only when an adequate relevant data base exists which can be used to develop and test the objective model. In its absence, subjective forecasts may be suspect, but they are "the only game in town."

Why Are Subjective Forecasts Poor?

Since we do not always have the option to choose, there is value in anything that we can do to improve the quality of subjective forecasts. We can distinguish two general sources of errors: conservatism and bias (intended and unintended).

Conservatism. Forecasters tend to anchor on the present and on the "reasonable." In the football example noted earlier, where the creator of the model was less accurate in his modifications than his own unmodified model, Harris (1963, p. 329) noted that

> 75% of (the) judgments involved . . . toning down of the mathematical predictions, and that the degree of diminuation increased with magnitude of the mathematical prediction.

In general, people (including forecasters) tend to distrust indications of major changes in the environment. Also, in many cases it is far more important to forecast the *direction* of a pending environmental change than to predict its exact magnitude, and there is a danger that users may overreact to forecasts of large changes. Finally, extreme forecasts tend to be more noticeable and thus expose the forecaster to more personal risk if the forecast proves wrong. All these factors tend to move the forecaster toward a more conservative position. An important exception is when the forecast is intended as propaganda. In such a case the tendency is to move a forecast to a more extreme position than the forecaster would otherwise choose.

Bias.   A frequent cause of bias in subjective forecasts is a system that differentially rewards the forecaster for positive and negative forecast errors. The most obvious example is the manager who is rewarded for exceeding the sales forecast or coming in under the project time estimate or budget, but is penalized for errors in the opposite direction. Equally important are the unintended sources of bias which arise because of misinterpretation of the information available to the forecaster or because of the subjective procedures used to interpret those data.

In technological forecasting, experts in the various scientific fields tend to be overly pessimistic in their forecasts because they think in terms of existing technologies and are acutely aware of the problems and limitations of those technologies. Nonexperts, on the other hand, tend to be overly optimistic. They do not know how the problems will be resolved but simply rely on the historical evidence that, when needs have existed, problems have been solved. By contrast, in the social sciences, experts who have developed rational or logical solutions to social problems tend to understate both the problems of making the institutional changes necessary in implementing those solutions and the ability of societies to undergo major changes within existing structures and systems.

Sources of Forecast Error

Tversky and Kahneman in a 1974 paper suggest three major types or sources of error which can arise in dealing with the uncertainties typical of forecasting. They term these representativeness, availability, and anchoring.

Representativeness.   In interpreting information we tend to classify data according to our past experience. If, for whatever reason, we believe that A tends to be followed by B and we now observe something we interpret as an A, we are likely to predict that B will follow. The problem arises in correctly identifying the current situation as an A. This can happen, for example, in estimating the degree of public support for or opposition to some government policy or program. If "all" of our friends or co-workers hold opinions similar to ours, we tend to interpret this as a reflection of general public support or opposition, without recognizing that our friends are not a random sample of the population but are much more likely to hold opinions similar to our own.

Availability.   People tend to place higher weight on more readily available data or easily imaginable situations. Immediately after a major crash or hijacking of a commercial airliner, people tend to overestimate their chances of being involved in such an incident. They are much less sensitive to the greater probability of being involved in an automobile accident because the one large accident is publicized and is more easily recalled than are the details of a large number of individually smaller automobile fatalities. Forecasts of sales for new technologies such as the current generation of supercomputers are typically understated, because the demand forecasts are based on extrapolations of current applications using existing computers without foreseeing the new applications that will be enabled by the new technology and that are much more difficult to conceptualize.

Anchoring.   When people create forecasts by starting from some base point and then making adjustments, the final forecast will be heavily influenced by the initial base point chosen. In forecasting how long it takes to complete some activity, people commonly start by estimating the "most likely" time and then making adjustments to obtain "optimistic" and "pessimistic" estimates. Typically, the latter two estimates tend to understate the extremes, leading to overly narrow probability distributions. If the same person were to start by giving an optimistic or pessimistic estimate and then adjusting, the results would be quite different. Similarly, in forecasting changes in existing conditions, institutions, or technology, the tendency is to understate the magnitude of the changes that will occur because the forecasts anchor on current conditions and make insufficient adjustments for the changes.

TECHNIQUES FOR ELICITING INDIVIDUAL JUDGMENTS

In this chapter we are concerned almost entirely with forecasting for strategic programs and projects, although the ideas presented certainly have broader applications. In Chapter 10 we identified activities, events, and trends as the three types of factors or elements that would enter into our planning models. Table 11–1 outlines the characteristics of each of these for which forecasts may be required.

There are important differences between the qualitative and quantitative characteristics of both activities/events and trends. The qualitative factors create the structure while the quantitative factors deal with aspects of magnitude or importance. Of the two, developing forecasts of the qualitative structure is clearly the more challenging. Indeed, much of the early literature of technological forecasting or futurism dealt with ways of encouraging oi improving human creativity in conceptualizing "alternative futures."

Developing forecasts of quantitative factors is a more easily structured procedure. Most frequently, they are expressed as probabilities or probability distributions. For events, these will be single discrete values: What

TABLE 11-1

Characteristics of Events, Activities, and Trends

	Activities/Events	*Trends*
Qualitative factors	What	What trend model
	Where	What variable(s)
	How	Scope or coverage of the trend model
Quantitative factors	When	Magnitude of the variable at a
	Duration	specific time
	Level of activity	
	Probability of event occurring	Rate of change of the variable

is the probability that new product *X* will first be commercially introduced in country *Y* using technology *Z*? Quantitative variables are forecasted as probability distributions or as averages and ranges.

Probabilities of Discrete Events

The most obvious approach to obtaining a person's judgment of the probability that a particular event will occur is to ask the question directly. This requires that the person understand, as clearly as possible, the characteristics of the event in question and can accurately report their probability judgment.

In describing an event, it is not enough to ask for an assessment of the probability that "technology Z will prove successful." One person may interpret this to mean "successful in the laboratory" and assign a relatively high probability, while another with the same available information and same beliefs will assign a low probability because that person will interpret the question to mean "commercially successful." There can be confusion over the issue of "when" with different interpretations ranging from "soon" or "within the relevant future" to a vague "someday." This problem can arise even in trying to develop one's own probability assessments, but it becomes particularly acute when attempting to obtain and combine the opinions of multiple assessors.

Even with a well-defined event, it is not always clear that a person can adequately verbalize probability judgments. People have different perceptions of the concept. Some people think more easily in terms of *odds* than of probabilities (a probability of $\frac{1}{4}$ or 0.25 would be expressed as odds of 3 to 1 against). In some cases it may be helpful to use a line with the end points marked 0 (impossible) and 1 (certain) and to ask the respondent to mark a point on the line corresponding to their probability judgment.

Reference events can sometimes be helpful. For example, the person might be asked if they felt the event were more or less likely than having a tossed coin come up heads, or a poker player might be asked to compare it to the event of being dealt a full house. Respondents might be offered a real or hypothetical payoff depending on their choice of a probability and on whether or not the event occurs. Techniques for selecting appropriate payoffs are referred to as *proper scoring rules*. As an example, the respondent might be offered a choice between two bets: "Win $10 if the event occurs; lose $10 if it does not," and "Win $10 if a tossed coin comes up heads; lose $10 if it is tails." If the individual chooses the former, it can be assumed that they think the probability of the event occurring is greater than 0.5.

Probability Distributions

When dealing with quantitative variables, the concept is the same but the number of different probabilities needed to create an entire distribution is much greater. A procedure often used with PERT scheduling is to assume a standard type of probability distribution and then obtain judgments on the parameters of the distribution. The beta distribution is frequently used for this purpose. As shown in Figure 11–1, this is a bell-shaped but not necessarily symmetric distribution. If estimates are obtained of the most likely (T_m), most optimistic (T_o), and most pessimistic (T_p) times as indicated, the mean of the distribution is estimated by

$$\bar{T} = \frac{T_p + 4 \times T_m + T_o}{6} \tag{1}$$

and the standard deviation by

$$S = \frac{T_p - T_o}{6} \tag{2}$$

These estimates are then used, as in Chapter 10, to develop time forecasts along the critical path and other characteristics of the overall planning model.

A second approach is to locate points on the cumulative probability distribution by direct questioning, as with the estimation of probabilities of discrete events: for example, to ask for an estimate of the probability that the activity will take more than 17 days or less than 12 days. To minimize

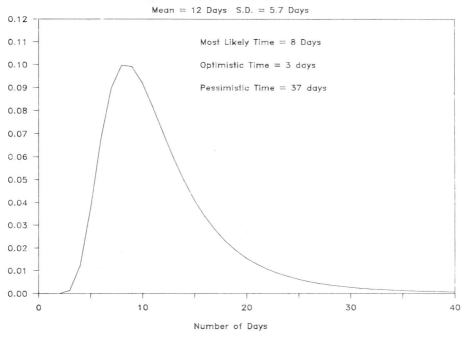

# The Beta Distribution
Mean = 12 Days   S.D. = 5.7 Days

Most Likely Time = 8 Days

Optimistic Time = 3 days

Pessimistic Time = 37 days

Number of Days

FIGURE 11-1

The beta distribution: Mean = 12 days, S.D. = 5.7 days

the "anchoring" phenomenon noted earlier, it is best to start with points toward the ends of the distribution and to present the values of the variable in random order.

A large number of other approaches have been suggested by various authors, although the two presented here are certainly the simplest. References to other possibilities will be found at the end of the chapter. If the importance of the problem warrants it and the available time and resources allow, it is wise to check the consistency of the respondent by using two or more different approaches and comparing the results. It can also be helpful to repeat the questioning after some lapse of time to test the reliability of the responses. A third way of improving judgments is to ask the respondents to cite evidence to support their opinions or to verbalize scenarios in which the variable would be unusually large or small. Some studies have suggested that individuals can be trained to make better probability assessments by completing a series of assessment exercises.

COMBINING GROUP JUDGMENTS

In some cases, probability judgments can be improved by combining the opinions of a group of different evaluators. Well-chosen groups can increase the breadth of information brought to bear on the estimation of probabilities and other quantitative aspects and potentially generate wider ranges of possible events. The use of groups *may* help to balance opposing biases of group members. It is equally possible that the group members will simply reinforce each other's biases. A major danger in combining group opinions is to mistake consensus for accuracy. As with judging the representativeness of information, consensus can often be an indication of bias and insufficient variety of opinion within the group, rather than a basis for confidence in the forecast.

Three basic types of group processes can be identified:

1. Nominal or statistical
2. Unstructured interactive or face-to-face
3. Structured interactive

Nominal Groups

When information or opinions are collected from a group of individuals and summarized or averaged statistically, the group is referred to as *nominal*.[2] The important characteristic is that group members never meet or interact directly or indirectly. The primary advantage is one of efficiency or convenience. Although interaction and discussion among group members can be helpful through pooling of information and shared analysis of the issues, for many applications any gains will not outweigh the costs. Nominal groups remain the most effective.

Unstructured Interactive Groups

An alternative term might be "self-structured," because nothing precludes the group from adopting its own rules to limit or control the interaction process. Sometimes a distinction is made between groups where a group leader is appointed in advance and "leaderless" groups. Two com-

---

[2]The use of the term nominal in this context should not be confused with something called the nominal group technique (NGT), which is actually a form of structured group interaction.

monly cited problems with this type of face-to-face interaction are the *expert effect,* where the group tends to be dominated by a perceived or self-appointed "expert," and the *bandwagon effect,* where the group is moved to premature consensus by the dominance of a strong majority position. Although these are certainly dangers, the choice of an effective leader can minimize the effects.

Structured Interactive Groups

Starting in the 1950s, concern with some of the potential sources of bias inherent in group interaction led to an interest in designing ways of structuring the interaction process. One of the best known of these is the *Delphi process* developed between 1948 and 1963 at the Rand Corporation, a government-sponsored research organization. It will be described here because many of its early applications were directed toward developing forecasts of the introduction of new technologies, and it therefore gained the reputation of being a forecasting technique. Over time, Delphi has undergone many changes and modifications. Here we describe some of the basic elements that appear to be common to most of the applications.

Delphi starts with the recruiting of a group of individuals willing to participate in the exercise. Generally, the individual identities and opinions of the participants are kept anonymous. A series of questions, normally requiring a quantitative response, is presented to the participants. Since early applications dealt with the introduction of new technologies, questions were often of the form "By what date do you expect event X to occur."

Responses are collected, summarized (usually by giving the medians, quartiles, and ranges of the variables), and reported to the participants, who are asked to reconsider their earlier responses and submit new forecasts. Some or all of the respondents (for example, those in the top and bottom quartiles) are asked to supply reasons for their forecasts. This information, including the reasons given, is summarized and reported, and the participants are asked for a third and final set of forecasts.

Despite early enthusiasm for the approach, overall experience has been mixed to negative. Group opinions over the three stages of the process do tend to converge. Usually this convergence is toward a value close to the initial median, suggesting that a bandwagon effect is still present and that equivalent results could have been obtained from a well-designed one-stage nominal group. Unfortunately, this convergence is sometimes interpreted as an indication of increased accuracy or reliability, which is usually incorrect. Certainly the exchange of information may be helpful, although, for this purpose, face-to-face interaction with a skilled leader is usually more effective. When the intent is to create a consensus rather than to forecast, Delphi can be effective. One modification of the basic process designed with this in mind is called the *Policy Delphi*.

Delphi is an example of a *consensus*-oriented structured interaction. It is also possible to structure interaction to create an *adversarial* process. One such procedure, strategic assumption surfacing and testing, developed by Mason and Mitroff (1981), has been effectively used in planning as an alternative to the multiple-scenario approach described in Chapter 10.

Finally, it should be noted that when records exist of the past forecast accuracy of managers or other sources of subjective forecasts, this information can be used to develop models combining the subjective and objective forecasts as described in Chapter 9.

SUMMARY

In general, experience and research support the idea that, whenever possible, objective forecasting procedures should be used in preference to subjective evaluation. This does not preclude using management or sales-force judgments as inputs, for example, to a regression model of the type discussed in Chapter 9. Unfortunately, in many situations objective approaches to forecasting may not be applicable. This happens during the initial stages of constructing an objective forecasting model when decisions must be made on the techniques to be used or on the variables to be included. It also occurs when forecasting for new or changing situations where historical data are no longer relevant. In such cases, human judgment is our only source of forecasts.

READINGS

Limitations of Judgment

The references cited in this section are

Paul E. Meehl, *Clinical vs. Statistical Prediction*, Minneapolis, University of Minnesota Press, 1954.

JESSE G. HARRIS, JR., "Judgmental vs. Mathematical Prediction: An Investigation by Analogy of the Clinical vs. Statistical Controversy," *Behavioral Science*, vol. 8, no. 4 (October 1963), pp. 324–335.

VINCENT A. MABERT, "Statistical Versus Sales Force—Executive Opinion Short Range Forecasts: A Time Series Analysis Case Study," *Decision Sciences*, vol. 7, no. 2 (April 1976), pp. 310–318.

AMOS TVERSKY and D. KAHNEMAN, "Judgment under Uncertainty: Heuristics and Biases," *Science*, vol. 185 (1974), pp. 1124–1131.

The counterexamples can be found in

ALLAN H. MURPHY and BARBARA G. BROWN, "A Comparative Evaluation of Objective and Subjective Weather Forecasts in the United States," *Journal of Forecasting*, vol. 3, no. 4 (October/November 1984), pp. 369–393.

J. SCOTT ARMSTRONG, "Relative Accuracy of Judgemental and Extrapolative Methods in Forecasting Annual Earnings," *Journal of Forecasting*, vol. 2, no. 4 (October/November 1983), pp. 437–447.

For an excellent discussion of the nature and limitations of human judgment, see

DAVID FAUST, *The Limits of Scientific Reasoning*, Minneapolis, University of Minnesota Press, 1984.

Also worth reading are

J. SCOTT ARMSTRONG, *Long Range Forecasting: From Crystal Ball to Computer*, New York, Wiley, 1978, Chapter 6.

ROBERT CARBONE and WILPEN L. GORR, "Accuracy of Judgmental Forecasting of Time Series," *Decision Sciences*, vol. 16, no. 2 (Spring 1985), pp. 153–160.

Eliciting Individual Judgments

The literature here is extensive. A good initial article, which will lead you into the rest of the literature, is

THOMAS S. WALLSTEN and DAVID V. BUDESCU, "Encoding Subjective Probabilities," *Management Science*, vol. 29, no. 2 (February 1983), pp. 151–173.

Combining Group Judgments

An interesting experiment comparing forecasting with nominal and interactive groups can be found in

> GARY L. H. LORENZ, *An Analysis of the Relationship between Selected Aptitudes, Decision Methods, and Forecasting Accuracy in a Business Problem,* unpublished Ph.D. dissertation, University of Minnesota, Minneapolis, June 1977.

Anyone interested in the Delphi method should read

> HAROLD A. LINSTONE and MURRAY TUROFF (eds.), *The Delphi Method: Techniques & Applications,* Reading, Mass., Addison-Wesley, 1975.

> HAROLD SACKMAN, *Delphi Critique,* Lexington, Mass., Lexington Books, 1975.

For more on strategic assumptions surfacing and testing, see

> RICHARD O. MASON and IAN I. MITROFF, *Challenging Strategic Planning Assumptions,* New York, Wiley, 1981.

PROBLEMS

1. In Problem 3 of Chapter 10, you were asked to discuss how you could use scenarios to help Carl Schmitt decide whether or not to buy a small-town newspaper. Review the scenario elements (events and trends) that you proposed in answer to that question. For which of these elements would objective forecasts be possible? What would be your possible sources of data? Suppose for the other elements you wanted to obtain from Carl Schmitt values that he considered plausible, but at the same time would enable him to foresee possible threats and opportunities in the options open to him. How would you go about obtaining this information from him?

2. Newspaper columnists and writers of letters to the editor frequently indulge in forecasting what is or is not going to happen in areas of economics, politics, social change, or technology. Go back 5 to 10 years and find some examples in old newspapers. In the reasoning or argument that they use, try to identify some possible sources of forecast error, such as the use of unrepresentative samples or anchoring

on an overly conservative base point. Attempt to discover what actually happened and how it compared to the forecast made.

3. In Problem 5 of Chapter 10, you were asked to chair a community festival. Assume that this is the first time such a celebration has been held in the area and that you have never before been involved in this type of event. Discuss how you would forecast the time, money, and resources required.

4. If you have a number of friends and/or colleagues to work with, choose some near to mid-term event where it will be possible to observe the actual outcome. Develop forecasts using nominal and interactive groups and allowing some subjects access to objective or informed forecasts (such as published weather, economic, political, or stock-market forecasts). Compare the results obtained under the different conditions.

5. Find some routinely published forecast on a topic in which you have some interest or competence and for which the variable or event forecasted can later be determined. Independent of that forecast, develop for each period your own subjective forecasts. At the end of 6 to 10 periods, develop a regression model using your forecasts and the published forecasts as independent variables and the actual outcome as the dependent variable. Discuss your results.

CHAPTER 12

Trends and Models in Scenario Development

In Chapter 10 we considered problems of forecasting and planning during periods of environmental change where historical patterns could not be automatically projected as a basis for forecasting. Even in strategic or long-range forecasting, however, not all change is random or erratic. Environmental variables have periods of smooth, evolutionary growth, as well as periods of turbulent shifting. Historic trends can be usefully studied to observe how the variables have changed over time and to analyze how the variables have reacted to past environmental discontinuities. What we cannot do is to assume that, because a variable has tended to increase at a rate of $X\%$ per year in the past, it will continue to do so for some indefinite future.

To analyze historical trends, we must try to create models to describe the changes observed. In the same way, if we are to develop future scenarios which are internally consistent and understandable, we must create models that describe how the component events and trends interact. To the extent that the components are qualitative, these "models" will tend to be subjective and expressed in words, rather than in the symbolic or mathematical structures that we usually associate with the term. In either case, there are some simple tools which can aid in this process. In this chapter we first consider some simple trend models and then some relationship models that can prove useful in the scenario-building process.

Major Points to be Noted

1. *The differences between time and structural models of change; the relationships between the two types of models.*
2. *The ways of including limits and bounds in models of growth and change.*
3. *Using trend models to detect points where discontinuous changes, caused perhaps by political or technological events, have occurred.*
4. *Procedures for creating and evaluating scenarios.*

TRENDS AND PROCESSES OF GROWTH

The concept of the trend was introduced previously in Chapter 4 as part of a general discussion of the analysis of time series. For relatively short range projection, seasonal and cyclical factors tend to dominate the forecasting process; the trend component can be approximated with a very simple model. As long as the basic direction of movement is correct, the specific mathematical form of the trend is relatively unimportant. As the forecast horizon increases, the underlying trend begins to dominate the forecast. In the long run, seemingly small differences in the form of the trend equation used can have major impacts on the trend projections. In Chapter 4, the analysis of the trend was illustrated using data on motor vehicle registrations. Three different models were considered: linear, logarithmic, and square root. At the time the slight differences in curvature which resulted probably did not seem too important, particularly in view of the much greater magnitude of the fluctuations that could be observed in the other components. Figure 12–1 (p. 350) shows the data on passenger car registrations but with the three possible trends projected to the year 2000. At that range, the log projection is more than 50% greater than the linear. For many strategic planning applications, looking 15 to 20 years into the future can be necessary, so the choice of the trend model becomes important.

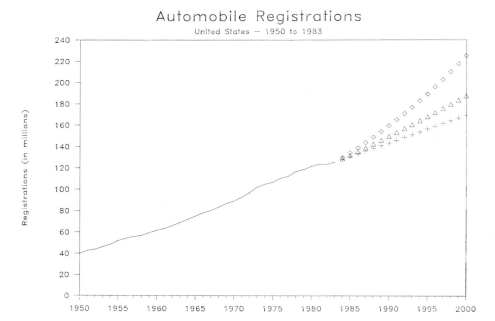

FIGURE 12-1

Automobile registrations: United States, 1950–1983

Time Versus Structural Trend Models

For purposes of trend projection, it is most convenient to express the trend as a function of time:

$$Y = a + bt \quad \text{or} \quad Y = A(1 + g)^t \qquad (1)$$

From a structural point of view, time t does not "cause" Y to take on a particular value and cannot be thought of even as explaining why Y has that particular value. That it is now 1985 says nothing to explain the current size of the population of the United States or the number of motor vehicles registered. In dealing with trends, we therefore face two problems: (1) to develop models that will help explain past patterns of change and (2) to convert those structural models into functions of time that can be used to develop projections.

Also, the *level* of a trend variable can never be directly explained. The statistic that the 1980 population of the United States was 226.5 million can only be accounted for by describing the changes which led up to this figure, the birth and death rates and the rates of in and out migration that caused the population to change from its previous level to the new value. We cannot directly explain Y_t, but we can attempt to explain the change, $Y_t - Y_{t-1}$.

Univariate Versus Multivariate Trend Models

Univariate models attempt to explain changes in terms of previous values of the variable. A common model in population studies is

$$Y_t - Y_{t-1} = gY_{t-1} \qquad (2)$$

where the change in Y is proportional to the size of the population at the beginning of the period. We can certainly understand why this might be so. The larger the population is, the more births and the more deaths and thus the greater the change. At the same time, it is clear that the size of the population cannot be said to "cause" the increase. To deal with causes of change requires multivariate models.

Univariate models can help us gain some understanding into the processes of change. In this section, therefore, we deal only with univariate models; we will return to multivariate forms at the end of the chapter.

Linear and Constant Growth Rate Trends. In Chapter 4 we saw that a linear trend was equivalent to a constant first difference.

$$Y_t - Y_{t-1} = b$$

implied $\qquad\qquad\qquad\qquad\qquad\qquad\qquad\qquad\qquad\qquad (3)$

$$Y_t = Y_0 + bt$$

Expressed another way, if period-to-period changes seem to be independent of any outside factors, including size of the variable itself, the trend will be linear. This can be a reasonable assumption for very short range projection; it is hard to imagine how it would hold over long periods of time.

Similarly, if the first differences are proportional to the magnitude of the variable, an exponential or constant growth rate model is appropriate.

$$Y_t - Y_{t-1} = gY_{t-1}$$

implies   (4a)

$$Y_t = Y_0(1 + g)^t$$

As in Chapter 4, this can also be written as a constant first difference in the logarithms.

$$\text{Log } Y_t - \text{Log } Y_{t-1} = \text{Log}(1 + g) \tag{4b}$$

Both models (3) and (4) can be thought of as special cases of a more general relationship:

$$Y_t - Y_{t-1} = gY^c_{t-1} \tag{5a}$$

If c is 0 or 1, the linear or constant growth trends, respectively, result. It c is between 0 and 1, the differences increase with Y but less than proportionally; if greater than 1, the differences increase at an increasing rate; if less than 0, the differences decrease.[1]

It can be shown that this leads to a general difference model

$$Y_t^{1-c} - Y^{1-c}_{t-1} = b$$

or $$Y_t^{1-c} = Y_0^{1-c} + bt \tag{5b}$$

In the case of $c = \frac{1}{2}$, we obtain the square-root transformation used earlier on passenger car registrations and the quadratic trend

$$Y_t = a_0 + a_1t + a_2t^2 \tag{5c}$$

In Chapter 4, this appeared to be the best trend model, implying that, since 1950, registrations have been increasing by increasing amounts but less than proportionally to the number of cars registered. It can be seen that each of the trend transformations of Figure 4–5 corresponds to a different assumption about the value of c.

Limits and Bounds

The trend models considered so far all assume that the trend variable can increase (or decrease) indefinitely. As a practical matter, there would seem to be a limit to the extent that any variable can increase even if the

[1]This expression is not precisely correct. For c other than 0 or 1, it should be written

$$Y_t - Y_{t-1} = gY^c_{t-a}$$

for some a between 0 and 1. In most cases the difference is negligible.

magnitude of that limit is not completely clear. In the other direction, most variables cannot be negative, so there is an effective lower limit of 0. When the variable being analyzed and projected is well removed from any possible limit, this issue may not be important. In Figure 12–1, there clearly is some upper limit to the number of cars which can fit onto the roads and parking lots of this country. Despite the appearance of some of our cities and highways, it is unlikely that we will approach that limit within the next 15 to 20 years. On the other hand, if we were to study television coverage of the United States, currently more than 99% of U.S. households own at least one TV set, so the increase in that variable is essentially complete; the limit has been reached.

In short-range forecasting, determining the limit for a variable rarely is relevant; as planning and forecasting time horizons lengthen, the problem can become critical. Three basic situations can be distinguished:

1. Upper and/or lower limits are known and relevant.
2. Limits are unknown but have known upper (or lower) bounds.
3. Limits are completely unknown.

Limits Which Are Known.   For trends which are declining toward a known lower limit of 0, the logarithmic or *constant growth* curve can be quite useful. If the period-to-period changes are proportional to the magnitude of the variable

$$Y_t - Y_{t-1} = -gY_{t-1} \qquad (6a)$$

then the changes become progressively smaller and, as shown in Figure 12–2a (p. 354), the trend equation

$$Y_t = Y_0 (1 - g)^t \qquad (6b)$$

approaches zero without becoming negative.

In some cases, upper limits are known or can be theoretically determined. The upper limit to the proportions of a total such as market share or the proportion of households with TV sets cannot be greater than 1 and may be substantially less. Measures of relative efficiency, as in the generation of electric power, are similarly bounded. If an upper limit L is relevant and known, then the trend can be fitted by considering $L - Y_t$, the amount left to go, rather than Y_t. Thus the difference model

$$(L - Y_t) - (L - Y_{t-1}) = -g(L - Y_{t-1}) \qquad (7a)$$

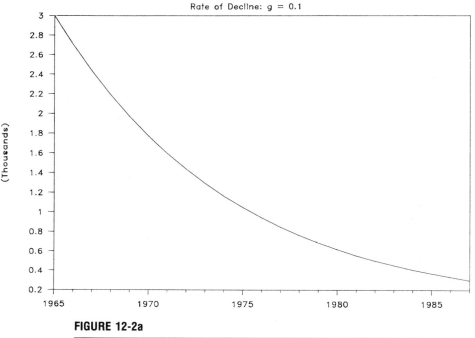

FIGURE 12-2a

Lower limit of zero, rate of decline: $g = 0.1$

leads to the trend model

$$Y_t = L - (L - Y_0)(1 - g)^t \tag{7b}$$

as in Figure 12–2b.

Limits Which Are Bounded but Not Known.   Ninety-nine percent of U.S. households own TV sets, but it is unlikely that an equivalent proportion will ever own air conditioners. In both cases the proportion will never exceed 1, but in the latter case the actual limit is almost certain to be substantially lower. In this situation, often a simple solution is to try several different possible values for L, plotting $\mathrm{Log}(L - Y_t)$ for each and observing which comes closest to giving a linear trend. An alternative and simpler approach is described in the next section. In any case, knowing the upper bound can be useful. If you attempt to fit a trend to a company's market share data and obtain an upper limit greater than 1, clearly something is wrong with your model or your calculations.

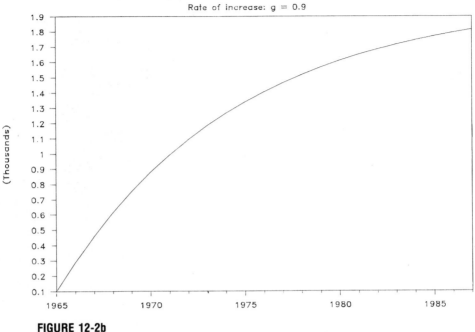

FIGURE 12-2b

Upper limit of 2000; rate of increase, g=0.9

When Neither the Limit nor Bound Is Known. This is the most common situation and the most difficult to deal with. It is actually the same as the previous case except that there are usually no guidelines to help in deciding what the upper limit might be. A good example is the passenger car data of Figure 12–1. There clearly must be an eventual upper limit to the number of cars which we can allow on our streets and highways, but there is no reason to believe that it will be reached within the relevant future, and there is little historical information to help in estimating what its long-run value might be.

Also, limits tend to change. Figure 12–3 (p. 356) is an example. Davis (1941) looked at the problem of determining upper limits in trend projection. As shown in the figure, one of the series he examined was the annual production of pig iron in the United States. Based on the assumption that the country had become industrially mature, he argued that production should level off at about 48 million tons per year. He recognized the need for preparing for World War II and suggested that the upper limit might be temporarily exceeded, but saw no basis for believing that this would be anything more than a short-term exception. What he could not foresee were the tremendous social, economic, and technological changes that would fol-

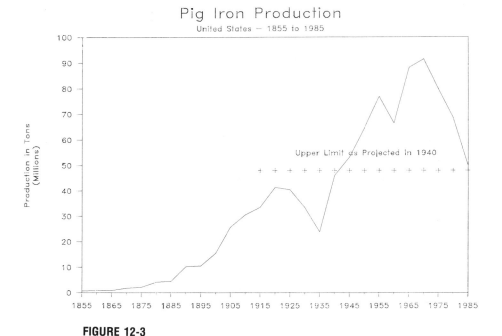

Pig Iron Production
United States — 1855 to 1985

FIGURE 12-3

Pig iron production: United States, 1855–1985

low the war and more than double his estimate. Pig-iron production is now dropping back to the upper limit he projected, but for very different reasons.

The Logistic Trend.   For many planning applications, our major interest is not in the time trend itself but rather in determining L and in detecting past points in time where L changed. A trend model which incorporates many of the ideas developed previously and which has been used extensively in long-range trend projection is appropriate here. It is the logistic or Pearl–Reed curve, more frequently known as the *S-shaped curve* from its characteristic shape as shown in Figure 12–4a (p. 358). The basic underlying model is

$$Y_t - Y_{t-1} = \frac{gY_t (L - Y_{t-1})}{L}$$

(8a)

When Y_t is small, the ratio $(L - Y_{t-1})/L$ is close to 1, and the model is essentially that of the simple exponential. When Y_t becomes large, the ratio of Y_t/L is approximately 1, and the trend approaches the upper limit of L. It is relatively easy to show that the time trend is given by

$$Y_t = \frac{L}{1 + a(1 - g)^t}$$

(8b)

If L is known, this can be easily fitted as

$$\text{Log}\left(\frac{L}{Y_t} - 1\right) = A + Bt \tag{8c}$$

where $A = \log a$ and $B = \log (1 - g)$.

Our concern is with the case when L is not known. To estimate L, plot the ratio Y_{t-1}/Y_t against Y_{t-1} as shown in Figure 12–4b (p. 359). Notice that this ratio is the *inverse* of the growth rate. It is sometimes called the *discount rate*. If the data can be appropriately described by this model, the graph will form a straight line.

$$\frac{Y_{t-1}}{Y_t} = (1 - g) + \frac{g}{L} Y_{t-1} \tag{9}$$

Project this line until it intersects a horizontal line at 1. The corresponding X coordinate will be the upper limit L. In Figure 12–4a, notice that the upper limit is 2000. Compare this to the value shown in Figure 12–4b.

Figure 12–5a (p. 360) shows an actual example of its use. Most writers on the subject of trend projection at some point apply their technique to the U.S. census data (the author is clearly no exception). During the 1920s and 1930s, several different forms of the logistic were tried by different authors. Estimates of the upper limit for the population of the United States were between 195 and 200 million. Examination of the data to 1930 by the method proposed here and shown in Figure 12–5b (p. 361) would lead to essentially the same result. What this simple analysis could not foresee was the tremendous impact of World War II and the changes that continued to take place after that war. By 1970 the projected upper limit of 200 million had already been exceeded. Projecting only from the three points since 1950 would lead to a new limit slightly greater than 300 million. Clearly, there is no inherent reason why it might not change again.

As illustrated by this last example, trend projection techniques can be very helpful in scenario development but must be interpreted with a great deal of caution. Trends can only reflect the patterns of the past; they say nothing directly about the future.

MODELS FOR SCENARIO DEVELOPMENT

Scenarios as we have introduced them here consist of a set of statements about future events and trends developed around some underlying theme. For a scenario to be persuasive and thus usable as a basis for planning, it is important that these statements be consistent with the theme and, inter-

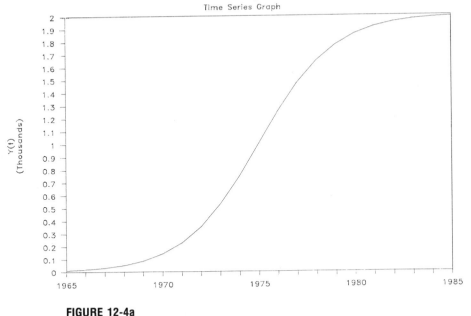

FIGURE 12-4a

Theoretical logistic curve: Time series graph

nally, with each other. In this section we outline some of the concepts and techniques which have been suggested for maintaining this consistency.

In choosing a theme, one or more critical events and trends are identified and given specific values or descriptions. It is then necessary to examine each of the other events and trends to consider the possible indirect impacts. For example, in the case of the hardware store, construction of the flood-control dam can be expected to lead to increased vacation traffic as the resulting lake becomes an attraction to campers and boaters. As a second-order effect, this may put pressure on the state to improve the roads and highways leading to the area. The improved roads may encourage local industrial development and increase the rate of population growth in the region. This may then affect land-use patterns and change the importance of dairy farming to the local economy. Clearly, this chain of potential higher-order impacts is never ending.[2] As a practical matter, we will normally be lucky if we can accurately identify even first-order effects.

[2]Tracing the chain of indirect effects is particularly interesting in considering the possible long-term impacts of new technological developments. In 1979, a public television series, *Connections*, made very effective use of this as a device for presenting the history of science and technology.

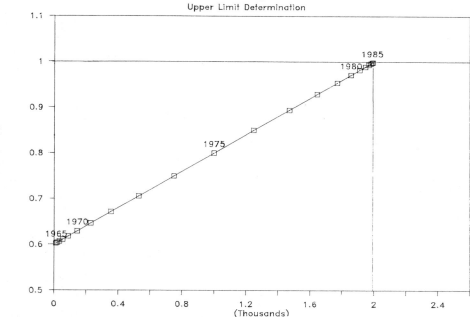

FIGURE 12-4b

Upper limit determination

In examining potential first- and higher-order impacts, we can distinguish four different situations, as in Table 12-1 (p. 360). Events have an effect on other events and on trends. Similarly, trends can affect other trends or events. Each has somewhat different implications for the methodology required.

Cross-impact Analysis

Relationships among events can be studied through use of a cross-impact table, as in Table 12-2 (p. 361). For simplicity, this example is limited to only three events; in practice the number would usually be substantially greater.

The impact of an event on another event can take many different forms. It can affect *what* occurs, that is, the specific details of the affected event, *where* it occurs, and *how* it occurs. At the quantitative level, it can affect the *probability* that the second event occurs, *when* it occurs, and the potential *magnitude* of the impact. As a practical matter, most proposed cross-impact techniques have limited themselves to evaluating the changes

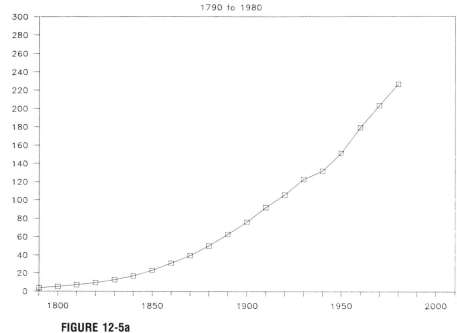

United States Population
1790 to 1980

FIGURE 12-5a

United States population, 1790–1980

TABLE 12–1

Studying the Indirect Effects of Event and Trend Assumptions

Occurrence of an:	*As it Affects an:*	
	Event	*Trend*
Event	Cross-impact analysis	Trend-impact analysis
Trend	Critical-level analysis	Dynamic modeling

in the probability of occurrence of the other events, given that each of the events listed in the first column of Table 12-2 is assumed to occur. This probability estimation can be carried out using the judgmental techniques proposed in Chapter 11. Notice that the impact of *A* on *B* is not the same as *B* on *A*; $I_{AB} \neq I_{BA}$.

In most cases of scenario development, these probabilities are not going to be used for prediction, but only for maintaining internal consis-

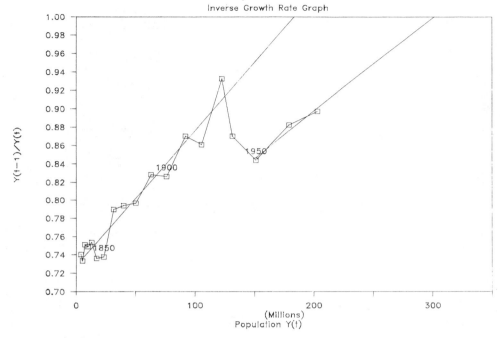

United States Population 1790 to 1980
Inverse Growth Rate Graph

FIGURE 12-5b

Inverse growth-rate graph

TABLE 12–2

Cross-impact Table

		On Event:		
Impact of:	*Event*	*A*	*B*	*C*
A	Construction of the flood-control dam	—	I_{AB}	I_{AC}
B	Government grant for local redevelopment	I_{BA}	—	I_{BC}
C	Creamery replaced by high-tech manufacturing company	I_{CA}	I_{CB}	—

tency in the scenarios, and it will be adequate to estimate the likely impacts using a 5- or 7-point scale, as illustrated in Table 12-3 (p. 262). Table 12-4 (p. 262) shows the type of cross-impact table that might result. A scenario based on event *B*, the government grant, might omit the flood-control proj-

TABLE 12–3

Seven-point Scale for Event Probability Assessment

Value	Interpretation
−3	Event almost certain to not occur
−2	Moderate decrease in probability of occurrence
−1	Slight decrease in probability of occurrence
0	No impact on occurrence
1	Slight increase in probability of occurrence
2	Moderate increase in probability of occurrence
3	Event almost certain to occur

TABLE 12–4

Cross-impact Table for Regional Development

Impact of:	Event	On event: A	B	C
A	Construction of the flood-control dam	—	−1	1(?)
B	Government grant for local redevelopment	−2	—	3
C	Creamery replaced by high-tech manufacturing company	0	0	—

ect but would certainly include a change in the character of local industry. A scenario based on event *A*, the flood-control dam, might or might not include some redevelopment grant money as well. A question mark has been placed after the 1 in the upper right cell. In the short scenario presented, it was suggested that construction of the dam could, in the long run, lead to other industrial development. Whether such third- and fourth-order effects should be part of a scenario is a difficult question. The forecaster would have to consider the scenario time horizon in deciding whether or not 1 was the correct value to be used here.

Critical-level Analysis

The assessment of the impact of a trend on a event can be carried out by identifying potential critical values or levels of the variable described by the trend. As this is being written, the demand for petroleum is down and the price is low. Not too many years ago when this situation was much different, a number of alternative sources for oil were considered. One, for example, was the use of oil shales in the western United States. These projects are now effectively on hold because the costs of development are too high. There is every reason to believe that the current low price of oil will at some future time increase until the price reaches the level where mining oil shale becomes profitable; the event "mining of oil shale commences" will occur. For purposes of scenario development, it would be necessary to identify that critical price level.

Trend-impact Analysis

Events affect trends by influencing the rate of change of the trend variable. This impact may be transient or permanent, it may occur immediately or after some delay. As shown in Figure 12-6, for each event-trend

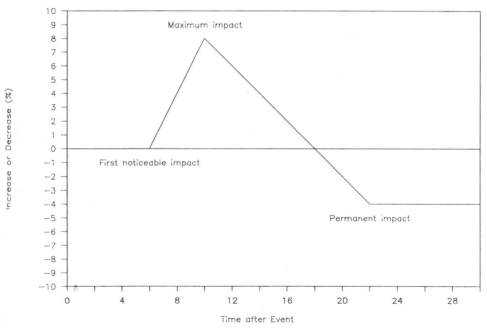

FIGURE 12-6

Trend-impact model

pair, five characteristics of the relationship must be estimated. The degree
of impact is relative to the base rate of change or growth prior to the event
and is in addition to any other changes in this growth rate that may be
projected. Notice that the short-term impact may be quite different from
the long-term or "steady-state" impact. Three time estimates are needed:
(1) to the first noticeable impact, (2) to the maximum short-term impact,
and (3) to the final, stable long-term impact (if any).

For many trends the impacts of past events may give clues to future
impacts. Figure 12-7 returns to the example of productivity in the printing
and publishing industry first introduced in Chapter 8. There we looked at
the changing relationship between an index of production and data on
average weekly hours worked. For simplicity, we reduce this to a single
productivity index by dividing the output or production index by the data
on hours worked. Figure 12-7a shows the productivity index from 1947 to
1984. The general upward curvature suggests that, overall, productivity
may have been increasing at a constant rate (slightly greater than 2.5% per
year). Figure 12-7b shows the inverse growth rate graph as discussed earlier for the logistic. At first the picture may appear a bit chaotic. Closer

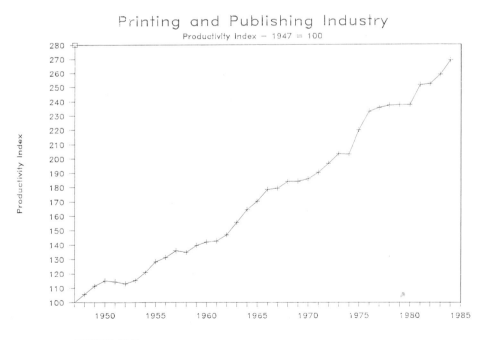

FIGURE 12-7a

Printing and publishing industry: Productivity index (1947 = 100)

examination shows a series of periods during which the points tended to move upward (approaching an upper limit), interspersed with relatively sharp drops (1957 to 1961, 1968 to 1974, and 1979 to 1983 are the clearest), corresponding to technological innovations in the industry. The period from 1968 to 1974, for example, corresponds to the replacement of hot-metal type casting (linotype machines) by photocomposition, as noted earlier. In general, it appears that these changes were introduced and absorbed fairly rapidly, since both the downward and upward changes in the underlying movement appear to be quite abrupt. In itself, of course, this says nothing about the possibility or the nature of the impact of future innovations. It does suggest that, if a new innovation in this industry were to be included as part of a scenario, the resulting impact on productivity might also be described as being rapidly absorbed.

Dynamic Modeling

A full discussion of the techniques for modeling the relationships among different trends is beyond the scope of this book. Some of the

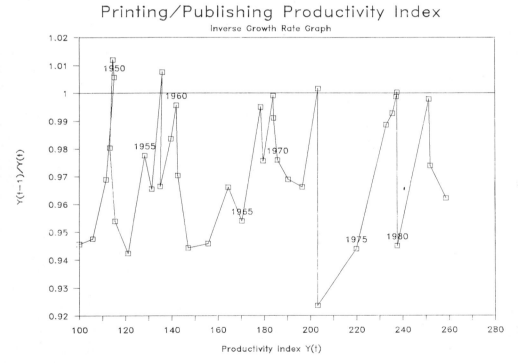

FIGURE 12-7b

Printing/publishing productivity index, inverse growth-rate graph

problems have already been introduced in Chapter 8. Chief among the problems is that regression techniques are for the most part not applicable. Any two trends will always appear to be correlated since both can be described as functions of time and thus will always appear to move together, even if they are completely unrelated.

In some cases it may be possible to identify variables which are *leading indicators*. A frequently cited example is the relationship between the speeds of military and commercial aircraft with innovations appearing first in military applications and then later in commercial aircraft. Aircraft speed is also a good illustration of the caution that must be used in interpreting leading indicators. Since 1970, speeds of commercial aircraft for practical purposes have remained constant, while military aircraft speeds have continued to increase. Although one SST, the Concorde, is still in operation, this innovation did not spread, but for economic and political rather than technological reasons.

In some cases, dynamic models can be constructed by making logical assumptions about the underlying structure, rather than by statistical modeling. This is essentially the approach used in one of the early attempts at large-scale social forecasting, the world model of Forrester and Meadows. For this, equations relating different trends are specified based on available (not necessarily statistical) data and on subjective interpretation of that data. Coefficients are estimated and modified in a similar way. Simulation, as discussed earlier, is then used to generate possible future paths of the variables included in the model. In the world model just cited, the major variables were world population, world nonrenewable resources, arable land, capital, and pollution. An earlier version also included a measure of quality of life. Because of the complexity of these dynamic models, they can be very costly to construct, and substantial computer time is needed for the simulation runs. Particularly because of the visual impact of the graphically displayed output of the model(s), they can be very effective in planning. For most planning applications, however, it appears that equivalent results can be obtained using much simpler methods.

EVALUATING SCENARIOS

The criteria for a "good" scenario are quite different from those discussed for shorter-range forecasts in Chapter 9. Time horizons are such that forecast accuracy is not an operationally relevant criterion. Even if it were possible to eventually check the accuracy of a scenario, each situation is substantially different, so any learning from past forecast errors will be limited. Equally important, the uses of scenarios are quite different from those of the types of forecasts discussed earlier.

In judging scenarios, four basic criteria should be used:

1. Responsiveness
2. Comprehensiveness
3. Documentation
4. Plausibility

Responsiveness.   Scenarios, as they have been considered here, should not be merely exercises in creativity designed to stimulate management's vision. Although there is often a place for this type of activity, for our purposes scenarios should be developed in the context of the specific strategic issues facing management. It must be remembered that the scenarios will have to be used in conjunction with specific strategic alternatives to generate and evaluate outcome scenarios. Both the included elements, events and trends, and the form in which the scenario is presented should be responsive to this need.

Comprehensiveness.   All the relevant environments should be addressed in the scenario, not just the economic factors. The scenarios should not simply describe alternative futures which may face the organization; they should also develop the "time line," the path of events which would lead up to that future.

Documentation.   The background material used in developing each scenario should be available to the planner/manager. The model structure should be explicit and understandable. Any included statements of fact should be correct and supported. All underlying assumptions should be explicit. Available evidence which would support or limit the assumptions should be included.

Plausibility.   The final risk in any strategic decision must be borne by the manager. No matter how good a scenario may be technically, if to the manager it does not describe a plausible future, it will have only limited impact. This does not mean that it must necessarily appear to be likely. It must, however, be internally consistent, it must address real issues, and the assumptions and path by which that future can evolve from the present must be clear.

SUMMARY

Scenarios can be very effective tools in focusing managerial attention and in highlighting opportunities and risks in planning. To be effective, scenarios must be plausible, well documented, internally consistent, and relevant to the decisions which must be made. It is too easy to dismiss the issue by simply asserting that scenario development is an "art form" and can only be learned by doing. Techniques have been developed to guide and facilitate this essentially creative process. These last chapters have introduced a few that may be particularly helpful.

READINGS

The pig-iron example came from

> HAROLD T. DAVIS, *The Analysis of Economic Time Series,* Blooming-ton, Ind., Principia Press, 1941, Chapter 6.

This chapter also gives a good general introduction to a wide range of different trend models.

Other material on trends and growth models can be found in

> JAMES P. CLEARY and HANS LEVENBACH, *The Professional Fore-caster,* Belmont, Calif., Lifetime Learning Publications, 1982, Chapter 6.
>
> ROBERT U. AYRES, *Technological Forecasting and Long Range Planning,* New York, McGraw-Hill, 1969, Chapter 6.
>
> JAMES R. BRIGHT, *Practical Technological Forecasting,* Austin, Tex., Industrial Management Center, Inc., 1978, Chapter 6.
>
> RAYMOND E. WILLIS, "Statistical Considerations in the Fitting of Growth Curves," *Technological Forecasting and Social Change,* vol. 15 (1979), pp. 107–125.

The book by Bright noted previously has a good introduction to cross-impact and trend-impact modeling. Material on cross-impact tables can also be found in

> HAROLD A. LINSTONE and MURRAY TUROFF (eds.), *The Delphi Method: Techniques and Applications,* Reading, Mass., Addison-Wesley, 1975, Part V.

The BBC TV show "Connections" had a companion book also dealing with historical cross-impacts.

> JAMES BURKE, *Connections,* Boston, Little, Brown, 1978.

A similar but shorter paper on the same theme is

LYNN WHITE, JR., "Technology Assessment from the Stance of a Medieval Historian," *American Historical Review*, February 1974, pp. 1–13.

Much of the work in dynamic modeling has been due to Jay W. Forrester. See particularly

JAY W. FORRESTER, *World Dynamics*, Cambridge, Mass., Wright-Allen Press, 1971.

JAY W. FORRESTER, *Principles of Systems*, Cambridge, Mass., Wright-Allen Press, 1968.

DONELLA H. MEADOWS et al., *The Limits to Growth*, New York, Universe Books, 1972.

A slightly different view of evaluating scenarios can be found in

JOSEPH P. MARTINO, "Evaluating Forecast Validity," in James R. Bright and M. E. Schoeman (eds.), *Guide to Practical Technological Forecasting*, Englewood Cliffs, N.J., Prentice-Hall, 1973, pp. 26–52.

PROBLEMS

1. In late 1977, McGure and Sams, Inc., entered a market dominated by two major firms. Results to date have been disappointing despite several changes in the company's marketing strategy. Using the following data on the company's market share for the last 10 years, evaluate the possible long-run market share for the company.

Year	Market Share (%)	Year	Market Share (%)
1978	3.0	1983	13.9
1979	6.8	1984	14.8
1980	9.9	1985	16.4
1981	11.8	1986	18.0
1982	12.8	1987	19.4

2. The Arrowgant Company manufactures a mechanical variable-speed control which is used extensively for industrial applications. Several years ago the company came out with an electronic control which they believed would, over time, completely replace the mechanical version. Because the new control required other modifications in any machine in which it was installed, they did not expect this change-over to take place "overnight." It now appears, however, that the new control may not be as generally applicable as was at first thought. This could cause problems for the company because their long-range plans were developed on the assumption that the mechanical control would gradually be phased out. They have asked you to investigate the question and assess whether you think their initial assumption that the mechanical control should be phased out was reasonable. You have 3 years of data on the sales of the electronic control including the following. What is your assessment?

Quarter		Percent of Unit Sales from Electronic Control
1985	I	3.3
	II	4.5
	III	6.0
	IV	8.0
1986	I	10.5
	II	14.0
	III	18.0
	IV	23.0
1987	I	29.0
	II	34.0
	III	37.0
	IV	39.0

3. In mid-1978, the Truetime Company entered a market with a new product that they felt would be a major technological innovation and would make existing units obsolete. The market at the time was dominated by three large national firms. Results to date have been less satisfactory than predicted by studies made prior to the product's introduction, despite several changes in the product and in the company's marketing strategies. Data on the company's sales and on the estimated market share are as shown. Based on these data, identify possible sources of the problem and discuss the implications for future strategies.

Year	Sales ($000)	Est. Size of Market ($000)	Market Share (%)
1978	3,459	116,305	2.97
1979	9,005	127,833	7.04

(continued on next page)

Year	Sales ($000)	Est. Size of Market ($000)	Market Share (%)
1980	14,350	140,014	10.25
1981	17,249	152,189	11.33
1982	21,995	165,964	13.25
1983	27,232	180,004	15.13
1984	30,339	191,290	15.86
1985	34,322	199,469	17.21
1986	40,031	206,063	19.43
1987	41,426	210,483	19.68

4. Smith's Crossing is a small semirural community located on a railroad line. The nearest city is approximately 35 miles away. Local industry consists of a sawmill and a railroad loading facility used by the local farmers. A state two-lane highway connects the town to the city. As the children of local families have grown, they have tended to move away and few families have moved into the community. The population in 1970 was 3740 and has been dropping at an average rate of 1% per year since then. There are also currently about 60 people who work at the sawmill and for the railroad facility but do not live in the town.

Joyce and Tom Hawthorne run a combination general store, gas station, and lunch room on the state highway and about $\frac{1}{2}$ mile from the sawmill and railroad facility. An interstate bus line stops at their store twice a day in each direction. They have been very contented both with the town and with their business but are concerned with rumors of possible changes.

The railroad has indicated that the line through Smith's Crossing is no longer profitable and will have to be shut down within the next 5 years unless circumstances change. Many groups have expressed concern over the changes that are taking place and the effects on Smith's Crossing and other small communities in the region around the city. A number of ideas have been suggested that could directly affect the town. These include:

    A. *Industrial park:* Several sites have been considered, including the area now used by the sawmill and railroad in Smith's Crossing. If this were built at that location, it would mean that the railroad would continue to operate the line. On the other hand, the sawmill and about 50 homes between the railroad and the Hawthorne's store would have to be removed. It is not clear that these would be relocated in the area.

    B. *Light rail transit:* The existing right-of-way has been suggested for light rail transit to the city. The state planning agency has suggested this as a way of developing the towns along the railroad into "bedroom" communities for the city. It is believed that this would cause substantial new residential construction in and around Smith's Crossing. This could not occur unless the railroad line first closed.

C. *Upgrading and widening the state highway:* This has been suggested to the state highway department, although to date nothing has been done. Widening the highway would allow trucks better access to the city and might be given a higher priority if the railroad were to close the line.

D. *Apartments:* There is an area across the highway from the store that has been considered for a very large multibuilding apartment complex. While it has been clear that the city, for many years, has been short of adequate apartment space and the site in Smith's Crossing has been considered several times, it has been rejected as too inconvenient to the city.

E. *Housing development:* One of the more ambitious ideas has been the development of a large residential area stretching about two miles along the highway in the direction of the city. This would consist of both single-family homes and townhouses.

The Hawthorne's business comes from three different groups:

1. Local residents and area farmers who use the store for groceries and gas and sometimes drop in for coffee.

2. Day workers at the sawmill and railroad who eat lunch and to a lesser extent breakfast at the lunch counter and buy gas.

3. Transits traveling along the highway who stop for gas and coffee and sometimes light meals.

Based on discussions with a number of different people, the Hawthornes believe that, in the absence of other developments, the railroad has a high probability of closing. They think that there is a 50–50 chance that a developer will start the housing development and about the same chance for the industrial park. They don't see someone building an apartment complex based on current conditions. Similarly, under current conditions, neither the highway improvements or the light rail would have much chance.

An informal cross-impact study has given the following estimates based on a 7-point scale with 3 almost certain and −3 almost impossible.

The events considered are:

O. Closing of the railroad

A. The industrial park

B. Light rail transit

C. Highway improvement

D. Apartments

E. Housing development

The Impact of	On Event:					
Event:	O	A	B	C	D	E
O	—	−3	1	2	−1	0
A	−2	—	−1	3	2	−3
B	a	−2	—	−1	2	2
C	2	1	−2	—	2	2
D	0	0	2	2	—	0
E	0	−3	1	2	0	—

ªThe light rail transit would not be built unless the railroad line were to first close.

The events are anticipated to have the following effects if they occur:

Railroad closing

> Resident population decreased by 20 people
>
> Day workers decreased by 25 people
>
> No change in passenger-car traffic
>
> Truck traffic doubled, then increasing by an additional 5% per year

Industrial park

> Resident population an immediate drop of 200 due to land clearance
>
> Day workers drop by 35, then increase by 500 over the following year and 5% per year thereafter
>
> Road traffic doubles the first year, then increases by 5% per year thereafter

Light rail transit

> Population increasing at 3% per year.
> All other effects negligible

Highway improvement

> Population, no effect the first year; 10% increase over the next 2 years
>
> Day workers increased by the road crews; 200 for 3 years

All road traffic decreased by 75% for 3 years; then return to current levels plus 15% and an additional 5% per year thereafter

Apartments

No change in resident population the first year, then increasing by 500 people per year for 5 years

Day workers increased by 200 for 6 years

Road car traffic increased by an additional 2% per year

Housing development

Resident population unchanged for 2 years, then increasing by 400 per year for 10 years

Day workers increased by 300 for 12 years

Road car traffic increased by an additional 3% per year

a. Using the information given, develop an internally consistent scenario based on the development of the industrial park.

b. What other internally consistent scenarios are suggested by the information given?

c. Discuss how the Hawthornes might use these scenarios in planning for the future of their store.

CHAPTER 13

A Planner's Guide to Developing and Evaluating Forecasts

Planning has to do with the future; one of the major issues facing the planner is dealing with the fact that the future is inherently uncertain. A wide variety of tools is available for coping with this uncertainty, starting with the organization's initial choice of a business to be in. This book has been concerned with one particular aspect of this problem, the analysis and projection of the past as a way of better anticipating the future events and trends which may affect the organization. The emphasis has been on the interface between planning and forecasting, not on the technical needs of the professional forecaster; nor have we tried to cover all the problems facing the planner. Two broad areas have been considered: (1) the use of techniques of analyzing and projecting time series and relationships among time series and (2) the development and use of scenarios or "alternative futures."

The concerns of the planner and forecaster are in general quite different. The fundamental job of the forecaster is to study and interpret the past so that the planner can look to the future. Planners do need to understand the potential and limitations of forecasting; they have to be able to evaluate forecasts both when they are initially used and after the events forecasted have come about. In many cases, particularly in small- to medium-sized companies and divisions, planners must be their own forecasters and need the tools for making simple forecasts. In any case the planner needs to have some forecasting skills for "quick and dirty" applications and as a check on the projections of technical analysts.

This book has examined some typical planning situations and their implications for the forecaster's choice of an appropriate approach. With only a few exceptions, the actual analytical methods presented have been those which require no more than graph paper and a hand calculator. At the same time, the day is rapidly approaching when every manager will have available (and be comfortable using) a personal computer or computer terminal. All the techniques we have considered can easily be adapted to current spreadsheet and graphics software. Thus, it will increasingly be possible and even necessary for the planner/manager to be involved in the forecasting process. This final chapter reviews and summarizes some guidelines for the planner who is also a part-time forecaster or who is a major user of forecasts.

ON BEING YOUR OWN FORECASTER

A distinction should be made between forecasts which are developed by analyzing and projecting patterns in single time series and forecasts which are based on relationships among several time series. It is also useful to make a distinction between the two stages of the *analysis* of the time series and of its *projection*.

Steps in Time-series Analysis

1. Select and Edit the Time Series.   In most instances the planner will be concerned with time series that someone else, in the company or outside, collected. In selecting a time series for analysis, always double-check the source and how it was collected; do not rely solely on descriptive titles. Some questions to consider might include:

> How was the data collected? By direct observation or indirect reporting? Or was it estimated? What exactly was included in the reported data?

What is the relationship between the reported data and the variables in the underlying planning model? Frequently, the planner is interested in analyzing *demand*. It is rare that this can be directly observed. More frequently, the available data are for sales, orders received, shipments, or billings. These variables may be closely related to demand; then again, they may not. What data were recorded and how were they related to demand? Where there have been frequent stockouts, it will be necessary to estimate "lost sales." Was this done? How?

Even with direct observation, the data recorded are not always completely accurate. How accurate are they? What are the possible sources of errors?

Are there discontinuities or changes in the definition of the time series? The coverage of a time series can increase or decrease. The meaning of terms may change. The base year for an index number may be shifted. Underlying conditions may change either temporarily or permanently because of factors such as strikes, weather conditions, price reductions, or changes in product quality or design.

The time series should also be double-checked for clerical errors and coverage omissions. Errors in coding and transcribing data are the hardest to detect but can still cause a great deal of trouble. At every stage of the analysis, apparent outliers should be checked. They often turn out to be clerical errors.

2. Make Appropriate Data Adjustments. Data are rarely collected in exactly the form needed for any specific application; some adjustments to the time series will be necessary. A number of possible adjustments were discussed in Chapter 3. Two of the most common are *working day adjustments* and *price adjustments*. In many cases, also, the analysis can be simplified by breaking the time series down into subcomponents before analysis. A common situation is the separation of *total demand* into *per capita demand* and *size of the population*.

3. Make Necessary Data Transformations. This step is not usually possible at the beginning. As the analysis proceeds, however, it may become apparent that the process could be simplified by some transformation or "re-expression" of the data. One of the most common is the use of logarithms. When transformations are indicated, they should be applied before any attempts are made at trend removal or seasonal adjustment. When a data transformation is indicated, it is necessary to "back up," make the appropriate data transformation, and start again.

4. Seasonally Adjust the Data If Appropriate. Data reported on an annual basis have no seasonal component. Sometimes time series, particularly government statistics, are already seasonally adjusted. In other cases the forecaster must remove the seasonal component from the data. If a seasonal index is required, it almost always involves the use of a computer. In many applications, a simpler alternative is to combine seasonal adjustment with trend removal by using *seasonal first differences*.

5. Remove the Trend Component. This can be done by taking successive differences (or seasonal differences) or by fitting an appropriate trend model and taking deviations from the trend. If first differences or a linear trend equation do not remove the trend, back up to step 3.

6. Smooth the Data. Isolate the residuals to study the fluctuations around the trend. These fluctuations include the *cyclical* component, outliers, and the residual. Outliers should be checked to make sure that they are not simply clerical errors.

7. Summarize the Residuals. The residual is the statistical component of the time series. It is not the same as the forecast error, although it is related. That is, if the residuals showed no obvious pattern in the past, it is likely that a similar unpatterned component will exist in the future and will be *one* of the sources of errors in the forecast.

Steps in Forecast Development

The process of forecast development involves the same basic steps but in reverse order.

1. Make Projections of the Cyclical Component. At the simplest level of analysis, this may have to be done subjectively. It is usually helpful to make a number of different projections based on different assumptions about the factors that might have an influence on the cyclical component.

2. Sum and Project the First Differences or Deviations from the Trend. The inverse operation of differencing is summing. Having projected the period-to-period changes or deviations from the trend in step 1, they are now added sequentially to the last available actual value or to the trend projections.

3. Reintroduce the Seasonal Component. If the seasonal component was removed by using a seasonal index, it should be reintroduced into the projections. If it was removed by division, it should be multiplied; if by subtraction, then it should be added. If the seasonal pattern is changing, appropriate adjustments should first be made to the seasonal index.

4. Transform the Projections Back to Their Original Form.   If in step 3 of the analysis the data were transformed to logarithms, the inverse log should now be used; if the transformation was the square root, the projections should be squared, and similarly for any of the other possible transformations.

5. Readjust the Projections.   If any initial adjustments were made to the data to simplify the analysis, reverse adjustments should now be applied. For example, if trading-day adjustments were made, the projections should be multiplied by the projected number of trading days in the future period. If price adjustments were made, separate price projections are needed for the reverse adjustments.

6. Adapt the Projections to the Planning Model or Use.   The final projections should now be re-expressed, if necessary, in a form and in units appropriate to the specific application. If there is any information on future discontinuities or other changes in the variable, appropriate adjustments should be made. For example, suppose that it is known that a retail chain is planning to open 10 new units during the period forecast; some adjustment to a projection based only on past sales would almost certainly be necessary. Remember, if the forecast is to be presented directly to management in a meeting or report, it must be put in a form that can be easily understood. You may use logs or square roots in your analysis, but go back to the original units when you present it.

7. Evaluate Possible Sources of Forecast Error.   The residual component is only one possible source of forecast error. Others include misspecification of the cyclical component, errors in estimating the trend and seasonal, inadequate transformations and data adjustments, and unanticipated discontinuities and outliers. The possibility of errors from each of these sources should be considered. Equally important, the impact of any of these errors on the underlying plan should be evaluated.

Developing Multivariate Forecasting Models

The development and use of multivariate models almost always involves computations requiring the use of computers and technical specialists. Even if the planner is not primarily concerned with development of the model, she or he will be involved at many stages in the process and should be aware of the issues involved. Two extreme situations can be identified: (1) the underlying theoretical model is well known and all that is necessary is to estimate the appropriate parameters, and (2) theoretical knowledge is completely absent and the model must be determined empirically. In practice, the situation will lie somewhere between these extremes. The underlying model will not be known completely, but enough knowledge will exist to help guide the process of model construction. Since it is the planner who most often has this knowledge, it is desirable for that individual to understand the model-development process and the necessary inputs.

1. Identify Model Variables.   Four categories of variables enter into planning/forecasting models: dependent variable(s), key independent variables, promising independent variables, and those that Mosteller and Tukey descriptively refer to as "the haystack," that is, all other possible variables. Because in most time-series applications the available data are severely limited, the modeler is also limited in the number of different variables which can be included in the model. The initial identification of the key variables can be critical to the success of the final model.

2. Adjust Individual Variables.   Before starting the development of the actual model, it is important to first make appropriate adjustments to each individual variable following the first five steps of time-series analysis described previously. Trend adjustments, if necessary, can either be made by differencing or by including a function of the time variable (t) in the final model.

3. Develop the Model One Step at a Time.   The development of the model should proceed one step and one variable at a time. Chapter 8 describes one possible guided approach to model building. At each stage the process should be influenced by whatever theoretical knowledge is available. With time series, special attention should be paid to the possibility of lagged relationships and to the possibility that the relationship itself may differ from one seasonal period to the next.

4. Develop Multiple Models.   When several different interpretations of the data and thus several different models are possible, all should be explored. Differences among the projections from the different models can point up possible sources of forecast error.

5. Test the Model(s).   Before starting the modeling process, some of the available data should be put in a separate "set-aside" sample which can be used for testing the models developed and for estimating the component of the forecast error that may arise from model misspecification.

Forecasting with Multivariate Models

As with single-variable analysis, the process of developing the forecast is the reverse of the process of analysis. In addition, since it is usually necessary to use *forecasts* of the independent variables to develop the final projections, the forecast error component which arises from errors in the independent variable forecasts should be estimated as well.

ON BEING YOUR OWN SCENARIO WRITER

In this book, scenarios have been presented primarily in their role in strategic program planning. In fact, for the planner/manager, the potential uses of scenarios are much broader. They can aid in contingency planning, in exploring the possible magnitude and sources of forecast errors, and in judgmental forecasting to reduce the problems of "anchoring." They can be useful in interpreting forecasts to nontechnical audiences and in making forecasts more plausible to the user.

Although scenario development and use is much less structured than for other types of forecasts, a number of steps can be taken to facilitate the process.

1. Identify the Use or Uses of the Scenario. It is much too easy to let a scenario turn into an exercise in creative writing or wishful thinking. To be effective, a scenario should be no longer than absolutely necessary. This means that every aspect of the scenario or scenarios developed should be directed toward some specific application. At the same time, each scenario must be responsive to the needs of the user and contain all necessary detail. It is wise to start by explicitly formulating the purpose of the scenarios, at every stage checking the developing scenario against that purpose.

2. Identify and Document Relevant Events and Trends. Events should be specified in terms of *what, when, where,* and *how.* Trends should be specific about the variable to be projected. To the extent possible, data and background material should be collected for each event and trend.

3. Specify the Scenario Themes. Decide on the number of themes to be developed and the central subject of each. Separate your personal beliefs of what you think is "likely" to happen from the need to develop scenarios which will expose potential risks and test underlying assumptions.

4. Decide on the Structure of the Scenarios.   The structure depends on the audience and the use. For some purposes a rather terse outline format is best; in other cases an informal case description structure is more effective. In some cases, extensive tabular and graphical documentation are needed; for other uses only a general description of the scenario events and trends is adequate.

5. Develop and Maintain a Range Table.   The scenarios collectively should have sufficient breadth to cover the range of issues under study. At the same time, each scenario should be internally consistent. As discussed in Chapter 12, there are a number of different analytical procedures, such as cross- and trend-impact models, to aid in this. Such elaborate devices are not always necessary. At a minimum, a range table should be used to facilitate the comparison of the different scenarios developed.

6. Be Sensitive to Changing Needs.   The use of scenarios is an evolutionary process. As the planning process proceeds, conditions and needs change. Scenarios should be changed, modified, or expanded to meet these needs.

ON EVALUATING FORECASTS

The ultimate responsibility for the direct and continuing evaluation of the forecasts lies with the manager who is the user. In earlier chapters a distinction was made between ex ante and ex post evaluation. *Ex ante* evaluation refers to the process by which forecasts and the forecasting process are monitored and controlled while the forecasts are being developed and before they are used. *Ex post* evaluation occurs after the actual outcome has occurred and is a direct comparison between the outcome and the forecast. Both are an important aspect of all forecasting and planning.

Ex Ante Forecast Evaluation

A distinction can be made between qualitative and quantitative methods of evaluation. Qualitative ex ante evaluation requires the use of multiple models or scenarios based on clearly different underlying theories or sets of assumptions. When faced with multiple models or forecasts, there is a natural tendency to try to choose the "best" among them. A far safer practice is to use *all* of them. If they all lead to the same operational conclusions, the user has additional assurance of the stability of the actions planned. If the conclusions are different, potential warning signals are raised.

As part of the qualitative evaluation, the planner/manager should be particularly sensitive to factors which are not included in the models, such as possible future discontinuities in the system. At the same time, as noted in Chapter 11, the manager should be careful not to overreact to such nonincluded factors.

Qualitative evaluation is directed toward the internal structure of the forecasting model. Many useful statistical techniques exist for testing how well a given model fits the historical data. It is important to recognize that historical fit is not the same as future accuracy. Many modeling techniques have an unfortunate tendency to tailor the model to the data and thus give an erroneous view of probable future accuracy. This risk can be reduced by testing the model against data different from those used to create the model. It is even more important to try to understand the underlying structure of the process and to see if the structure of the model is consistent with that of the process.

Ex Post Evaluation

Once forecasts have been made and plans implemented, there is a tendency to forget the forecasts and move on to new problems. Ex post evaluation is an essential learning process with a view to the improvement of future forecasts. When forecast time horizons are short and forecasts are made routinely, techniques such as the CUSUM and P–R diagram discussed in Chapter 9 can be very helpful. In any case, a study should be made not just of the magnitude of the forecast errors, but of the probable causes as well. Several specific areas of questioning were cited in Chapter 9: specification errors and problems of extrapolation, omitted factors, errors in the independent variables used as inputs to the forecast model, and outliers. Each of these raises different issues that are relevant to future forecasting. With very long forecast horizons, it can be very helpful to include some shorter-range milestones in the forecast. These can be evaluated as a check on the overall forecast.

Finally, as with any other managerial process, some form of cost-benefit analysis should be applied to the forecasting process. There is a tendency to equate a "good" forecast with an accurate forecast. This is only partially true. If the increased accuracy has no effect on the choice of managerial action or if the cost of the increased accuracy outweighs any potential gains, then trying for additional accuracy may be inappropriate. As noted in Chapter 1, forecasting is only one of the possible ways of dealing with uncertainty about the future; it is not always the best way.

SOME FINAL GUIDELINES

It will be useful to end with some random thoughts on forecasting collected from a variety of sources. Most have already been noted, but all are worth restating.

1. When relying on forecasts made by others, don't look just at the forecasts. Find out as much as possible about the assumptions behind the forecasts. You may agree with them; then again, you may not.

2. Beware of consensus. Agreement is not the same as accuracy. All that it usually means is that the forecasts are all based on the same data, assumptions, and biases. If one forecast proves to be wrong, the others will probably turn out to be wrong—in the same direction and for the same reasons.

3. With multiple forecasts, pay special attention to those at the extremes (the outliers). They are likely to include factors that the "middle of the road" forecasts have omitted. You may not agree with these forecasts, but you should at least understand them.

4. Don't confuse correlation with causation. The fact that two variables have moved together in the past is no guarantee that they will continue to do so. Be particularly careful when both variables have strong trends; such variables will always be correlated.

5. Don't use past residuals as your sole measure of probable forecast accuracy. Remember that the model or procedure used was designed to specifically fit the data. It will never fit any other as well.

6. Avoid overfitting and tailoring your model to your data. To the extent that your model reflects nonrecurring historical idiosyncrasies, you will have built in another potential source of forecast error. Be parsimonious; the simpler your model, the less likely will be the chance that you have overfitted.

7. Don't try to focus on some single "best" forecast or model. Recognize that all the forecasts will probably be wrong although by different amounts and for different reasons. A better evaluation of the potential magnitude of the forecast error can be obtained by comparing several different models based on different sets of assumptions and observing the range of forecasts that result. Don't choose a forecast model solely on the basis of how well it fits. That is only one indication of a potentially useful forecast (and not always the most important).

8. To the extent possible, err on the side of overstating rather than understating the probable magnitude of the forecast error. There will always be sources of error that you have not even thought of.

9. Don't base your forecast model on independent variables that are as hard to forecast as the dependent variable. It will just add one more layer of potential forecast error.

10. Don't confuse wishful thinking or ideological commitment with forecasting. Neither need nor morality can assure the future course of events.

11. Particularly with long forecast horizons, develop milestone forecasts to check your accuracy along the way.

12. In looking back, don't evaluate your forecasts solely on the basis of whether they were right or wrong (they will almost never be right anyway). Instead, try to analyze *why* they were wrong. Was it the assumptions, the structure of the forecast model, or some completely unpredictable factor that caused the error?

13. Don't keep track of only your successes. In fact, forget your successes (as long as others don't); you will learn a lot more from your mistakes.

14. Remember that the purpose of forecasting is to improve your planning and decision making; it is not an end in itself. If *any* of the factors in *any* of the alternative futures or forecasts could have an adverse effect on the plan or decision outcome, they highlight a potential threat and should not be ignored.

Appendix

TABLE A1

NORMAL DISTRIBUTION: CUMULATIVE DISTRIBUTION AND DENSITY FUNCTION

z	F(z)	1 − F(z)	f(z)	z	F(z)	1 − F(z)	f(z)	z	F(z)	1 − F(z)	f(z)
.00	.5000	.5000	.3989	.30	.6179	.3821	.3814	.60	.7257	.2743	.3332
.01	.5040	.4960	.3989	.31	.6217	.3783	.3802	.61	.7291	.2709	.3312
.02	.5080	.4920	.3989	.32	.6255	.3745	.3790	.62	.7324	.2676	.3292
.03	.5120	.4880	.3988	.33	.6293	.3707	.3778	.63	.7357	.2643	.3271
.04	.5160	.4840	.3986	.34	.6331	.3669	.3765	.64	.7389	.2611	.3251
.05	.5199	.4801	.3984	.35	.6368	.3632	.3752	.65	.7422	.2578	.3230
.06	.5239	.4761	.3982	.36	.6406	.3594	.3739	.66	.7454	.2546	.3209
.07	.5279	.4721	.3980	.37	.6443	.3557	.3726	.67	.7486	.2514	.3187
.08	.5319	.4681	.3977	.38	.6480	.3520	.3712	.68	.7517	.2483	.3166
.09	.5359	.4641	.3973	.39	.6517	.3483	.3697	.69	.7549	.2451	.3144
.10	.5398	.4602	.3970	.40	.6554	.3446	.3683	.70	.7580	.2420	.3123
.11	.5438	.4562	.3965	.41	.6591	.3409	.3668	.71	.7611	.2389	.3101
.12	.5478	.4522	.3961	.42	.6628	.3372	.3653	.72	.7642	.2358	.3079
.13	.5517	.4483	.3956	.43	.6664	.3336	.3637	.73	.7673	.2327	.3056
.14	.5557	.4443	.3951	.44	.6700	.3300	.3621	.74	.7704	.2296	.3034
.15	.5596	.4404	.3945	.45	.6736	.3264	.3605	.75	.7734	.2266	.3011
.16	.5636	.4364	.3939	.46	.6772	.3228	.3589	.76	.7764	.2236	.2989
.17	.5675	.4325	.3932	.47	.6808	.3192	.3572	.77	.7794	.2206	.2966
.18	.5714	.4286	.3925	.48	.6844	.3156	.3555	.78	.7823	.2177	.2943
.19	.5753	.4247	.3918	.49	.6879	.3121	.3538	.79	.7852	.2148	.2920
.20	.5793	.4207	.3910	.50	.6915	.3085	.3521	.80	.7881	.2119	.2897
.21	.5832	.4168	.3902	.51	.6950	.3050	.3503	.81	.7910	.2090	.2874
.22	.5871	.4129	.3894	.52	.6985	.3015	.3485	.82	.7939	.2061	.2850
.23	.5910	.4090	.3885	.53	.7019	.2981	.3467	.83	.7967	.2033	.2827
.24	.5948	.4052	.3876	.54	.7054	.2946	.3448	.84	.7995	.2005	.2803
.25	.5987	.4013	.3867	.55	.7088	.2912	.3429	.85	.8023	.1977	.2780
.26	.6026	.3974	.3857	.56	.7123	.2877	.3410	.86	.8051	.1949	.2756
.27	.6064	.3936	.3847	.57	.7157	.2843	.3391	.87	.8079	.1921	.2732
.28	.6103	.3897	.3836	.58	.7190	.2810	.3372	.88	.8106	.1894	.2709
.29	.6141	.3859	.3825	.59	.7224	.2776	.3352	.89	.8133	.1867	.2685

TABLE A1 (Continued)

Z	$F(z)$	$1 - F(z)$	$f(z)$	Z	$F(z)$	$1 - F(z)$	$f(z)$	Z	$F(z)$	$1 - F(z)$	$f(z)$
.90	.8159	.1841	.2661	1.25	.8944	.1056	.1826	1.60	.9452	.0548	.1109
.91	.8186	.1814	.2637	1.26	.8962	.1038	.1804	1.61	.9463	.0537	.1092
.92	.8212	.1788	.2613	1.27	.8980	.1020	.1781	1.62	.9474	.0526	.1074
.93	.8238	.1762	.2589	1.28	.8997	.1003	.1758	1.63	.9484	.0516	.1057
.94	.8264	.1736	.2565	1.29	.9015	.0985	.1736	1.64	.9495	.0505	.1040
.95	.8289	.1711	.2541	1.30	.9032	.0968	.1714	1.65	.9505	.0495	.1023
.96	.8315	.1685	.2516	1.31	.9049	.0951	.1691	1.66	.9515	.0485	.1006
.97	.8340	.1660	.2492	1.32	.9066	.0934	.1669	1.67	.9525	.0475	.0989
.98	.8365	.1635	.2468	1.33	.9082	.0918	.1647	1.68	.9535	.0465	.0973
.99	.8389	.1611	.2444	1.34	.9099	.0901	.1626	1.69	.9545	.0455	.0957
1.00	.8413	.1587	.2420	1.35	.9115	.0885	.1604	1.70	.9554	.0446	.0940
1.01	.8438	.1562	.2396	1.36	.9131	.0869	.1582	1.71	.9564	.0436	.0925
1.02	.8461	.1539	.2371	1.37	.9147	.0853	.1561	1.72	.9573	.0427	.0909
1.03	.8485	.1515	.2347	1.38	.9162	.0838	.1539	1.73	.9582	.0418	.0893
1.04	.8508	.1492	.2323	1.39	.9177	.0823	.1518	1.74	.9591	.0409	.0878
1.05	.8531	.1469	.2299	1.40	.9192	.0808	.1497	1.75	.9599	.0401	.0863
1.06	.8554	.1446	.2275	1.41	.9207	.0793	.1476	1.76	.9608	.0392	.0848
1.07	.8577	.1423	.2251	1.42	.9222	.0778	.1456	1.77	.9616	.0384	.0833
1.08	.8599	.1401	.2227	1.43	.9236	.0764	.1435	1.78	.9625	.0375	.0818
1.09	.8621	.1379	.2203	1.44	.9251	.0749	.1415	1.79	.9633	.0367	.0804
1.10	.8643	.1357	.2179	1.45	.9265	.0735	.1394	1.80	.9641	.0359	.0790
1.11	.8665	.1335	.2155	1.46	.9279	.0721	.1374	1.81	.9649	.0351	.0775
1.12	.8686	.1314	.2131	1.47	.9292	.0708	.1354	1.82	.9656	.0344	.0761
1.13	.8708	.1292	.2107	1.48	.9306	.0694	.1334	1.83	.9664	.0336	.0748
1.14	.8729	.1271	.2083	1.49	.9319	.0681	.1315	1.84	.9671	.0329	.0734
1.15	.8749	.1251	.2059	1.50	.9332	.0668	.1295	1.85	.9678	.0322	.0721
1.16	.8770	.1230	.2036	1.51	.9345	.0655	.1276	1.86	.9686	.0314	.0707
1.17	.8790	.1210	.2012	1.52	.9357	.0643	.1257	1.87	.9693	.0307	.0694
1.18	.8810	.1190	.1989	1.53	.9370	.0630	.1238	1.88	.9699	.0301	.0681
1.19	.8830	.1170	.1965	1.54	.9382	.0618	.1219	1.89	.9706	.0294	.0669
1.20	.8849	.1151	.1942	1.55	.9394	.0606	.1200	1.90	.9713	.0287	.0656
1.21	.8869	.1131	.1919	1.56	.9406	.0594	.1182	1.91	.9719	.0281	.0644
1.22	.8888	.1112	.1895	1.57	.9418	.0582	.1163	1.92	.9726	.0274	.0632
1.23	.8907	.1093	.1872	1.58	.9429	.0571	.1145	1.93	.9732	.0268	.0620
1.24	.8925	.1075	.1849	1.59	.9441	.0559	.1127	1.94	.9738	.0262	.0608

(continued on next page)

TABLE A1 (Continued)

Z	F(z)	1 − F(z)	f(z)	Z	F(z)	1 − F(z)	f(z)	Z	F(z)	1 − F(z)	f(z)
3.00	.9987	.0013	.0044	2.30	.9893	.0107	.0283	2.65	.9960	.0040	.0119
3.01	.9987	.0013	.0043	2.31	.9896	.0104	.0277	2.66	.9961	.0039	.0116
3.02	.9987	.0013	.0042	2.32	.9898	.0102	.0270	2.67	.9962	.0038	.0113
3.03	.9988	.0012	.0040	2.33	.9901	.0099	.0264	2.68	.9963	.0037	.0110
3.04	.9988	.0012	.0039	2.34	.9904	.0096	.0258	2.69	.9964	.0036	.0107
3.05	.9989	.0011	.0038	2.35	.9906	.0094	.0252	2.70	.9965	.0035	.0104
3.06	.9989	.0011	.0037	2.36	.9909	.0091	.0246	2.71	.9966	.0034	.0101
3.07	.9989	.0011	.0036	2.37	.9911	.0089	.0241	2.72	.9967	.0033	.0099
3.08	.9990	.0010	.0035	2.38	.9913	.0087	.0235	2.73	.9968	.0032	.0096
3.09	.9990	.0010	.0034	2.39	.9916	.0084	.0229	2.74	.9969	.0031	.0093
3.10	.9990	.0010	.0033	2.40	.9918	.0082	.0224	2.75	.9970	.0030	.0091
3.11	.9991	.0009	.0032	2.41	.9920	.0080	.0219	2.76	.9971	.0029	.0088
3.12	.9991	.0009	.0031	2.42	.9922	.0078	.0213	2.77	.9972	.0028	.0086
3.13	.9991	.0009	.0030	2.43	.9925	.0075	.0208	2.78	.9973	.0027	.0084
3.14	.9992	.0008	.0029	2.44	.9927	.0073	.0203	2.79	.9974	.0026	.0081
3.15	.9992	.0008	.0028	2.45	.9929	.0071	.0198	2.80	.9974	.0026	.0079
3.16	.9992	.0008	.0027	2.46	.9931	.0069	.0194	2.81	.9975	.0025	.0077
3.17	.9992	.0008	.0026	2.47	.9932	.0068	.0189	2.82	.9976	.0024	.0075
3.18	.9993	.0007	.0025	2.48	.9934	.0066	.0184	2.83	.9977	.0023	.0073
3.19	.9993	.0007	.0025	2.49	.9936	.0064	.0180	2.84	.9977	.0023	.0071
3.20	.9993	.0007	.0024	2.50	.9938	.0062	.0175	2.85	.9978	.0022	.0069
3.21	.9993	.0007	.0023	2.51	.9940	.0060	.0171	2.86	.9979	.0021	.0067
3.22	.9994	.0006	.0022	2.52	.9941	.0059	.0167	2.87	.9979	.0021	.0065
3.23	.9994	.0006	.0022	2.53	.9943	.0057	.0163	2.88	.9980	.0020	.0063
3.24	.9994	.0006	.0021	2.54	.9945	.0055	.0158	2.89	.9981	.0019	.0061
3.25	.9994	.0006	.0020	2.55	.9946	.0054	.0155	2.90	.9981	.0019	.0060
3.26	.9994	.0006	.0020	2.56	.9948	.0052	.0151	2.91	.9982	.0018	.0058
3.27	.9995	.0005	.0019	2.57	.9949	.0051	.0147	2.92	.9983	.0017	.0058
3.28	.9995	.0005	.0018	2.58	.9951	.0049	.0143	2.93	.9983	.0017	.0055
3.29	.9995	.0005	.0018	2.59	.9952	.0048	.0139	2.94	.9984	.0016	.0053
3.30	.9995	.0005	.0017	2.60	.9953	.0047	.0136	2.95	.9984	.0016	.0051
3.31	.9995	.0005	.0017	2.61	.9955	.0045	.0132	2.96	.9985	.0015	.0050
3.32	.9996	.0004	.0016	2.62	.9956	.0044	.0129	2.97	.9985	.0015	.0048
3.33	.9996	.0004	.0016	2.63	.9957	.0043	.0126	2.98	.9986	.0014	.0047
3.34	.9996	.0004	.0015	2.64	.9959	.0041	.0122	2.99	.9986	.0014	.0046

TABLE A1 (Continued)

Z	F(z)	1 − F(z)	f(z)	Z	F(z)	1 − F(z)	f(z)	Z	F(z)	1 − F(z)	f(z)
3.00	.9987	.0013	.0044	3.35	.9996	.0004	.0015	3.70	.9999	.0001	.0004
3.01	.9987	.0013	.0043	3.36	.9996	.0004	.0014	3.71	.9999	.0001	.0004
3.02	.9987	.0013	.0042	3.37	.9996	.0004	.0014	3.72	.9999	.0001	.0004
3.03	.9988	.0012	.0040	3.38	.9996	.0004	.0013	3.73	.9999	.0001	.0004
3.04	.9988	.0012	.0039	3.39	.9997	.0003	.0013	3.74	.9999	.0001	.0004
3.05	.9989	.0011	.0038	3.40	.9997	.0003	.0012	3.75	.9999	.0001	.0004
3.06	.9989	.0011	.0037	3.41	.9997	.0003	.0012	3.76	.9999	.0001	.0003
3.07	.9989	.0011	.0036	3.42	.9997	.0003	.0012	3.77	.9999	.0001	.0003
3.08	.9990	.0010	.0035	3.43	.9997	.0003	.0011	3.78	.9999	.0001	.0003
3.09	.9990	.0010	.0034	3.44	.9997	.0003	.0011	3.79	.9999	.0001	.0003
3.10	.9990	.0010	.0033	3.45	.9997	.0003	.0010	3.80	.9999	.0001	.0003
3.11	.9991	.0009	.0032	3.46	.9997	.0003	.0010	3.81	.9999	.0001	.0003
3.12	.9991	.0009	.0031	3.47	.9997	.0003	.0010	3.82	.9999	.0001	.0003
3.13	.9991	.0009	.0030	3.48	.9997	.0003	.0009	3.83	.9999	.0001	.0003
3.14	.9992	.0008	.0029	3.49	.9998	.0002	.0009	3.84	.9999	.0001	.0003
3.15	.9992	.0008	.0028	3.50	.9998	.0002	.0009	3.85	.9999	.0001	.0002
3.16	.9992	.0008	.0027	3.51	.9998	.0002	.0008	3.86	.9999	.0001	.0002
3.17	.9992	.0008	.0026	3.52	.9998	.0002	.0008	3.87	.9999	.0001	.0002
3.18	.9993	.0007	.0025	3.53	.9998	.0002	.0008	3.88	.9999	.0001	.0002
3.19	.9993	.0007	.0025	3.54	.9998	.0002	.0008	3.89	1.0000	.0000	.0002
3.20	.9993	.0007	.0024	3.55	.9998	.0002	.0007	3.90	1.0000	.0000	.0002
3.21	.9993	.0007	.0023	3.56	.9998	.0002	.0007	3.91	1.0000	.0000	.0002
3.22	.9994	.0006	.0022	3.57	.9998	.0002	.0007	3.92	1.0000	.0000	.0002
3.23	.9994	.0006	.0022	3.58	.9998	.0002	.0007	3.93	1.0000	.0000	.0002
3.24	.9994	.0006	.0021	3.59	.9998	.0002	.0006	3.94	1.0000	.0000	.0002
3.25	.9994	.0006	.0020	3.60	.9998	.0002	.0006	3.95	1.0000	.0000	.0002
3.26	.9994	.0006	.0020	3.61	.9998	.0002	.0006	3.96	1.0000	.0000	.0002
3.27	.9995	.0005	.0019	3.62	.9999	.0001	.0006	3.97	1.0000	.0000	.0002
3.28	.9995	.0005	.0018	3.63	.9999	.0001	.0005	3.98	1.0000	.0000	.0001
3.29	.9995	.0005	.0018	3.64	.9999	.0001	.0005	3.99	1.0000	.0000	.0001
3.30	.9995	.0005	.0017	3.65	.9999	.0001	.0005	4.00	1.0000	.0000	.0001
3.31	.9995	.0005	.0017	3.66	.9999	.0001	.0005				
3.32	.9996	.0004	.0016	3.67	.9999	.0001	.0005				
3.33	.9996	.0004	.0016	3.68	.9999	.0001	.0005				
3.34	.9996	.0004	.0015	3.69	.9999	.0001	.0004				

Source: Adapted from *Standard Mathematical Tables*, 27th edition, William H. Beyer, ed., 1984, pp. 526–553. Copyright, CRC Press, Inc., Boca Raton, Florida.

390

TABLE A2

CRITICAL F VALUES: PROBABILITY OF BEING EXCEEDED BY CHANCE = 0.1

| | | | | Number of coefficients | | | | | |
n \ m	1	2	3	4	5	6	7	8	9	10
1	39.86	49.50	53.59	55.83	57.24	58.20	58.91	59.44	59.86	60.19
2	8.53	9.00	9.16	9.24	9.29	9.33	9.35	9.37	9.38	9.39
3	5.54	5.46	5.39	5.34	5.31	5.28	5.27	5.25	5.24	5.23
4	4.54	4.32	4.19	4.11	4.05	4.01	3.98	3.95	3.94	3.92
5	4.06	3.78	3.62	3.52	3.45	3.40	3.37	3.34	3.32	3.30
6	3.78	3.46	3.29	3.18	3.11	3.05	3.01	2.98	2.96	2.94
7	3.59	3.26	3.07	2.96	2.88	2.83	2.78	2.75	2.72	2.70
8	3.46	3.11	2.92	2.81	2.73	2.67	2.62	2.59	2.56	2.54
9	3.36	3.01	2.81	2.69	2.61	2.55	2.51	2.47	2.44	2.42
10	3.29	2.92	2.73	2.61	2.52	2.46	2.41	2.38	2.35	2.32
11	3.23	2.86	2.66	2.54	2.45	2.39	2.34	2.30	2.27	2.25
12	3.18	2.81	2.61	2.48	2.39	2.33	2.28	2.24	2.21	2.19
13	3.14	2.76	2.56	2.43	2.35	2.28	2.23	2.20	2.16	2.14
14	3.10	2.73	2.52	2.39	2.31	2.24	2.19	2.15	2.12	2.10
15	3.07	2.70	2.49	2.36	2.27	2.21	2.16	2.12	2.09	2.06
16	3.05	2.67	2.46	2.33	2.24	2.18	2.13	2.09	2.06	2.03
17	3.03	2.64	2.44	2.31	2.22	2.15	2.10	2.06	2.03	2.00
18	3.01	2.62	2.42	2.29	2.20	2.13	2.08	2.04	2.00	1.98
19	2.99	2.61	2.40	2.27	2.18	2.11	2.06	2.02	1.98	1.96
20	2.97	2.59	2.38	2.25	2.16	2.09	2.04	2.00	1.96	1.94
21	2.96	2.57	2.36	2.23	2.14	2.08	2.02	1.98	1.95	1.92
22	2.95	2.56	2.35	2.22	2.13	2.06	2.01	1.97	1.93	1.90
23	2.94	2.55	2.34	2.21	2.11	2.05	1.99	1.95	1.92	1.89
24	2.93	2.54	2.33	2.19	2.10	2.04	1.98	1.94	1.91	1.88
25	2.92	2.53	2.32	2.18	2.09	2.02	1.97	1.93	1.89	1.87
26	2.91	2.52	2.31	2.17	2.08	2.01	1.96	1.92	1.88	1.86
27	2.90	2.51	2.30	2.17	2.07	2.00	1.95	1.91	1.87	1.85
28	2.89	2.50	2.29	2.16	2.06	2.00	1.94	1.90	1.87	1.84
29	2.89	2.50	2.28	2.15	2.06	1.99	1.93	1.89	1.86	1.83

Degrees of Freedom

(continued on next page)

TABLE A2 (Continued)

Number of Coefficients

Degrees of Freedom n \ m	1	2	3	4	5	6	7	8	9	10
30	2.88	2.49	2.28	2.14	2.05	1.98	1.93	1.88	1.85	1.82
40	2.84	2.44	2.23	2.09	2.00	1.93	1.87	1.83	1.79	1.76
60	2.79	2.39	2.18	2.04	1.95	1.87	1.82	1.77	1.74	1.71
120	2.75	2.35	2.13	1.99	1.90	1.82	1.77	1.72	1.68	1.65
∞	2.71	2.30	2.08	1.94	1.85	1.77	1.72	1.67	1.63	1.60

PROBABILITY OF BEING EXCEEDED BY CHANCE = 0.05

Number of Coefficients

Degrees of Freedom n \ m	1	2	3	4	5	6	7	8	9	10
1	161.4	199.5	215.7	224.6	230.2	234.0	236.8	238.9	240.5	241.9
2	18.51	19.00	19.16	19.25	19.30	19.33	19.35	19.37	19.38	19.40
3	10.13	9.55	9.28	9.12	9.01	8.94	8.89	8.85	8.81	8.79
4	7.71	6.94	6.59	6.39	6.26	6.16	6.09	6.04	6.00	5.96
5	6.61	5.79	5.41	5.19	5.05	4.95	4.88	4.82	4.77	4.74
6	5.99	5.14	4.76	4.53	4.39	4.28	4.21	4.15	4.10	4.06
7	5.59	4.74	4.35	4.12	3.97	3.87	3.79	3.73	3.68	3.64
8	5.32	4.46	4.07	3.84	3.69	3.58	3.50	3.44	3.39	3.35
9	5.12	4.26	3.86	3.63	3.48	3.37	3.29	3.23	3.18	3.14
10	4.96	4.10	3.71	3.48	3.33	3.22	3.14	3.07	3.02	2.98
11	4.84	3.98	3.59	3.36	3.20	3.09	3.01	2.95	2.90	2.85
12	4.75	3.89	3.49	3.26	3.11	3.00	2.91	2.85	2.80	2.75
13	4.67	3.81	3.41	3.18	3.03	2.92	2.83	2.77	2.71	2.67
14	4.60	3.74	3.34	3.11	2.96	2.85	2.76	2.70	2.65	2.60

(continued on next page)

TABLE A2 (continued)

n / m	1	2	3	4	5	6	7	8	9	10
15	4.54	3.68	3.29	3.06	2.90	2.79	2.71	2.64	2.59	2.54
16	4.49	3.63	3.24	3.01	2.85	2.74	2.66	2.59	2.54	2.49
17	4.45	3.59	3.20	2.96	2.81	2.70	2.61	2.55	2.49	2.45
18	4.41	3.55	3.16	2.93	2.77	2.66	2.58	2.51	2.46	2.41
19	4.38	3.52	3.13	2.90	2.74	2.63	2.54	2.48	2.42	2.38
20	4.35	3.49	3.10	2.87	2.71	2.60	2.51	2.45	2.39	2.35
21	4.32	3.47	3.07	2.84	2.68	2.57	2.49	2.42	2.37	2.32
22	4.30	3.44	3.05	2.82	2.66	2.55	2.46	2.40	2.34	2.30
23	4.28	3.42	3.03	2.80	2.64	2.53	2.44	2.37	2.32	2.27
24	4.26	3.40	3.01	2.78	2.62	2.51	2.42	2.36	2.30	2.25
25	4.24	3.39	2.99	2.76	2.60	2.49	2.40	2.34	2.28	2.24
26	4.23	3.37	2.98	2.74	2.59	2.47	2.39	2.32	2.27	2.22
27	4.21	3.35	2.96	2.73	2.57	2.46	2.37	2.31	2.25	2.20
28	4.20	3.34	2.95	2.71	2.56	2.45	2.36	2.29	2.24	2.19
29	4.18	3.33	2.93	2.70	2.55	2.43	2.35	2.28	2.22	2.18
30	4.17	3.32	2.92	2.69	2.53	2.42	2.33	2.27	2.21	2.16
40	4.08	3.23	2.84	2.61	2.45	2.34	2.25	2.18	2.12	2.08
60	4.00	3.15	2.76	2.53	2.37	2.25	2.17	2.10	2.04	1.99
120	3.92	3.07	2.68	2.45	2.29	2.17	2.09	2.02	1.96	1.91
∞	3.84	3.00	2.60	2.37	2.21	2.10	2.01	1.94	1.88	1.83

Degrees of Freedom

PROBABILITY OF BEING EXCEEDED BY CHANCE = 0.01

Number of Coefficients

n / m	1	2	3	4	5	6	7	8	9	10
1	4052.	4999.5	5403.	5625.	5764.	5859.	5928.	5982.	6022.	6056.
2	98.50	99.00	99.17	99.25	99.30	99.33	99.36	99.37	99.39	99.40
3	34.12	30.82	29.46	28.71	28.24	27.91	27.67	27.49	27.35	27.23
4	21.20	18.00	16.69	15.98	15.52	15.21	14.98	14.80	14.66	14.55
5	16.26	13.27	12.06	11.39	10.97	10.67	10.46	10.29	10.16	10.05
6	13.75	10.92	9.78	9.15	8.75	8.47	8.26	8.10	7.98	7.87
7	12.25	9.55	8.45	7.85	7.46	7.19	6.99	6.84	6.72	6.62

Degrees of Freedom

(continued on next page)

393

TABLE A2 (Continued)

| | | Number of coefficients | | | | | | | | |
	1	2	3	4	5	6	7	8	9	10
n \ m										
8	11.26	8.65	7.59	7.01	6.63	6.37	6.18	6.03	5.91	5.81
9	10.56	8.02	6.99	6.42	6.06	5.80	5.61	5.47	5.35	5.26
10	10.04	7.56	6.55	5.99	5.64	5.39	5.20	5.06	4.94	4.85
11	9.65	7.21	6.22	5.67	5.32	5.07	4.89	4.74	4.63	4.54
12	9.33	6.93	5.95	5.41	5.06	4.82	4.64	4.50	4.39	4.30
13	9.07	6.70	5.74	5.21	4.86	4.62	4.44	4.30	4.19	4.10
14	8.86	6.51	5.56	5.04	4.69	4.46	4.28	4.14	4.03	3.94
15	8.68	6.36	5.42	4.89	4.56	4.32	4.14	4.00	3.89	3.80
16	8.53	6.23	5.29	4.77	4.44	4.20	4.03	3.89	3.78	3.69
17	8.40	6.11	5.18	4.67	4.34	4.10	3.93	3.79	3.68	3.59
18	8.29	6.01	5.09	4.58	4.25	4.01	3.84	3.71	3.60	3.51
19	8.18	5.93	5.01	4.50	4.17	3.94	3.77	3.63	3.52	3.43
20	8.10	5.85	4.94	4.43	4.10	3.87	3.70	3.56	3.46	3.37
21	8.02	5.78	4.87	4.37	4.04	3.81	3.64	3.51	3.40	3.31
22	7.95	5.72	4.82	4.31	3.99	3.76	3.59	3.45	3.35	3.26
23	7.88	5.66	4.76	4.26	3.94	3.71	3.54	3.41	3.30	3.21
24	7.82	5.61	4.72	4.22	3.90	3.67	3.50	3.36	3.26	3.17
25	7.77	5.57	4.68	4.18	3.85	3.63	3.46	3.32	3.22	3.13
26	7.72	5.53	4.64	4.14	3.82	3.59	3.42	3.29	3.18	3.09
27	7.68	5.49	4.60	4.11	3.78	3.56	3.39	3.26	3.15	3.06
28	7.64	5.45	4.57	4.07	3.75	3.53	3.36	3.23	3.12	3.03
29	7.60	5.42	4.54	4.04	3.73	3.50	3.33	3.20	3.09	3.00
30	7.56	5.39	4.51	4.02	3.70	3.47	3.30	3.17	3.07	2.98
40	7.31	5.18	4.31	3.83	3.51	3.29	3.12	2.99	2.89	2.80
60	7.08	4.98	4.13	3.65	3.34	3.12	2.95	2.82	2.72	2.63
120	6.85	4.79	3.95	3.48	3.17	2.96	2.79	2.66	2.56	2.47
∞	6.63	4.61	3.78	3.32	3.02	2.80	2.64	2.51	2.41	2.32

Degrees of Freedom

Source: Adapted from *Standard Mathematical Tables,* 27th edition, William H. Beyer, ed., 1984, pp. 526–553. Copyright, CRC Press, Inc., Boca Raton, Florida.

TABLE A3

CRITICAL t VALUES: PROBABILITY OF BEING EXCEEDED BY CHANCE $(+$ or $-)$

Degrees of Freedom	0.50	0.20	0.10	0.05	0.02	0.01	0.001
1	1.000	3.078	6.314	12.706	31.821	63.657	636.619
2	.816	1.886	2.920	4.303	6.965	9.925	31.598
3	.765	1.638	2.353	3.182	4.541	5.841	12.941
4	.741	1.533	2.132	2.776	3.747	4.604	8.610
5	.727	1.476	2.015	2.571	3.365	4.032	6.859
6	.718	1.440	1.943	2.447	3.143	3.707	5.959
7	.711	1.415	1.895	2.365	2.998	3.499	5.405
8	.706	2.397	1.860	2.306	2.896	3.355	5.041
9	.703	1.383	1.833	2.262	2.821	3.250	4.781
10	.700	1.372	1.812	2.228	2.764	3.169	4.587
11	.697	1.363	1.796	2.201	2.718	3.106	4.437
12	.695	1.356	1.782	2.179	2.681	3.055	4.318
13	.694	1.350	1.771	2.160	2.650	3.012	4.221
14	.692	1.345	1.761	2.145	2.624	2.977	4.140
15	.691	1.341	1.753	2.131	2.602	2.947	4.073
16	.690	1.337	1.746	2.120	2.583	2.921	4.015
17	.689	1.333	1.740	2.110	2.567	2.898	3.965
18	.688	1.330	1.734	2.101	2.552	2.878	3.922
19	.688	1.328	1.729	2.093	2.539	2.861	3.883
20	.687	1.325	1.725	2.086	2.528	2.845	3.850

(continued on next page)

TABLE A3 (Continued)

Degrees of Freedom	0.50	0.20	0.10	0.05	0.02	0.01	0.001
21	.686	1.323	1.721	2.080	2.518	2.831	3.819
22	.686	1.321	1.717	2.074	2.508	2.819	3.792
23	.685	1.319	1.714	2.069	2.500	2.807	3.767
24	.685	1.318	1.711	2.064	2.492	2.797	3.745
25	.684	1.316	1.708	2.060	2.485	2.787	3.725
26	.684	1.315	1.706	2.056	2.479	2.779	3.707
27	.684	1.314	1.703	2.052	2.473	2.771	3.690
28	.683	1.313	1.701	2.048	2.467	2.763	3.674
29	.683	1.311	1.699	2.045	2.462	2.756	3.659
30	.683	1.310	1.697	2.042	2.457	2.750	3.646
40	.681	1.303	1.684	2.021	2.423	2.704	3.551
60	.679	1.296	1.671	2.000	2.390	2.660	3.460
120	.677	1.289	1.658	1.980	2.358	2.617	3.373
∞	.674	1.282	1.645	1.960	2.326	2.576	3.291

Source: Adapted from *Standard Mathematical Tables*, 27th edition, William H. Beyer, ed., 1984, pp. 526–553. Copyright, CRC Press, Inc., Boca Raton, Florida.

Index

Accuracy, 164, 384
Actions
  alternative, 30, 173
  relationships with environment and outcome, 23
Activities, 338
  dummy, 320
  and events, 319, 320
  ordering relationships among, 319
  planning for short-term, 141
  time slack for, 323
Activity levels, 238
Activity planning, 20, 141–58, 199
Adapt, increased flexibility to, 4
Adaptive smoothing, 193–96
Adjustments
  other, 62–63
  preliminary, 60–62
  price, 61
  trading-day, 60–61
Aggregate resource planning, 141, 318
Aggregation, level of, 319
Allison, Graham T., 20, 37
Alternative futures, 311
Analog: Science Fiction/Science Fact, 11
Analogy, forecasting by, 5, 44
Analysis
  confirmatory, 213
  critical-level, 362–63
  cross-impact, 359–62
  of data, 44–45, 204
  decomposition approach to, 125–27
  exploratory, 68, 213
  of residuals, 63–76, 81
  steps in time-series, 376–78
  trend-impact, 363–65
  of trends, 85–98
  of trends in time-series, 70
Anchoring, 338
  ARIMA model, 230
  basic types of, 230–34
  identification of, 231–33
  multivariate, 235
Armstrong, J. Scott, 245, 298, 336
Array, 70
Assumptions
  categories of, 309
  sets of environmental, 311
Autocorrelation coefficient, 231
Autoregression, 228
Autoregressive model, 228, 230
Availability, 337–38
Average
  centered versus uncentered, 101
  length of, 101
  1-2-3 macros for moving, 132–33

type of, 101
  weighted versus unweighted, 101
Averaging tendencies, of groups, 6

Base line, 56, 115
Bell, Daniel, 9, 10
Bell-shaped curve, 151
Beta distribution, 340, 341
Bias, 336, 337, 343
Bounds, and limits, 352–57
Box, George, 230, 260
Box-and-whiskers diagram, 75–76
  data table for, 78–79
  example of, 76
  illustration of for probability distribution, 164
  Lotus 1-2-3 template for, 78
Buchan, John, 2, 11
Budgeting model, 158–65
Budgets, 17
  as annual process, 21
  development of, 19
  financial, 159
  pro forma, 159–61
Business Economics, 11
Business units, operating, 19

Capital, working, 17
Carriers, 205
Cash-flow estimates, 17
Causation, 384
Census program X-11, 125, 134
Change, organizational, 304–5
Christmas Tree Problem, 142
Coefficient, choosing, 176
Coefficient of correlation, 231, 278
Coefficient of determination, 218, 231, 278
Coefficients, 204, 220–22, 231
Confirmatory analysis, 213
Connected scatter diagram, 240, 241, 256
Conservatism, 336
Constant dollars, 61
Constant growth curve, 353
Consumer Price Index (CPI [W]), 58
Contingency planning, 238
Continuity, 9, 139, 140
Continuous variable, state of environment as, 32–35
Correlation, 384
Correlogram, 231, 232, 233, 236, 237
Cost, expected opportunity, 30
Cost-benefit analysis, 383
Costs, 238